THEATRE BACKSTAGE
FROM A TO Z

THEATRE
BACKSTAGE

FROM

TO

A Z

WARREN C. LOUNSBURY
NORMAN C. BOULANGER

Fourth edition, revised and expanded

by NORMAN C. BOULANGER

University of Washington Press   Seattle and London

Theatre Backstage from A to Z is a revised and expanded version of *Backstage from A to Z* copyright © 1959 by Warren C. Lounsbury and distributed by the University of Washington Press.

The illustration on p. xix from *Play Production in America* by Arthur Edwin Krows is reproduced by permission of Holt, Rinehart, and Winston, Inc. All rights reserved.

Library of Congress Cataloging-in-Publication Data

Lounsbury, Warren C.
       Theatre backstage from A to Z / Warren C. Lounsbury,
       Norman C. Boulanger.--4th ed., rev. and expanded / by Norman
       C. Boulanger
              p.   cm.
       Includes bibliographic references.
       ISBN 0-295-97717-5 (alk. paper)
       1. Stage machinery--Dictionaries. 2. Stage lighting--Dictionaries. 3.
       Theatre--Stage-setting and scenery--Dictionaries.
       I. Boulanger, Norman C. II. Title.
       PN2091.M3L68 1998
       792'.025'03--dc21
              98-4854

An Apple Computer® Macintosh Performa 6290CD was used in the preparation of this book. Drawings were generated in Deneba® Canvas v3.06, and page makeup was done in Aldus® PageMaker v4.02.

The paper used in this publication is acid-free and recycled from 10 percent post-consumer and at least 50 percent pre-consumer waste. It meets the minimum requirements of American National Standard for Information Sciences—Permanence of Paper for Printed Library Materials, ANSI Z39.48-1984. ∞

To Kay and Tyke
together again

Contents

Preface to the Fourth Edition

It was with some trepidation that I considered writing the fourth edition of this book without the wisdom, guidance, humor, and stabilizing influences of my mentor, friend, and coauthor, Warren C. (Tyke) Lounsbury. His passing not only has left a gap in my life and in his daughters' lives but has also impaired the dissemination of knowledge within our profession. He is sorely missed.

This edition is necessitated by the great strides that technology has made in such a short time. This is particularly true in the areas of automated lights and their control, trusses, and rigging. Also, the proliferation of the Internet is truly making people think in global terms. It is sobering indeed to realize that the literature of half a dozen countries can be accessed in an hour of computer searching for theatrical man-ufacturing companies. And even though it is exhilarating to contemplate this rapidly expanding method of research, the downside is that change is taking place so quickly that the change is, or appears to be, continuous. This became a serious consideration when I decided to include Web site URLs (addresses) in the manufacturers and distributors list. The inclusion of the URLs begs the question of how fast the addresses will change with the introduction of newer technologies. I gleaned a great deal of information from the Internet, and many thanks go to the companies who have Web sites. In particular I wish to thank the first thirteen organizations and companies in the WORLD WIDE WEB section of the bibliography; without them there would be no new edition.

We are in a high-tech revolution as we approach the millennium. It is a wondrous thing to watch or to be involved in the use of the new theories, tools, and machinery. Although this revolution necessitates the inclusion of new terms and definitions in a book of this type, it is also necessary to retain the older terminology and definitions. After all, the larger percentage of the world is not yet financially able to participate in the high-tech revolution.

I am indebted to many for their contributions to this book over the years. This edition would not have been possible without the time and effort of John Blixt, who is with Feld Entertainment's Walt Disney's World on Ice, "Toy Story." John looked over the new additions, made suggestions, and contributed much. My "picking up" his show on the road was a fine learning experience. Warren Houtz, Technical Director of the Tulsa Performing Arts Center, likewise was of great help and a great sounding board. I am grateful to Charlie and Karen Jones, who "monitored" my writing. Thanks also go to Pam Bruton, Veronica Seyd, Naomi Pascal, Bob Hutchins, Julidta Tarver, and Mary Anderson of the University of Washington Press. I also owe a debt of gratitude to those who have remained in the background but who are always adding to my store of knowledge, including Jacel and Helen Evans, Mike Boulanger, Don Mc-Laughlin, Don and Jude Thompson, and, of course, my former students, who were subjected to me as their teacher and who indeed taught me.

Norman C. Boulanger
1998

Preface to the Third Edition

A reference book has an interesting shelf-life. First it is useful, then helpful, then quaint, and finally historical over what seems to be an increasingly shorter time lapse. The 1972 edition of *Theatre Backstage from A to Z* comes precariously close to reaching the historical stage in the areas of sound, electronic control, and equipment. Therein lies the mandate for revision.

In attempting to put together a reference book for theatre a real confusion exists. For many theatres, much of the new and innovative equipment carries a prohibitive price tag and therefore, technicians are forced to mount this year's productions with equipment that was old 20 years ago. Consequently, because much of this "ancient" equipment is still in use, we are reluctant to eliminate the old and functional just because something new and exciting reaches the market. We are equally reluctant to eliminate the new and exciting because it carries an impossible price tag. We therefore ask the indulgence of the reader in accepting our decision to include both.

It is through the efforts of my co-author, Norman Boulanger, that this third edition of "A to Z" has come to fruition. Having retired from theatre responsibilities many years ago, I had no intention of returning to the fray. However, because of Norman's continued connections with both professional and academic theatre, his intimate knowledge of sound systems and computer boards, and his indomitable determination, I capitulated; at first with reluctance but soon with exuberance. My sincerest thanks to Norm.

Among the many to whom we are indebted for contributions, we are especially grateful to Luke Vorstermans, Pat Blakley, Bob Hutchins, Pam Bruton, Eddy DeBorde, Helen and Jacel Evans, Neil MacDonald, Jan A. Nelson, Charles V. Jones, Floyd E. Hart, Jr., Edie V. Evans, Mike Boulanger, and all the long-suffering students whom we have taught over the years.

Warren C. Lounsbury
1989

Introduction:
Scenery and Lighting Practices in the United States

The following broad survey of stage scenery and lighting practices in America is designed as (1) a quick review and (2) an encouragement for future stage technicians to continue research in this interesting and productive area of inquiry.

SCENERY

In the Beginning

More than one hundred years elapsed between the establishment of the first English settlement in Jamestown in 1607 and the building of the first American theatre. During this period there is scattered evidence of strolling players appearing in New York and Charlestowne (Charleston), South Carolina, but it is difficult to imagine complete productions with no established theatres in which to play and with transportation limited to horseback, wagons, and occasional sailing vessels.

Despite transportation difficulties, the rigors of colonial life, and the restrictive moral code of the Puritans, sufficient activity in the entertainment field was in evidence in 1709 to cause the Governor's Council in New York to issue a ban on playacting, cockfighting, and other disreputable forms of entertainment.

The first recorded theatre to be built in America was constructed in Williamsburg, Virginia, in 1716, for Charles and Mary Stagg. No further record has survived concerning the theatre, the company, the scenery, or the Staggs.

Scattered reports of theatre activities in and around Philadelphia, New York, Charlestowne, and Boston indicate a growing interest in the theatre during the first half of the eighteenth century: in 1735 *Flora or Hob in the Well*, the first production of an opera in America, was presented in Charlestowne; in 1736, William and Mary College in Williamsburg offered to the public Addison's *Cato*; in the same year the New Theatre in Dock Street, Charlestowne, was financed by subscription and opened to the public; in 1749 William Plumstead's warehouse in Philadelphia housed a company headed by Walter Murray and Thomas Kean. Little is known of these so-called theatres and even less is known of the scenery they used, although one can assume it was of the wing-and-drop or wing-and-shutter variety.

The First Professionals

In 1752 William Hallam, bankrupt manager of the Goodman's Fields Theatre in London, decided that the New World was ready for professional theatre. A newly formed company of twelve adults and three children, under the management of William's brother, Lewis Hallam, set sail in the *Charming Sally*, replete with scenery, properties, and a repertory of plays to be rehearsed during their forty-two-day voyage. The busy little company arrived in Williamsburg, Virginia, in July, bought and remodeled a warehouse, and opened to the public on September 15. This event marks the first professional British acting company and the first professional scenery to be seen in the colonies.

According to a notice in the *Virginia Gazette* a few days before the arrival of the company, "the Scenes, Cloaths, and Decorations, are entirely new, extremely rich, and finished in the highest taste, being painted by the best Hands in London, are excelled by none in Beauty and Elegance." It is not known whether Hallam's scenery was repainted during the voyage, but it is almost certain that, far from being new, it was part of the bankrupt stock of the old Goodman's Fields Theatre.

Although Hallam's scenery was new to Wil-

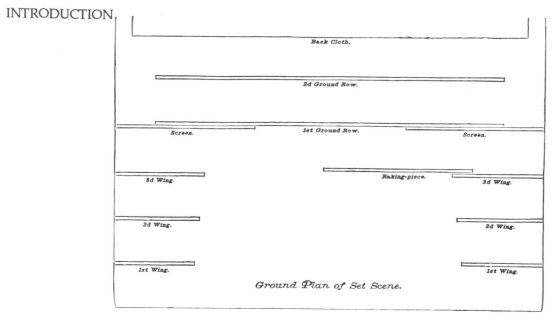

Back Cloth.

2d Ground Row.

Screen.   1st Ground Row.   Screen.

3d Wing.   Raking-piece.   3d Wing.

2d Wing.   2d Wing.

1st Wing.   1st Wing.

Ground Plan of Set Scene.

Typical plan for wing-and-drop settings (from F. Lloyds, *Practical Guide to Scene Painting in Distemper*)

liamsburg, the style of staging was familiar to all and was destined to continue through most of the nineteenth century. Indeed, even now, many musicals and operas are staged with modifications of the old wing-and-drop sets of the 1750s.

Wings, Borders, and Drops

The wing was a rectangular frame made of lightweight lumber, usually pine or spruce. In all probability, wing construction followed other building principles of the time, using dowel and glue or mortise and tenon joints. Because of its durability and resiliency, linen canvas was used for covering flats and wings.

Wings were placed at the side of the stage at proper intervals to form masking and entrances. Tracks (grooves) on the floor and overhead provided support, and scene changes were made by simply sliding one wing offstage and revealing another directly behind it.

Painted strips of canvas were used as borders to complete overhead masking. Suspended from pulleys in the ceiling, borders were raised during the scene change, revealing the borders behind them.

Drops, or "cloaths," forming the upstage background were made of canvas on battens and were either rolled or tripped to expose the next scene behind. Where seaming of the canvas was necessary, a lap joint was made and glued horizontally. An alternative backwall was a pair of "shutters,"

Front elevation for the floor plan above

built like flats and supported by "grooves" in the same manner as the side wings.

A well-equipped wing-and-drop stage would have five sets: fancy interior, plain interior, garden, woods, and street scene. With a limited amount of money a company could get along with three sets of wings, doubling wood wings for street and garden scenes. On at least one such occasion, however, the Lewis Hallam, Jr., Company was brought to task. The *New York Advertiser* of April 4, 1787, stated that "frequently where the author intended a handsome street or a beautiful landscape, we only see a dirty piece of canvas . . . nor is it uncommon to see the back of the stage represent a street, while the side scenes represent a wood." Eight days later the same paper reported that "the scenery is now got up with great taste." One can assume that the Hallam Company built and painted its own scenery and, undoubtedly, spent a busy week.

The four sets of borders required for the well-equipped stage included ceilings for fancy and plain interiors and leaf borders and sky borders for exterior scenes. With wings and borders forming the frames for drops, and with the above-mentioned combinations, almost any number of drops could be used. It was therefore possible, and probably necessary, to have between a dozen and two dozen backdrops depicting everything from battlefields to waterfalls, from palatial interiors to hovels.

Scene changes were so simple they were made in full view of the audience by stagehands dressed as servants. Furniture, apparently kept to a bare minimum, was also slid on- and offstage by "servants."

Three-dimensional Scenery

Although a cutout ship with possibly some third-dimensional features was used in the Charlestowne production of *The Tempest* in 1793, the beginning of constructed, rather than painted, scenery is generally credited to John Burke. In a letter describing his Boston production of *The Battle of Bunker's Hill* in 1796, Burke stated: "The hill is raised gradually by boards extended from the stage to a bench. Three men should walk abreast on it, and the side where the English march up should, for the most part, be turned towards the

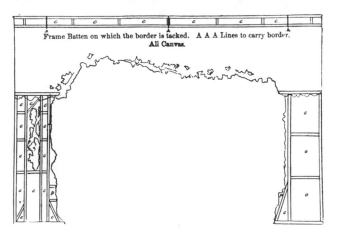

Frame Batten on which the border is tacked. A A A Lines to carry border.
All Canvas.

Rear elevation of an exterior wing-and-drop, ca. 1883: "the wings as made of light wooden framing, and where it is marked C it is fitted with canvas, and where it is marked P with profile" (from F. Lloyds, *Practical Guide to Scene Painting and Painting in Distemper*).

wings; on our hill, there was room for 18 or 20 men, and they were concealed by a board painted mud colour, and having two cannon painted on it—which Board was three feet and a half high . . . firing commences—they are beaten back—windows on the stage should be opened to let out the smoak. . . . A square piece about nine feet high and five feet wide, having some houses and a meeting house painted on fire with flame and smoak issuing from it . . . the window and doors cut out for transparencies. . . . We had painted Smoak suspended. . . . Small cannon should be fired during the battle, which continued with us for 12 or 15 minutes."[1]

Beginning of Realism

During the eighteenth century American theatrical productions paid little attention to historical accuracy. Costumes for the most part were either contemporary, traditional (such as the long black gown and red wig for Shylock), or improvised from material at hand. Furniture and properties were used as found, crudely built of wood or papier-mâché, or painted on the backdrop. A garden drop or street might serve equally well for plays set in London, Paris, or Venice.

Probably the first attempt at historical accuracy in this country was made for the 1809 revival of *De Montfort* in New York's Park Theatre, where John Holland painted the necessary Gothic settings for the production. It was Charles Kean, however, who brought the first historically accurate spectacle to New York in 1846. In his presentation of *King John*, with a reported cast of two hundred, all costumes, properties, and scenery were designed according to the best scholarly information of the time. Wings and drops were executed in minute detail, conforming to the architectural styles of the thirteenth century.

Five years before Kean's production of *King John*, Dion Boucicault was experimenting with another attempt at realism: the box, or "sealed," set. Still a novelty in London, the box set, with three walls enclosing the stage as a realistic room, formed a fitting background for Boucicault's *London Assurance* and gave the Park Theatre an unprecedented three-week run. Such a simple inno-

1. William Dunlap, *A History of the American Theatre* (New York: J. & J. Harper, 1932), pp. 161-63.

vation, as it might seem to us now, was the talk of New York in 1841 and set a style of staging that has persisted for well over a century.

The box set was quickly adopted by the larger and more important theatres, but wings and drops continued to be the staging style through the turn of the century on less well equipped stages. In fact, plain and fancy sets and fancy center doors were apparently frequently used during the first quarter of the twentieth century.

Early Spectaculars

Theatre has always thrived on novelty. Guest appearances, entr'actes, star systems, historicals, realistic sets, stage machinery, and extravaganzas are all outgrowths of a desire to build audience interest.

In all probability it was the need for just such a stimulus that prompted the Charlestowne, South Carolina, company to produce *The Tempest* as a spectacle that showed, according to the *City Gazette* of April 20, 1793, "a troubled horizon and tempestuous sea, where the usurper's vessel is tossed a considerable time in sight." Thunder and lightning, rain and hail accompanied as "the vessel sinks in full view of the audience." The performance concluded with Ariel in a chariot in the clouds.

Such a glowing report from a newspaper stimulates an interest in the mechanics of such a production, but unfortunately our knowledge of the methods used to achieve these effects is purely conjectural. One can reasonably assume, however, that current British practices were in use in America. The fact that trapdoors have been standard equipment in stages for many centuries suggests that the sinking of a ship could be accomplished by placing a portion of the deck on the trap and fastening a ship cutout painted on canvas to the deck. As the trap is lowered, the cutout merely folds up on the floor. It is not known when the practice of using stagehands under a blue floorcloth to simulate an undulating sea began, but it is not unlikely that this was the method used to heighten the storm effect in *The Tempest*.

The thunder sheet was invented in 1708 by John Dennis, whose possessive nature was responsible for the introduction of the phrase "stealing my thunder" to the English language. It is possible that a sheet of metal produced the necessary thunder sound effects for *The Tempest*. However, prior to that date and long afterward, thunder effects were usually produced by the thunder-run, a machine with reversing chutes along the side and back walls of the stage through which cannonballs, released from a series of pens commonly known as the "rabbit hutch," were rolled; weighted rumble carts filled with stone or scrap iron and provided with cleated wooden wheels that rumbled across the stage; or cannonballs in wooden drums. These traditional methods of producing storm effects depended greatly upon timber house-construction for resonance.

In the years before electricity, the lycopodium pipe was used to produce lightning flashes. The pipe was similar to our simple fixative spray pipe, and when the operator blew into one end, the highly combustible lycopodium powder was sprayed onto the open flame of a candle. At later dates magnesium powder was sometimes substituted for lycopodium, but *The Tempest* would have used the latter since it was readily available in the neighborhood apothecary, where it was needed as a coating for hand-rolled pills and as a dusting powder for the skin.

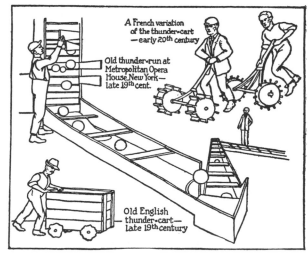

Thunder in old wooden theatres (from Louis Hartmann, *Theatre Lighting*).

Later Spectaculars

Spectaculars reached another high point in the 1830s when New York's Park Theatre and the Bowery were in great competition. While the Park catered to the carriage trade, Bowery managers Hamblin and Hackett deliberately introduced a

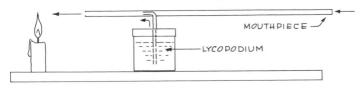

Lycopodium pipe

program of blood, thunder, and spectacle in an effort to woo the lower classes. Such a production was the 1833 presentation of *Mazeppa*. With an actor strapped to his back, Mazeppa, a wild horse, raced up precipices. Thunder, lightning, a falling tree, a moving panoramic background, and a mechanical bird flown from above to peck at the unfortunate rider contributed to the realistic horror of the scene. In this show the moving panorama was made by painting scenery on a long strip of canvas and rolling it off one roller onto another on the opposite side of the stage. Dim light provided by oil and gas during this period made possible quite realistic effects from rather crude devices.

A New Era

From the beginning of theatre in America through the first half of the nineteenth century, staging customs were basically wing-and-drop style. Stages, too, for the most part followed a given pattern. A large apron extended into the auditorium, the stage was raked (slanted toward the audience), proscenium doors were located on each side, and grooves were permanent fixtures in the wing position.

According to Barnard Hewitt, the opening of Booth's Theatre in 1869 marked the beginning of a new era in the theatre.[2] Booth not only did away with conventional raking, grooves, proscenium doors, and apron, but he also built the stagehouse to a seventy-six-foot height so that he could frame his drops tautly and fly them out of sight. Although wings were still used most of the time, they were individually braced and set at irregular intervals in accordance with the dictates of directors and not of stages. Hydraulic-powered traps were used to lower heavy pieces of scenery to the basement, where other scenery could be slid in place and raised to the stage level.

2. Barnard Hewitt, *Theatre U.S.A., 1668 to 1957* (New York: McGraw-Hill Book Co., 1959), p. 217.

Although Booth's Theatre was probably not the first in this country to introduce any of these innovations, it undoubtedly was the first to include them all in a total disregard for traditional staging conventions. In any event the next forty years witnessed prodigious changes in stage mechanization. Cities in Germany, France, England, and America experimented with revolving stages, wagon stages, hydraulic stages, and combinations of these, plus new grid systems. Power to operate this array of inventions ranged from hand, to counterweight, to hydraulic devices, and finally to electricity. The stage had become fully mechanized.

The Double Stage

One of the most fascinating of the "gadget stages" of the last quarter of the nineteenth century was that of Steele MacKaye. As a solution to the ever increasing problem of shifting heavy realistic scenery, MacKaye designed a double stage for New York's Madison Square Theatre, which was opened in 1884. The stagehouse consisted of an elevator shaft 114' high, 22' wide, and 31' deep in which two stages 25' apart were suspended by cables at the four corners. The forty-eight ton stages were counterweighted, and a hoisting cable running to a drum operated by four men provided the necessary 25' 2" movement. The time allotted for changing from one stage to the other was forty-five seconds.

Each of these two stages contained its own set of traps, and 6' of space was provided between the two stages, allowing room for machinery necessary to operate the traps on the upper stage. A double set of gaslights provided illumination, and rubber-hose connections allowed for the travel.

In addition to his novel theatre, Steele MacKaye is credited with many other theatrical devices, including rising theatre seats, sliding stages, adjustable proscenium, flameproofing for scenery, and various complicated lighting effects.

Scenery Construction

Whether the scene technician has been too busy to write, totally uninterested, or incapable is a moot question. The fact remains that there is practically no record of how American scenery was built prior to the twentieth century. Indeed,

Interior of Booth's Theatre, New York, on its opening, February 3, 1869, of *Romeo and Juliet*, Act III, Scene 5, showing the loggia leading to Juliet's chamber (engraving from Frank Leslie's *Illustrated Newspaper*, February 27, 1869)

one of the first books to deal specifically with scenic problems was written by Arthur Edwin Krows in 1916. In his book, *Play Production in America*, Krows devotes several chapters to scenery, lighting, and painting and appears to be describing old and established methods of the period. This could reasonably take us back to such standardization of construction as existed at the turn of the century and, perhaps, long before that. Flats, even as they are today, were made of seasoned white pine, with mortise and tenon joints "clout nailed together with corner blocks and keystones."[3] Plywood was a Russian invention of the 1880s, but it was not used in connection with scenery in this country until well after the turn of the century. According to records as far back as the eighties, the use of profile board probably dates back to the eighteenth century. Profile board used for corner blocks and cutouts was made of 1/4" x

12" white pine with canvas glued on both sides. In Krows's words: "Each [flat] usually has two stiles, or vertical side pieces; two toggle-irons, or pairs of rods strained together by reverse threads with nuts; two braces, and top and bottom rails. Doors and arches have flat, iron sills to keep them firmly in shape. All frames are provided with cleats, lash-lines, and so forth. . . . Pieces in the round, like tree trunks, are usually made of hollow cylinders of light lath, or frames covered with wire netting over which canvas is stretched and twisted."[4] With the exception of "toggle-irons" there appears to have been very little change in construction methods over the next fifty years.

Exactly when hinges were first used with scenery is not known, but in 1916 Krows wrote of twofolds, threefolds, and loose-pin hinges for temporary fastening in a most matter-of-fact manner.

Since the major portion of the life of any set of

3. Arthur Edwin Krows, *Play Production in America* (New York: Henry Holt & Co., 1916), p. 141.

4. Ibid.

Steele MacKaye's double stage in the Madison Square Theatre, New York (engraving from *Scientific American*, April 5, 1884)

this period was spent on the road, "the American Carpenter makes all his pieces of a size that will go through a [box] car door that measures five feet nine inches."[5] This standard flat width persisted in professional theatre for many years; however, since road show scenery is almost always shipped by truck at the present time, this restriction is no longer valid.

Stock Scenery

By the beginning of the twentieth century virtually every town with a population over one thousand had its opera house or equivalent, and there were over five hundred separate companies touring the United States. The vast majority of these theatres maintained a supply of reserve scen-

ery known as "stock sets," which included wings, borders, and drops for the familiar street scene, a woods scene, plain and fancy interiors, and a garden scene. Plays could thus be mounted locally, or if scenery for a road show were damaged or delayed, the play could go on in stock settings.

An ingenious use of stock scenery was found by some road companies during the second decade of the twentieth century through the use of what was known as "aniline dye stuff." Drops painted with aniline dyes were flexible enough to be folded rather than rolled, and in this way an entire set could be carried in a trunk and simply stretched and tacked over existing stock sets in any theatre.

It is interesting to note that sets constructed according to these same principles were used in

5. Ibid., p. 142.

the Italian theatre shortly after World War II as an economy measure. Subsequently, similar scenery was shipped to the Metropolitan, Chicago, and Dallas opera companies, where it was heralded as the modern Italian concept of stage design. Peter Wolf Associates of Dallas, Texas, were soon making "scenery by the bag," shipped anywhere in the country.

Center Door Fancy

In addition to wings and drops, three-dimensional set pieces found their way into the permanent equipment of many theatres. Probably an outgrowth of the realistic box set, these pieces were practical doors and windows that could stand alone, braced by the stage brace (patented in 1888), and could therefore be used with either drops or flats. One of the most persistent of these pieces was known as the "center door fancy," given the dubious honor of being the only set piece to be "suspended in the flies when not in use." The importance ascribed to this piece inspired a poem by Howard Lindsay, then stage manager for Margaret Anglin, which begins:

> O Center-Door-Fancy that hangs in the flies
> Do you feel that you have been given a raise?
> As you room with the borders—the kitchens and skies
> Do you join them in play—or only in plays?[6]

Other practical doors and windows, although of lesser importance than the center door fancy, were equally rigid in construction and were braced by jacks or stage braces.

Floors

Along with the growing popularity of the realistic box set came the more extensive use of the groundcloth, or floorcloth. A large piece of canvas painted to represent a floor appropriate to a play, the groundcloth was laid over the entire visible acting area. Many such cloths were painted in great detail to represent parquet floors, lawns, or pavement. In plays calling for several different types of floors, the various cloths were laid in sequence and peeled off during the scene change to reveal the next cloth.

6. Ibid., pp. 121-22.

The floor for Margaret Anglin's 1914 production of *Lady Windermere's Fan* was made of strips of shellacked linoleum glued on a canvas back to simulate a hardwood floor. Since this type of floor could be rolled for easy transportation, it became popular with vaudeville of the era, especially with clog dancers.

The Run

As wings and drops gradually gave way to box sets and realistic scenery, it became commonplace to force perspective, particularly with backings, to give the illusion of greater depth. Practical ramps, known as "runs," were used in conjunction with painted perspective to further this illusion behind doors, arches, and windows. Many exterior scenes used runs as a road leading to the wings, where the actor dropped character long enough to climb down a ladder to the stage level.

Scene Painting

A Practical Guide to Scene Painting and Painting in Distemper by F. Lloyds, printed ca. 1883, was probably the first comprehensive treatment of the subject to be published in this country. In great detail Lloyds describes paint frames, brushes, paints, binders, drops, wings, profiles, architectural drawings, and painting techniques. Among the colors found on the scene painter's palette of that era were the familiar whiting, lemon chrome, orange chrome, yellow ochre, raw and burnt sienna, raw and burnt umber, vermillion, venetian

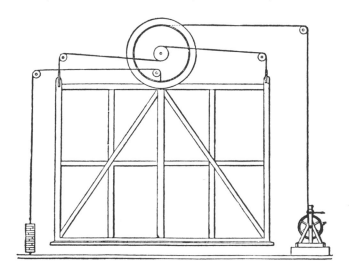

Front elevation of a paint frame, ca. 1883 (from F. Lloyds, *Practical Guide to Scene Painting and Painting in Distemper*)

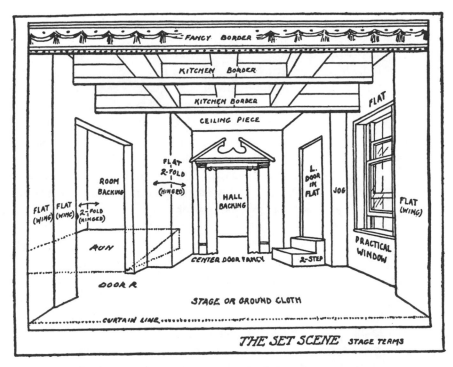

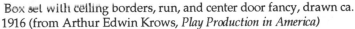

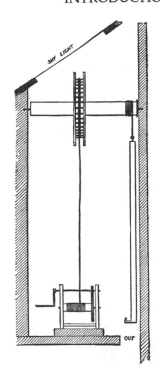

Box set with ceiling borders, run, and center door fancy, drawn ca. 1916 (from Arthur Edwin Krows, *Play Production in America*)

Cross section of a paint frame (from F. Lloyds, *Practical Guide to Scene Painting and Painting in Distemper*)

red, ultramarine blue, dark and light green lake, prussian blue, and vandyke brown. Although some of these colors were available in powder form, the majority were purchased in lumps and had to be crushed or ground in water with a palette knife.

The most common binder used for these distemper colors was known as "size" and was used in a one-to-four ratio with water. Where size was not available, a good grade of carpenter's glue (flake or ground amber) was substituted, or, lacking this, Lloyds suggests cuttings of leather, parchment, or any kind of skin, simmered in water until "converted into a strong jelly." The stench of size decomposition was as familiar to Lloyds as it is to us today: "A little carbolic acid, however, mixed with the size will prevent its decomposition."[7]

During the nineteenth century it was common practice to place a paint frame on the backwall of the stage and hang a scaffold known as the "flying bridge" in front of the frame. Painters on the bridge would adjust their height while painting drops by

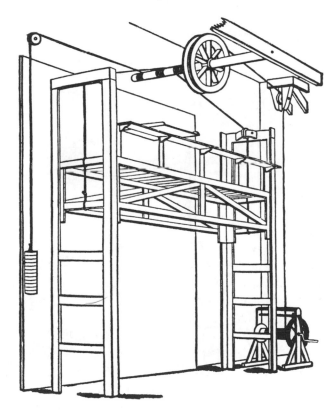

The flying bridge, drawn ca. 1883 (from F. Lloyds, *Practical Guide to Scene Painting and Painting in Distemper*)

7. F. Lloyds, *Practical Guide to Scene Painting and Painting in Distemper* (New York: Excelsior Publishing House, [1883]), p. 20.

raising or lowering the bridge. More stringent fire laws introduced in the eighties curbed the use of paint frames on city stages because of the hazard from the stoves necessary to heat the paint binder. However, in places where fire laws were not strictly enforced, "flying bridges" continued in use through the first quarter of the twentieth century, but the space was gradually taken over by lighting equipment used to light the cyclorama.

As paint frames moved out of theatres, studios were acquired for building and painting scenery. English and American methods of painting at that time employed either a stationary frame with a movable bridge or the less-common movable frame that dropped through a slot in the floor. During this same period the French and Italians used the technique, currently employed for most painting in New York, of stretching drops on the floor and painting with long-handled brushes.

In 1915 business was so brisk in New York that the Lee Lash Studio employed as many as twenty painters, who often worked a double shift. The

peak season for building and painting ran from May through January.

Help for the Amateur

Amateur theatrical groups choosing to produce plays from the Samuel French acting editions of the second half of the nineteenth century must have taken considerable comfort in the advertisement appearing on the inside covers of Mr. French's scripts. The front cover offered colored paper scenery to fit all demands while the back cover promised a most effective proscenium, complete with a picture of Shakespeare in the center. The reproduction appearing here was taken from French's acting edition of *Camille*, ca. 1856, but an identical advertisement appeared in many of French's Standard Drama series during this era.

Decentralization

The advent of motion pictures contributed to the demise of the majority of road shows and curtailed the activities of many scene studios. With fewer shows on the road, however, amateur theatrical groups and community theatres began to develop throughout the country. Inexperienced help and low budgets were probably responsible for some of the worst scenery in our brief theatrical history. In an effort to inform amateurs of proper construction methods, Dariel Fitzkee of the American Stu-

Flying horses, F. Lloyds's suggested alternative to the flying bridge (*Practical Guide to Scene Painting and Painting in Distemper*)

SCENERY.

With a view to obviate the great difficulty experienced by Amateurs (particularly in country houses) in obtaining Scenery, &c., to fix in a Drawing Room, and then only by considerable outlay for hire and great damage caused to walls, we have decided to keep a series of Scenes, &c., colored on strong paper, which can be joined together or pasted on canvas or wood, according to requirement. Full directions, with diagrams showing exact size of Back Scenes, Borders, and Wings, can be had free on application. The following four scenes consist each of thirty sheets of paper.

GARDEN.

The above is an illustration of this scene. It is kept in two sizes. The size of the back scene of the smaller one is 10 feet long and 6½ feet high, and extends, with the wings and border, to 15 feet long and 8 feet high. The back scene of the large one is 13 feet long and 9 feet high, and extends, with the wings and border, to 20 feet long and 11½ feet high. It is not necessary to have the scene the height of the room, as blue paper to represent sky is usually hung at the top. Small size, with Wings and Border complete, $7.50 ; large size, do., $10.00.

WOOD.

This is similar in style to the above, only a wood scene is introduced in the centre. It is kept in two sizes, as the previous scene, and blue paper can be introduced as before indicated. Small size, with Wings and Borders complete, $7.50 ; large size, do., $10.00.

FOLIAGE.—This is a sheet of paper on which foliage is drawn, which can be repeated and cut in any shape required. Small size, 30 in. by 20 in., 25 cts. per sheet ; large size, 40 in. by 30 in., 35 cts. per sheet.

TREE TRUNK. This is to be used with the foliage sheets and placed at the bottom of the scene.—Price and size same as foliage.

DRAWING ROOM.

This scene is only kept in the large size. The back scene is 13 feet long and 9 feet high, and extends, with the wings and borders, to 20 feet long and 11½ feet high. In the centre is a French window, leading down to the ground, which could be made practicable if required. On the left wing is a fireplace with mirror above, and on the right wing is an oil painting. The whole scene is tastefully ornamented and beautifully colored, forming a most elegant picture. Should a box scene be required extra wings can be had, consisting of doors each side, which could be made practicable. Price, with Border and one set of Wings, $10.00 ; with Border and two sets of Wings, to form box scene, $12.50.

COTTAGE INTERIOR.

This is also kept in the large size only. In the centre is a door leading outside. On the left centre is a rustic fireplace, and the right centre is a window. On the wings are painted shelves, &c., to complete the scene. A box scene can be made by purchasing extra wings, as before described, and forming doors on each side. Price, with Border and one set of Wings, $10.00 ; with Border and two sets of Wings, to form box scene, $12.50.

The above Scenes, mounted, can be seen at **28 West 23d St.,** New York. Full directions accompany each Scene.

PROSCENIUM AND DROP SCENE.

PROSCENIUM.—A most effective Proscenium can be formed by utilizing the paper made for this purpose. Three pieces of wood are merely required, shaped according to this design, and covered with the paper ; the proscenium having the appearance of light blue puffed satin panels, in gold frames, with Shakespeare medallion in the centre.

Puffed satin paper, Light Blue, size 20 inches by 20 inches, per sheet, 25 cts.
Imitation Gold Bordering, per sheet, 25c., making 14 feet.
Shakespearian Medallion, 18 inches in diameter, 50 cts.

DROP SCENE. The picture shown above is an illustration of this scene. It comprises four sheets of paper which are to be pasted in the centre of any sized canvas that may be requisite for the drop curtain. Size 6½ feet by 5 feet. Price $2.50.

DOORS.—These comprise three sheets of paper each, and can be had either for drawing-room or cottage purposes. Size, 7 feet by 3 feet. Price, complete, $1.25 each.

WINDOW.—This is a parlor window formed with two sheets of paper, and could be made practicable to slide up and down. The introduction of curtains each side would make it very effective. Size, 3 feet by 4½ feet. Price. $1.00, complete.

FRENCH WINDOW.—Consisting of four sheets of paper, representing a window containing four large ornamental frosted glass panes with colored glass around. Size 6½ feet high by 5 feet. Price $1.50.

FIREPLACE.—This is also made with two sheets of paper. The fire is lighted, but should this not be required a fire-paper can be hung over it. It will be found most useful in many farces wherein a character has to climb up a chimney, and many plays where a fireplace is indispensable. By purchasing a door, window, and fireplace an ordinary room scene could easily be constructed with the addition of some wall-paper. Size, 3 feet by 4½ feet. Price, complete, $1.25.

dio wrote a book called *Professional Scenery Construction*. This book represents a conscientious effort on the part of the author to divulge, as he explains in his preface, "for the first time, the real, true, trade-secrets of the professional scenery builder."[8]

In 1932 Cleon Throckmorton approached the same problem from a different angle. Throckmorton conceived the idea of prefabricating scenery and shipping it by the piece from his scene studio to the buyers. His catalogue included everything needed for the stage, from a variety of painted and unpainted flats to platforms, stairs, doors, windows, fireplaces, lights, and switchboards. Con-

siderable ingenuity was shown in creating modules permitting the interchange of various scenic effects.

With the introduction of drama courses in colleges and universities in the late twenties and thirties came a certain standardization of construction methods, in many cases differing somewhat from scenery bearing the union label, but generally following sound structural procedures. Evidence of some training and understanding is found in most community and amateur theatres of today, even though the results may not be of the highest standards.

What has happened to the many studios in New York that were so busy during the first quarter of the century? They have dwindled to a few, the

8. Dariel Fitzkee, *Professional Scenery Construction*, ed. Ellen M. Gall (San Francisco: Banner Play Bureau, 1930), p. 8.

largest of which is the Nolan Scene Studio, claiming 80 percent of the Broadway business. Television studios maintain their own shops, the movie industry builds its own scenery, colleges and universities provide shops for their needs, and even the community theatres have shop spaces, or the stage, on which they can build and paint their scenery. The New York theatre remains the parent theatre, but the secrets of the trade are indeed far-flung.

LIGHTING

Early Lighting

Candles were the only means of artificial illumination available to our first American theatres. Before the invention of the mold in 1708, candles were made by repeatedly dipping a stringlike wick into melted tallow until a sizable diameter was built up. Considering the number of candles necessary to light a theatre, one can imagine the enthusiasm with which a theatre manager would accept the simple candle mold.

A reasonably well equipped theatre of the last quarter of the eighteenth century might boast two chandeliers in the auditorium and one on stage. Additional candles lined the front of the stage in the footlight position, and still more candles, mounted in brackets, were hung on the upstage side of the wings. It was the custom of the times for theatres to have a swab and tub of water on each side of the stage, and all members of the cast and crew were alerted to possible duty. All candles were lighted before the play began and were tended during the evening by the "snuff boy," who often walked on stage during a scene to trim a smoking wick. Other snuff-boy duties sometimes included "dimming" the lights by snuffing some of the candles for darker scenes. Since the brightest part of the stage was the center, where all rays converged, this location, known as the "focus," became the most desirable acting area.

Spermaceti and Tallow

From the meticulous records of David Douglass, we learn something of the cost of lighting a mid-eighteenth-century theatre. During a benefit performance on a November night in 1761, in the Chapple Street Theatre, New York, Douglass recorded the use of 26 pounds of spermaceti and 14 pounds of tallow at a cost of about $13.00, approximately 4 percent of the total gross receipts of about $333.[9]

Chandeliers of this period caused considerable grumbling among the pit patrons, who were constantly showered by candle drippings from above. In an effort to placate the patrons, a few managers introduced oil lamps before the turn of the century, but this only led to further complaints about the unpleasant odor of burning oil. Some astute managers partially solved both problems, the dripping of candles and the stench of oil, by moving chandeliers to the sides of the auditorium, introducing ventilators in the ceiling, and in some cases adding venetian blinds in the boxes.

The end of the eighteenth century saw the development of the Argand burner for oil, which used a tube-shaped wick and a glass chimney and produced a steadier, brighter light. Although green chimneys were alternated with white in the Haymarket Theatre in London prior to this time, one of the first mentions of colored light on the American stage appeared in the *Royal Gazette* of June 10, 1778, in reference to a New York production celebrating the king's birthday: "Lamps 'of every color' and a band of music 'cheered' the company."

The Age of Gas

In 1816 the Chestnut Street Theatre in Philadelphia became the first in the United States to use gas as a means of illumination. The added "brilliancy and neatness" was advertised as certain to please the audience.

Apparently the expense of installing gas was a deterrent to other theatres, for it was not until 1825 that the Chatham Theatre introduced gaslight to New York. One year after that, however, in 1826, both the Bowery and the Lafayette Theatres converted to gas, and in 1827 the Lafayette introduced the gas border light, thus temporarily freeing the wings from the ladders and trees formerly used for hanging lights.

Improvement in gaslights continued until the turn of the century. In border lights and footlights, jets were placed closer together so that they could be lighted at one end and the flame would travel to

9. William Dunlap, *A History of the American Theatre*, p. 46.

Gaslights of yesterday. The cage was a fire precaution; the trailing hose was connected to the gas main (from Louis Hartmann, *Theatre Lighting*).

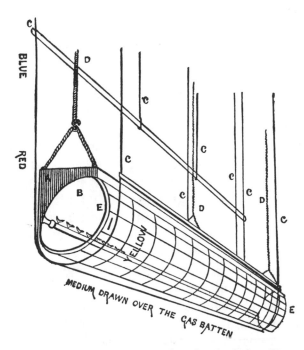

A method of changing colors of gas border lights. Pieces of blue, red, and yellow silk were sewn together and looped around the gas batten. A. Downstage lines holding silk. B. Sheet-metal reflector painted white. C. Upstage lines holding silk. D. Lines supporting gas batten. E. Wire protecting silk from gas flame. By lowering line A and raising line C, the color was changed from yellow to red to blue (from F. Lloyds, *Practical Guide to Scene Painting and Painting in Distemper*).

the other, producing a continuous light; special mesh screens were placed over and around lights to protect scenery from the flames; guard chains were placed in front of footlights to protect costumes; the olivette, a crude tin box on a standard that could be moved around the stage, was developed as a side light to once again usurp wing space; a system for lighting all gas jets by means of electricity was installed in the Booth Theatre in New York in 1868; the Argand burner was adapted to gas to give a brighter, steadier light.

The last, but by no means the least, gaslight improvement came in the nineties with the invention of the Welsbach burner, which surrounded the flame with a mantle and produced a white light when the mantle was heated to incandescence. The Welsbach burner, similar to the Coleman lantern of today, was enclosed in a protective screen, which kept scenery hanging from the flies at a safe distance. The burner could be used in border, wing, and footlight positions, with a guard rope behind the footlights to prevent trailing robes from catching fire.

In the Limelight

The limelight, variously known as calcium light, oxyhydrogen light, or Drummond light, after its inventor Thomas Drummond, was developed as a geodetical survey light and was first used in Ireland about 1825. The first recorded use of this light onstage was in London in 1837, but it was not until the midsixties that it gained general acceptance in

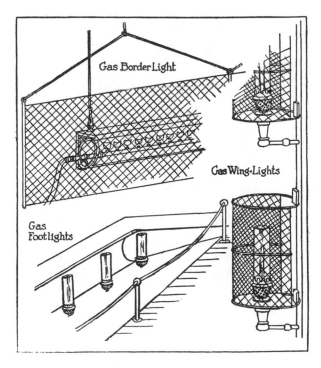

Welsbach burner (from Louis Hartmann, *Theatre Lighting*)

this country. The point source of light, derived from playing an oxygen-hydrogen flame on a cylindrical piece of lime, made possible the use of a lens and gave the theatre its first practical spotlight.

The limelight, however, was not without drawbacks. It was a bulky instrument, requiring two containers (originally india rubber bags), one of oxygen and one of hydrogen, plus the necessary double hose running to the light. It was mandatory that an operator be in attendance at all times to adjust both flame and lime, and not infrequently the audience was startled by a loud pop, followed by a blackout, when the attendant attempted to adjust light intensity but added too much oxygen.

During this period, the man in charge of illumination was quite naturally referred to as the "gas man" and was usually a plumber who resorted to a little moonlighting to supplement his income. Later, when electricity was installed, the "gas man" usually became the electrician.

The Arc Light

Theatres were experimenting with electricity before the invention of the electric lamp, and the extremely bright light caused by a spark leaping between two carbon electrodes was the beginning of a new kind of light for the stage. At first the arc was used as a means of providing lightning and other special effects, but in the early 1880s a few olivettes were converted from gas to arc lights, powered by dynamos installed in individual the-

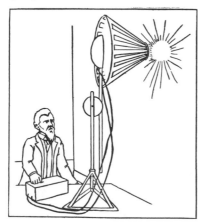

Electric light instrument of 1873. A simple arc placed in the focus of a parabolic mirror and projected through a slotted funnel against the transparent back of a drop produced the effect of a rising or setting sun, with broad surrounding shafts of light (from Louis Hartmann, *Theatre Lighting*).

atres. A little later a nickel-plated parabolic reflector was placed behind the electrodes to give direction and concentration to the arc flood.

Because the general light provided by gas was soft and diffused, the contrasting harshness and intensity of the arc were originally considered detrimental to stage lighting except for special effects such as sun, moon, or lightning. The softer rays of the limelight were much preferred by lighting experts for what we might term area or accent lighting. However, the inconvenience and expense of shipping oxygen and hydrogen containers back for refill (the cost was said to be about $2.00 per light per evening) soon tipped the balance from the more artistic limelight to the more economical arc light.

David Henderson, founder and promoter of the Chicago Opera House, is said to have been among the first to light an extravaganza with arc lights. The year was 1900. Henderson had his own lighting expert design and build his arc lights, which came to be known as Kruger Lamps.

Electricity Takes Over

Edison's newly developed electric lamp was placed on the market in 1879, and by 1885 theatres in New York, Boston, Chicago, and San Francisco were using electric lights. Theatre managers, as might be expected, took full advantage of the publicity value of the new development and measured efficiency in terms of quantity, advertising their installations as having "thousands of the electric lamps."[10]

Early Installations

The crude manner in which electricity was first used in theatres would have given a present-day inspector nightmares. Anyone who could fasten two wires to terminals and get light was immediately hailed as an electrician. It was common to find inflexible single-strand wire, covered with tape for insulation, connecting open knife switches mounted on wooden panels with wooden sockets in tin-lined borders and footlights. Wire was occasionally threaded through gas hose as an extra precaution and for added insulation.

10. "Stage Lighting—A Survey since 1906," *Illuminating Engineering* 51 (January 1956):113.

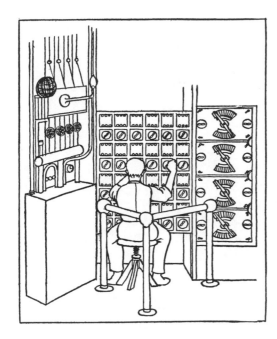

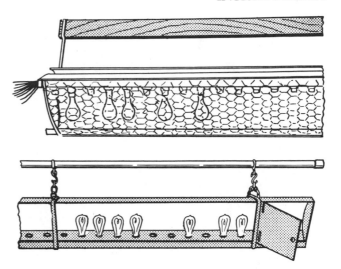

Border lights ca. 1900, with sockets above for lamps and gas jets below for emergencies (from *Illuminating Engineering*, January 1956).

Light control on the stage of Proctor and Turner's Theatre, New York, in the late nineteenth century, with the gas table, still needed for emergencies, and the electrical board at the left. The operator is working the switches, and the dimmers are at his right. This was only seven years after Edison had opened the first central power stations in New York and only ten years after he had demonstrated his first practical incandescent lamp (from Louis Hartmann, *Theatre Lighting*).

Since neither lamp nor power source was particularly reliable in the early days of electricity, border lights and footlights were generally equipped with both gas jets and sockets, and it was not uncommon to see switchboards and "gas tables" side by side in theatres. On more occasions than one, the newly appointed electrician found himself back in his old job as plumber or gas man.

Lamp Efficiency

In 1906 the largest, brightest light available on the market was the 32-candlepower carbon filament lamp. Heat emanating from this lamp was sufficient to fade silk and gelatine color mediums, and most directors were therefore content to use the 50-watt, 16-candlepower lamp. When we realize that our present 100-watt household lamps are rated at approximately 125 candlepower, or almost eight times the intensity of the 1906 lamp, we can readily appreciate the relatively low intensity of light from each instrument on the stages of this era. Approximately sixty 16-candlepower lights

would be needed to equal the intensity of one present-day 500-watt ellipsoidal spotlight lamp.

Equipment in the Early 1900s

During the first decade of the twentieth century, one might expect to find the following equipment on the stage of one of our largest theatres:

Footlights and border lights, equipped with both gas jets and lamp sockets. The sockets were generally wired for four circuits—red, amber, white, and blue. According to Krows, the simple ratio used for most shows was three amber to one white,[11] but elaborate plays might call for two whites to one blue and one amber, with no mention of the red circuit.

Olivettes: simple, open-box arc lights used in the wings.

Bunch lights: the familiar open-box floodlight with ten to twelve sockets for 16-candlepower lamps.

X-rays: a form of border light designed for incandescent lamps and equipped with a highly efficient silvered glass reflector. The process of manufacturing this reflector was developed in 1896, the same year Professor Wilhelm Roentgen announced his discovery of the X-ray. Since "X-ray" seemed descriptive of the power of the reflector, the name was given to this type of border light. Although the actual reflectors are rarely, if ever,

11. *Play Production in America*, p. 210.

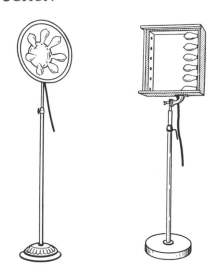

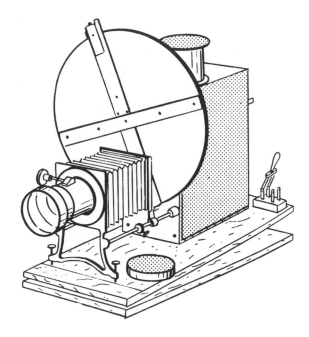

Bunch lights used in the first decade of the twentieth century (from *Illuminating Engineering*, January 1956).

Stereopticon of early twentieth century used for moving effects (from *Illuminating Engineering*, January 1956).

Gallery reflector ca. 1905, using carbon arc and nickel-plated parabolic reflector (from *Illuminating Engineering*, January 1956).

found on the stage today, the term is still in common use.[12]

Gallery reflectors: balcony arc lights with parabolic reflectors and spill rings.

Special effects projectors and stereopticons of various forms, using carbon arcs as the light source and capable of projecting moving effects of snow, clouds, rain, and water ripples painted on moving mica disks.

Switchboards using resistance dimmers manu-

12. See Joel Edward Rubin, "The Technical Development of Stage Lighting Apparatus in the United States" (Ph.D. diss., Stanford University, 1959), p. 57.

factured by Ward Leonard or Cutler Hammer, individually controlled or, toward the end of the decade, in interlocking banks.

By this time several manufacturers of lighting equipment were in existence, including Universal Electric Stage Lighting Company, later to become Kliegl Brothers. New lights were advertised in catalogues and old equipment was dropped as it became obsolete. Thus, by 1909 combination gas and electric border lights and footlights were no longer advertised, although it was certainly not uncommon to see them in theatres for a number of years thereafter.

The Followspot

One of the first records we have of using a spotlight to follow an actor onstage refers to the 1866 production of *Black Crook*, presented in Niblo's Garden, New York. For many years after that, stars of a production were followed around the stage by the limelight. Sarah Bernhardt, during her 1900 "farewell" tour in *Camille*, managed to bundle a stagehand and limelight into a basket and send them aloft to follow her throughout the show.

In all probability, the custom of following actors influenced David Belasco in his 1911 New York production of *The Return of Peter Grimm*, although

AA-Light Bridge | DD-Proscenium Lights
BB-Tormentor Lights | EEE-Border Lights
C-Portable Switchboard | F-Fly-Gallery Lights
for Light Bridge | G-Main Switchboard

Diagram of the major scene for Louis Hartmann's lighting of *The Return of Peter Grimm* (from Louis Hartmann, *Theatre Lighting*).

his technique showed considerable refinement. In this famous production, in which David Warfield appeared for so long in the role of Peter, Louis Hartmann used what he claimed to be his newly invented 7-volt lamps as the light source for his "baby lenses."[13] Nearly a dozen men, each with a baby lens, were stationed in the proscenium and on a specially constructed bridge overhead. Each attendant was given a character in the play to follow with his light and had the responsibility of adjusting intensity and color in accordance with predetermined cues.

Since these early days, the followspot has increased in efficiency and intensity and has a somewhat different role in present lighting practice. For extravaganzas, musicals, ballet, and ice shows, the followspot is almost essential in calling attention to the important act or actor. However, through the use of area lighting and greater dimmer control, it is rarely necessary to use such a blatant light as the followspot for dramatic productions.

Equipment Development

During the second decade of the twentieth century, manufacturers answered requests for larger, more efficient lamps for theatre use, and new lighting equipment was developed for the stage. In 1913, 500-watt and 1,000-watt nitrogen-filled lamps superseded bunch lights, the arc flood, and

13. Louis Hartmann, *Theatre Lighting* (New York: D. Appleton & Co., 1930), p. 35.

the gas olivette. In 1915 catalogues listed disappearing footlights for the first time. A new 1,000-watt concentrated filament lamp made its debut in 1918 in a much more intense plano-convex spotlight. Improvements in reflectors resulted in the long-throw "Caliban" flood, advertised as suitable for outdoor pageants. The "Caliban" derived its name from Percy MacKaye's production of the masque *Caliban*, presented at the stadium of the College of the City of New York in 1916. This light was essentially a floodlight with a parabolic reflector and louvres to shield spill light from the audience. The 1,000-watt nitrogen-filled incandescent lamp was probably used in this instrument, although neither the lamp nor the "Caliban" was shown in catalogues until a year or two later.

Portion of the control board at the old Metropolitan Opera House in New York. An oil lantern hangs over the gas table in case of emergencies (from Louis Hartmann, *Theatre Lighting*).

Similar larger lamps used in border lights made compartmentalizing possible and provided slots for frames to facilitate the use of color.

Perhaps the greatest improvements in lighting instruments came during the brief period between 1930 and 1936. In 1932 the newly developed "downlights," installed as house lights in the Radio City Music Hall auditorium, introduced the potential of ellipsoidal reflectors. By 1934 both the Century Lighting Equipment Company and Kliegl Brothers were advertising ellipsoidal spotlights. Century named their light the Lekolite, taken from the first two letters of the last names of the company's founders, Joseph Levy and Edward Kook; the Kliegl Brothers light was called the Klieglight.

During this same period experimental work was being done with the fresnel lens, which proved so successful that the 1936 catalogues showed a complete line of fresnel spotlights ranging in size from 250 to 5,000 watts. The Alzak process of manufacturing reflectors replaced the old electrolytic process in 1935, increasing efficiency up to 85 percent reflectance.

With better reflectors and better lenses, the ellipsoidal and fresnel spotlights became the major instruments of stage lighting and have remained unchallenged in the many years that have followed.

Intensity Control

Not counting the chores of the snuff boys of the eighteenth century, one of the first evidences of attempted light control came in 1794, when a special footlight trough was built in the Chestnut Street Theatre in Philadelphia. Across the 36-foot proscenium was constructed a trough that lowered the footlights—described as "wicks floating in lard"—into the stage, thus "dimming" the lights for night scenes.

In the middle of the nineteenth century came the invention of the "gas table." From its humble beginnings as a few valves used to turn lights on and off, the gas table was developed over the next thirty years into a complicated maze of pipes and valves controlling the intensity of individual lights and permitting complete light changes during the performance. For the first time, through unified lighting control, house lights could be dimmed, moods could be established, and changes in the time of day could be shown effectively onstage.

By the time electricity reached the theatres, the necessity of lighting control was well established; consequently, resistance dimmers, with patents as early as 1885, were added to the new systems. The height of perfection for resistance dimmers was reached in the 1920s with both manual and motor-controlled interlocking dimmers and masters.

According to Joel Edward Rubin, the first resistance-controlled reactor dimmer in the United States was installed in the Cleveland Public Auditorium in 1920, and the first tube reactor was built for the Chicago Civic Opera in 1929.[14] A number of tube reactors were installed throughout the country during the next few years, including the giant

350-control, five-preset board in Radio City Music Hall in 1932.

In the midthirties, the first autotransformer dimmers became available for theatres equipped with alternating current, but this unfortunately included very few professional theatres. The thyratron tube, developed in the late forties, formed the basis for another kind of remote control and presetting dimmer board. Shortly after the magnetic amplifier switchboard was introduced in the fifties, the silicon rectifier was developed for theatre use.

Electronic controls made possible presets, card readers, and tapes that could record unlimited numbers of dimmer readings in a memory circuit to be played back on cue. It was only a matter of time before microcircuits and solid state conductors reduced controls to a fraction of their previous size and at the same time increased their efficiency and flexibility.

Research

David Belasco is considered responsible for much of the early development in lighting. When he took over New York's Republic Theatre in 1902, Belasco built a laboratory for lighting research high in the dome of the theatre. It was in this laboratory that Belasco's electrician, Louis Hartmann, spent countless hours developing new spotlights and experimenting with new techniques in lighting.

Among the inventions claimed by Hartmann in his book, *Theatre Lighting,* are concentrated filament lamps; low-voltage lamps; baby spotlights, which he called the "baby lens"; the "tube," known to us as the top hat; various color mediums; and diffusers made of laminated sheets of mica rubbed with emery and oil to frost the outside.

With the help of Henry Irving, Maude Adams made some notable contributions to lighting around the turn of the century. After completing a three-year run of *The Little Minister,* Adams requested a rest so that she could experiment with lighting. During this period she developed a lamp stain for coloring lamps and a compartmentalized border that, together with the three-circuit footlights, were introduced by Henry Irving.

14. "Technical Development of Stage Lighting Apparatus," p. 219.

Munroe Pevear's investigations in color (1911) made possible the manufacture of color mediums of unusual spectral purity. In addition to his experimental work with colors, which included advocating the use of the primary colors of light (red, blue, and green) for complete color control, Pevear designed several new types of spotlights, including those with built-in swivel barndoors and a soft-edge spotlight made possible by grinding the periphery of the lens to help diffuse and blend areas.

Methods versus Madness

With the exception of a handful of visionaries who could see the use of light as an expression of art, most lighting as practiced before World War I consisted of flooding the stage with as much light as possible. Indeed, there are too many instances where this method is still in use.

Formalization of methods of area lighting, accent lighting, and lighting for dramatic effect began with the creation of a graduate course in drama at Yale University in 1925. Within surprisingly few years, most major universities in the country had added drama to the curriculum, and through analysis and research in these schools, many changes have been made. As drama majors have graduated and filtered into manufacturing companies as well as theatres, their impact has been felt throughout the entire industry.

Potentially, lighting can achieve some of the most dramatic effects in the theatre. Directors and technicians of today have at their command the best instruments, the highest intensities, and the greatest control over light ever known in the history of theatre. The possibilities of bathing the stage in a light of any color in the spectrum, piercing the shadows with a pencil-thin shaft of light, or creating naturalistic lighting from motivated light sources are finally all within easy grasp of the technician.

THEATRE BACKSTAGE
FROM A TO Z

A

AB. Abbreviation for ASBESTOS CURTAIN.

ABERRATIONS

Chromatic aberration. Colored rings, rainbows, or lens leaks emanating from spotlights and caused by unequal refractive powers of lens or reflector. Diffuse light beam with frost color media and use spotlight for general lighting only. Replacement of lens or reflector (whichever offends) is the only true correction for aberrations.

Spherical aberration. Failure of a lens or reflector to focus all rays of light from source to a given point. A common fault in inexpensive lenses, spherical aberration may cause stray beams of light to spill in a most objectionable manner. Corrections same as above or realign instrument. See ALIGNMENT, INSTRUMENT.

ABSORPTIVE. Dark neutral shades and black are said to be absorptive because they reflect little or no light. In general, a pigment will reflect its own color and absorb others.

ABSTRACT. Term used to describe nonrepresentational settings, which suggest, rather than duplicate or simulate, appropriate surroundings.

AC. Abbreviation for ALTERNATING CURRENT.

ACCENT. To emphasize one particular action or phase of a scene or play. Methods of accenting include concentration of light; use of elevations or platforms; use of unusual or attractive furniture or properties; creation of center of interest in the setting; use of color in setting or properties; distinctive costumes.

ACETATE. See under PLASTICS.

ACETONE. See under SOLVENTS.

ACHROMATIC. A lens is achromatic when it transmits light without separating it into its spectral colors. Lenses in spotlights should be achromatic.

ACOUSTICAL BARRIER BOARD. Sound-absorbing material used in speaker enclosures. Similar to CELOTEX.

ACOUSTICS. The qualities of a room in respect to transmission of sound. Acoustical problems are generally complex in nature, and many hours of labor, and often a great deal of money, may be saved if acoustical engineers are consulted at the outset.

ACRYLIC. See under PLASTICS.

ACRYLIC LATEX. See under PAINT AND PAINT COLORS.

ACT CURTAIN. A curtain used at the beginning of, during, and at the end of a production.

ACTING AREA. Space on stage in which action of a play takes place. See AREAS; STAGE SPACE.

ADAPTOR (pigtail, jumper, patchcord)

Short length of wire used with equipment having different types of plugs.

Screw-type plug that changes mogul base receptacle to standard, or standard base to candelabra base, etc.

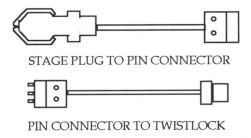

STAGE PLUG TO PIN CONNECTOR

PIN CONNECTOR TO TWISTLOCK

ADAPTORS

AD CURTAIN. An older style of roll curtain with advertising of local business painted on it. See **Roll curtain** under CURTAIN.

3

ADDITIVE METHOD OF COLOR MIXTURE

Lights. Producing color by mixing lights in the primary colors of red, green, and blue. A red light, a blue light, and a green light focused on a given area will produce a white light, providing all colors are pure and intensities of light transmitted are equal. Varying the intensity of individual lights makes it possible to reproduce any color of the spectrum. See also LIGHTING COLORS; SUBTRACTIVE METHOD OF COLOR MIXTURE.

Paints. Producing different colors by adding one color to another, e.g., red and yellow make orange. See also COLOR; COLOR WHEEL.

AIR CASTERS. Used to move platforms, slip stages, and revolvers on a thin film of air. The air caster consists of a neoprene "doughnut" in which air pressure builds up to exceed the total load, thereby breaking the seal and floating the doughnut. The noise of escaping air can be loud enough to offend. Low air pressure, 5 to 10 pounds per square inch (psi), is sufficient to activate the casters, but the relatively high volume of 5 to 15 cubic feet per minute (cfm), is mandatory. A positive displacement pump is recommended for the air supply. If a plant air system is to be used, a simple pressure regulator is required to reduce moving pressure to no more than 15 psi. Connecting hose (3/4") is adequate for air delivery to the casters providing no restrictions of less than 3/4" occur between the supply and the intake. Advantages of the air caster include almost frictionless movement in any horizontal direction, firm contact with the floor when the platform settles in place and practically unlimited load capacity. Air casters operate well only on a smooth, nonporous surface such as Masonite (glossy side up), heavy plastic, or a surface painted with urethane or the equivalent. All cracks or joints must be sealed reasonably air-tight, duct tape will often suffice.

AIR OVER OIL. Term used for compressed air powering a hydraulic cylinder.

AIRPLANE (sound effect). Recordings should be used. An obsolete method for simulating the sound of a propeller plane was to use short leather thongs with knotted ends, fastened to the pulley of a variable speed motor to beat on a snare drum. Intensity was varied by adjusting position of drum in relation to thongs and motor speed or adjusting tension of drum head.

AIR TOOLS. Various tools that use compressed air as a power source. Air tools used in the scene shop include air guns, caulking guns, saber saws, sanders, staplers, and power wrenches. Air nailers in particular are a very commonly used tool for driving brads, nails, staples, and **Tee nails** (see under NAILS).

AISLE. Passageway between seats in auditorium. Aisle widths vary with seating capacity of auditoriums and local and state fire laws. Local architects or fire departments should be consulted before decisions on aisles are made. See also FIRE CODE; SEATING, AUDITORIUM.

A-LADDER. See under LADDERS.

ALARUM. Shakespearean trumpet call to arms. Recordings can be used for distant calls, but live talent is considered more satisfactory for most use.

ALCOHOL. A solvent for shellac, also a wetting agent for making mineral colors water soluble. See also PAINT AND PAINT COLORS; SOLVENTS.

ALCOVE. A recess in a room, frequently used in scene design to accommodate large pieces of furniture, e.g., beds, tables, window seats. May also be used to heighten interest in design or to separate simultaneous action on the stage. See also DESIGN.

ALDER. A semihardwood, easily worked and often used for furniture construction. See also FURNITURE.

ALIGNMENT, INSTRUMENT. A condition where all major components of a lighting instrument are aligned perpendicular to the optical axis. New instruments need to be aligned when received, and spotlights should be aligned on a regular basis; failure to do so can cause ABERRATIONS. See also OPTICAL AXIS.

ALLIGATOR CLIPS. A spring-loaded clip used for temporary electrical connections. Usually used for testing equipment.

ALTERNATING CURRENT (abbr. AC). Current that reverses direction 120 times, or 60 complete cycles, per second as contrasted with DIRECT CURRENT (DC), which flows in one direction only. Since DC cannot be carried great distances economically, AC is widely used in this country, although the odd theatre still has DC. Resistance dimmers and incandescent lamps will operate on either AC or DC, and many kinds of motors, amplifiers, radios, etc., if so designated, will also operate on either current.

ALUMINUM. Soft metal available in a variety of sizes, shapes, thicknesses and hardnesses. Used in many areas backstage.

ALUMINUM PAINT. See under PAINTS, MISCELLANEOUS.

ALZAK REFLECTOR. Trade name for a highly efficient reflector used in many lighting instruments and made by a patented method of processing aluminum developed in the 1930s.

AMBER. A yellowish-orange hue used in color media for lights. See also COLOR MEDIA; LIGHTING COLORS.

AMBER GLUE. A type of water-soluble animal glue used as a paint binder as well as a furniture and covering glue. See also GLUE.

AMBIENT LIGHT. Stray light, either diffused or reflected into areas where it is not wanted. For example, when projections are used on stage, a high ambient light level will tend to wash out the projected picture.

AMBIENT SOUND. Sound that re-creates the space in which it was originally recorded. Background noise, echoes, reverberation, etc., are all components within this concept.

AMERICAN PLAN SEATING. See SEATING, AUDITORIUM.

AMMONIA. Obsolete; used with hydrochloric acid to produce SMOKE EFFECTS.

AMPERE (abbr. amp, A). A measure of current, or rate of flow of electricity, and generally associated with capacities of dimmers or fuses. Fuses and breakers are always rated in amps, dimmer capacities may be given in either watts or amps. Wattage ratings of lights are stamped on the bulbs. Since dimmers and fuses should never be loaded with more watts than they are rated to carry, it is often necessary to change an ampere rating to watts and vice versa. Two simple equations are used, the PIE and the W. VA. See ELECTRICITY.

AMPLEX. Older trade name of a reflector lamp with colored bulb available in many nonfade colors. Reflector lamps, or R-types, cover wider areas at lower intensities than parabolic reflector spotlights of the same wattage. See LAMPS.

AMPLIFIER. A mechanical, electronic device capable of making a sound louder. See under SOUND EQUIPMENT.

AMP TRAP. Special fast-action fuse designed to protect rectifiers in silicon controlled rectifier (SCR) dimmer circuits. Amp traps should never be replaced with other types of fuses.

ANCHOR (verb). To fasten to the floor, as in anchoring a wall of a set, a flat, a groundrow, or a set piece.

ANGLE IRON. See under STRAP IRON.

ANILINE DYE. Dyes of various colors, made from benzene derivative combined with other substances. Transparent dyes that stain as opposed to pigment paints that cover a surface. Aniline is the most potent dye used for costumes, draperies, drops, and glazing sets. For directions in using, see DYE. See also PAINT AND PAINT COLORS.

ANIMAL GLUE (amber, ground gelatine glue). An amber-brown glue usually extracted from animal matter. When more refined it forms gelatine glue. See also GLUE.

ANODE. The positive terminal of an electric source, the terminal through which current enters, as opposed to the negative terminal, called the cathode. Usually refers to radio tubes or arc lights.

ANSI. Abbreviation for American National Standards Institute, an independent organization that establishes standards to promote consistency and interchangeability among manufacturers. For example, ANSI has assigned arbitrary code letters to electric lamps indicating that any lamps bearing the same code letters, regardless of the manufacturer, will have similar characteristics and be interchangeable. Formerly known as the United States of America Standards Institute (USASI or ASI). See also **Incandescent, Tungsten halogen** under LAMPS.

ANTEPROSCENIUM. Areas in front (auditorium side) of house. Front of house (FOH) stage lights can be referred to as anteproscenium lights. See also LIGHTING STAGE, PROSCENIUM.

ANTEROOM. A room before, or leading to, another room. In theatre architecture, it is good practice to plan an anteroom between dressing rooms and stage to serve as a sound and light trap. Similarly, anterooms between auditorium and lobby will help eliminate disturbances caused by late arrivals.

ANTICIPATE. Actors and technicians learn to anticipate cues for exact timing. Warning cues can be memorized or written on cue sheets to facilitate timing. Electricians sometimes anticipate cues by several words or even lines to compensate for the delayed reactions of certain types of dimmers.

ANTIQUE (verb). To paint furniture or props to appear old or worn. Antiquing can be done effectively with any light-colored oil base paint and a tube of oil base burnt umber or with antiquing kits, available in paint stores. After base coat has dried, wipe burnt umber over the object with a soft cloth dipped in paint thinner. Apply burnt umber sparingly, streaking flat surfaces slightly and concentrating heavier applications in corners and recesses. Water base paints can be used for antiquing if base coat contains extra glue and proper care is taken in application of burnt umber. Scrubbing will cause base coat to bleed through. A thinned shellac over water base paints will prevent paint from wiping off on hands and clothes. Clear latex or Varathane will serve the same purpose and will provide a glossy surface.

ANTIQUE PROPS. Antique props are continually needed for period plays. Furniture should be built or remodeled from inexpensive second-hand pieces. A relatively high breakage rate of props is to be expected because of the constant pressure under which stage personnel work. Never use antiques of any value.

APERTURE (gate). The opening in an ellipsoidal reflector spotlight through which the light crosses. In spotlights, the shutters and the pattern slot are located at the aperture . See illustration under GOBO; see also **Ellipsoidal spotlight** under LIGHTING INSTRUMENTS, SPECIFIC.

APPARITION. Appearance of something unreal or intangible. Apparitions are common to plays of the Elizabethan period and may be suggested in a number of ways. Very realistic images can be projected by laser holography on moving plastic film (see HOLOGRAPHY). Shadowlike images can be projected on the cyc (see PROJECTORS).

Realism can also be attained more simply by flying ghostlike cutouts on black wire. The effect will by enhanced by lighting from above or below at a steep angle and by using bizarre colors. Scrim is commonly used (see SCRIM) to diffuse the view and heighten the effect. If no equipment is available, the simple solution is to have only the actor see the apparition.

APPLAUSE (sound effect). Applause recordings should always be supplemented with live applause from members of the crew or cast off stage.

APPLIQUE. Decoration cut from one material and applied to another. Commonplace articles are often appliquéd with papier-mâché, wood, metal, or cloth to make them appear more authentic for period and locale of a play. See also PAPIER-MACHE.

APRON. The part of a stage in front of the main curtain. The apron once constituted the greatest portion of the acting area. Its extended use was first abolished by the Haymarket Theatre in London in 1834. On many present-day proscenium stages, aprons are no more than a few feet in depth. A return to Elizabethan staging practices has gained popularity in the form of thrust stages, where aprons extending into auditoriums constitute the major acting area. Also increasingly popular are **extended-apron** stages (see STAGES) where the apron area is less than that of the thrust stage but still forms an acting area. See also PROSCENIUM DOORS.

ARBOR (carriage, cradle). Metal frame used to support counterweights in a system for flying scenery. See COUNTERWEIGHT SYSTEM.

ARC

Lights. An electric spark jumping across a gap. Poor wiring connections sometimes arc and may result in serious fires. All wiring of a permanent nature should conform to safe wiring practices set forth in the National Electrical Code (NEC). Arcs occurring between pin connectors can often be solved by spreading the split prongs with a knife blade. See **Arc light** under LIGHTING INSTRUMENTS, SPECIFIC.

Scenery. Any part of a circle. A "sweep" cut in wood or plywood to make an ARCH.

ARCH. An opening, as for a door, window, or bookcase. In some theatres the term arch can mean the proscenium. In theatre terminology,

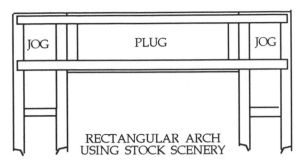

RECTANGULAR ARCH
USING STOCK SCENERY

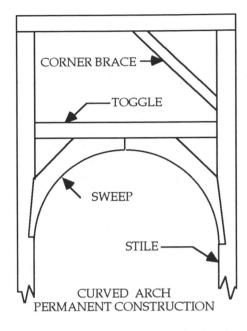

CURVED ARCH
PERMANENT CONSTRUCTION

however, an arch does not necessarily imply a curve. Proscenium arches may or may not be curved. Similarly, a recessed alcove or separate room may be constructed with a straight beam, and the resulting division may be called an arch.

Standard construction of an arch flat. Proceed as in flat construction (see under FLAT), making flat according to designed dimensions. Arch angle enclosing outside dimensions of opening is formed with toggle rails and inner stiles as illustrated; sweeps are laid out with compass on 3/4" plywood or 1" x 12" stock lumber; sweeps are cut with bandsaw or sabersaw, and the inner stiles are notched as illustrated. Glue and nail into place.

Detachable thicknesses. Cut double sweeps for arch thickness and space with 1"x 3" stock to provide total thickness desired; cut 1/4" or 3/16" plywood or door skin to designed thickness, with outside grain running opposite the length; nail plywood to frame of sweeps with twopenny or threepenny nails at 2" or 3" intervals; bolt to

flat with 3/8" carriage bolts 2 1/2" long and wingnuts, or fasten with loose pin hinge to flat using 1 1/2" or 2" backflap loose pin hinges. Entire arch thickness can be made as one unit, fastened at bottom with a sill iron or a plywood threshold.

Temporary construction. Use stock door or window flat; proceed as for standard construction except for notching inner stiles; butt sweeps to inner stiles and rail and fasten with **Keystone** (see under FLAT) and 3/4" no. 8 flathead wood screws; do not use corrugators or glue; cover triangular openings in upper corners with a

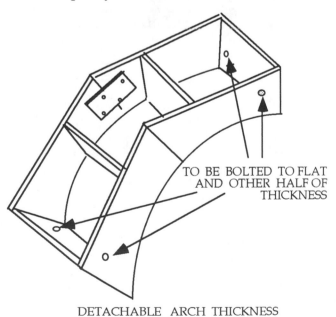

DETACHABLE ARCH THICKNESS

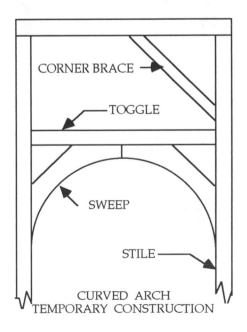

CURVED ARCH
TEMPORARY CONSTRUCTION

muslin patch applied as DUTCHMAN. After run of show is completed, remove patches and sweeps and return flat to stock.

Temporary thicknesses. Cut BEAVER-BOARD or corrugated cardboard to width of thickness as specified in design, plus 3/4"; cut to correct length to fit around arch, plus 3"; bevel or feather both ends with sander or wood rasp; nail sweep into place with twopenny nails, allowing 1 1/2" to extend down on each side; nail vertical thicknesses on back of inner stiles with eightpenny nails put in from face of flat; tack feathered ends of beaverboard to vertical thicknesses. *Warning:* Corrugated cardboard has a greater tendency to buckle under scene paint than does beaverboard.

ARCHITECTURAL STYLE. The conscientious scene designer, faced with the creation of a realistic setting, may spend hours in research to determine the architectural style suited to the location and period of the play. Good design usually concentrates on line, color, and overall characteristics of setting rather than on details that will be lost onstage. See also DESIGN.

ARC LIGHT (abbr. arc). See **Arc light** under LIGHTING INSTRUMENTS, SPECIFIC; see also SPOTLIGHT.

AREAS (stage locations). For convenience in directing, acting, lighting, and placing of furniture, stages are usually divided into six, nine, or fifteen areas depending on the size of the stage. Areas closest to the footlights are designated *downstage*; those closest to the backwall are *upstage*. The areas in between are *right stage, center*

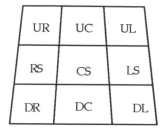

UR	UC	UL
RS	CS	LS
DR	DC	DL

9 STAGE AREAS

UR	UC	UL
DR	DC	DL

6 STAGE AREAS

stage, left stage for the nine-area stage and additionally *rightcenter* and *leftcenter* for the fifteen-area stage as illustrated. *Right* and *left* directions refer to the performer's right and left when facing the audience. Abbreviated for obvious reasons of simplification, DR is downright, UC is upcenter, URC is upright center, etc.

ARENA STAGE. A stage that has audience on two, three, or four sides. See under STAGE.

ARIELITE. An obsolete trade name for lighting equipment used in the 1950s and 1960s.

ARM

Lights. A pipe used to support a spotlight; usually called a side arm or hanger.

Scenery. A batten or support projecting from the main frame holding a curtain or cyclorama. The arm is generally used to form wings or entrances on stage.

ARMOR. See SHIELDS.

UR	URC	UC	ULC	UL
RS	RC	CS	LC	LS
DR	DRC	DC	DLC	DL

15 STAGE AREAS

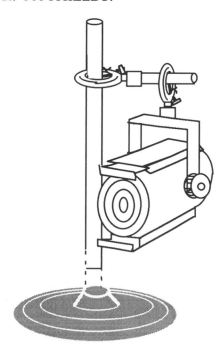

FRESNEL ON A SIDE ARM
MOUNTED ON BOOM

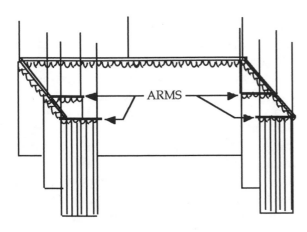

USE OF ARMS TO HANG LEGS

ARMS. See GUNS; SWORDS.

ART DIRECTOR. Name sometimes given to film or television scene designer. It is generally the art director's responsibility to coordinate color, style, and period in costumes, scenery, and properties. See also SCENIC ARTIST.

ARTWORK. Term loosely applied to stage decor, costumes, properties, program layout, etc.

ASBESTOS CURTAIN (abbr. AB). Fire curtain. In accordance with fire laws, all proscenium theatres are required to have some sort of protection for the audience in case of fire. For many years that protection was in the form of a fire curtain made of asbestos or other incombustible material. Located in front of the act curtain, the asbestos curtain slides in metal grooves (smoke pockets) on either side of the proscenium, forming a flameproof seal between stage and auditorium. States have required the asbestos to be lowered until five minutes before curtain time and lowered again after the final curtain. Fire departments will advise about current precautions because asbestos has been banned in the United States. See also DELUGE SYSTEM; FAN AND DELUGE SYSTEM.

ASH. A semihardwood, particularly suited to furniture construction.

ASYMMETRIC DESIGN. Aesthetic irregularity and disproportion, lacking symmetry, often used in contemporary plays in keeping with modern design trends. Period designs are apt to be more formal or symmetrical.

ATMOSPHERE. Atmosphere of a play pertains to the mood, as conceived by the author and expressed through staging, design, costumes, light, color, props, and sound effects combined to produce suggested atmosphere.

ATTRIBUTES (PARAMETERS). The functions of AUTOMATED LIGHTS and of AUTOMATED LIGHT CONTROL. Attributes and parameters are the same but different companies use one or the other of the terms within their firm.

AUDITORIUM (the house, out front, the audience). The part of the theatre devoted to the audience. See also SEATING, AUDITORIUM; FOYER; LOBBY.

AUDITORIUM LIGHTS. See HOUSE LIGHTS.

AUGER. Cutting bit used for boring holes. See also BIT.

AUTOFOLLOW (follower). A CUE that comes automatically after a called cue.

AUTOMATED LIGHT CONTROL. A computer especially designed to control the functions of AUTOMATED LIGHTS. These light boards are much larger in memory circuits and control logic than the modern conventional COMPUTER LIGHT BOARDS. Many modern boards are capable of controlling a limited number of automated lights if they have DMX 512 PROTOCOL capability. There are different protocols for control such as DMX, DMX 512, and PMX. The parameters and subparameters controlled include the following.

    Beam shape. Round, triangle, square, star, and almost any shape imaginable can be achieved by variable and insertion-type lens systems and GOBOS. Beam shape can also be modified by refraction.

    Beam size. The physical space a beam of light takes. Commonly manipulated with an IRIS or a ZOOM LENS.

    Blackout. Stopping the light beam from showing, usually accomplished by a shutter device.

    Calibration. Allows the computer to find the home position or starting point of the luminaire's focus.

    Color. Usually achieved by insertion of one or more dichroic filters into the beam.

    Diffusion. Softer, less intense light usually achieved by a glass diffusion filter. This effect is similar to using FROST.

Focus. Sharpening the beam relative to a GOBO or other parameter within a LUMINAIRE.

Zoom. Moving from narrow to wide focus.

Gobo. A cutout pattern or a pattern painted on glass that can be inserted into the light beam.

Gobo rotation. Moving a GOBO in a clockwise or counterclockwise direction. Different speeds of rotation are possible.

Light intensity. Manipulated by changing the voltage applied to the lamp, or by changing the reference level of a mechanical shutter in a unit with an encapsulated arc lamp. See **Arc type** under LAMP.

Pan. Moving a light from side to side.

Fine pan. Panning the light in very small increments.

Prisms. Used to break down white light into many and variously shaped rainbow effects.

Prism rotation. Moving the prism at various speeds in a clockwise or counterclockwise direction.

Speed of movement. Time allotted to a motion.

Steps. Inserting pauses in all functions; also referred to as beats or timed pauses.

Strobe. Usually achieved by a mechnical device that momentarily blocks the light.

Tilt. Moving up and down.

Fine tilt. Moving the tilt in extremely small increments.

AUTOMATED LIGHTS (automated LUMIN-AIRE, moving lights). These lights are designed to be computer controlled. Generally available in two different styles. The so-called moving-yoke type pans and tilts the entire instrument housing, and the moving-mirror type pans and tilts a mirror to direct the light beam. The units have a number of PARAMETERS that can be modified for various cues and effects. These parameters, or functions, include tilt, pan, gobos, beam size, beam shape, color, diffusion, insertion of prisms, light intensity, mechanical strobe, speed of movement, and blackout devices. Additionally, there are subparameters such as rotation of the gobo, fine pan, fine tilt, rotation of prisms, and zoom lenses. Sophisticated computers are capable of controlling each parameter and subparameter, and virtually any number of steps are possible in each function.

Parameters and subparameters can utilize 24 or more control channels for larger units. Some lights have built-in memory chips, and some use memory built into the control computer. If 8 to 10 parameters are available for a light and each function has various settings, the number of possibilities within one light alone are staggering, and if that were not enough, multiply the number of parameter possibilities times the number of instruments needed or wanted for a particular effect, then the computer is into some amazing command numbers. Add to that the number of cues in the show and the complexity is almost frightening. It is not unusual for a 90-minute show to have 400 to 500 cues, and that may not include the "normal" lighting. One 90-minute show may have a million bytes of information going from AUTOMATED LIGHT CONTROL to 100 automated units.

The use of automated lights is increasing at a rapid rate. When first introduced in the early 1980s, they were used primarily in rock concerts and celebrity attractions. In the past 5 years, their use has spread to variety shows, musicals, and other types of book shows.

The price of these lights, $4,000 to $12,000 per unit, has been a prime factor in keeping them out of educational theatre. As the price of the units drops, the more they will be used. University theatre students are now being trained in the programming and use of the instruments with the assistance of the manufacturers. Automated lights can only be rented from some companies, while other companies allow units to be purchased. Fortunately, many COMPUTER LIGHT BOARDS have DMX and DMX 512 PROTO-COLS, which allow a modern conventional light board to control the units. Beyond the cost of the unit, the cost of AUTOMATED LIGHT CONTROL is a major capital outlay. See also CLAY PACKY; INTELLABEAM; PAN AND TILT LIGHTS; VARI-LITE.

AUTOMOBILE (sound effects). Recordings are the most practical solution for the sound of starting, shifting, running, and stopping. Horns should be real, and the correct vintage is sometimes available at local junkyards. A storage battery can be used for voltage supply, but a transformer to reduce voltage to 6 or 12 volts plus a rectifier to change from AC to DC is a more trouble-free source of power. If correct intensity of volume cannot be obtained by moving the horn to a different location, the horn can be muffled with sound-absorbing material.

AUTOPAN. See PAN AND TILT LIGHTS.

AUTOTRANSFORMER. See under DIMMER.

AUTRASTAT. Obsolete; trade name for an autotransformer no longer manufactured. See also DIMMER.

AVISTA. Move or change of scenery in view of the audience.

AWL. Pointed tool used for punching holes in leather or canvas.

B

BABY SPOT. See under LIGHTING INSTRU-MENTS, SPECIFIC; see also chart under SPOT-LIGHT.

BACKCLOTH. British expression for BACKDROP.

BACKDROP (drop). A screen, curtain, or painted drop in back of a scene, usually for vista or panorama effects. The backdrop has long been used as a means of establishing the confines of a set and/or changing scenery. See also DROPS.

BACKFLAP. See under HINGES.

BACKGROUND (cyclorama, groundrow, back-ing, projection, drop). Appropriate setting.

BACKGROUND MUSIC. Appropriate music, enhancing the mood of a play.

BACKING. A unit of scenery, often a twofold or threefold, used to mask behind doors or windows of a set. Also, a curtain, drapery, or cyclorama used to mask doors or windows of a set.

BACKING LIGHT. Any instrument used to light a backing or light through an opening from off stage. See also LIGHTING BACKINGS.

BACKLIGHTING. Illumination of actors or objects from above and behind to produce a highlight or separation light from the background.

BACK-PACKING TRAVELER (rearfold). See TRAVELER.

BACK PAINTING. Painting back of scenery with any scene paint in order to remove wrinkles in canvas or muslin, or with any dark scene paint to make scenery opaque.

BACKSAW. See under SAWS.

BACKSTAGE. The portion of a theatre behind the main curtain, including dressing rooms, wing space, storage dock, etc.

BACKUP. A protection copy of anything, e.g., audio tape. See **Computer terminology** under LIGHTING CONTROL.

BACKWALL. The rear wall of a set or of a stage.

BAFFLE, LIGHT. A piece of metal used in light-ing instruments to prevent escape of light through ventilation holes.

BAFFLEBOARD. A board usually made of 3/4" plywood, 18" to 36" square, used to increase the tonal qualities of a loudspeaker. It has a hole in the center large enough to accommodate the speaker, which should be screwed or bolted to the board with a rubber or cork gasket between the metal rim of the speaker and the board. See also BASE REFLEX CABINET; **Speakers** under SOUND EQUIPMENT.

BAG (noun). See SANDBAG.

BAG (verb)

To counterweight a set of lines with sandbags or to tie a sandbag on a line or set of lines in place of a batten or scenery. If only two lines in a set are needed, the third can be bagged.

To put curtains, legs, tabs, and drops (un-painted) into a bag for transit or storage. See also WESTCOASTING.

BAG LINE. A pickup line for a sandbag used to relieve weight while raising the bag higher on a set of lines or while trimming the set of lines.

BAG TIE. The practice of using two modified stopper hitches with a bight between for tying sandbags to a set of lines. See **Stopper hitch** under KNOTS.

BAKELITE. Trade name for a plastic made of phenol and formaldehyde, used extensively as an insulation material for electrical work. Con-trol panels for switchboards and sound equip-ment are often faced with Bakelite. It withstands heat without melting and can be drilled with drills and cut with a hacksaw or a skip-tooth bandsaw.

BALANCE

Paints. Weighting hue, chroma and value to

form a harmonious relationship.

Lights. Adjusting the intensity of light color from one area to another.

BALCONY LIGHTS (rail lights). Spotlights, usually 750- to 2,000-watt capacity, mounted on a balcony rail or a hanger in front of the rail. The balcony angle of 10° to 30° is generally too flat for best results, but it is widely used because of convenience or lack of better positions. A position used often for color washes for the front of the stage or apron. See also LIGHTING STAGE, PROSCENIUM.

BALLAST. A resistance wired in series with an arc light, used to control flow of current through electrodes.

BALL-PEEN HAMMER. See under HAMMERS.

BALSA. A very soft, lightweight, tropical American wood, useful for making props, models or ornamental appliqués. See also STYROFOAM.

BALUSTER (spindle). An upright support of a rail. See illustration under STEPS.

BALUSTRADE. A row of balusters supporting or joined by a handrail, usually referring to exterior railings. Garden balustrades to be used in background are usually two-dimensional cutouts. Medium-sized balusters for settings requiring three-dimensional railings are available from house-wrecking companies. Larger replicas can be made of PAPIER-MACHE or STYRO-FOAM.

BANDSAW. See under POWER TOOLS.

BANISTER. Staircase railings for interiors. Railings are approximately 32" high and newel posts approximately 36" high. Measurements are taken from the tread at the riser. See also BALUSTRADE.

BANK

Lights. Occasionally, where heavy concentration of light is required, a group of sockets arranged in banks is used. Individual lights of higher intensity are gradually replacing older, banked forms, but certain types of footlights and border lights are available in banks which tend to give a more continuous line of light.

Switchboard. Switchboards are often arranged in tiers of dimmers known as banks. There are usually three or four banks arranged for the convenience of the operator.

BARNDOOR. See under LIGHT SPILL CONTROL.

BAROQUE. Extravagant architectural style of the seventeenth and eighteenth centuries. Ornate, fantastic, grotesque.

BASE. A cast-iron weight used as a footing for a pipe standard (boom) to which lighting equipment can be attached. Available through theatrical supply houses or can be cast to order at foundries. See also **Bases** under LAMPS; **Floodlights** under LIGHTING INSTRUMENTS, GENERAL.

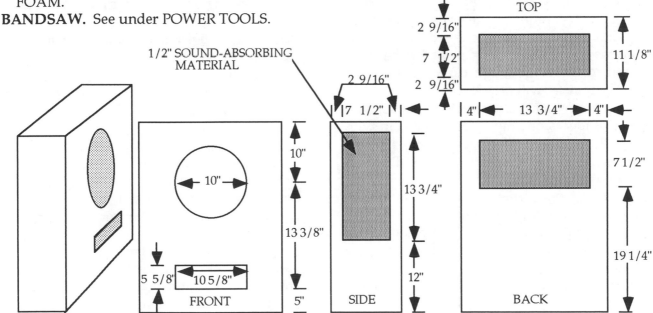

BASS REFLEX CABINET

BASEBOARD (mopboard). A decorative trim on a wall at floor level. For realistic interiors, baseboards of 1" x 6" or 1" x 10" lumber are applied to flats at floor level. Picture molding or 3/4" x 3/4" lumber can be used to obtain a similar effect if applied to flats at the prescribed height and if the portion of the flats below the molding is painted woodwork color. Baseboards should be painted on folding flats.

BASKET

    Lighting. An enclosure that hangs from a TRUSS, beam, or crane and that holds a FOLLOWSPOT and an operator.

    Rigging (basket hitch). A particular kind of rigging point that loops a wire rope around a beam with a forged shackle to hang a wire rope from the underside of the beam. Often used in TRUSS works.

BAS-RELIEF. Sculpture or pattern in low relief. Bas-relief can be simulated with PAPIER-MACHE or STYROFOAM.

BASS REFLEX CABINET. A speaker cabinet designed to produce excellent tonal qualities. Illustrated is a cabinet designed for a 12" speaker, using 3/4" plywood and 1/2" fibrous wallboard or acoustical material. Illustration on previous page; all dimensions are inside. See also BAFFLEBOARD; **Speakers** under SOUND EQUIPMENT.

BATIK. Fabric dyed in designs of several colors, using the technique of covering with wax or paraffin the parts not to be dyed at each stage. Patterns for costumes or draperies can be transferred to fabrics through carbon paper. The waxlike transfer will help to prevent colors from running together. Bolder patterns for stained-glass windows or drapes can be laid out with colored crayons and dye brushed into different panels. See also **Dye drop** under DROPS.

BATTEN (noun)

    Lights. A pipe, truss, or extruded aluminum raceway from which lighting instruments may be hung. In permanent installations circuits are often included on this mounting device. See also ELECTRICS.

    Pipe. Lengths of pipe permanently or semi-permanently tied to lines from grid and used for flying scenery, lights, or curtains. Pipe battens are usually 1 1/4" (inside dimension) black

pipe but may be smaller or larger depending upon the length required. Most C-clamps for lighting equipment are designed for 1 1/4" or 1 1/2" pipe.

    Wooden. 1" x 3" lumber used as framework of a flat or used to support scenery to be flown. See also **Battening** under FASTENING FLATS.

BATTEN (verb). To fasten scenery together with a batten. See FASTENING FLATS: **Battening**.

BATTEN CLAMP. See under CLAMPS.

BATTEN HOOK. See **S-hook** under HOOKS.

BATTERIES. In common usage backstage are batteries made for flashlights and portable tools: 1.5, 3, 6, 7.2, 9, 9.6, and 12 volt sealed units; 1.5 volt D, C, AA, and AAA sealed batteries; rechargeable batteries; and 12 volt, automobile wet cell or gel cells.

BATTERY HOOKUP. See BELLS.

BATTERY LIGHTS. Lights that look somewhat like strip lights and are gimbal lights mounted together that pan and tilt in unison. These are controlled by DMX PROTOCOL. See also AUTOMATED LIGHT CONTROL.

BATTERY OF LIGHTS. A bank or many banks of lights, usually spotlights, used to obtain great intensities. Generally used for extravaganzas or outdoor staging.

BATTING. Wool, cotton, or polyfill prepared in sheets and used for quilting, costume padding, or upholstering. Available in most fabric stores and department stores.

BAY. Structural division in a building marked by piers or buttresses.

BEAD. Narrow piece of molding, such as half round, used ornamentally to frame windows, pictures, doors, etc. See also MOLDING.

BEAM

    False. Pertains to L-shaped beams or coves in auditoriums, used to conceal spotlights from audience. Angle from beam to apron edge should be between 45° and 60°.

    Light. The cone of light from a reflector, lens, or spotlight.

    Structural. A structural member in a building or setting. Beams used in settings are L-shaped and generally have no structural value. Usual practice is to fly beams used in settings, and occasionally it is necessary to cut holes in a ceiling of a set to allow lines to pass through to support beams.

BEAM ANGLE. The cone of light within the total field with an intensity of 50% of the maximum candlepower of a lighting instrument. See also FIELD ANGLE; **Ellipsoidal spotlight** under LIGHTING INSTRUMENTS, SPECIFIC.

BEAM LIGHTS (cove lights, bridge lights, catwalk lights). Spotlights, usually 500- to 2,000-watt capacity with plano-convex or step lens, located on false beam or equivalent position in auditorium. The beam angle to the stage should be between 45° and 60°.

BEAM PROJECTOR (BP). See **Beam projector** under LIGHTING INSTRUMENTS, FIXED FOCUS.

BEAVERBOARD (Upsonboard, easycurve). Laminated cardboard used in scene construction as thickness pieces for arches or curved openings; also used for silhouette cutouts or profiles as an inexpensive substitute for plywood. Most useful thicknesses are, 1/8", 1/16", and 1/4". Available in 4' x 8' and 4' x 12' sizes.

BECKET (martingale). See BRIDLE.

BELAYING PIN. A round hardwood or metal pin about 1" in diameter by 12" to 16" in length. Belaying pins are inserted in holes in the pin rail and used as tie-off pins for lines from the grid.

BELL. Various types of bells are used on stage for bell, buzzer, and telephone cues. It is customary to make self-contained units with at least one bell, one buzzer, and a door chime with either batteries or a transformer as a power supply. Batteries are used for more portable units, enabling cues to be given from any location on stage. Bell transformers, available in hardware stores, are more reliable and less expensive in the long run.

BELLYLUGGER. See GRUNT.

BELT. Used for power transfer. Often power equipment requires a V-belt between motor and equipment. Replacements are necessary from time to time. Belt measurements are given in inches of circumference and can be made by stretching a tape or rope around the two pulleys in the exact position of the belt. V-belts are available at hardware and auto stores.

BENCHES

Cutting. A table built on each side of a radial saw to hold lumber being cut.

Tailing. A table placed behind a table saw to facilitate ripping long lengths of lumber.

Template. A heavy table used as an aid in constructing flats. The template table is built to the dimensions of the most commonly used flat, and has metal lips on the corners to square flats as they are assembled. Built-in clinching plates at corners and joints ensure clinching of nails holding corner blocks and keystones.

BEVEL. To cut the end or edge of material to any angle other than 90°.

BEVEL GAUGE (sliding tee bevel, bevel square). Tool used to determine and reproduce angles.

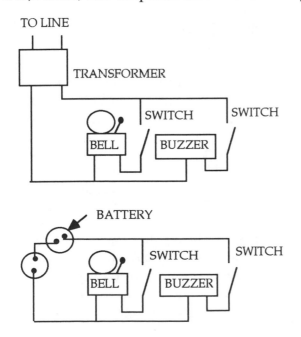

BELL HOOKUP

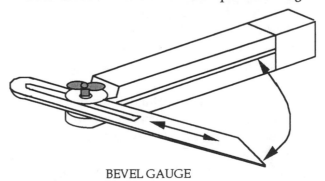

BEVEL GAUGE

BEVERAGES (props). Stage beverages are often tea, appropriately diluted for color. Soft drinks are generally avoided because of the effects of sugar and carbonation on diction. Pure food dyes in water can also be used.

BIGHT. A bend or loop in a rope. Most knots begin with a bight. See also KNOTS.

BINDERS. See GLUES.

BIPOST BASE. See **Bases** under LAMPS.

BIRDCALL (sound effect). Best simulated by whistling or with Audubon birdcall, available through Audubon Societies. The birdcall is a small cylinder of wood with a keyed metal shank that turns in a rosined hole. The calls are easily varied and of reasonable volume, although amplification through a microphone may be necessary. Dime-store water whistles are often suitable for nondescript birdcalls. Recordings are available and should be used for specific calls.

BIT. A cutting tool for drilling holes. See also DRILL.

Auger bit. A sharp spiral-fluted or sharp-edged tool used with a brace for boring holes in wood. Bits are numbered according to diameter in sixteenths of an inch; e.g., no. 2 equals 1/8 " diameter, no. 3 equals 3/16", and no. 4 equals 1/4", etc.

Center bit (center drill, pilot bit). A short small bit with a larger shank, often used in a lathe to start a pilot hole for a larger drill. Often used to start holes for nails and screws.

Expansion bit. A bit with an adjustable outer cutting edge, generally designed to cut any size hole from 1" to 3".

Extension bit. An adjustable tool for boring very deep holes.

Paddle bit (scraper bit). A wood drill consisting of a tapered point for centering and starting the cut and flat chisel-like blades on either side for cutting the hole.

Reamer. A tapered bit for enlarging or tapering holes.

Screwdriver. The metal driving end that fits into the screw head. Screwdriver bit is used with electric screwdriver tools and ratchet screwdrivers.

BIT PART. A small role in a play. In nonprofessional theatre actors playing bit parts are often used as stage managers, electricians, crew, etc. In professional theatre stage managers and assistant stage managers may play bit parts. See also WALK-ON.

BLACK LIGHT (UV). See ULTRAVIOLET LIGHT.

BLACKOUT (noun)

Acting. A performer's short sketch usually comic.

Lights. Complete darkness on the stage caused by pulling the main switch or master dimmer or blackout (BO) switch. Many scenes can be ended effectively by means of blackouts. Landmarks of phosphorescent (glow) paint or tape will help actors find their way offstage.

BLACKOUT (Command verb). The order to go to a blackout, used often by directors, designers, and stage managers.

BLACK PAINT. See PAINT AND PAINT COLORS.

BLACKS. Draperies and cycloramas are frequently referred to by color; hence, blacks would be a section or sections of black drapes. Many plays are most effectively staged in blacks with set pieces, platforms, and furniture.

BLANKS. See GUNS.

BLAST. To set volume control on sound equipment too high. Volume controls should be accurately calibrated and intensity readings should be taken for each cue.

BLEED

Lights. Lighting is said to bleed through when it shows through a flat. Either backpainting the flat with black or hanging a piece of black fabric on the back of the flat will solve the problem.

Paints. If one coat of paint fails to cover another, the first coat is said to bleed through. Scenic aniline dyes and paints containing dyes will bleed. Scrubbing with a paintbrush will cause a water base undercoat to bleed. A coat of shellac or rubber base paint will check bleeding of dye paints. See also **Shellac** under PAINTS, MISCELLANEOUS.

BLENDING

Lights. Washing light over the acting areas in order to smooth out the overall effect.

Paints. Smoothing one color into another to avoid lines of demarcation. Wet-blending (puddle painting) allowing one color of paint to flow into a another with extra water or solvent to make an effect such as marble. See also PAINTING TECHNIQUES.

BLINDER

   Lights. Device to control beam spread of light. See **Barndoor** under LIGHT SPILL CONTROL.

   Scenery. A 3"- to 7"-wide strip of fabric used to opaque cracks where flats join.

BLIND RECORDING. See **Computer terminology** under LIGHTING CONTROL.

BLINKER. A signal light in series with a push button, used for relaying cues. See also SIGNAL LIGHT and CUE LIGHT.

BLOCK (noun). A pulley or pulleys in a frame. See also BLOCK AND TACKLE.

   Electrical. Special groupings of control. Groups of CUES.

   Eye block. A pulley with a ring on top.

   Floor block (tension sheave, idler). A pulley or sheave mounted on the floor, as for a curtain control, or on the bottom of the overhaul line in a COUNTERWEIGHT SYSTEM.

   Head block. A block with three or more pulleys mounted on a single axle. The head block is located directly above the counterweights or pin rail and serves to bring together all lines in a given set.

   Kick-up block (kicking block, tension sheave, welsh block). A pulley near the floor that can be pressed with the foot to allow the back of the sheave to slide up the TEE-BAR in order to TAKE A WRAP.

   Lead block. A block with three or more pulleys fastened in tandem in one frame. The lead block is mounted on the grid in direct line with each set of lines. All lines from each set are brought together through the pulleys of the lead block and dropped to the pin rail or counterweight.

   Loft block. A sheave or pulley used on a grid for each line.

   Take-up block (tension sheave, idler). A sheave below the counterweight arbor through which a hand line or overhaul line passes.

BLOCK. Acting direction instructing actors to move in a prescribed manner for various scenes.

BLOCK AND TACKLE (block and fall). A pair of blocks with rope strung through the pulleys to gain a mechanical advantage in lifting or pulling.

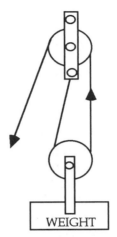

BLOCK AND TACKLE

BLOOD. Liquid or dry panchromatic makeup or special makeup blood that washes out is available from most major distributors. "Blood" is available in liquid, powder, and capsule form from the various supply houses. Catsup is sometimes used on stage to simulate a fresh wound or bloodstain.

BLOW. To make a mistake. "Juice blew the cue!" (the electrician made a mistake on the light cue). See also BLOWOUT.

BLOWOUT (blow)

   Melting of a fuse link due to a short circuit or an overload in an electrical circuit.

   A breaker switching to the off position.

   The burning out of a lamp.

BLUE. Primary color in lights and paints. See PAINT AND PAINT COLORS.

BLUEPRINT. A white line print on a blue background made by placing a tracing on a light sensitized paper and exposing to strong light. A fast and inexpensive method of duplicating working drawings. The process is also used for black on white, brown on white, and blue on white backgrounds. Original drawings must be made on tracing paper.

BOARD. A term used for the controlling device for either lights or sound. See AUTOMATED LIGHT CONTROL; LIGHTING CONTROL; SOUND EQUIPMENT.

BOARD FOOT. A name for lumber measuring or equal to 1" x 12" x 12". To find out how many board feet are in a given length of wood the formula is thickness (in inches) times width (in inches) times length (in feet) divided by 12. Thus to find out the board feet in a piece of lumber 1" x 12" x 10', the calculation is (1 x 12 x 10)/12 = 120/12 = 10 board feet.

BO-BAR. A 2/3 length JOHNSON BAR that allows the lever to be used in confined spaces.

BOBBINET. Machine-made netting with a hexagonal mesh available through supply houses in widths up to 30' for theatrical use. Used to simulate glass in windows or as transparent drops. Gauze, scrim, or netting may also be used. See also SCRIM.

BOLT. A folded or rolled quantity of cloth, usually ranging between 40 and 60 yards in length.

BOLTS. A rod used for temporary or permanent fastening. Bolts 1/4" in diameter and larger are designated by diameter in inches, threads per inch, and length in inches. Smaller bolts are coded by number, e.g., 12 x 24, 8 x 32, in which diameter decreases as first number, and threads per inch increase as second number. See Table under TAP AND DIE SETS.

    Carriage bolt. Has a round head and is reasonably inconspicuous. Used extensively for ceiling plates, structural supports, casters, etc., where the head is exposed to view.

    Eye bolt. Has a loop, ring, or eye on one end.

    Machine bolt. Has a square or hexagonal head which permits the use of a wrench on both nut and bolt.

    Stove bolt. Slotted to receive a screwdriver. Stove bolts have either round or flat heads, the latter type being designed to fit into a countersunk hole.

    U-bolt. Shaped like the letter U and threaded on both ends.

BOMBS (sound effect). For distant bombs, use recordings; for close bombs, use a 12-gauge shotgun firing blanks into a metal barrel or ashcan. Check with local fire department.

BOOK (noun).

    Acting. The script of a play, or the prompter's copy.

    Flat. To vee a TWOFOLD so it is self-standing.

    Scenery. A TWOFOLD.

    Set dressing. In order to facilitate handling and reduce weight, books in stage bookcases are usually faked. Methods of faking books include: removing pages and mounting bindings on a

board; cutting silhouettes of varying heights and painting to resemble backs of books; mounting sample bindings on a board. Libraries

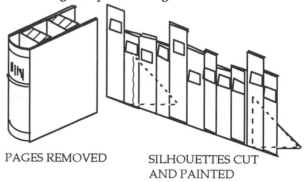

PAGES REMOVED   SILHOUETTES CUT
                   AND PAINTED

BOOKS FOR SET DRESSING

and binderies are good sources for finding books and bindings to be converted into stage books.

BOOK (verb). To vee hinged flats together to make self standing.

BOOK CEILING. See under CEILINGS.

BOOK SHOW. A production that is scripted as opposed to an unscripted show or an improvisation. See also CLASSIFICATION OF SHOWS.

BOOM. A light standard, usually includes a base, pipe upright, and sidearms for the mounting of lighting instruments. See also LIGHT MOUNTING DEVICES.

BOOM BASE. A heavy, often cast-iron, base that supports a light standard. See also LIGHT MOUNTING DEVICES.

BOOMERANG

    Paint. A platform on casters having two or

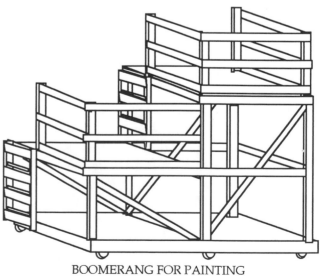

BOOMERANG FOR PAINTING

more levels, used for painting scenery or drops.

Lights. Any of several types of devices used to change colors in followspots by remote or manual operation.

A tower on which lights are mounted on either side of stage. See under LIGHT MOUNTING DEVICES. See also LIGHT TOWERS; BOOM; GENIE LIFT.

BOOTH, CONTROL. See CONTROL ROOM.

BOOTH, PROJECTION. The enclosed area near the extreme back of auditorium used as a projection room for movies in many theatres. A good location for high-intensity spotlights used for general coverage or as followspots for special productions. Many theatres use the booth for lighting and sound control. Projection booths must be made with fireproof walls.

BOOTH LIGHTS. Spotlights of 1,000- to 3,000-watt capacity used in booth location at rear of auditorium.

BORAX. A chemical compound mixed with sal ammoniac and water to make a flameproofing solution for scenery. See also FLAMEPROOFING.

BORDER (teaser, valance). Canvas, cloth, draperies, or any material used to mask the upper portion of stage from the view of the audience. Cut borders were formerly used for all settings, but now their use is generally limited to exterior or nonrealistic settings. See also TREE LEAVES.

BORDER LIGHTS (X-ray). See under LIGHTING INSTRUMENTS, GENERAL.

BOSUN'S CHAIR. A rope chair made by tying a doubled rope into a bowline (see KNOTS) using one bight to support the back of the person and the other bight to act as a seat. A notched board will sometimes be inserted into the seat bight to make it a little more comfortable.

BOTTLES

Lights. Professional term for the glass enclosing the filament in a lamp.

Set dressing. If used in quantity for shelf dressing, bottles should be cut from balsa wood or Styrofoam or made of papier-mâché.

BOULDERS (rocks). See PLASTIC SETS.

BOUNCE

Lights. Refers to stray light reflecting off areas of the stage to other areas. Usually solved by relocating instrument or changing its angle.

Sound. Sound reflecting off a surface such as walls, floors, ceilings, baffles, etc.

BOUNCE IT (Command verb). On a hemp SET OF LINES, hold the set several feet from the low TRIM and let it fall sharply to stretch out the ropes. This is often necessary in dry weather because the low trim may be a bit high due to the lack of humidity. In some theatres this term is used for the fast raising and lowering of the house curtain, actually bouncing it off the floor, for quick BOWS.

BOW KNOT. See under KNOTS.

BOWLINE. See under KNOTS.

BOWS (curtain calls). The action of performers taking a bow for their performance.

BOXES. In a large show, more than one of each of the boxes referred to below may be needed.

Carp box. The master carpenter's box which holds tools and hardware.

Electrical box. Used for electrical tools, testing equipment, spare parts for AUTOMATED LIGHTS, INSTRUMENTS, and LIGHTING CONTROL.

Personal box. Used for an individual's tools, departmental records, clothing, and luxuries such as a TV or CD player and perhaps even a hot plate or microwave. A hanging clothes closet is common in this box.

Prop box. Holds all things pertaining to properties and their maintenance.

Road box. Any box that is built to go on tour. This type of box always has WRAP for longer life plus metal-enclosed corners to prevent damage. Tops of road boxes sometimes have special indented trays so that another box with casters may be set on top.

BOX BOOM. Location of temporary FOH lights in the box positions in the auditorium. Not legal in some cities. When used it is imperative that the box boom with its lights are secured with wire guides.

BOXING PAINT. The practice of pouring paint back and forth from one bucket to another or to several buckets to ensure complete mixing of a color for uniform color and consistency. Often done when mixing large amounts of dry pigment.

BOX RENTAL. Money paid by the show to a individual crew member for the use of personal tools.

BOX SET (hard set). An interior setting with three walls and often a ceiling, as opposed to earlier staged interiors of wings, borders, and drops. See also SOFT SET.

BRACE. See **Corner brace** under FLAT: **Components**; STAGE BRACE.

BRACE AND BIT. A tool for boring holes in wood. See also BITS.

BRACE CLEAT. See under FASTENING FLATS: **Lashing.**

BRACING SCENERY. See **Design for solidity** under DESIGN; JACK; STAGE BRACE.

BRACKET. A metal or wooden piece used to support a shelf. See also WALL BRACKET.

BRAD. A small wire nail, usually 1" or less in length.

BRANCH CIRCUIT. The final electrical circuit protected by the lowest amperage fuse or breaker. See also CIRCUITS, ELECTRICAL.

BREAKAWAY SCENERY. Scenery that breaks in a predetermined manner in full view of the audience. Props or scenery requiring this treatment are usually broken by force beforehand and mended temporarily so that future breaks will always occur in the same place. Glass, tumblers, or bottles to be broken should be scored with a glass cutter first to ensure breakage and guard against excessive shattering. Breakable glasses and bottles are available in most theatrical supply houses. See also GLASS.

BREAKER, CIRCUIT. See under SWITCHES.

BREASTING (curtains or scenery). Tying special lines to a pipe batten for the purpose of moving curtains or scenery upstage or downstage from the normal hanging position. See illustration under TRIP.

BREAST LINE (Paddy Cleary). See BREASTING; CLEARING LINE.

BRICK. A generic term for counterweight.

BRICK EFFECT. Beaverboard, plywood, or Styrofoam "bricks" applied to a flat in staggered courses achieve a most realistic effect. Painted bricks are satisfactory for more distant effects. Brick sizes should be exaggerated for stage use.

BRIDGE. A catwalk or hanging platform above the audience on which FOH lights are hung. See also LIGHT BRIDGE.

BRIDLE (becket, martingale). A means of distributing weight of a flown object over two

fastening points instead of one. See also under PIPE EXTENSION.

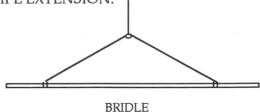

BRIDLE

BRIGHAM COLORS. Obsolete; a lighting color media company. One of the few companies that made variegated color media (i.e., three or more colors on a base color).

BRILLIANCE. Intensity or amount of light. See also COLOR.

BRING IT IN (let it in, come in) (Command verb). To lower a pipe batten or any flown unit.

BRISTOL BOARD. Thin laminated cardboard with a smooth surface, commonly used for color sketches and models of set designs.

BRONZING POWDER. See **Gilding paint** under PAINTS, MISCELLANEOUS.

BRUSH, ELECTRICAL (shoe). Carbon contacts on the movable arm of a dimmer. Brushes and points should be cleaned periodically with rouge paper or a very fine grit (6/0) sandpaper. Alcohol and tuner cleaner can also be used for cleaning electrical points and contacts.

BRUSH, PAINT. See PAINTBRUSHES.

BUCKLE. To warp or curl. See also WARPED LUMBER.

BULB (envelope, bottle). Technically the glass portion of a lamp; commonly the lamp in a lighting instrument or fixture. See also ENVELOPE; BOTTLE.

BULL LINE. A large-diameter rope tied to a hemp set that pulls lines down to fly floor in order to attach sandbags. Used on pipes that are heavy in the down position, e.g., fully loaded electric pipes. Also used in reverse to take bags off when lights are taken off pipe. Name comes from the circus, where bull elephants pulled on ropes to erect the "big top."

BULL ROAR (sound effect). Apparatus for producing groans, roars, squeaking doors, etc. The bull roar is made with a large metal can and a short length of heavy cord or fishline. One end of the can is removed, and cord is run through a hole in the center of the other end. By holding the cord taut and rubbing it with a rosined cloth, a variety of noises can be made. Variations in tautness of the cord and the speed of rubbing will produce corresponding variations in sound. Amplification through a microphone can provide greater control.

BUMPER (scenery guard). A round metal device that clamps on a pipe to allow flown scenery to slide by without bumping the protected pipe. Often used to protect lighting instruments from closely hung scenery.

BUMP IT (Command verb)

　　Lights. To increase light intensity suddenly.

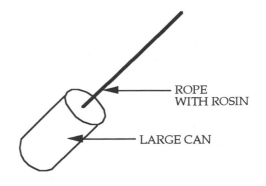

ROPE WITH ROSIN

LARGE CAN

BULL ROAR

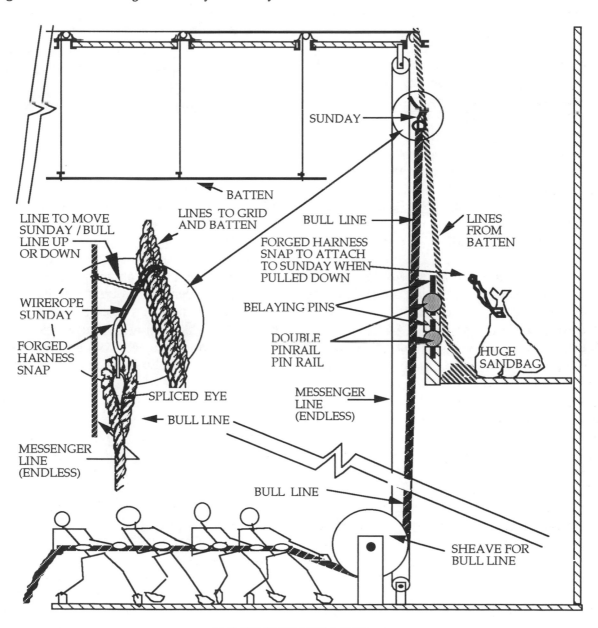

SUNDAY

BATTEN

LINES TO GRID AND BATTEN

LINE TO MOVE SUNDAY / BULL LINE UP OR DOWN

BULL LINE

LINES FROM BATTEN

FORGED HARNESS SNAP TO ATTACH TO SUNDAY WHEN PULLED DOWN

WIREROPE SUNDAY

FORGED HARNESS SNAP

BELAYING PINS

DOUBLE PINRAIL PIN RAIL

HUGE SANDBAG

SPLICED EYE

BULL LINE

MESSENGER LINE (ENDLESS)

MESSENGER LINE (ENDLESS)

BULL LINE

SHEAVE FOR BULL LINE

MANNING THE BULL LINE

21

Scenery (bounce it). To hit the floor force-fully with a flown piece of scenery in order to restore trim. Heavy walls that are flown may occasionally lose trim during the run of a play. Trim can often be temporarily restored if walls are deliberately bumped (bounced) several times on the floor when they are let in. If this method fails, it will be necessary to retrim the lines.

BUMP UP (slam up). The act of increasing light intensity suddenly.

BUNCH LIGHT. Obsolete; a type of floodlight designed to use several low-wattage lamps instead of the single higher-wattage lamp used in modern floodlights.

BUNGEE CORD. A cord or rope made with many rubber strands to give great elasticity to the material. Used as temporary restraint that doesn't require great strength.

BURNDY. A SOLDERLESS CONNECTOR that uses a bolt or set screw to tighten the wire in one end and has a large opening on the flat end so it can be attached with bolts to light boards or distribution panels.

BURNT SIENNA. An earth color. See PAINT AND PAINT COLORS.

BURNT UMBER. An earth color. See PAINT AND PAINT COLORS.

BURY THE SHOW (strike, drag out, takeout, the out). Obsolete; term for taking out and putting away all components of a show after the final performance. See also STRIKE A SET.

BUS BAR (bus). A heavy copper bar used as a conductor for electricity. Bus bars are usually found in panel boxes, panel boards, fuse boxes, and company patches. See also COMPANY PATCH.

BUSHES (exterior set pieces). Two-dimensional bushes are usually made from beaverboard or plywood. If three-dimensional bushes are needed, real bushes are sometimes used for short runs or wire frames can be covered with fabricated leaves of flameproofed material. Styrofoam is another popular material for making stage bushes. See GROUNDROW.

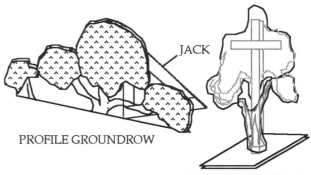

PROFILE GROUNDROW

JACK

THREE DIMENSIONAL

BUSHES

BUTT HINGE. See under HINGES.

BUTT JOINTS. See under JOINTS.

BUTTRESS. A pier or column built against a wall and used for structural support. Flying buttresses, which were an architectural feature of the Gothic period, can be simulated to make a setting of that period more realistic.

BX WIRE. Obsolete; electrical wires encased in flexible armored steel. Not usually legal to use. See GREENFIELD; WIRE, ELECTRICAL.

CABLE. See WIRE.

CABLE, ELECTRICAL. See **Stage wire** under WIRE, ELECTRICAL.

CABLE CLAMP. See under CLAMPS.

CABLE CYLINDER. A two-way cylinder rigged with cable and pulleys used for moving scenery. This device can be powered by air or oil and usually is remote controlled.

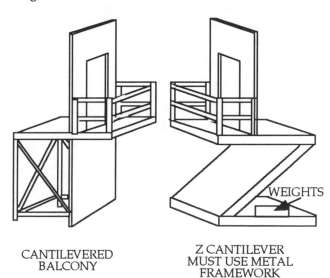

PISTON INSIDE GOES BOTH WAYS WITH CABLE ATTACHED OVER PULLEYS

AIR IN OR OUT

TURNBUCKLE AND ATTACHMENT DEVICE CONNECTING OBJECTS TO BE MOVED

CABLE CYLINDER

CABLE HOOK (J-hook). See under HOOK.

CABLE PIPE (carpenter's pipe). A regular flying pipe dedicated to carrying cable from one side of the stage to the other, used by professional touring shows.

CAD (computer-aided design). A software program for computers that makes it possible to DESIGN or to do DRAWINGS.

CAGE. Wire enclosure sometimes used to separate lighting control or sound control installations from stage.

CALCIUM LIGHT. See LIMELIGHT.

CALIBRATION. System of placing numbers on dimmers or potentiometers to facilitate recording of accurate readings of light or sound intensities.

CALIPER. An instrument with two prongs, resembling a compass, and used to measure diameters of rods or pipes. An outside caliper measures outside diameter (OD). An inside caliper measures inside diameter (ID).

CALL BOARD. A theatre bulletin board for rehearsal or work calls or general theatre announcements.

CALL BOY. Obsolete; usually an assistant stage manager, who called actors for cues and places for scenes and was generally responsible for the personnel of a show. Intercommunication systems have eliminated the need for call boys in most theatres.

CAMLOCK. A brand name for a fastener that uses a headed smooth pin that locks with a friction device on the headless end. Often used in TRUSS assemblies.

CANCEL (Command verb). Often used to refer to killing or striking a particular property, costume, or bit of scenery.

CANDELABRA BASE. A socket or base for a lamp slightly smaller than standard. Usually found in wall brackets, large Christmas tree lights, or chandeliers.

CANTILEVERED BALCONY

Z CANTILEVER MUST USE METAL FRAMEWORK

WEIGHTS

CANDLEPOWER. Luminous intensity. See also FOOTCANDLE; ILLUMINATION.

CANNON (sound effects). Recordings very effective or use bass drum or shotgun in ashcan, etc. See also BOMBS.

CANTILEVER. A beam or truss firmly supported at one end and hanging free at the other. Used as the structural element of a balcony setting.

CANVAS. A coarse, heavyweight fabric. For uses, see under COVERING FLATS: **Materials;** FLOORCLOTH.

CAP (noun). Abbreviation for CAPITAL.

CAP (verb). To place a capital or top on a column or post.

CAPACITY, ELECTRICAL. The amount of current a conductor can carry without overheating. Usually used in reference to dimmers. See also AMPERE; WIRE.

CAPCOLITE. Obsolete; trade name for Capitol Stage Lighting Company's fresnel spotlights.

CAPITAL (abbr. cap). Ornamental top of a column. Most common types are Doric, Ionic, and Corinthian. For illustrations, see COLUMNS.

CAR. A professional term for a skeletal wagon (framework wagon) used to support scenery to be moved.

CARABINER. An enclosed elongated device with a spring gate on it. Originally a piece of mountaineering equipment, it is often used in the theatre for the rigging of SAFETY LINES for lights, color frames, and other light-duty applications.

CARBOLIC ACID. Obsolete; formerly added in small quantities to scene paint as a disinfectant, delaying decomposition. Carbolic acid has been declared toxic and too dangerous for casual use. Substitute the safer oil of wintergreen or hospital disinfectant. See also PAINT MIXING. For disposal of toxic material, see HAZARDOUS WASTE.

CARBON ARC. See **Arc light** under LIGHTING INSTRUMENTS, SPECIFIC.

CARBON TETRACHLORIDE. Obsolete; formerly stocked as a cleaning fluid in costume departments and used also to clean contact buttons and brushes of dimmers. Carbon tetrachloride has been declared extremely toxic and dangerous. Substitute 6/0 sandpaper or rouge cloth (not Carborundum paper) for cleaning contact brushes. For disposal of toxic materials see HAZARDOUS WASTE.

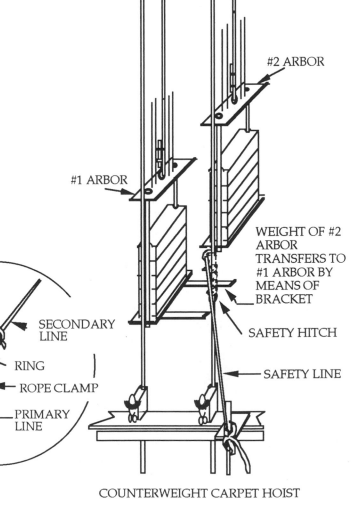

SANDBAG CARPET HOIST

COUNTERWEIGHT CARPET HOIST

CARBORUNDUM PAPER. An abrasive paper, available in different grades, for smoothing and polishing wood or metal. Also available as power sander wheels and belts. For coarse work no. 2 and no. 4 are common grades; for finish work no. 1/0 and no. 2/0 are used. See also WET OR DRY PAPER; SANDPAPER.

CARPENTER. See STAGE CREW.

CARPET HOIST. Device used to transfer counterweight from one set of lines to another during a scene change in which flown scenery must be detached from its lines. The first illustration represents a carpet hoist for rope rigging, showing the counterweight (sandbag) securely tied to a ring which rides freely on the primary line until engaged by a rope clamp or trim block. The secondary line is tied to the ring and is used to hold the counterweight in high position, leaving the primary set free to be detached from the scenery and raised out of sightlines. The second illustration shows how this same transfer is made with a counterweight system on which two cleats are attached to the bottom of the arbor on the primary set of lines and are engaged by the arbor of the secondary set of lines. Never trust the rope lock on the lock rail to hold a counterweighted set of lines that is out of balance. Use a safety hitch from the hand line to the lock rail. See **Safety hitch** under KNOTS.

CARRIAGE (arbor)

An arbor for holding counterweights in a COUNTERWEIGHT SYSTEM.

A stringer supporting the risers and treads in STEPS.

CARRIAGE BOLT. See under BOLTS.

CARRIER. Roller in a traveler track to which curtains are tied.

CARRYING FLATS. See HANDLING FLATS.

CARRY OFF (escape, get away). Offstage steps leading down from a platform. See STEPS.

CARTOONING. See LAYOUT.

CARTRIDGE

A kind of container, e.g., a brush holder for a dimmer.

A holder for a needle in a phonograph arm. See under SOUND EQUIPMENT.

CARTRIDGE FUSE. A fuse shaped like a cylinder. Fuses of more than 30-amp capacity are of the cartridge type. See also FUSE.

CARTRIDGE TAPE (cart tape). See **Cartridge** under SOUND EQUIPMENT.

CARVED DESIGN. For properties or stage design. Intricate carvings are not generally necessary for proscenium staging, but demands of central staging may be more exacting. Balsa or black walnut are easy woods to carve if papier-mache is not feasible. Styrofoam, if not abused in handling or if protected by a coat of acrylic modeling paste, may also be used for intricate designs of ornamental nature

CASEIN PAINT. See under PAINT AND PAINT COLORS.

CASEMENT (casing). See DOOR; WINDOW.

CASTER. A small wheel used in making wagons, tilt jacks, and lift jacks for shifting scenery. Swivel casters turn in all directions; stationary casters are fixed for movement in one direction only. Because of irregular floors, casters should not be less than 3" in diameter and should be of ball-bearing type, equipped with rubber tires. See also GLIDES; SCENERY, SHIFTING.

CATALYST. A secondary chemical added to the primary chemical for the purpose of activating the primary. In Styrofoam and other plastic foams, the catalyst causes foaming and hardening. With plastic resins, the catalyst usually changes the plastic from liquid to solid.

CATWALK. A walk usually suspended or cantilevered in the air. A term sometimes given to a fly gallery, loading platform, or a lighting position in the auditorium.

C-CLAMP. See under CLAMPS.

C-CYC. See under CYC, C.

CEDAR. A soft, lightweight wood sometimes used for special construction or for bulky scenery not requiring too much strength. Not recommended for permanent scenery because it is brittle and splinters easily. See also LUMBER.

CEILING BEAM

Box-type dead hung. Usually a false beam masking a second electric pipe needed to light the upstage areas of a box set with a ceiling. The box ceiling beam can be, and often is, designed in such a way that the audience is unaware the ceiling is not one piece.

Flipper type, to fly. A narrow flat, 12" to 36" wide, fastened at right angles to downstage edge of ceiling and used to mask the flies. Ceil-

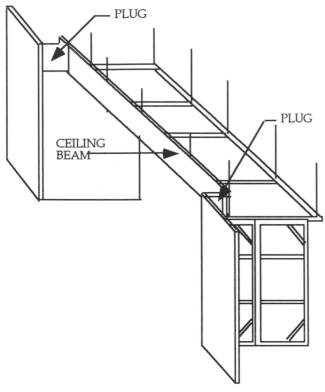

CEILING BEAM IN POSITION

ing beams are painted the same color as the ceiling. If further masking is necessary, a border or teaser can be hung behind beam. See illustration next page.

CEILING PLATE. Stage hardware consisting of a plate 4" to 6" long with a 1" or 2" ring attached; the plate is drilled to accommodate both screws and a bolt. Used to tie off lines supporting ceilings or other scenery to be flown. See illustration under CEILINGS; see also **Hanger iron** under STRAP IRON; **Flying scenery** under SCENERY, SHIFTING.

CEILINGS. Large covered frames, suspended horizontally from two or three sets of lines, used to enclose a box set. Conventionally, ceilings are trapezoidal, with sides raked to conform to sightlines; however, a rectangular shape is often more versatile for repertory or stock theatre. All-purpose ceilings designed to fit many different sets are 16' to 18' deep and 1' to 4' wider than acting area on stage. Downstage edge of ceilings finish in a CEILING BEAM, 1' to 3' wide and as long as the ceiling, fastened perpendicularly with 2" backflaps and diagonal braces of 1" x 3"

stock. If ceiling beam does not mask vertical sightlines, a cloth border can be dropped behind beam on another set of lines. Upstage edges of ceilings can use a flap of muslin or canvas to prevent light leaks where backwall and ceiling meet. Ceilings are hung 3' to 4' upstage of terminal points of set to allow ample space for lighting from the first pipe. Ceilings reflect less light and are unobtrusive if painted dark colors. Smaller, temporary ceilings may be made by battening stock flats together, dutchmanning cracks, and adding ceiling plates as needed.

Book ceiling. Two flats hinged to fold face to face and suspended from three sets of lines. Requires less grid height in flying than a plain ceiling. Build rectangles of 1" x 3" or 1" x 4" stock lumber in same manner as for FLAT, omitting corner braces; if stock lumber is not long enough to make stiles, join two lengths with a **scarf joint** (see under JOINT); place toggles on approximately 6' centers; mount CEILING PLATES on approximately 6' centers on both sides of downstage flat and one side of upstage flat; turn flats face up and countersink 2" **backflaps** (see under

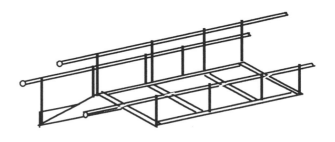

BOOK CEILING

HINGES) not more than 6' apart. Cover in same manner as flat (see COVERING FLATS); if canvas or muslin is not wide enough, seam with a double-stitched flat seam running parallel with proscenium; dutchman crack with strip of muslin no wider than combined width of stiles; turn face down and hinge ceiling beam to ceiling with 2" backflaps not more than 6' apart, allowing beam to overlap edge of ceiling; paint a dark color and hang as illustrated.

Plain ceiling for single set. Designed and built like one section of a book ceiling and flown

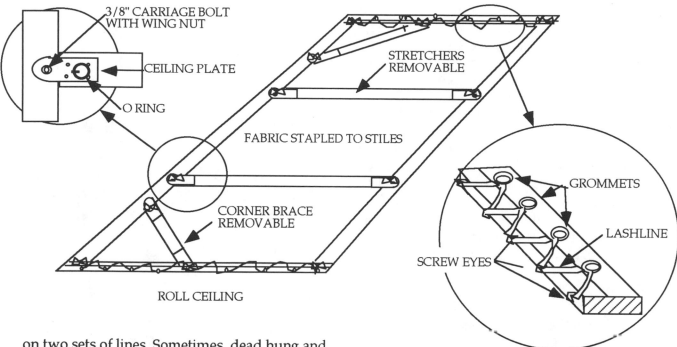

3/8" CARRIAGE BOLT WITH WING NUT

CEILING PLATE

O RING

STRETCHERS REMOVABLE

FABRIC STAPLED TO STILES

CORNER BRACE REMOVABLE

ROLL CEILING

GROMMETS

LASHLINE

SCREW EYES

on two sets of lines. Sometimes dead hung and used in conjunction with a box ceiling beam to provide a second position for instruments needed to light upstage.

Plain ceiling for multiple sets. This can be the same ceiling as described for the single set; however flying the plain ceiling, which is necessary with multiple sets, requires a high grid in order to raise it out of sight. The book ceiling may have to be substituted.

Roll ceiling (road ceiling). The roll ceiling is designed to be taken apart for storage or transporting. Like the plain ceiling, it is hung from two sets of lines. Construction is as follows: Cut rails and toggle rails to same length and fit between stiles; screw ceiling plates to toggles with 3/4" no. 8 flathead wood screws; space toggles not more than 6' apart and drill a 3/8" hole in stiles, corresponding to hole in ceiling plates; fasten toggles to stiles with 3/8" x 1 1/2" carriage bolts with wing nuts through ceiling plate; nail one stile of ceiling beam perpendicular to downstage stile of ceiling, using eight penny nails; hinge toggles and rails of ceiling beam to both stiles with 2" loose-pin backflaps; assemble ceiling and turn face up. Sew muslin lengthwise to obtain necessary width; cut muslin exact length of ceiling and sew 2" webbing, double seam, on each end; grommet webbing

with no. 2 grommets on 12" centers; glue and tack muslin to stiles of both ceiling beam and ceiling; place 1" no. 10 roundhead wood screws or 1 5/8" screw eyes on 12" centers on inside edges of the two end rails, allowing about 3/8 " to project up as a hook for lash line run through grommeted ends of cloth.

CELASTIC (Sculpt-o-fab). Cellulose impregnated fabric resembling stiff felt. When softened with acetone or methyl ethyl ketone (MEK) Celastic can be formed in either positive or negative molds to make a variety of objects, including masks, armor, and many props. MEK is more toxic and does not seem to have the shelf life of acetone, which is highly combustible. Celastic is stronger and more durable than papier-mâché and equally versatile. Use aluminum foil in or on molds for easy separation. Celastic is used commercially for marine decking and roofing and is available in many marine supply houses. Use medium weight and 46" width.

CELLULOSE ACETATE. See under PLASTICS.

CELLULOSE ACETATE BUTYRATE. See under PLASTICS.

CELOTEX (firtex). Trade name for a fibrous wallboard used as an acoustic board to absorb sound; also good for bulletin boards, motor mounts, turntable mounts, etc. Available in 1/2", 3/4", and 1" thicknesses, 4' x 8' sheets.

CEMENT. Plastic adhesive used for model making, china repairing, etc. Not generally recommended for heavier work. See also GLUES.

CENTER BIT (center drill). See under BITS.

CENTER LINE

Drawing. A broken line (usually dot-dash) running through the center of a floor plan from the apron to the back wall, indicating center of the stage. Symbol: ⎯ ⎯ ⎯ ⎯ ⎯ ⎯ ⎯ ⎯ ℄

Rigging. In a three-rope system, the rope nearest the pin rail is the short line, the next is the center line, and the farthest is the long line. See also COUNTERWEIGHT SYSTEM.

CENTRAL STAGE. See **Arena stage** under STAGE.

CFM Abbreviation for cubic feet per minute; unit for measuring liquids and gases, used often in reference to air pressure.

CHAIN

Passing link chain. Lightweight chain, used in the lower hem of curtains and draperies to keep the material from blowing and to improve hanging. Sold by the foot at hardware stores.

6 gauge, 2/0 chain = 33 pounds per 100 feet;
5 gauge, 3/0 chain = 39 pounds per 100 feet;
7/32 gauge, 4/0 chain = 43 1/2 pounds per 100 feet.

Safety chain. A length of chain fastened between a spotlight or other hanging object and a wall, pipe batten, or ceiling, and used as a safety measure.

Trim chain (snatch chain). Short lengths of chain with a ring and snap hook, used to fasten pipe battens to scenery.

CHAIN BAG (climbing bag). A container that holds chain not in use for a CHAIN HOIST.

CHAIN HOIST (chain motor, chain winch). A motorized winch (hoist) that uses a specially shaped drive to move a chain. Often associated with these units is a CHAIN BAG, which holds the chain not in use.

CHAIN HOIST CONTROL (motion control, winch control). A multiswitch or computer control that allows chain hoists or winches to be individually controlled or to have GANG control.

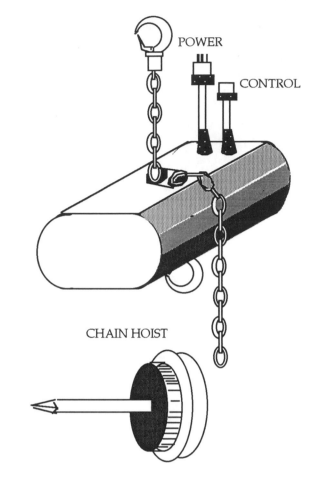

POWER

CONTROL

CHAIN HOIST

CHAIR GLIDE

CHAIN POCKET. See **Dye drop** under DROPS.

CHAIR GLIDE. Small metal disks used on the bottom of furniture to make sliding easy.

CHAIR RAIL. Stock lumber placed on a wall at a height corresponding to a chair height and used as protection for the wall. See also WAINSCOTING.

CHAISE LOUNGE. A sofa with a back rest on one end only.

CHALK BAG (pounce bag). See STENCIL.

CHALK LINE (snap line). Long length of twisted cotton string rubbed with colored chalk or charcoal and used to snap straight lines for baseboards, wainscotings, cornice moldings, etc. After line is chalked, it is held to mark on each end and snapped, thereby transferring

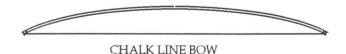

CHALK LINE BOW

chalk powder to flat surface. A one-person chalk line can be made by using a 3/4" x 3/4" x 6' to 12' length of lumber as a bow and stretching string from one end to the other. Snapping chalked line against a flat surface will transfer chalk powder to flat.

CHAMFER. To bevel an edge (remove the CURSE).

CHANNEL

    Lights. See **Computer terminology** under LIGHTING CONTROL.

    Rigging. The space between girders in a gridiron, accommodating sheaves or pulleys and allowing clearance for fly lines. Most gridirons are divided by three, four, or five channels (depending on stage size) running upstage and downstage and permitting installation of as many lines as desired. See also GRID.

CHANNEL IRON. A U-shaped bar of rolled iron used for structural purposes.

CHASE CONTROL. A type of control, either computer or noncomputer, that handles the following:

    Range. A numeric value of lamp range or cue range.

    Level. Light intensity.

    Rate. The speed of movement.

    Go. Begins the movement.

    Step. The number of lamps used.

    Hard. In fine or close focus.

    Soft. Somewhat out of focus.

    Beat. The timing of a pause.

    Clear entry. Removes last numeric entry.

CHASER. Mechanical or electronic device that makes a grouping of lights go on and off in a sequential manner. See also SPECIAL EFFECTS.

CHATTER. Excessive vibration of a cutting tool that is either improperly adjusted or dull.

CHEESECLOTH. An open-weave cotton cloth used to strain paints and polish furniture.

CHESEBOROUGH. A double half-clamp arrangement often associated with TRUSS assemblies. Since there is a pivot between the two parts, pipes may be clamped at almost any angle to each other.

CHEMICALS. See SMOKE EFFECTS; HAZARDOUS WASTE.

CHICKEN WIRE. A fencing material with 1 1/2"

or 2" hexagonal holes available in 24", 30", and 36" widths.

CHIMES (sound effect). Chimes may be borrowed from orchestras or music stores. Tolling bells, town clocks, etc., are easily simulated by striking suspended brake drums, wrecking bars, circular saw blades, pipes, etc. Use a lightly padded wooden hammer as a striker. Sound effects for great variety of bells, chimes, etc., are available on records.

CHIMNEYPIECE. Mantelpiece on a FIREPLACE.

CHIPPED FLAT. Flat with chipped or splintered ends. Repair by sawing the chipped portion from the batten and replacing with a new, carefully fitted piece. Flats with chipped paint should be washed or re-covered. See **Flat recovering** and **Flat washing** under COVERING FLATS.

CHISEL. A flat tool having a cutting edge on one end and a handle on the other. Generally used for gouging, recessing hinges, locks, etc. Most popular sizes are 1/2" and 1" chisels. See also TOOLS, HAND.

CHOPPER. See DOUSER.

CHROMA

    Lights. The amount of pure color within a

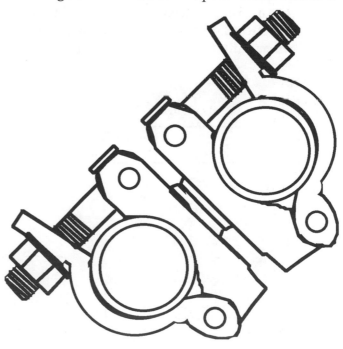

CHESEBOROUGH

HUE. Chroma can be altered by intensity change from a dimmer.

Paint. The amount of saturation (pure color) within a HUE. Chroma is altered in painting by adding black or white.

CHROME PAINTS (mineral colors). See also **Dry pigments** under PAINT AND PAINT COLORS.

CHUCK

A device for holding drills or bits.

A device on the head of a lathe used to hold the material to be cut or drilled.

CINEMOID. English trade name for color media used in lighting instruments. See COLOR MEDIA.

CIRCLE THEATRE. See **Arena stage** under STAGE.

CIRCUIT, ELECTRICAL. A circuit is the complete path of a current, from source to load and back to source.

Branch circuit. The final electrical circuit protected by the lowest-amperage fuse or breaker.

Hot circuit. An electrical circuit carrying a current.

Parallel circuit. The most common way of ganging electrical lights together for the theatre is to use a multiple electrical circuit in which the current flows independently through each socket or outlet. In a parallel circuit battery

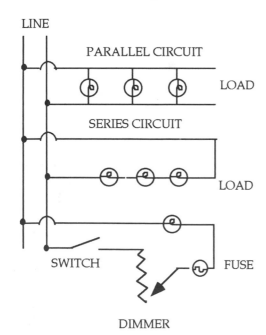

LINE

PARALLEL CIRCUIT

LOAD

SERIES CIRCUIT

LOAD

SWITCH   FUSE

DIMMER

hookup, each positive pole is fastened to one wire, each negative pole to another wire. The resulting voltage is not changed, but the amperage is equal to the sum total of each battery in the circuit.

Series circuit. Equipment wired to form a conductor, e.g., a series of lamp sockets with alternate binding posts connected so that the current must flow through each lamp in order to complete the circuit. The path of electricity passes through each lamp filament before continuing to the next, resulting in a voltage loss in direct relation to the number of lamps in the circuit. Thus, in a 110-volt circuit wired in series with ten lamps of equal capacity, the voltage for each lamp would be 11, and intensity would be lessened accordingly. Batteries wired in series increase total voltage to the sum of the voltage of each battery. Although lights are seldom put in series for stage use, switches, most dimmers, and fuses are always placed in series with the lights they control.

Short circuit. To complete an open circuit by a shunt of low resistance. Short circuiting can be caused by worn insulation, accidental cutting of the wire, careless handling of an open circuit, etc. The results of a short circuit are usually blown fuses, but burned out equipment can also result. Try to determine cause of the short before replacing fuse or resetting breaker.

Three-wire single-phase circuit. Two hot lines with a common (neutral) wire. 110-volt potential exists between the hot line and the common wire, and a 220-volt potential exists between the two hot lines. The common line is the same gauge as the other two lines but must not be fused.

Four-wire three-phase circuit. A circuit involving three hot lines and one common (neutral) wire serving all three hot lines. The potential between any hot line and the common wire is 120-volts and that between any two hot lines is 208-volts. Three-phase services offer the greatest capacity for the least initial installation cost, and three-phase motors are cheaper and smaller than single-phase motors of equal horsepower. The stage electrician should be aware that certain installations using only 208-volts may omit the common wire in the service

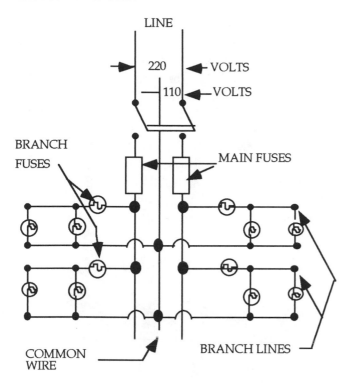

THREE-WIRE SINGLE-PHASE CIRCUIT

panel, making the circuit look like a three-wire single-phase circuit; this does not usually happen on stage in a COMPANY PATCH. The common line is not fused. Always check the voltage between wires before installing 120-volt equipment.

CIRCUIT BREAKER. A device that protects a circuit in a similar manner as a fuse but can be reset if blown. Circuit breakers look somewhat like electrical switches.

CIRCULAR SAW. See under POWER TOOLS.

CIRCULAR STAIRS. See **Steps** under CURVED SCENERY.

CLAMPS. Devices that hold things together. See also COUPLER.

Bar clamp. A screw clamp with a tail jaw that slides on a metal bar or a length of pipe to allow clamping over varied distances up to about 6'. Useful in furniture construction and repair.

Batten clamp. A metal clamp used to fasten fly lines to flats. Batten clamps are used for scene changes in which it is necessary to disconnect flown scenery from the pipe batten. See also CARPET HOIST.

Cable clamp. A small metal clip used to hold cable or wire to a ceiling or wall.

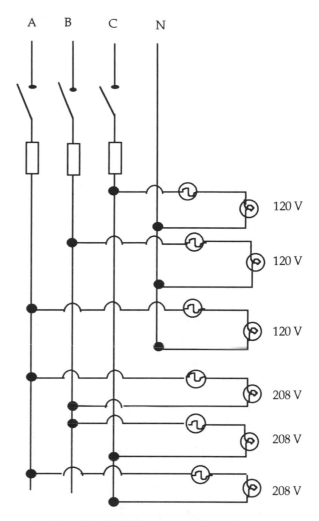

FOUR WIRE THREE-PHASE CIRCUIT

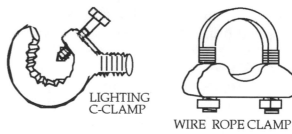

LIGHTING C-CLAMP

WIRE ROPE CLAMP

YOKE OR BRIDGE CLAMP

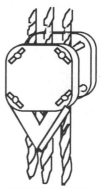

TRIM CLAMP

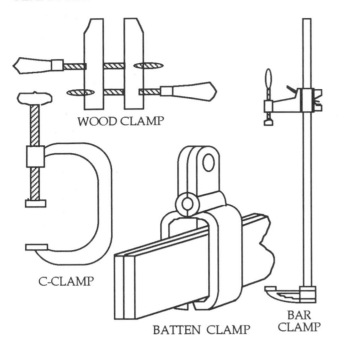

WOOD CLAMP

C-CLAMP

BATTEN CLAMP

BAR CLAMP

C-clamp, electric. Used on lighting equipment to fasten equipment to pipe battens or standards.

C-clamp, wood. C-shaped clamp with a single bolt for tightening. Generally used for holding glued pieces together or temporarily fastening platforms together.

Pipe clamp. A clamp for fastening electrical equipment to pipes. The two most common types are small C-clamps and yoke clamps.

Trim clamp (trim block). A metal clamp designed to clamp a set of lines together for counterweighting. Trim clamps are available in theatrical hardware supply houses for three-, four-, or five-line sets.

Wire rope clamp (clip, crosby, fist grip clip). A U-shaped bolt with a yoke designed to clamp wire rope or cables together.

Wood clamp. A double screw clamp with wooden jaws. Useful in furniture construction and repair.

Yoke clamp (bridge clamp). A clamp made in two pieces to grip a pipe from two sides. Used to fasten spotlight arms or hangers to pipe battens.

CLAPBOARD. Boards used as an exterior finish, usually tapered from 1/4" thickness on one side to 5/8" on the other and designed to overlap in horizontal lines. Strips of beaverboard, over-

lapped and nailed to flats, adequately simulate clapboard exteriors.

CLASSIFICATION OF SHOWS (type of show). Productions are often referred to as certain types or kinds of show, such as BOOK SHOW, COSTUME SHOW, HIGH-TECH SHOW, IMPROV, SCENERY SHOW.

CLAW HAMMER. See under HAMMERS.

CLAY PACKY. A company that makes moving-mirror-type AUTOMATED LIGHTS. The name is sometimes used as a generic name for any of the larger instruments made by this company.

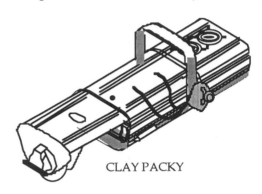

CLAY PACKY

CLEARING LINE. One or two sandbagged lines let in during a scene change for the purpose of creating room in the flies for another piece of scenery to be flown into place. The bagged lines are let in and tied off and stagehands clear room for the new piece to come in by taking strain on the bagged lines and tripping anything in the way either upstage or downstage.

CLEAR PLEASE (Command verb)

Order to strike props.

Order to get out of the way.

Order to erase a given bit of information.

Warning that curtain is going up and crew is to get offstage. Next command is usually PLACES.

CLEAT

Various types of metal pieces used for hardwaring flats. See **Lashing** under FASTENING FLATS.

A strip of wood fastened to the floor or wall or under a shelf and used to fasten scenery to the floor, brackets to a wall, etc.

CLEW. A metal plate with holes, designed to tie together several lines to be handled by a single line.

CLEWING (marrying). Tying lines together with knots or a clew so they can be handled as one line.

CLINCHING PLATE (clinch iron). See CLOUT PLATE.

CLIP. See CLAMPS.

CLIP, TERMINAL (gator clip). Fastener with spring and jaws, used as a temporary electrical contact for a terminal.

CLOUD EFFECTS. See PROJECTED SCENERY.

CLOUT NAIL. See under NAILS.

CLOUT PLATE. A metal plate 1/8" to 1/4" thick and 10" to 12" square, used during flat construction to clinch nails of corner blocks and keystones on reverse side of flat. Professional shops often weld handles to top of plates to facilitate handling.

COBWEB EFFECT. A cobweb spinner creates realistic cobwebs quickly and simply. A special liquid placed in the tank of a cobweb machine is blown from the machine in a fine thread to make the web configuration in any desired location. The web will not stain furniture or scenery and is easily removed. Cobweb dust and a pumplike duster are available in conjunction with the spinner.

COCOA MATTING. Coarsely woven rush, twine, or other fibrous material, used for padding platforms, stage armor, etc.

CODE. Refers to city, state, or national building and electrical regulations for the construction and installation of wiring and equipment. Check with local architects, contractors, or building authorities. See also FIRE CODE; NATIONAL ELECTRICAL CODE; NATIONAL UNDERWRITER'S CODE.

COFFIN LOCK (roto locks). A fastening device utilizing a rotary principle to lock the two parts of the lock together with a large hexagonal wrench. Excellent lock capable of holding and pulling two scenic units tightly together. Available from scenery supply houses.

COHERENT LIGHT. Light of the same wavelength, all waves being in phase and polarized. Lasers are coherent light.

COIL HOSE OR WIRE. See STRETCH HOSE OR WIRE.

COLD CHISEL. A chisel of tempered steel used to cut metal.

COLD CHISEL

COLD MIRRORS. See DICHROIC FILTER.

COLLET. A cylindrical steel tube with cuts in the side, used as a chuck in lathes or small drills.

COLLISIONS (sound effects). See CRASH BOX; CRASH MACHINE.

COLOR. One of the four aspects of visual manifestation, the other three being line, texture, and form. Color has three qualities or attributes: hue is designation of color, i.e., red, blue, yellow, etc.; value is tone, ranging from light to dark;

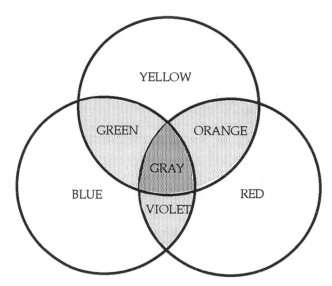
PIGMENT PRIMARIES AND MIXING OF PIGMENTS

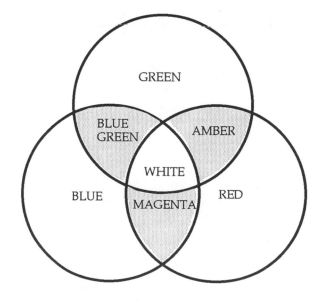
LIGHT PRIMARIES AND MIXING OF LIGHTS

33

intensity is the degree of pureness or saturation. See COLOR WHEEL; LIGHTING COLORS; PAINT AND PAINT COLORS.

Pigment primaries. Red, yellow, blue.

Pigment secondaries. Orange, green, violet.

Light primaries. Red, green, blue.

Light secondaries. Yellow, blue-green, magenta.

Warm colors. Red, yellow, and combinations.

Cool colors. Blue, green, and combinations.

Neutral colors. Black, gray, white, with a little or no hue.

	WHITE	
	HIGHLIGHT	YELLOW
YELLOW GREEN	LIGHT	YELLOW ORANGE
GREEN	LOWLIGHT	ORANGE
BLUE GREEN	MEDIUM	RED ORANGE
BLUE	HIGH DARK	RED
BLUE VIOLET	DARK	RED VIOLET
VIOLET		
	LOW DARK	
	BLACK	

COLORS IN RELATION TO GRAY SCALE

COLOR BEAM. Obsolete; trade name for a colored reflector lamp. See also AMPLEX.

COLOR CHANGERS. See **Lights** under BOOMERANG; SCROLLER.

COLOR CODE

Lights. In multiple conductor cables, inner insulations are often given different colors to facilitate tracing circuits or wires.

COLOR CHANGER
(GREAT AMERICAN MARKET)

Scenery. In repertory theatre, scenery is often color coded on the back as an aid to spotting and spiking sets by show, act, and scene.

COLOR FRAME. Wooden, paper, or metal frame designed to hold color media in front of lighting units. Sizes vary according to manufacturers; frames are not always interchangeable from one manufacturer's equipment to that of another. See also SAFETIES.

COLOR MEDIA (filter). A transparent material (gelatine, glass, plastic, etc.) used to color a light beam. Most suppliers have over 100 colors, available in sheets or rolls, and some diffusion media. See also CINEMOID; GELATINE.

COLOR TEMPERATURE. The color of light as expressed in kelvins on the KELVIN SCALE.

COLOR WASH. FOH spotlights focused on front areas of stage in same toning colors as overhead lights onstage. Color washes and toning lights are often in light primary or secondary colors. See LIGHTING COLORS.

COLOR WHEEL

Lights. A form of boomerang used to change color media in front of a spotlight.

Painting. A circle upon which the colors of the spectrum are placed to facilitate reading. See illustration on next page. See also MUNSELL SCALE; POPE COLOR WHEEL.

COLUMN. Upright pillar, generally used on the stage for ornamentation only. Square or rectangular columns are made of plain wood, flats, or both. Round columns are made from cardboard mailing tubes, corrugated cardboard, concrete form tubes, linoleum on frames, papier-mâché, or a special fluted cardboard sold by supply houses for window display. Columns include shaft and ornamental bases and capitals. Columns are usually designed to conform to one of the three basic styles of Greek architecture:

Corinthian. Characterized by bell-shaped capitals topping slender, often fluted, columns.

Doric. The simplest and oldest style, characterized by heavy, fluted columns and simple capitals.

Ionic. Characterized by fluted columns, spiral volutes on capitals, and scroll-like decorations.

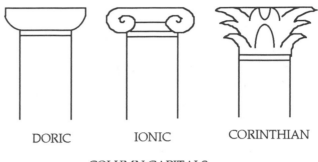

DORIC   IONIC   CORINTHIAN

COLUMN CAPITALS

COMBINATION SAW. A circular saw blade equipped with teeth for both ripping and cross-cutting. The combination saw is most practical for theatre workshops.

COMMAND. See **Computer terminology** under LIGHTING CONTROL.

COMMON NAIL. See under NAILS.

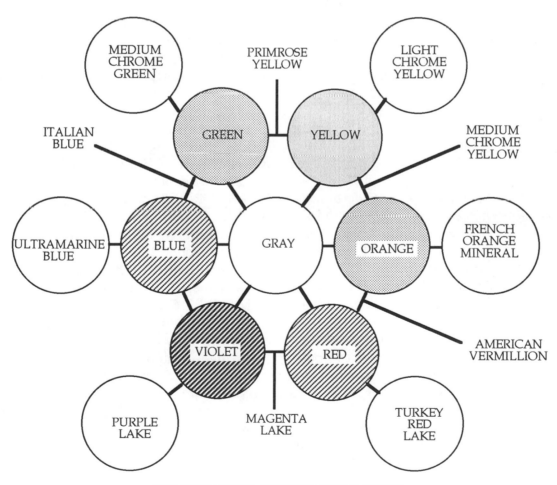

PIGMENTS IN RELATION TO COLOR WHEEL

COMPACT DISK (CD). A digitally recorded disk capable of very high quality playback. See also DIGITAL AUDIO TAPE.

COMPANIES. Touring companies under a single management are often designated by names such as company #1, company #2, red unit, blue unit, gold unit. Anything that works is acceptable.

COMPANY PATCH. A panel which allows a touring company to patch into internal permanent wiring circuits that go from backstage to remote areas such as the rail and booth positions. Utilizing the company patch saves the touring company many thousands of feet of cable running.

COMPANY SWITCH (company panel). Auxiliary electrical panel used to hookup portable dimmers to electricity. Used in theatres that cater to road shows carrying their own lighting equipment. The company switch is usually located on the service side of the stage and has a large capacity of alternating current on three phase. See **Four-wire three-phase** under CIRCUITS, ELECTRICAL.

COMPARTMENTALIZED LIGHTS. Border lights, footlights, and strip lights, having separate compartments for each lamp and usually equipped with slots for color frames. See also LIGHTING INSTRUMENTS, GENERAL.

COMPASS. An instrument used for drawing circles. See also TRAMMEL POINTS.

COMPLEMENTARY COLORS. Colors opposite each other on the color wheel, e.g., red and green, blue and orange, yellow and violet. Complementary colors of pigments when mixed together form a neutral gray color.

COMPUTER (microprocessor). A control system with a microprocessor at its heart, usually associated with memory systems.

    Lighting computer. Microprocessor that dims or intensifies light. The lighting computer can often handle many of the operations listed below. See **Computer board** under LIGHTING CONTROL.

    Scenery computer. Microprocessor that operates motors or switch-operated scenery units to allow them to be remotely controlled.

    Moving-light computer. Specially developed microprocessor that runs AUTOMATED LIGHTS. See AUTOMATED LIGHT CONTROL.

    Chaser. Specialty control unit that is not always a microprocessor but rather a grouping of switches and individual function SEQUENCERS. See CHASE CONTROL.

    Sound board. Controls all functions of sound recording and playback, from music and sound effects to the live production amplification of the human voice. See also SOUND EQUIPMENT.

CONCERT BORDER. Border lights mounted on the first electric pipe upstage of the proscenium. See also LIGHTING INSTRUMENTS, GENERAL.

CONDENSER LENS. One or two lenses used to concentrate, or bring together, rays of light. Condenser lenses are used in projection equipment to concentrate an even distribution of light on slides. See also PROJECTORS.

CONDUCTOR, ELECTRICAL. A wire or bar, usually of copper, used to transmit electricity. See also WIRE, ELECTRICAL.

CONDUIT (EMT, electrician's metal tubing, thin wall). A lightweight, thin walled pipe used to carry electric wires for permanent wiring. Since a conduit is relatively easily formed, it is often used on the stage for ornamental purposes also.

CONNECTION, ELECTRICAL. A splice or union of wires, joined by means of plugs. See also SOLDERLESS CONNECTOR.

CONNECTOR

    Automotive style or multicable type. Low-voltage connectors originally used in the automotive industry. These connectors are often used inside control boards and in AUTOMATED LIGHTS. Color codes used most often are pink for 18 to 22 gauge wire, blue for 14 to 16 gauge, yellow for 10 to 12 gauge, and red for 6 to 8 gauge. Common types are butt splice, spade, bullet, round, and open terminal. All of these can be bare or insulated (shrouded). The various connectors are mechanically attached to wire with CRIMPERS.

    Pin (slip connector). See **Pin connector** under PLUGS, ELECTRICAL.

CONSOLE. Control center for lights, sound, etc.; tends to refer to remote controlled boards.

CONSTRUCTIVISM. A popular theatre movement in Russia during the twenties, with emphasis upon machines, mechanical devices, and skeletal construction.

CONTACTOR. Remote, electromagnetically controlled switch.

CONTINENTAL PARALLEL. See under PARALLEL.

CONTINENTAL SEATING. See under SEATING, AUDITORIUM.

CONTINUITY TESTER, ELECTRICAL. Any of a number of testing devices used to detect a break in a circuit. A simple continuity tester can be made with a battery and buzzer, bell, or lamp.

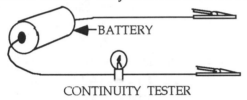

CONTINUITY TESTER

CONTOUR CURTAIN. See under CURTAIN.

CONTROL BOARD. See under LIGHTING CONTROL.

CONTROLLER

Usually a small potentiometer used to control one or more groupings of dimmers, controllers, or channels.

The electrician who has control of dimmers. See also LIGHTING CONTROL.

CONTROL ROOM (control booth). Space designated to hold control boards, sound and or lights, is often the stage manager's station as well.

CONVENIENCE OUTLET (handy box). The common household duplex wall receptacle.

CONVEX LENS. See **Plano-convex** under LENSES.

COOL COLORS. See under COLOR.

COPING SAW. See under SAWS.

CORD, SASH. No. 8 sash cord (1/4") is used for lash lines on flats.

CORE, ELECTRICAL. Soft iron bar or lamination forming the center of a transformer or autotransformer dimmer.

CORE SOLDER. See SOLDER.

CORINTHIAN. See under COLUMNS.

CORNER BLOCK. See **Components** under FLAT.

CORNER BRACE. See **Components** under FLAT.

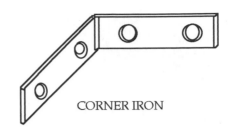

CORNER IRON

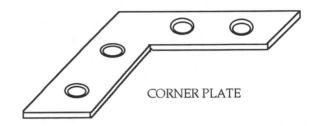

CORNER PLATE

CORNER IRON. Small piece of strap iron cut in a right angle and used as a plate to support the corners of screens, frames, etc.

CORNER PLATE. L-shaped metal plate used to join corners of screens, frames, and sometimes flats.

CORNICE. Ornamental molding placed on wall near ceiling. See **Cornice molding** under MOLDING.

CORNMEAL

Paint. Sometimes used in paint to give the texture of fine plaster. See also PAINTING TECHNIQUES.

Props. Coarse-ground white cornmeal is sometimes used to simulate snow on stage.

CORRUGATED CARDBOARD. An inexpensive substitute for beaverboard, Upson board, or profile board. Double-faced corrugated cardboard is relatively stiff and can be used for temporary facing. Single-faced cardboard rolls readily and can be adapted as a material for columns, steam pipes, etc. Corrugated cardboard is sometimes used for platform and step padding under muslin or canvas. Available from box manufacturers and, in limited quantities, from bookstores and department stores, where it is used in wrapping. Mattress boxes obtained from department stores offer a generous supply of corrugated cardboard at a reasonable cost. *Warning:* Painting tends to buckle corrugated cardboard. Painting both sides may help relieve buckling.

CORRUGATOR

CORRUGATOR (corrugated fastener). Fluted metal fastener, 1/2" x 3/4", with points on one end, used to hold two pieces of wood together. Most helpful in holding a flat together before applying corner blocks and keystones. Use 1/2" no. 5 or 5/8" no. 5. Place two to a joint, running at a slight angle to grain of wood.

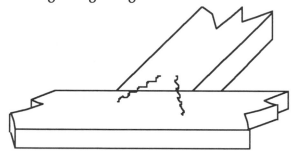

PLACEMENT OF CORRUGATORS

COSTUME SHOW. Often a historical show, which implies a number of complicated period costumes.

COUNTERSINK (noun). A cone-shaped drill used for countersinking.

COUNTERSINK (verb). To set the head of a flat-head screw or bolt into wood or metal.

COUNTERWEIGHT SYSTEM. A system for flying scenery, composed of pipe battens, cables or ropes, sheaves, head blocks, and arbors, in which weights are added to the arbor to offset the weight of scenery being flown. See also under RIGGING; **Flying scenery** under SCENERY, SHIFTING; SYNCHRONOUS WINCH.

COUPLER

Half-coupler. A pipe clamp that attaches to only one pipe, usually with a bolt for attachment to other objects.

Rota-lock (Rota-lok). A special pipe clamp that attaches a pipe at a 90° angle to another pipe.

Swivel coupler. See CHESEBOROUGH.

COVE LIGHTS. Lighting instruments placed in vertical slots in the side walls of the auditorium.

Similar to the BOX BOOM position. See BEAM LIGHTS.

COVERING FLATS

Materials. See also DRAPERY, SET; FLAMEPROOFING; FLOORCLOTH.

Canvas. A coarse, heavyweight fabric. The linen canvas formerly used for covering flats in professional theatre has been replaced by lighter weights (7 or 8 ounces per square yard) of cotton canvas. Although nonprofessional theatre generally uses **Muslin** (see below) for covering flats, canvas is recommended for flats used for touring or subjected to abnormal abuse. Seven-ounce canvas is adequate for most flat covering. Flameproofed canvas is available at a slightly higher price and does not shrink up as well.

Duck. A strong cotton or linen material; 7- or 8-ounce duck can be used interchangeably with **Canvas** (see above) for covering flats. Duck is often used for groundcloths in 10- to 16-ounce weights.

Muslin. Muslin, which is easier to apply than canvas, is generally used for covering flats in nonprofessional theatre. Heavy, at least 128 to 140 threads per square inch, unbleached muslin is used. Unbleached muslin is often sold under the name of sheeting and is available in a variety of widths. Flameproofed muslin is also available through theatrical supply houses, but since flameproofing preshrinks material, care must be taken while covering to stretch material tautly. Many technicians prefer to do their own flameproofing after covering in order to take advantage of shrinkage and ensure tautness. Available at fabric stores and scenery supply houses.

Velour (plush). Any of various fabrics with a pile or napped surface. Sometimes used for covering flats.

Directions for covering. Place flat face up on table or sawhorses; check rails, toggles, and stiles for unclinched nails. Cut canvas or muslin 2" longer than flat; place material on flat with selvage edge either flush with edge of stile or set in approximately 1/8"; partially set no. 4 tacks or 3/8" staples at 12" intervals on inside edge of stile; stretch material from opposite stile and repeat tacking on inside edge of stile; stretch material and continue tacking on two rails, adjusting to remove puckers. Turn material back and apply GLUE to stiles, brushing carefully to ensure complete coverage with no holidays or puddles; smooth material on glued surface with block of 1" x 3" lumber. Trim surplus material with sharp knife or razor blade, 1/8" to 1/4" from outside edge of flat, using thumb as guide; after trimming continue tacking or stapling on outside edge of flat at 6" intervals staggered with inside tacks. **Alternate, preferred method** requiring three people: Place material on flat and turn back on one stile; brush glue, as above; hold material approximately 1' above flat, with one person on each end. Third person smooths muslin onto flat with 1" x 3" block of wood, beginning in the middle and working first to one end and then to the other. Repeat process on other stile, then on two ends; trim and tack or staple as above. *Warnings:* Glue used is a hot glue; work rapidly before it cools and sets. If material does not stick in places, lift and reglue. Avoid spilling glue on face of material and pulling glue through material with fingers; scene paint will not cover such **Glue burns** (see under STAINS).

Covering flat with openings. Proceed as above, gluing, trimming and tacking material to stiles and rails. Cut material from opening, allowing approximately a 1" overhang; cut a diagonal in each corner to allow material to be folded back; glue, trim and tack as on stiles and rails. **Alternative method** to use scraps: Cover door flat in three pieces, window flat in four pieces; glue, trim, and tack material above door and above window opening; with window flat, repeat below window opening; glue, trim, and tack material to sides of legs, allowing ends to remain as flaps to be painted down as DUTCHMAN when the size coat is applied.

Flat patching. Patch holes or tears in a flat with muslin and scene paint with a high glue content. Paint back of flat around tear; paint patch; hold a board against face of flat and apply patch to back; paint patch on, paying special attention to the edges, which may curl if not painted down. To prevent the puckering caused by different rates of shrinkage, patch painted flats with painted muslin and new flats with new muslin. If patches must be applied to the face of a flat, use the lightest weight muslin possible, patch as above, and give two coats of paint to blend patch into flat.

Flat re-covering. If paint becomes too thick on flats, or if a former coat of dye paint bleeds through, rip off old canvas or muslin and replace with new. Frames should be free from all tacks and irregular surfaces before applying new cover. Proceed as above (**Directions for covering**).

Flat washing. Flats with too many coats of scene paint can be washed and reused. Washing tools are sawhorses, hose, and stiff fiber-bristled brushes. Place flats on sawhorses and hose with warm water; allow a few minutes for water to soak in, then scrub gently with brush and more water; continue scrubbing until all paint is off flat. *Warnings:* Too much or too hot water will loosen glue holding muslin or canvas to flat. Too vigorous use of brush will break down fibers and the natural resilience of material, causing future sagging. Be gentle!

COVERING MATERIAL FOR FLATS. See **Materials** under COVERING FLATS.

CRACKS BETWEEN FLATS. When two or more flats are hinged or battened together on the same plane, the cracks between the flats are covered with a strip of muslin called a DUTCHMAN.

CRADLE

Curved support used to help hold the center of flying electrical lines.

Obsolete. A metal frame in first border position in which baby spots are mounted.

CRADLE, SNOW. See SNOW CRADLE.

CRASH BOX. A portable sound effects box made of wood or metal filled with glass and/or metal and designed to make noise when it is upended.

CRASH MACHINE. A drum with pins contacting hardwood slats of various lengths. When the

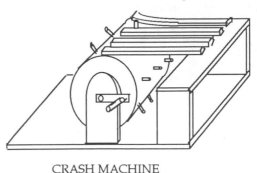

CRASH MACHINE

drum is revolved, pins force slats away and allow them to snap back onto drum, giving a crashing sound. Crash machines, with or in place of recordings and thunder sheets, make good sound effects for many types of crashes.

CRESCENT WRENCH. See under WRENCHES.

CREW. See STAGE CREW.

CRIMPER. A plier-type tool used to attach various electrical connectors. Used primarily in control wiring. See **Automotive style or multicable type** under CONNECTORS.

CROSBY. See **Wire rope clamp** under CLAMPS.

CROSS FADE (Command verb). The process of simultaneously fading one cue out and another cue in.

CROSS-FADER. A devise, often a dimmer, used to fade one cue out simultaneously as a second cue fades in. See **Computer terminology** under LIGHTING CONTROL.

CROSSHATCH. See **Dry brush** under PAINTING TECHNIQUES.

CROSSPIECE. Horizontal structural members of a flat, known as **Rails** and **toggles**; see **Components** under FLAT.

CROSS-SECTION DRAWING. A drawing of a section made at right angles to the main axis of a three dimensional object. See illustration under DRAWINGS.

CROWBAR (wrecking bar). Tempered steel bar used for prying, loosening, and dismantling. Most useful sizes for theatre work are 12" and 24".

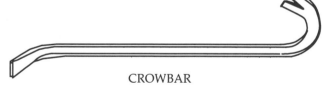

CROWBAR

CRT (display, monitor, VDU). See under LIGHTING CONTROL.

CUE. An order to perform an action. Cues are normally given to lights, sound, carpenters, flys, props, and anyone who may need an order to perform a given deed. WARNING CUES usually precede a cue, and often AUTOFOLLOWERS come after a cue. In the days before computers, cues were numbered as 1, 1a, 1b, etc. Since computer light boards, cues are numbered as 1, 1.1, 1.2, etc.

CUEING SYSTEM. Often a combination of voice calls (see INTERCOM SYSTEM) and light cueing system (see CUE LIGHTS).

CUE LIGHTS. A system of lights and switches with controls at the stage manager's station allowing him to signal cues to other members of the crew. A good cueing system will have two lights per circuit at each work station in case one burns out. The normal procedure is for the stage manager to give a vocal warning as he turns on the cue light, followed in 15 to 30 seconds by the **GO** cue, which is not necessarily verbal but may be simply turning the cue light off.

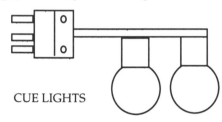

CUE LIGHTS

CUE SHEET (cue card). A sheet of paper or a card that gives a setting to be used by light and sound boards. Usually will include specific information on how to execute the cue in terms of time, sequential information, and AUTO FOLLOWERS. See also PLOT; WARNING, CUE.

CURRENT. The rate of flow of electricity, expressed in amps. See also AMPERE.

CURSE OF A BOARD. Sharp corners of a board. It is sometimes necessary to plane the edges of a board to prevent splintering and to remove the curse.

CURTAIN (act curtain, grand drape, house curtain, main curtain). Draperies separating stage from auditorium. See also ASBESTOS CURTAIN; DRAPERY, STAGE.

Contour curtain (braille, waterfall). Permanently tied on top with individually controlled lines dropping through rings 12" apart to ties at intervals across lower hem. Designs or contours are made by raising the lines to various heights. Nylon or Orlon fishline should be used for the lines, and curtain weights, or sinkers, should be attached to the ends to ensure return of curtain to floor.

Draw curtain (traveler, traverse). Curtain rigged on a wire, traveler, or track to part in the center and open to each side of the stage. Draw curtains overlap in the center a minimum of 2'.

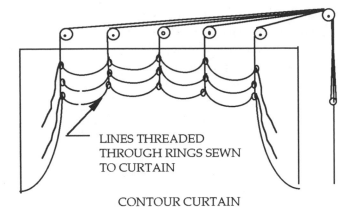

LINES THREADED
THROUGH RINGS SEWN
TO CURTAIN

CONTOUR CURTAIN

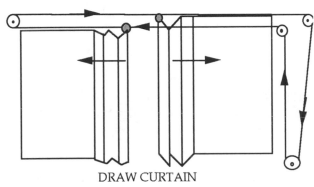

DRAW CURTAIN

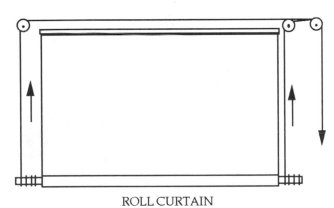

ROLL CURTAIN

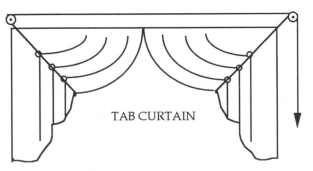

TAB CURTAIN

Lift curtain (flyaway). Curtain rigged on counterweights to raise and lower.

Roll curtain (oleo). Permanently tied to top batten and glued and tacked to a round wooden

pole or a plastic or aluminum pipe on bottom. Ropes wound around each end of the pole and threaded through pulleys overhead provide the necessary mechanism for rolling curtain up or down. The roll curtain, or oleo, was formerly used extensively for vaudeville, melodrama, and light musicals. Although it was principally used as an interact curtain allowing action to continue downstage while scenery was being changed upstage, the oleo also sometimes represented street scenes or forest scenes or carried advertising from local merchants (AD CURTAIN). The oleo is an amusing and authentic touch for staging melodramas.

Tab curtain. Permanently tied on top with diagonal lines running through rings to lower inside edges. Tension on diagonal lines raises and parts the curtain. Tab curtains almost always need a stagehand on each side to ensure closure, a process known as "paging the curtain."

CURTAIN CALLS. See BOWS.

CURTAIN GOING UP. Warning given by stage manager to actors and technicians that scene is about to begin.

CURTAIN LINE

A line drawn on the stage floor marking the position of curtain when closed.

Acting. The last line in a scene, used as a cue line to bring curtain down.

Rigging. The overhaul line controlling the curtain.

CURTAIN TRACK. See also **Draw curtain** under CURTAIN; TRAVELER.

CURTAIN WARMER. Using lights to illuminate (warm) the ACT CURTAIN or SHOW CURTAIN. When these lights go out, they heighten anticipation that the show will start.

CURVED OPENING. See ARCH.

CURVED SCENERY

Flats. Construction: Cut sweeps from 3/4" plywood to desired radius; fasten as illustrated on 2' or 4' centers, using 1" x 3" batten as stringers; glue and nail with eightpenny box nails to sweeps. Cover sweeps with plywood or beaverboard, nailing to sweeps with threepenny nails on 3" centers. Glue muslin onto plywood or beaverboard with **sizing** (see under GLUES). On concave curve, use preshrunk muslin to prevent pulling away from surface while drying.

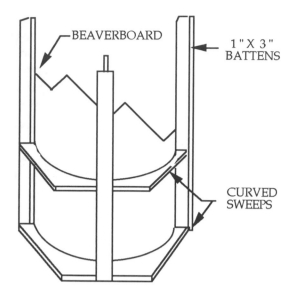

CURVED FLAT

and nail risers to stringers with sixpenny nails; leg up stairs to proper height with 1" x 3" lumber fastened to stringers by 1 1/2" wood screws; face downstage edge with 1/4" plywood or beaverboard.

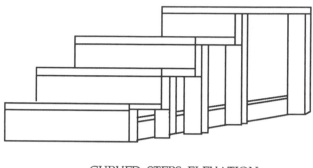

CURVED STEPS ELEVATION

Steps. Construction: Curved steps are laid out from a radial point, generally not less than 4' from inside curve. Lay out full-scale plan on floor or on plywood; determine size of treads and cut all treads alike from 3/4" plywood; make stringers in sections, running as tangents to inside arcs and as chords to outside arcs. Cut stringers from 3/4" plywood 2' wide; the span between stringers should not exceed 3'; cut 1" x 3" legs for each joint of stringers. Cut risers 6" wide by length determined from layout; glue

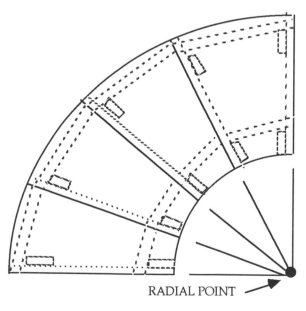

RADIAL POINT

CURVED STEPS PLAN

CUTOFF. Framing shutters in ERS to shape and size a light beam. See also **Barndoor** under LIGHT SPILL CONTROL; DOUSER.

CUTOFF, ELECTRICAL. A switch for one portion of a given circuit.

CUTOUT. Silhouettes or profiles cut from canvas, muslin, plywood, beaverboard, etc., and painted. See also GROUNDROW.

CUTOUT DROP. See under DROPS.

CYC, C (surround a cyc, full cyc). Cyclorama enclosing three sides of acting area in a U- or C-shape. See also CYC, SKY .

Linnebach cyc. Designed and invented in the early twentieth century by Adolphe Linnebach (1876–1963). Hung on a curved track and rolled when not needed on a cone at one side of the stage.

Trip cyc. A cyc designed to be raised by tripping. See TRIP.

CYC, SKY (cyclorama). A backdrop, either permanent or temporary, used to simulate the sky. Best effects are obtained from a permanent plaster cyc. Stitched canvas cycs, portable and much less expensive than plaster, are more popular. Light blue or blue-green are the favored colors.

CYCLORAMA ARM. See **Scenery** under ARM.

CYCLORAMA DRAPES. The basic drapes surrounding the stage with legs, borders, tabs and backdrops, not to be confused with sky cyclorama. Often called by the color of the fabric, e.g., the blacks.

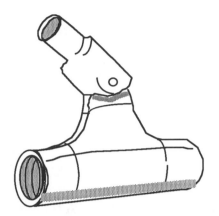

CYCLORAMA KNUCKLES

CYCLORAMA KNUCKLE. A swiveled coupling attached to a tee, permitting cyclorama arms to be extended in any direction.

CYCLORAMA LIGHTS (cyc lights) Border lights, floodlights, or strip lights used to illuminate the cyc. On some stages, floor lights are called cyc foots. See **Floodlight, Scoop, Striplight** under LIGHTING INSTRUMENTS, GENERAL; **Cyclorama colors** under LIGHTING COLORS.

CYLINDER. Remote-controlled single- and double-acting cylinders powered by air, gas, or oil. Cylinders have a piston and rod that move back and forth under the powering source. See also AIR OVER OIL; CABLE CYLINDER; HYDRAULICS; PNEUMATICS.

CYM. Refers to cyan, yellow, and magenta, a method of color blending using light secondary colors. This method of blending is often used in AUTOMATED LIGHTS and DICHROIC FILTERS. See also COLOR; RGB.

D

d. Symbol for penny, length designation of a nail. See NAILS.

DADO. Rectangular slot cut in a board to add strength to a joint. Ends of bookcases are usually dadoed to receive shelves. See also PLOUGH.

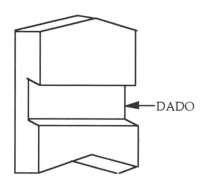

DAGGERS (props). Rubber replicas are generally used, as a safety precaution. Wooden facsimiles or strap iron ground to shape and fitted with wooden handles can also be used if rigidity is necessary.

DAISY CHAINING. A method of cabling between automated lights. The instruments have an "in" and an "out" receptacle.

DANCE FLOOR

Stage floor covering (Marley, Harlequin, Rosco Floor). A portable floor covering for a stage that is used for dance. It helps prevent injury to the dancers.

Truck trailer. The step in a trailer above the fifth wheel is called the dance floor. Often heavy items like road boards and cable boxes travel in this area to put weight over the drive wheels of the truck's tractor. A dance ramp is used to roll BOXES up to the step.

DARK (dark house). Said of theatres when no show is playing. A dark theatre has no show running at the moment. A theatre may be dark for one night a week or dark for an extended period between productions.

DAVIS BOARD. Older trade name for a versatile, portable, compact switchboard of autotransformer type, operating six sliders from a single coil.

dB. Abbreviation for DECIBEL

DC. Abbreviation for DIRECT CURRENT.

DEAD CIRCUIT. Circuit with no current flowing in it.

DEAD FRONT. Said of a switchboard or electrical panel having no exposed wires or parts carrying a current. All electrical equipment should be dead front though some obsolete boards are open fronted.

DEAD HUNG (dead off). Tied off to grid and therefore not able to be raised or lowered as part of the action of a show.

DEAD SPOT

Lights. Improperly lighted acting area that is not as bright as other areas. Refocus key lights.

Sound. A place in the auditorium where sound from the stage is muffled or unclear. If possible, adjust balance of absorptive and reflective acoustical materials.

DEAD STACK. See under STACK.

DEAD WEIGHT. Weight of an inert body as opposed to a moving body. Platforms should be built to withstand live weight, approximately twice the thrust of dead weight. See also LIVE WEIGHT.

DECIBEL (abbr. dB). A unit of measure expressing the gain (volume) of an amplifier

DECK. Any floor. See also FALSE DECK.

DECOMPOSITION OF P AINT. See under PAINT MIXING, DRY PIGMENT.

DEFAULT. This refers to settings on electronic

boards, computers, or other high-tech equipment. Default settings can be set by the factory or by the user. See **Computer terminology** under LIGHTING CONTROL.

DELAY. Holding or stopping a cue in progress for a prescribed effect. This process often involves the use of split faders. See **Computer terminology** under LIGHTING CONTROL.

DELAYED REACTION. See TIME LAG.

DELUGE SYSTEM. A fan shaped curtain of water at the proscenium line used instead of an asbestos curtain. See FAN AND DELUGE SYSTEM.

DENATURED ALCOHOL. See **Alcohol** under SOLVENTS.

DEPTH, STAGE. Distance from the curtain line or apron edge to the upstage wall. A stage should be one to one and a half times as deep as the proscenium is wide

DESIGN. Scene design should take into account the mechanical limitations of a given stage, the structural plausibility of a given solution, and the suggestions of the playwright. The designer should prepare floor plans, front elevations, rear elevations, working drawings, and color samples. Many designers like to include a model and/or a colored perspective. Working drawings should be in at least 1/2" scale with details worked out at 1" or larger scale. Special construction should be indicated in rear elevations and cross section as well as by using different drawing formats such as orthographic and isometric projections, if necessary for clarity. See also DRAWINGS; SIGHTLINES.

Choice of style. Realistic or nonrealistic, as determined by script and by interpretation of designer and director. If realistic, authenticate according to period, locale, time of year, social strata of characters, etc. Details such as windows, fireplaces, wallpaper, pictures, and furnishings are revealing features which should be authentic. If nonrealistic, design should suggest or symbolize mood within structure of play: struggle, tragedy, levity, satire, or comedy. Line, color, and form will determine the theme for nonrealistic settings.

Economical design. Nonprofessional theatres, as far as possible, use flats in stock. If new flats are to be made, design to standard dimensions so that they can become part of stock and be used again. Design odd scenery (forced perspectives, groundrows, rooftops, etc.) as smaller pieces that can be built from scrap lumber and temporarily attached to stock flats (see also PERSPECTIVE, FORCED). Buy second-grade lumber for battening and building throwaway scenery and save good lumber for permanent scenery. Use inexpensive muslin for throwaway scenery and design for widths of muslin available in economical grades. Be on alert for houses and buildings being wrecked and inquire about carpeting, newel posts, spindles, chandeliers, wall brackets, moldings, door hardware, etc. Design around available materials. Visit window display suppliers for new and reasonable ideas and materials.

Practical design. Determine sightlines on stage by drawing stage and first row seats to scale. Rake stage walls to angle of sightline so that actors will not move out of sight of audience. Design sets so that all cracks between flats can be dutchmanned. If breaks must come in the middle of a wall, offset wall with a jog or a 6" board so that a corner is formed at the break.

Stage design. Avoid attempting to force an "acting edition" floor plan on a stage not suited to it. Attempt to incorporate stage peculiarities and limitations into designs rather than fight them. If possible, design settings so that electrician can see stage. For plays demanding difficult lighting, if light controls are located on stage, offset downstage proportion of setting so that electrician can see. Design for available lighting equipment. If lighting forestage is difficult, use false prosceniums and tormentors to force set upstage where it can be lighted from first electric. Allow wing space, tormentor space, or windows for adequate cross lighting. Design for maximum efficiency of shifting multiple set plays. Know stage dimensions and plan for stacking space. Choose shifting methods best suited to stage limitations. See also SCENERY, SHIFTING.

Design for solidity. Design of a set largely determines its stability on stage. Three straight walls with doors and windows have a greater tendency to shake when doors are closed than walls braced by offsets and alcoves. A door cutting the diagonal of a side wall and backwall will be more stable than a door in a straight wall. Bay windows add stability and interest to a box set. Bracing can be accomplished with backings if they are designed to lash or hook to back of door flats they are masking. Ceilings contribute greatly toward making interior settings solid.

Choice of color. A setting is a background and should be painted as such. Low intensity, light absorbing colors should be used in order to keep light reflection to a minimum. Good background colors are black, brown, green, blue, and dark gray. Lighter colors may be used if they are spattered with one or more of the darker shades. Nontextured coats of paint tend to show imperfections and blemishes, causing flats to look two-dimensional, whereas textured coats of two or three different colors give the appearance of solidity and three dimensions. See also PAINTING TECHNIQUES.

DESIGNER. See SCENE DESIGNER.

DETAILED DRAWINGS. See under DRAWINGS.

DIAGONAL BRACE. See **Corner brace** under FLAT: **Components.**

DIAGONALS (dikes). Side cutting pliers used for cutting wire, available in 4" to 7" lengths. For nonelectronic uses, the 6" and 7" lengths are recommended.

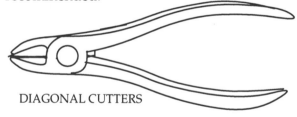

DIAGONAL CUTTERS

DICHROIC FILTERS

Cold mirrors, hot mirrors. A mirror coated with alternate layers of materials of high and low refractive index, designed to reflect only desired wavelengths of light. A cold mirror reflects only visible rays of the spectrum, allowing heat rays (infrared) to pass through the glass. Conversely, hot mirrors allow visible rays to pass through the glass and reflect only the heat rays. Because of their high cost they were largely confined to heat filtration for certain projection lamps and other high-intensity lamps.

Color. By selectively stripping out wavelengths, dichroic filtration can produce pure color with a higher transmission factor (amount of light passing through) than conventional color media. Theatre use of dichroic colors is rapidly gaining acceptance as costs drop. In all AUTOMATED LIGHTS these colors are the only accepted method of adding color. The spectrum available is virtually unlimited in some of the larger LUMINAIRES. Additionally there are smaller automated FIXTURES which only change dichroic color and are taking the place of the older SCROLLERS. These units are stand-alone units, not hang-ons in front of other lights.

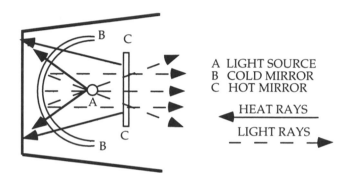

A LIGHT SOURCE
B COLD MIRROR
C HOT MIRROR

HEAT RAYS

LIGHT RAYS

DICHROIC FILTER

DIE

A metal tool used in stamping or cutting various materials.

A tool used for threading bolts or pipes (see also TAP AND DIE SETS).

DIE, SETTING. A tool used for setting GROMMETS.

DIELECTRIC. Having electrical insulating properties on a given material.

DIFFUSED LIGHT. Light spread over a wide area. Shadowless or nearly shadowless light produced by footlights, border lights, floods, or by frost color media, frosted glass, or other media used to disperse concentrations of light. Frost color media are widely used to diffuse light from spotlights and floodlights. See also **Star frost** under FROST.

DIGITAL AUDIO TAPE (DAT). Yields extremely fine quality of sound using digital technology on audio tape recordings. See also COMPACT DISK.

DIGITAL DELAY. See SOUND EQUIPMENT.
DILUTE PRIMARY. See LIGHTING COLORS.
DIM (noun). A lighting setup of low intensity.
DIM (dim up, dim down, dim out) (Command verb). To increase or decrease intensity of stage lights by means of a DIMMER.
DIMENSIONS ON DRAWINGS. See DRAWINGS.
DIMMER. Any of a number of devices that control intensities of stage lights. The most widely used dimmers have been **Resistance** and **Autotransformer**, and now **Silicon controlled rectifiers**.

   Autotransformer. The autotransformer is based on the principle of varying intensity by varying the voltage delivered to equipment, in contrast to **Resistance dimmers**. Autotrans-

RADIASTAT 3,600-WATT
AUTOTRANSFORMER (WARD LEONARD)

LUXTROL MOTOR OPERATED
AUTOTRANSFORMER (SUPERIOR ELECTRIC)

VITROHM NONINTERLOCKING
RESISTANCE DIMMERS (WARD LEONARD)

LUMITRON 3,000-WATT MAGNETIC AMPLIFIER
(METROPOLITAN ELECTRIC)

formers consist of a soft iron core wrapped with copper wire to form a single coil. Size of wire and amount of core determine capacity of dimmer. A rotating or sliding arm containing a carbon brush makes contact either on the coil or on taps from the coil. The coil is placed in series with the input (line), and the brush and one side of the line are placed in series with the output (load). Current requirement to operate autotransformers is practically negligible, and they are therefore more economical than resistance dimmers. **Advantages**: Will dim any size lamp up to dimmer capacity, without GHOST LOAD; offer smooth dimming, with usually no more than a 1-volt variation in contact points; are economical to operate. **Disadvantages**: Will not operate on direct current, some models are bulky and are not readily adaptable to compact ganging. Autotransformers have been sold under a variety of trade names, including Autrastat, Davis, Luxtrol, Powerstat, Radiastat, Variac.

Inductor dimmer. Obsolete; an older form of dimmer consisting of a rotor and a stator, in which the rotor is turned through 90°. Has the advantage of no moving electrical contacts; however, its action is not considered as smooth as that of other types of dimmers.

Magnetic amplifier. Obsolete; an older form of dimmer based on saturable core principle, using a small current varied by means of a potentiometer or autotransformer, to control voltage output of a large coil. No tubes are involved in this system, and the only moving parts consist of relays and potentiometers. Magnetic amplifiers were manufactured in 3,000-watt to 10,000-watt sizes and were available in 2, 3, 4, 5, and infinite preset. Infinite preset control was set up on cards similar to the punch cards in older IBM systems, and the electrician simply turned preset fader, fading from one card setup to another.

Reactance dimmer. Obsolete; an older form of dimmer consisting of transformer-like windings placed in series with a lamp and equipped with a movable laminated core. When the core is inserted in the windings, the resulting disturbance in the field causes a voltage drop, decreasing the intensity of the lamp. The reactance dimmer is bulky and has never been used extensively in the theatre.

Resistance dimmer. Obsolete; an older type of stage dimmer or rheostat operating on the principle of adding a controlled amount of resistance in series with circuit to decrease intensity of lighting equipment. Resistance dimmers are usually rated according to minimum-maximum load, and for efficient, smooth results, loads cannot be below minimum rating. Thus, a dimmer rated 900-watt minimum and 1,200-watt maximum will not dim out a 500-watt light unless a GHOST LOAD is introduced somewhere in series with the dimmer. Overloading a resistance dimmer for a sustained period will overheat wires and cause a break in circuit. Sometimes a break in a resistance dimmer can be repaired temporarily by locating the dead contact button on dimmer plate and bridging or shorting it to the adjacent button with a piece of copper wire. This will cause a jump in intensity when the brush passes over the repaired point but may serve temporarily until replacement can be made. Clean contact buttons with tuner cleaner or rouge paper. Do not oil or grease contacts on any brush-contact-type dimmer.

Salt water dimmer. A crude, makeshift, unsafe dimmer, predating commercial light control, it is basically a resistance dimmer and provides an interesting classroom demonstration.

LUXTROL AUTOTRANSFORMER
(SUPERIOR ELECTRIC)

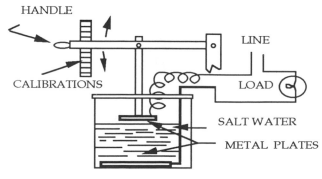

SALT WATER DIMMER

A salt water dimmer consists of a 5- or 10-gallon crock, one stationary electrode (iron plate) in the bottom of the crock, and an adjustable electrode attached to an arm to allow calibrated control of distance between electrodes, and salt water as the electrolyte. Insulated wires connect the two electrodes in series with the line (power supply) and the load (lamp), as illustrated. Sufficient water is placed in the crock to almost touch the top electrode in the highest position. Circuit is turned on, top electrode is lowered to barely touch water, and common salt is added to water until lamp starts to glow. As electrodes are brought closer together, intensity is increased until full intensity is reached when electrodes touch.

Silicon controlled rectifier (SCR). An SCR is composed of two rectifiers and two "gates" used to control the flow of electricity through the rectifiers. The function of an SCR can be explained with the aid of a few standard symbols. The symbol for alternating current in one complete cycle as shown by this pattern, , in which the top half-cycle represents forward flow of current and the lower half-rent. A rectifier, , placed in the circuit permits flow of current in one direction only, either forward or return. represents one half-cycle of alternating current.

If two rectifiers are placed in a parallel-inverse connection, (commonly called "back to back"), rectifier A blocks forward movement of current, and rectifier B blocks reversed movement of current. A "gate" (controlled by an electrical impulse) used in conjunction with a rectifier GATE allows intermittent passage of current through the rectifier. If a gate is used in each rectifier, a control is established over the length of time during each cycle when current is permitted to pass through the rectifiers, Actual time control is determined by a low voltage signal imposed upon the gates. If there is no signal, gates remain closed and a lamp connected with the SCR output is off. If the signal is varied with a small voltage control device such as a potentiometer, intensity of the

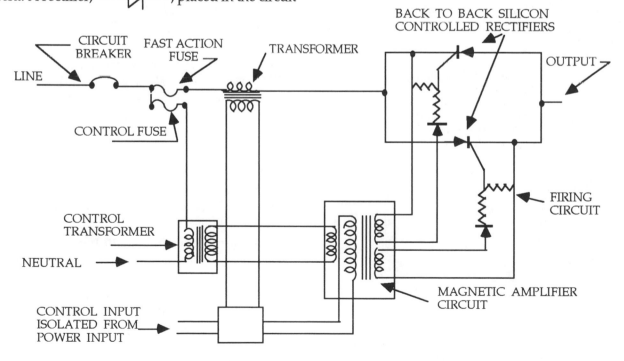

SILICON CONTROLLED RECTIFIER SCHEMATIC DRAWING

SILICON CONTROLLED RECTIFIER (KLIEGL)

lamp load varies correspondingly. Low-voltage signal control such as this makes possible a wide variety of mastering, presetting, and cross-fading. Although basic circuitries and explanations are relatively simple, the inherent peculiarities and sensitivities of the SCR require numerous protective devices, including amp traps, heat sinks, and RF chokes, which tend to complicate circuits. Some brands of SCRs require a GHOST LOAD because they cannot detect a load if it is under a certain wattage, e.g., 50 watts or less, such as a flame or candle flicker lamp. Certain designs of SCR are using plug-in-type printed

circuit boards (PCBs) for quick exchange in case of a defective part. Of interest to some designers is the ability to shape different dimmer curves to meet designer requirements; see LIGHTING CONTROL.

Thyratron tube dimmer. Obsolete; superseded by SCRs. This type of dimmer consists of two thyratrons (gas-filled electron tubes with control grids) that carry the load current. Since the thyratron tube is always a rectifier (a direct current device), two tubes must be connected back to back to permit alternating current circuitry. The thyratron acts as an electronic switch, and an analogy can be drawn between the thyratron and the SCR. Dimming is accomplished by varying the time in the half-cycle when conduction occurs, or, in other words, altering the duration of "firing periods."

DIMMER, MASTER. Any of a number of devices used to GANG a group of dimmers to a single control.

Group master. Controls a bank or a partial grouping of dimmers or switches.

Grand master. Controls all individual dimmers or switches on the board.

Electrical master. Either a high-capacity dimmer (autotransformer or electronic) wired in series with the individual dimmers on the board as a direct control of the load, or a smaller autotransformer wired in series with the low-voltage control of electronic dimmers. The latter is preferred because of compactness and versatility. With electrical mastering, individual dimmers should be provided with three-way switches for off, independent, and master positions, so that any dimmer can be switched to the master control at any time. Because of the variable load demand placed on the master dimmer, resistance dimmers cannot be used as masters. When lights are dimmed up or down with the electrical master, the same intensity ratio of all stage lights is maintained in what is called proportional dimming.

Mechanical master. A single lever that interlocks dimmers by means of a slotted shaft or a slip-clutch, so that several dimmers may be controlled. The conventional method of mechanically mastering switchboards is to mount all dimmer handles of each bank of dimmers on

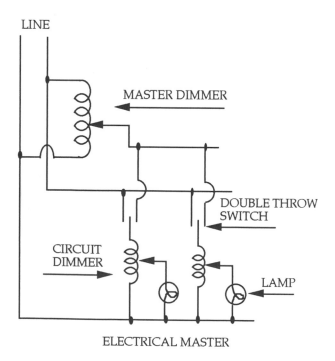

ELECTRICAL MASTER

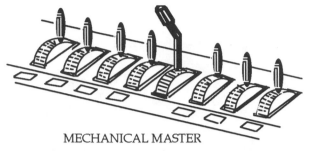

MECHANICAL MASTER

a single slotted shaft. Individual dimmer handles can then be locked into the shaft and controlled by one lever or a wheel control geared to the shaft. Some boards are equipped with a grand master, which will interlock all bank masters.

DIMMER CURVE. Used to calibrate dimmer controls with respect to light intensity as opposed to arbitrary linear scaling on a 0 to 10 basis. See also under LAW OF SQUARES.

DIMMING, PROPORTIONAL. See **Electrical master** under DIMMER, MASTER.

DIP. See LAMP DIP.

DIP IN INTENSITY. Involuntary lowering of intensity of stage lights. Many electronic dimmers show a slight dip in intensity or dimming while fading from one scene to another. Cause can be either in fader itself or in the potentiometers (pots) controlling individual dimmers. Mass-produced pots are not always perfectly linear and do not always match, resulting in a dip in intensity on a scene-to-scene fade, even though both scenes have dimmers set at the same readings. Mismatches on dimmer intensities seem to be more noticeable on the lower half of the dimming scale.

DIRECT BEAM (DB). Term describing lensless projection equipment used to cast a shadow or translucency on a screen. See **Linnebach projector** under PROJECTORS.

DIRECT CURRENT (abbr. DC). Current that flows in one direction, from positive to negative, in contrast to alternating current (AC), which reverses direction. For the uses of AC and DC, see ALTERNATING CURRENT.

DISK

Computer board. A (floppy) disk that stores data in a magnetic form for playback at a later time. See under LIGHTING CONTROL.

Scenery. A revolving stage superimposed on a stage. See also **Revolving stage** under SCENERY, SHIFTING.

DISPLAY. See **Computer terminology** under LIGHTING CONTROL.

DISTEMPER (scene paint). A paint prepared by mixing dry pigment with a binder.

DMX PROTOCOL. A standardized method, or interface, used to control dimmers via lighting controls. Prior to the use of this protocol, dimmers were controlled by individual wires or MULTIPLEXING over pairs of wires. DMX 512 is presently the standard adopted by USITT. This is the protocol of choice for sending signals to AUTOMATED LIGHTS. In this protocol 512 channels of control are considered to be one UNIVERSE.

DOCK. Scenery storage space or workshop; much more convenient when directly connected with stage.

DOLLY. A low truck with casters, used for moving heavy objects. See also AIR CASTERS.

DOME

A curved plaster cyc.

Polished metal furniture glides, sometimes useful on small platforms and furniture to facilitate moving.

DONKEY. Refers to a WINCH motor with a DRUM used to pull objects. The term was once used in logging camps for the lines used to pull logs in from the forest.

DOOR (shutter). Often consists of 1/4" plywood cut to dimension and framed with 4", 6", and 9" lumber to form desired panels. Panels are somtimes made with picture molding rectangles applied to plywood. See also **Window flat** and **Door flat** under FLAT.

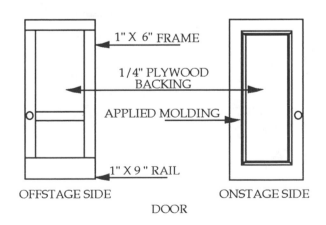

OFFSTAGE SIDE   ONSTAGE SIDE

DOOR

Door casing. Facing and/or molding around the door opening, plus the thickness (reveal) and threshold (saddle). Standard practice is to make casings separate from flats for ease in transportation and storing and to lock in place with strap hinges when in use.

Door hardware. Usually consists of loose-pin hinges, simplifying removal of doors for transport and storage; rim latches (when available) for doors that open offstage; mortise locks (see below) for doors opening onstage; doorknobs and escutcheon plates appropriate to the period. In the United States, standard height for doorknobs is 34" to 36" off the floor; in Europe, the doorknob is slightly higher.

Door locks. Sliding bolts or locks requiring keys should be mounted so as to appear to be locking doors without actually locking. Mishaps resulting from accidents or missed cues may thus be avoided.

Mortise lock. A door lock designed to be inserted in a slot or hole in the thickness of a door. Mortise locks are round in shape and can be set into a 3/4" hole, with a backset of 2 1/4" to 2 1/2". Rim latch is more commonly used on scenery doors that swing offstage.

Rim latch. A rectangular latch commonly used on stage doors because it can be surface mounted and requires less work to install than a mortise lock. Available at larger scenery supply houses.

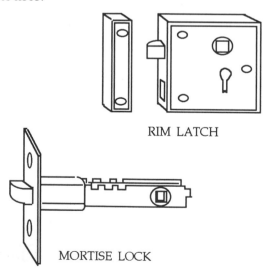

RIM LATCH

MORTISE LOCK

DOORBELL. See BELL; CHIMES.
DOOR FLAT. See **Window flat** and **Door flat** under FLAT.

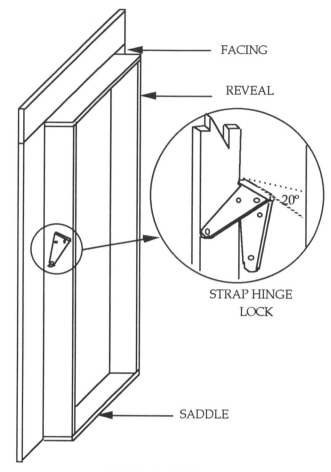

DOOR CASING

FACING
REVEAL
STRAP HINGE
LOCK
SADDLE
—20°

DOOR SKIN (lauan, mahogany underlay, wiggly ply). Originally 1/8" VENEER used as facing in hollow doors. Since it is relatively flexible and strong, it is also used to make thicknesses for arches and as a covering for high-tech flats. See Hardcover flat under FLAT, see also SCENERY PANELS.

DOOR SLAM (sound effect). Offstage sound made with a small portable door and casing made heavy enough to have a solid sound. Stock doors in casements are also used if available.

DOOR, SLIDING. For construction of the door, see DOOR. A track with rollers from which doors can be suspended is available in hardware stores. Stationary (one-way) casters can be mounted on the bottom of a door and a groove fashioned to guide the top. Either method is satisfactory; the latter is less expensive.

DOPE. Glue mixture for attaching canvas or muslin to flats: 1/3 melted gelatine glue, 1/3 Danish Whiting, 1/3 wheat paste. Dilute with water to spread easily. Dope has been superseded by white glue thinned 10% to 15% with water. See also GLUES.

DORIC. See under COLUMNS.

DOUBLE-HEADED NAIL. See NAILS.

DOUBLE LUFF. Mechanical advantage of 4 to 1 using BLOCK AND TACKLE.

DOUBLE POLE SWITCH. See **Toggle switch** under SWITCHES.

DOUBLE THROW SWITCH. See **Toggle switch** under SWITCHES.

DOUBLE WHIP. Mechanical advantage of 2 to 1 using BLOCK AND TACKLE.

DOUSER (chopper, fader). A cutoff device in a followspot used between light source and lens to black out by cutting the beam of light. See **Arc light** under LIGHTING INSTRUMENTS, SPECIFIC.

DOWEL. Round 3' to 4' lengths of wood varying in diameter from 1/8" to 1" in 1/8" increments. A dowel is used to pin wood together for furniture or for decorative designs; larger sizes, over 1" and up to 3", are often called closet or curtain poles or rods. Most useful sizes are 1/4", 3/8", 1/2", 3/4", 1", and 1 1/2".

DOWNSTAGE. Toward the front of the stage. Term derived from early theatres, in which stage was sloped (raked), and downstage was literally lower than upstage. See also STAGE DIRECTIONS; AREAS.

DRAPE FORMING. A technique where sheets of plastic are heated and allowed to drape into a female mold. See VACUUM FORMING.

DRAPERY, SET. Draperies for doors and windows are hung in a variety of ways:

　Permanent draperies. Stapled or tacked to a 1" x 3" batten which is screwed to the flat with 1 1/2" (no. 8) wood screws or stapled or tacked to a wooden header that is attached to the flat by picture hooks or loose pin hinges.

　Sliding draperies. Suspended by curtain rings from a pole held in place by metal or wooden sockets or from a wire stretched between two points on the flat and held taut with a turnbuckle. A wooden header may also be used. Traverse rods, available in department stores and hardware stores, can also be used for lightweight curtains up to 16' wide.

DRAPERY, STAGE (soft goods, rags, blacks, browns, blues, etc.). Hanging material used as part of scenery, background, or dressing for a stage; this includes legs, borders, etc. Draperies are made of any material that will hang well, including velveteen, duvetyn, velour (plush); however, the fabric must be strong enough not to sag. Best colors for cyclorama drapes are black, dark blue, dark browns. Grays and other colors are not as versatile. Draperies for the backwall should be made in 8' to 20' sections to permit openings in any desired location on stage. The top should be webbed and grommeted at 6" to 9" intervals for tie lines. A chain pocket should be sewn to bottom, 4" to 6" off the floor and large enough to accommodate a CHAIN for weight. Allow extra material of at least half the width for best draping; many theatre people prefer not to have fullness sewn in so they have the options of tying the drapes flat or making pleats. Some designers choose to sew the nap in velours facing up to form millions of little light traps, which is excellent for lighting but difficult to keep clean, since they must be swept up following the direction of the nap.

DRAW CURTAIN (traverse, traveler, one way). See under CURTAINS.

DRAWINGS. See also SYMBOLS. Drawings necessary for the theatre include floor plans, front elevations, detailed drawings, cross sections, sketches and painter's elevations. Rear elevations are also necessary if shop personnel are not familiar with a given designer's methods. See also DESIGN.

　Cross-section drawing. See **Section drawing,** page 56.

　Detailed drawing. Mechanical drawing drawn to a scale sufficiently large to clearly indicate the intricacies of construction of a given property or piece of scenery. Detailed drawings are necessary for complicated cornices, fireplaces, pediments, columns, etc.

　Elevation, front. A mechanical drawing showing the exact dimensions and details on front of set. For convenience in reading, front elevations are generally divided into stage right wall, backwall, and stage left wall. All offsets and irregularities in the floor plan appear in the same plane in elevation drawings. Thicknesses of windows, doors, etc., are **not** shown. There is

FRONT ELEVATION; STAGE RIGHT WALL

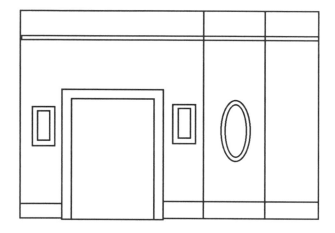

FRONT ELEVATION; STAGE LEFT WALL

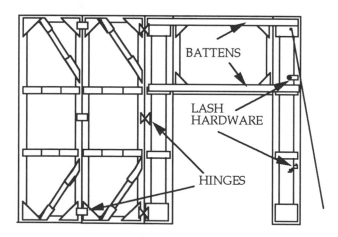

BATTENS

LASH
HARDWARE

HINGES

REAR ELEVATION; STAGE LEFT WALL

no perspective and no freehand drawing in elevations. Moldings, pictures, draperies, trim, and wall dressing are shown to scale.

Elevation, painter's. A mechanical drawing

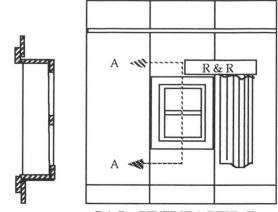

R & R = REVERSE & REPEAT

CROSS SECTION
THROUGH A-A

FRONT ELEVATION
UPSTAGE CENTER

of front elevation rendered in colors. Painter's elevations should include color samples and the texturing techniques to be used by painters.

Elevation, rear. A mechanical drawing indicating the exact dimensions and details of construction from rear of set. Rear elevations must be reversed as if drawn on back of front elevations. Flat details showing construction and fastening are included in rear elevations: small rectangles, indicate top, bottom, and center of flats to be hinged on back; small butterflies indicate top, bottom, and center of flats to be hinged on face; lash hardware and lash line are indicated where flats are to be lashed; battens are drawn in place at top, bottom, and center where flats are to be battened together.

Floor plan. A mechanical drawing showing exact outline of set on the stage. Proper symbols (see under SYMBOLS) should be used for windows, doors, stairs, etc. Double lines showing flat overlaps at joints are preferred.

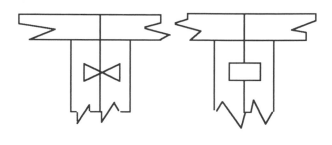

HINGE ON FACE   HINGE ON BACK

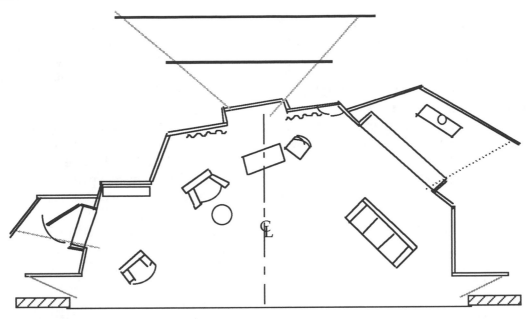

FLOOR PLAN

Floor plans should include sightlines, backings, and furniture to scale.

Perspective drawing. Many books are available explaining and illustrating the principles involved in converting floor plans and elevation drawings into perspectives. Perspective drawings of sets executed to dimension can be of great value, but one should avoid misleading,

haphazard drawings which merely confuse and distort the scale. An artist's rendering is a formal color perspective drawing. A sketch is a black and white informal perspective drawing.

Isometric projection. A method of drawing in three dimensions without regard for true perspective. The two planes are usually drawn at a 30° angle and kept to scale. Most useful for showing complicated three-dimensional details of fireplaces, platforms, canopies, cornices, gables, etc.

Oblique projection. A method of drawing in three dimensions in which the most compli-

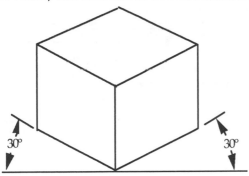

ISOMETRIC PROJECTION

OBLIQUE PROJECTION

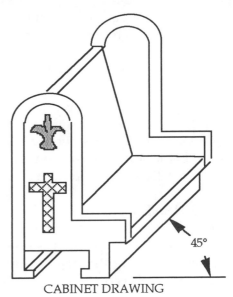

CABINET DRAWING

cated view is at right angles to line of sight; the remaining sides are drawn between 30° and 45°.

Cabinet drawing. A method of drawing in three dimensions in which the most complicated view is at right angles to line of sight; the remaining sides are drawn between 30° and 45°, and the long side is facing away from the viewer and is distorted (arbitrarily shortened by half). A fancy hand-carved end of a church pew, for example, might be drawn in this manner.

Section drawing. A drawing of a cutaway view through a three-dimensional object. A cross-section drawing is a drawing of a section made on a cutting plane at right angles to the main axis of a three-dimensional object. See illustration on page 54; the cutting plane is denoted by line A–A.

Working drawing. Dimensioned scale drawing showing details of construction. Working drawings include floor plans, elevations (front and rear), cross sections of complicated pieces, and enlarged-scale details of special pieces.

DRAW KNIFE (spokeshave). A tool consisting of a blade with a handle on each end, used for shaping wood.

DRESSING

A line. The art of making rope work neat by always keeping the pin rail tied correctly and excess line neatly coiled and hung off the belaying pins. Rope dressed properly never drags on the floor, and there is always room to sweep underneath.

The house. Practice of placing people in an auditorium in such a way that it sounds to performers on stage as if there are people in all areas of the house. A method of making the house not look so empty.

The set. Adding pictures, furniture, props, etc., to make set look "lived in."

DRESS PARADE. Onstage check of all costumes on each character in a production. Dress parade should be called preceding the first dress rehearsal.

DRESS REHEARSAL (dress). Final rehearsals of a production before opening. All scenery should be built and painted, properties and costumes ready, lights focused and colored, sound ready. This is the time for all the parts of the show to be integrated into a smoothly running production for an audience. Scenery cues and shifts, light cues and intensities, sound cues and levels are set with the stage manager and the cast and crew.

DRILL (bit) (noun)

Bit. Tool steel (a hard strong steel), with twist flutings, sharpened at one end, used for drilling metal or wood. High speed drills are recommended for metal. See page 57 for drill designations and their equivalent sizes. See also TAP AND DIE SETS.

Tool. A power driven or hand driven machine used to turn a drill. See also POWER TOOLS; TOOLS, HAND.

Yankee drill. Trade name for a spiral hand drill with small bits from 1/32" to 3/16" in diameter. Useful for starting holes in hardwood for screws and nails.

DRINKS (props). See BEVERAGES.

DROP BLACK (ivory black, Hercules black). A black pigment used in scene painting. See PAINT AND PAINT COLORS.

DROP BOX. An electrical plug-in or junction box dropped from overhead via a spot line.

DROPS. Large unframed expanses of material

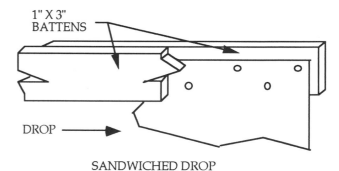

1" X 3" BATTENS

DROP →

SANDWICHED DROP

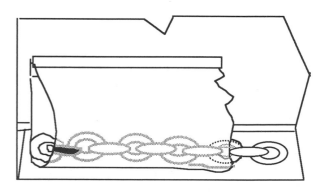

CHAIN POCKET

Drill	Diam. Inches	Drill	Diam. Inches	Drill	Diam. Inches	Drill	Diam. Inches	Drill	Diam. Inches
80	.0135	50	.0700	22	.1570	G	.2610	31/64	.4843
79	.0145	49	.0730	21	.1590	17/64	.2656	1/2	.5000
1/64	.0156	48	.0760	20	.1610	H	.2660	33/64	.5156
78	.0160	5/64	.0781	19	.1660	I	.2720	17/32	.5312
77	.0180	47	.0785	18	.1695	J	.2770	35/64	.5469
76	.0200	46	.0810	11/64	.1719	K	.2810	9/16	.5625
75	.0210	45	.0820	17	.1730	9/32	.2812	37/64	.5781
74	.0225	44	.0860	16	.1770	L	.2900	19/32	.5937
73	.0240	43	.0890	15	.1800	M	.2950	39/64	.6094
72	.0250	42	.0935	14	.1820	19/64	.2969	5/8	.6250
71	.0260	3/32	.0937	13	.1850	N	.3020	41/64	.6406
70	.0280	41	.0960	3/16	.1875	5/16	.3125	21/32	.6562
69	.0292	40	.0980	12	.1890	O	.3160	43/64	.6719
68	.0310	39	.0995	11	.1910	P	.3230	11/16	.6875
1/32	.0312	38	.1015	10	.1935	21/64	.3281	45/64	.7031
67	.0320	37	.1040	9	.1960	Q	.3320	23/32	.7187
66	.0330	36	.1065	8	.1990	R	.3390	47/64	.7344
65	.0350	7/64	.1094	7	.2010	11/32	.3437	3/4	.7500
64	.0360	35	.1100	13/64	.2031	S	.3480	49/64	.7656
63	.0370	34	.1110	6	.2040	T	.3580	25/32	.7812
62	.0380	33	.1130	5	.2055	23/64	.3594	51/64	.7969
61	.0390	32	.1160	4	.2090	U	.3680	13/16	.8125
60	.0400	31	.1200	3	.2130	3/8	.3750	53/64	.8281
59	.0410	1/8	.1250	7/32	.2187	V	.3770	27/32	.8437
58	.0420	30	.1285	2	.2210	W	.3860	55/64	.8594
57	.0430	29	.1360	1	.2280	25/64	.3906	7/8	.8750
56	.0465	28	.1405	A	.2340	X	.3970	57/64	.8906
3/64	.0469	9/64	.1406	15/64	.2344	Y	.4040	29/32	.9062
55	.0520	27	.1440	B	.2380	13/32	.4062	59/64	.9219
54	.0550	26	.1470	C	.2420	Z	.4130	15/16	.9375
53	.0595	25	.1495	D	.2460	27/64	.4219	61/64	.9531
1/16	.0625	24	.1520	E	.2500	7/16	.4375	31/32	.9687
52	.0635	23	.1540	1/4	.2500	29/64	.4531	63/64	.9844
51	.0670	5/32	.1562	F	.2570	15/32	.4687	1	1.0000

DRILL DESIGNATIONS AND SIZES

suspended from a batten on top and weighted by a batten or chain at bottom. Drops can be painted to represent a scene or background or can be colored fabric that fits in with the cyclorama drapes and is the backdrop to legs and borders.

General construction (sandwich drop). Make double-stitched flat seams, sewn horizontally; sew 2" hems in ends; sew 3" to 5" hem in bottom and insert a 1" x 3" batten or a 1" pipe for weight; and tack top of drop to a 1" x 3" or 1" x 4" batten and fasten a similar batten to the first with 1 1/2" x (no. 8) wood screws, sandwiching drop between the two battens. Drill 5/8" holes in ends of top battens and in center; at no more than 12' intervals, insert 3/8" or 1/2" sash cord as tie lines to fasten drop to pipe batten. Drops of this type are rolled for transporting and storing.

Drops fall into several categories, intended use determines the type chosen.

Cutout drop. Materials: canvas, duck, velour, or heavy muslin. **Construction:** Proceed as above; fasten drop to the paint frame with staples; treat with FLAMEPROOFING; transfer design by squaring painter's sketch, squaring drop, and plotting points as illustrated. Paint design with scene paint that has flexible GLUE as a binder, or with dye; when paint is dry, trim around contours of design with razor blade or sharp knife. If design is intricate or will not be supported by the natural hang of the fabric, remove from frame, place face down on floor, and apply netting to back of drop with SOBO or other suitable adhesive. For better bonding, sandwich net between drop and another piece of similar material. Make sure drop is square before applying netting; otherwise drop will sag when hung. See illustration under LAYOUT.

Dye drop. Materials: muslin of varying weight, depending upon degree of translucency desired. **Construction:** Proceed as for **General construction** with everything except top batten; double stitch 2" to 4" webbing to top of drop; grommet webbing on 6" to 12" centers with no. 2 grommets; sew chain pocket of muslin as illustrated, to hang 2" above the floor. Staple to paint frame and FLAMEPROOF; apply aniline dye with brush or spray; salt contained in fire retardant will set dye. Dye drops are folded into compact bundles for transporting and storing.

Framed drop. Drop with battens top and bottom and stiffener battens running vertically. **Construction:** Proceed as for **General construction.** Glue and staple top batten in place and inset 1" x 3" batten in lower hem. Place face down on stage floor and cut 1" x 3" battens (to be used as spacers) to full height of drop. Stretch drop taut and fasten spacers to top and bottom battens at right angles, framing drop. Use 1 1/2" (no. 8) wood screws. Stretch widthwise and staple drop to outside vertical battens, beginning in the center and working to the ends. Fasten additional vertical spacers as needed to keep drop taut and wrinkle-free, but do not staple to drop.

Leg drop. Drop with center cut out, forming two wings and border in one piece. **Construction:** Proceed as for **Cutout drops.**

Scrim drop. Materials: bobbinet, sharkstooth scrim. **Construction:** Materials are available from theatre supply houses in various widths up to 30', generally requiring no seaming. Webbing, grommets, and chain pockets are applied as in **Dye drops,** and drop is flameproofed and painted with aniline dyes. Scrims seem to disappear when front light is dimmed down and light behind scrim is brought up. Use care in handling scrims as they snag easily and are difficult to mend; minor tears can be patched with fabric glue.

Translucent drop. Material: lightweight muslin (80 to 100 thread count per square inch). **Construction:** Proceed as for **Dye drop.**

Translucent projection screen. Material: lightweight muslin. **Construction:** Can be made with 2" webbing sewn on all four sides; grommet webbing with no. 2 grommets on 6" to 12" centers; stretch screen on wooden or pipe frame. Plastic projection screens are often used for rear screen projections but the muslin screen is an inexpensive substitute.

DRUM (capstan). A revolving cylinder with flanges on which rope or wire rope is wound. Used as part of a WINCH OR HOIST. A specialized version is used in a CHAIN HOIST. See also DONKEY.

DRUM, THUNDER. See THUNDER.

DRY BRUSH. See under PAINTING TECHNIQUES.

DRY ICE. See under SMOKE EFFECTS.

DUCK. A strong cotton or linen material. See under COVERING FLATS: **Materials;** FLOORCLOTH; CANVAS.

DUTCHMAN

Lights. An objective lens mounted on a spotlight and used for projection.

Scenery. Strip of muslin about 5" wide, used to cover the crack between two flats that are fastened together. Dutchman should be made of light-weight muslin cut no wider than combined width of stiles to be covered and applied with size coating to which a little more glue has been added if necessary. Paint about 3' of dutchman on one side and then the top 3' of stiles. While still wet, place dutchman on stiles and paint down. Repeat the process until entire crack is covered. It is sometimes necessary to staple the end of a dutchman to allow proper stretching. Painted muslin makes the best dutchman material for painted flats; new muslin for new flats. Dutchman can be torn off and reused.

DUVETYN (duvetyne, duv). A smooth, lustrous, velvety fabric with a napped surface that obscures the twill weave. Made from wool, silk, rayon, cotton, or various combinations. Lighter weight than velour but heavier than flannel, cotton duvetyn is most commonly used on stage for inexpensive curtains and drapes.

DYE. It is best to dye costumes with standard brands of dyes, following directions on the package. Materials for draperies can be dyed with commercial aniline dyes available in all colors. Dyeing should be done in large vats with boiling water. Intensity of color depends upon amount of dye, amount of water, amount of material, and time in vat. For best results, experiment with small strips, keeping account of all variables, and run material through according to records. Since dyes are not paints, no binder is needed; however, approximately 1 pound of salt to 20 gallons of water will set dye and prevent rubbing. Drops to be dye painted should be flameproofed; the fire retardant contains sufficient salt to set dyes. See also **Dye drop** under DROPS.

DYE DROP. See under DROPS.

DYNA-BEAM SPOTLIGHT. Older trade name for a high-intensity followspot.

DYNAMIC MICROPHONE. See **Microphones** under SOUND EQUIPMENT.

E

ECHO (sound effect). An echo can be produced electronically through a reverberator or a digital delay allowing different time lags. Available from electronic supply houses.

EDKOTRON. Obsolete; trade name by Century Lighting for a portable SCR dimmer board. The Edkotron appeared in the late 1960s and was one of the first compact portable dimmers.

EFFECTS

Sound. See under individual entries: CHIMES; EXPLOSION; THUNDER; etc. See also SPECIAL EFFECTS.

Special. See SPECIAL EFFECTS.

Visual. See under individual entries: FOG EFFECT; LIGHTNING EFFECT; RAINBOW; etc. See also SPECIAL EFFECTS.

ELECTRICIAN (juicer, lights, electrics). The individual who operates the light board in a theatre. See also OPERATOR.

ELECTRICIAN'S PLOT. See LIGHT PLOT.

ELECTRICITY. Electricity is described as the flow of electrons through a conductor. The subject of electricity is infinitely complex. Theatre electricians, fortunately, need not be electrical engineers, but they do need to know basic terminology and a few equations. Comparison of water with electricity is a familiar method of clarifying terminology. Pressure of water is measured in pounds per square inch (psi). Pressure of electricity is measured in volts (units of electromotive force, EMF). A water meter measures flow of water in cubic feet per minute. An ammeter measures flow of electricity in amperes (amps) per second. A waterwheel or turbine converts flow of water to power, and an electric motor converts flow of electricity to power. Resulting power in both cases is measured in horsepower, but in the case of electricity, it is further subdivided into watts, 746 watts being equal to 1 horsepower. Even as a given waterwheel may require 100 psi and a flow of 50 cubic feet of water per minute to make it operate, so may a given motor require a 120-volt pressure and a flow of 5 amps per second to make it operate, and a lamp may require 120 volts and a flow of 8.3 amps per second to cause it to operate and produce approximately 1,000 watts (1 kilowatt) of power. Varying sizes of pipe will offer varying resistances to flow of water, and varying sizes (and kinds) of wire will offer varying resistances to flow of electricity.

Ohm's law. Direct current flowing in an electric circuit is proportional to the voltage applied to the circuit. The unit measure of resistance of a circuit is stated in ohms. Electrical terms and symbols are defined as follows: E = electromotive force (EMF, pressure, or volts), I = intensity (amps), R = resistance (ohms), P = power (watts). The German physicist Georg Simon Ohm (1787-1854) expressed equation relationships of these terms, the following being the most useful to the theatre technician:

$$E = IR, \ I = E/R, \ R = E/I,$$
$$E = P/I, \ I = P/E, \ P = IE.$$

West Virginia formula. One primary concern of stage electricians is to avoid overloading dimmers and circuits. Since lamps are rated in watts, and fuses and breakers protecting dimmers and circuits are rated in amps, one must determine the fuse and breaker size required to handle the cumulative wattage on a given circuit. The above equations are easier to remember if the letters are changed to W for watts, V for volts, and A for amps (called the West Virginia formula for mnemonic purposes): $W = V \times A$, $A = W/V$.

Rule of thumb. Rapid calculation with a 15 to 20 percent margin of safety (depending upon voltage supply) can be made by moving the decimal point two places to the left when determining amps from watts; thus, a 100-watt lamp requires a flow of approximately 1 amp, and a 500-watt lamp needs 5 amps. See also CIRCUIT, ELECTRICAL.

ELECTRICS

Pipe battens on which lighting instruments are hung. Usually numbered consecutively from proscenium to upstage: 1st electric, 2d electric, etc. See also **Plan** under LIGHTING STAGE, PROSCENIUM.

A name synonymous with electric department.

ELECTRODE. Either pole or terminal of an electrical apparatus.

ELEVATION

Drawings. Front and rear views of scaled mechanical drawings. See under DRAWINGS.

Scenery. Platforms and ramps used on stage are often called elevations. See also PLASTIC SETS.

ELEVATOR. A section or series of sections of stage floor that can be mechanically raised or lowered from the stage level. Hydraulically controlled orchestra pits are probably the most commonly used stage elevators in this country and the majority of those raise from basement to stage level, forming additional apron space in the high position. See **Elevator Stage** under SCENERY, SHIFTING.

ELLIPSOIDAL REFLECTOR. See under REFLECTORS.

ELLIPSOIDAL REFLECTOR FLOODLIGHT (ERF). See **Floodlight** under LIGHTING INSTRUMENTS, GENERAL.

ELLIPSOIDAL REFLECTOR SPOTLIGHT (ERS, leko, ellips). See under LIGHTING INSTRUMENTS, SPECIFIC.

EMBRYO SPOT (inky). See under LIGHTING INSTRUMENTS, SPECIFIC.

EMERGENCY LIGHT. Battery-powered lights that turn on automatically during power failure. Required installations in auditoriums, above exits, and in lobbies. See also FIRE CODE.

EMERY CLOTH. An abrasive used like sandpaper for smoothing and finishing. Emery cloth is tougher and more durable than sandpaper and can be used on metal as well as wood. Available in many grits from very fine (no. 3/0) to coarse (nos. 3 or 4). See also SANDPAPER; WET OR DRY PAPER; ROUGE CLOTH.

EMPHASIS. Concentration of attention or interest on a given actor, area, or object. Technical aids to emphasis include concentration of light; changes in color of light; use of elevations or platforms; use of color or line in settings and costuming; position of doors, stairs, and points of entrance or exit.

EMT (electrician's metal tubing). Conduit used to enclose electrical wiring.

ENCAPSULATE. To seal any material in a more long-lasting environment, such as a filament in a glass bulb or an electronic device in a solid plastic or phenolic mass. The process usually means the item cannot be repaired but must be replaced when it fails.

ENCLOSURE. Boxlike cabinet surrounding a speaker. See also SOUND EQUIPMENT.

ENDO (end for end). Term used to describe moving an object 180°, or reversing an object.

ENGLISH. Footing away from wall. Flats stacked against a wall should have the bottoms placed away from wall 18" to 24" to make certain they will not fall.

ENTER ABOVE. Direction in Elizabethan theatre pertaining to gallery extending over the stage used by both actors and audience.

ENTR'ACTE. From the French, "between acts," intermission. Also, used to refer to short scenes or skits performed in front of curtain or OLEO between acts or scenes of main performance.

ENTRANCE. A door, arch, window, or wing through which an actor may enter the acting area. Older acting editions of plays written for wing-and-drop staging often designate entrances and exits by letter and number, in which the letter refers to the actor's left or right and the number refers to the wing number, beginning with 1 at the proscenium and numbered consecutively upstage. Thus, L1 is left first wing entrance; R3 is right third wing entrance; etc. See **Defining stage space** under IN; STAGE DIRECTIONS.

ENVELOPE. Glass enclosing filament in LAMP.

61

EPOXY. See under PLASTICS

EQUALIZER, GRAPHICS (EQ). An electronic device that changes specific frequency ranges to help "shape sound" for a space. See also SOUND EQUIPMENT.

EQUATIONS. See AMPERE; ELECTRICITY; LENSES; PROJECTORS.

EQUITY. Actors Equity Association. See under UNIONS.

ERF. Ellipsoidal reflector floodlight. See LIGHTING INSTRUMENTS, GENERAL.

ERROR. See **Computer terminology** under LIGHTING CONTROL.

ERS. See **Ellipsoidal spotlight** under LIGHTING INSTRUMENTS, SPECIFIC.

ESCAPE (carry-off, getaway). Offstage steps leading down from a platform. See also **Offstage steps** under STEPS.

ESCUTCHEON PLATE. See under PLATE.

ETHAFOAM. See **Foam, Ethafoam rod** under PLASTICS.

EXECUTE (Command verb). See **Computer terminology** under LIGHTING CONTROL.

EXIT. Point of egress from the auditorium. Most states have stringent fire laws concerning numbers of exits, lights over exits, panic locks, draperies around exits, etc. Local fire departments should be consulted concerning regulations governing any particular area. See also under FIRE CODE.

EXPLOSION (sound effect). Fire blanks from a 12-gauge shotgun into a metal ashcan. A dynamite cap discharged electrically will also simulate the sound of an explosion (check with fire department). Use thunder sheets and records in the background.

EXTENSION BIT. See under BIT.

EXTENSION LADDER. See under LADDERS.

EXTERIOR. Settings for scenes requiring outside location. Adaptations of wing and drop stagings are often used for exteriors. Corners of buildings, bushes, trees, black draperies, etc., are used as wings framing a cyc or drop. Since realistic exteriors are difficult to construct, it is often best to devote the largest area possible to one building. Projections on the cyc may be helpful if equipment is available. See also PROJECTED SCENERY.

EXTERIOR SET

EYE, LASHLINE. See **Lash eye** under FASTENING FLATS: **Lashing.**

EYE, SCREW. See **Screw eye** under SCREWS.

EYE BLOCK. See under BLOCKS.

EYE BOLT. See under BOLTS.

F

FABRIC. See DRAPERY, SET; DRAPERY, STAGE; **Materials** under COVERING FLATS.

FAB SPRAY. A spray paint used to color fabric. Used for costumes, upholstery, and props. Tends to make fabric stiff.

FACING. Decorative trim, either painted or otherwise applied around doors, windows, etc. Facings may also be nondecorative pieces used to MASK construction. See under MOLDING.

FACTORY NOISES (sound effects). Use recordings supplemented by electric drills, sewing machines, or shop equipment, and amplified through SOUND EFFECT SYSTEMS. Where feasible, tape sounds on location.

FADE IN (sneak in, steal in) (Command verb). Gradual dim up of lights or sound.

FADE OUT (sneak out, steal out) (Command verb). Gradual dim down of lights or sound.

FADER. A device that fades any dimmer assigned to it, up or down. A device that fades from one bus, scene, or preset to another. See also CROSS-FADER; **Computer terminology** under LIGHTING CONTROL.

FALL. As in block and fall. A rope used with a pulley. Specifically, the end of the rope that is pulled by the operator.

FALSE DECK. A platformed floor put on top of regular stage floor, usually because the false deck has various kinds of mechanical devices within for quick changes of scenery, e.g., winch slots, turntables, etc.

FALSE PROSCENIUM (inner proscenium). See under PROSCENIUM.

FAN AND DELUGE SYSTEM (water curtain). A fan-shaped water curtain located at proscenium line, the same as DELUGE SYSTEM except for the addition of powerful exhaust fans above stage house intended to clear smoke. Designed to provide evacuation time for the audience in case of fire onstage.

FASTENING FLATS. Methods commonly used to fasten flats together include the following.

Battening. Scenery to be moved on stage in large sections or flown on pipes is battened together to ensure rigidity. Flats to be battened together are laid face down on floor and brought flush to a straight edge against bottom rails. Long battens, 1" x 3", are applied top, center, and bottom with 1 1/2" (no. 8) wood screws. Battens should be placed to allow a 1" clearance on both ends and edge. After battening, wall section is turned over and all cracks are dutchmanned before painting.

Hinging on back (hinge return). Flats to be fastened at right or obtuse angles, as returns, should be hinged on back with 1 1/2" or 2"

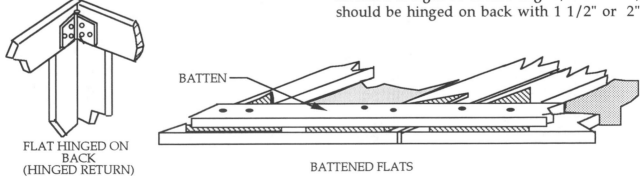

FLAT HINGED ON BACK (HINGED RETURN)

BATTEN

BATTENED FLATS

backflap hinges, or if subject to abnormal strain, with 4" strap hinges. At least three hinges (top, center, and bottom) are required for flats up to 14'. Taller flats require four or more hinges. Apply hinges with 3/4" (no. 8) flathead wood screws. It is sometimes necessary to take returns apart for painting on a paint frame, in such cases loose pin-hinges are used and pins are pulled for painting or transport.

Hinging on face (face hinge, twofold, three-fold). Scenery to be transported must be able to be folded. Three 1 1/2" or 2" backflaps on face of flats (top, center, and bottom) will hold flats together securely. By using a tumbler, three-folds and fourfolds can be hinged together for transportation and then be battened down for rigidity during final assembly on stage. Temporary battening is done with battens and S-hooks (see under HOOKS) or by placing a 1" x 3" batten at right angles to the back of the flat and hinging with loose-pin backflap hinges on alternate sides to form a STIFFENER. Cracks between flats of face-hinged flats should be dutchmanned before painting. There is sufficient resiliency in scene paint to withstand folding many times.

Lashing. Flats are lashed together when temporary joints are required for road shows or multiple-set shows. Lashing should be planned for angle joints only and preferably for outside corners, such as that formed by a side wall and

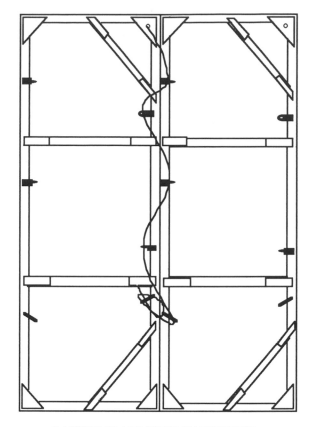

LASHED FLATS WITH HARDWARE

a back wall. Inside corners, returned side walls, are difficult to lash and should be hinged when possible. Flats lashed edge to edge in a straight line have no strength and show an unsightly crack, which cannot be dutchmaned. Flats intended as stock should carry standard hardware of lash cleats, brace cleats, tieoff cleats, and lash line. Hardwaring should be done before covering. Lash hardware includes the following.

Brace cleat. A metal plate with a 1/2" hole to accommodate the hook of a STAGE BRACE. The usual position is at about two-thirds the height of the flat, on the back of the right stile. In this location brace cleats can double as lash cleats.

Lash cleat. Any of a number of types of cleats made to fasten to stiles of flats and used to hold flats together by lashing. A round cleat with one screw hole and a clip to be driven into the edge of a stile is the most satisfactory for upper lash cleats.

Lash eye. A cleat, located in the upper right corner of the back of a flat, with a hole to

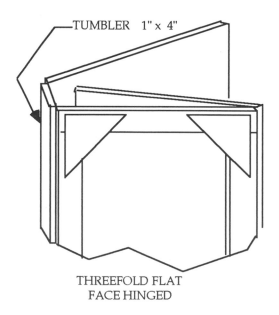

TUMBLER 1" x 4"

THREEFOLD FLAT
FACE HINGED

accommodate a lash line. A hole in the upper corner block is often used in place of a lash eye.

Lash hook. A cleat used in place of lash cleat on door flat stiles. The lash hook looks like a tie-off cleat that has been bent over to form a C-shape on the end.

Lash lines. No. 8 cotton sash cord, 1/4", tied through a 3/8" hole bored in top right corner block, or through a lash eye in top right corner. Lines are cut to the length of the flat.

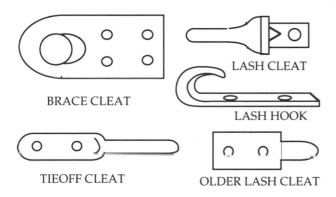

BRACE CLEAT

LASH CLEAT

LASH HOOK

TIEOFF CLEAT

OLDER LASH CLEAT

Stop block. A small block of wood screwed to the back of a flat 3/4" from the edge of the stile at top, center, and bottom, used as a positive stop for flats fastened at right angles as returns.

Stop cleat. A flat metal cleat fastened to the face or back of a flat to keep it from falling forward when lashed to another flat at right angles.

Tieoff cleat. Lowest cleat on each stile, 30" to 36" off the floor. Has two screw holes. Should

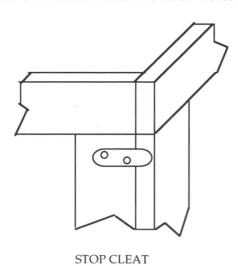

STOP CLEAT

be placed at a slight angle to the stile. In emergencies, 3" (no. 12) roundhead screws can be used as lash hardware.

Nailing. Permanent sets can be nailed together at all corners. **Double-headed nails** (see under NAILS) are best for this purpose since nails can be driven home to the first head and easily withdrawn by the second head. Use four eightpenny nails to hold each joint. Only flats at an angle to each other can be nailed.

FATIGUE. Weakening of material through age or continued strain. Ropes, guy lines, platforms, and counterweight systems are subject to fatigue and should be checked periodically.

FEATHER DUSTER. See under PAINTING TECHNIQUES.

FEATHER EDGE

An edge or end of lumber, plywood, or beaverboard that has been beveled or chamfered.

An edge of a cutting tool that is, or is likely to become, curled or turned over.

FEEDBACK. A hum or disturbance in a sound system, caused by a microphone or other electrical equipment being too close to a speaker or by unshielded wires, ungrounded set, disturbed wiring, or worn insulation. In older two wire systems, sometimes reversing prongs of plug in power supply will reduce hum. See also SIXTY-CYCLE HUM.

FEEDER (feed line). An electrical line used to power dimmers. See **Electrical** under LINE.

FEEDING LINE (paying out). Uncoiling rope or wire to prevent knotting or snagging at source.

FEEL IT UP (Command verb). Flyman's expression for taking up slack on each line of a hemp set, until a strain is felt, in order to trim the set.

FELT. Matted material usually made of wool, fur, or hair and useful in costuming and props. Often glued to the bottom of props to prevent marring of furniture or to deaden sound of a prop.

FEMALE PLUG (body). See PLUGS, ELECTRICAL.

FENCES. Exterior set piece. Usually made as a two-dimensional cutout, sometimes of lumber and sometimes of beaverboard or plywood, depending on type and design. Inexpensive lumber can be used for scenery of this type.

FENDER. A metal guard, sometimes in the form of a bench, used on the floor in front of the fireplace.

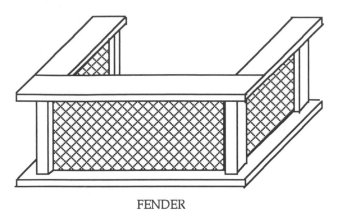

FENDER

FIBERGLASS. Cloth woven of glass fibers and saturated with polyester resin. Fiberglass is a plastic material useful in many ways in theatre. Costumers can use fiberglass for armor, headgear, masks, shields, etc. Bottles, vases, globes, etc., can be made of this tough, durable material. Materials necessary are glass cloth (8 1/2 ounce weight is most versatile), resin, and catalyst. Directions for mixing and applying are on resin labels and should be followed closely. A mold or form made of Plasticine, clay, or plaster of paris is greased with Vaseline or other releasing agent, and strips of glass cloth are smoothed in place. Vaseline not only acts as a releasing agent but also holds glass cloth in place while resin is being brushed on. Layers may be repeated to any given thickness, but two layers will produce a tough, resilient object that will not break when thrown or dropped. When molded object is almost dry, strip from mold to ensure release and then replace until dry (from several minutes to several hours, depending upon amount of accelerator used). Fiberglass is available in a variety of resins for specific purposes. Molded fiberglass cured for a few hours at about 150° F will withstand continuous heat up to 280° F or short exposure up to 400° F. After releasing agent has been thoroughly removed, fiberglass can be painted with any kind of paint; colored resins are also available.

FID. A tool, usually of wood, which helps separate the lay of rope for splicing.

FIELD ANGLE. Cone of light within the entire field with an intensity of 10% or more of the maximum candlepower of a lighting instrument. See also BEAM ANGLE.

FILAMENT. A resistance wire or coil of wire, usually of tungsten, inside a bulb. Illumination occurs as filament is heated to incandescence by a current.

FILAMENT IMAGE. A projection of filament from lens of a spotlight. Correct by widening focus of spotlight through adjustment or by aligning instrument. Some older instruments are misdesigned and the image cannot be removed; in such cases frost color media help.

FILES. Cutting tools with sharp furrows, used for smoothing and shaping.

Bastard mill file. Widely used for average metal filing.

Four-in-hand file (shoe rasp). A file combining four different files in one.

Rasp. A large file with coarse teeth, used for smoothing and shaping wood. Assorted rasps of round, semiround, and flat types are invaluable in shop.

Rattail file. A round file used for enlarging holes in metal or wood.

Sureform. A hand tool with a removable rasp-like blade.

Triangular file. Used for sharpening saw blades.

FILIGREE. Scrollwork of wood, metal, or plastic usually representing a decorative form of a particular architectural period.

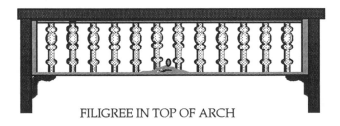

FILIGREE IN TOP OF ARCH

FILLER

Composition used to fill cracks or pores of wood before painting. Most fillers are applied with a brush to open-grain woods such as oak, mahogany, and walnut to seal the grain and ensure an even coverage of stain. All paint stores stock good fillers.

Material added to paint to either give it body or extend the paint. Whiting is considered a filler for scene paints rather than a color.

FILL LIGHT (base light). Light provided in addition to KEY LIGHT or area lights, to blend areas and reduce shadows. Instruments used for fill light may be floodlights, scoops, border lights, footlights, or spotlights, and the choice of the lighting designer will determine the extent of the secondary shadow that will be cast. In television, fill light is often called a "base light" and provides the minimum candlepower required for taking a picture. See also KEY LIGHT.

FILTER. See COLOR MEDIA; STRAINER.

FIN. A perpendicular projection from a flat surface, such as a 1" x 3" or 1" x 6" board nailed perpendicularly to a flat but not used as a thickness. Fins can be purely decorative, or used as a stiffening device, or both.

FIR. A medium-soft, somewhat grainy wood used extensively for the construction of houses, but not for scenery. Fir is adequate for platforms and similar rough construction but it is too splintery and heavy for flat construction.

FIREARM. See GUNS.

FIRE CLASSIFICATION

Class A: wood, paper, cloth, mattresses, furniture, drapes, etc. Use pressurized water; for very small, not deep-seated fires use dry chemical.

Class B: paint, gas, oil products, chemicals. Use foam, fog, CO_2, or, for relatively small fires, dry chemical.

Class C: electrical, nonmicrochip. Use CO_2 or dry chemical. Microchip component electrical fire: use Halon.

FIRE CODE. Laws set up nationally and locally for protection of people in public buildings and places of amusement. Local fire departments will gladly provide desired information for the vicinity. See also NATIONAL ELECTRICAL CODE; NATIONAL UNDERWRITERS CODE. Following are some of the regulations for proscenium theatres.

Aisles. Not less than 5' wide, and wider for large capacity or continental seating theatres.

Emergency lights. Auxiliary house lights and exit lights that turn on automatically in case of power failure. Emergency lights are battery powered, though exit signs usually are on a separate breaker from main house lights. Some states have stringent laws governing emergency or panic lights. Fire or safety inspectors in a given locale will cooperate in explaining laws.

Exits. No draperies, curtains, or anything else in the way of exits. No false indicators of doors, and all exits clearly marked with lighted signs. Panic bars and hardware on all doors, no chains allowed to lock doors.

Fire safety equipment. Fire axes, extinguishers, and fire hoses available at various locations in the auditorium, lobby, foyer, on stage, and at the various levels of the stage and house. Usually the switchboard, sound board, and dimmer space must have CO_2, dry chemical, or Halon extinguishers. Dressing rooms, halls, and rehearsal space must have extinguishers, usually pressurized water and dry chemical. Shops must have extinguishers of types necessary for hazards found in the area. Of course all mechanical rooms must also be equipped.

Fire hoses. 1 1/2" hose. 50' long is the standard hose on quick-release hangers.

No Smoking signs. On both sides of stage at stage level, in all dressing rooms, and in all storage areas. Many states forbid smoking in all public buildings.

Seats. Seating; not less than 34" back to back; not more than 14 seats per row; and no more than six seats from an aisle. See also SEATING, AUDITORIUM.

Smoke vents. One square foot of smoke vent for each 10 square feet of stage area. Smoke vents should be glazed with single-strength glass and equipped to open both automatically and manually.

Sprinklers. In theatre sprinklers should be installed above and below the grid, above all storage areas, and above or on the proscenium arch.

FIRE CURTAIN. See ASBESTOS CURTAIN; DELUGE SYSTEM; FAN AND DELUGE SYSTEM.

FIRE ESCAPE (emergency exit). Consult local fire code and fire department for rules governing fire escapes in a given locale.

FIRE EXTINGUISHER. Any of several types of portable fire-fighting equipment. Local fire departments will cooperate in determining number and locations of extinguishers; see also **Fire safety equipment** under FIRE CODE. All extinguishers should be checked and filled on a regular basis by a professional in that field. The following or their equivalents are recommended for theatre use.

Soda and acid. Obsolete; chemicals mix to pressurize water when extinguisher is inverted. Not recommended at all. Do not use on electrical fires. Replace with pressurized water.

Foam. Inversion mixes chemicals to form a foam, smothering flames at base. Since it is not a liquid, foam extinguishers are recommended for oil or gasoline fires.

Carbon dioxide (CO_2). The equivalent of dry ice under pressure, CO_2 spreads a blanket of heavy, white vapor, smothering flames. Nonliquid and recommended for electrical fires.

Dry chemical. A pressurized extinguisher filled with nonburning powder that smothers flames. Rated for small class A and B fires and class C.

Halon. These are dry chemical extinguishers especially designed for electronic and computer equipment.

Pressurized water. No chemicals, merely water under ca. 125 pounds of pressure. Not recommended for electrical or oil fires.

FIRE IRONS. Shovel, poker, and tongs used in fireplace sets.

FIREPLACE. Generally a free-standing unit of scenery, stored as part of stock equipment. One of the best ways of establishing mood, time, and place is to use authentic fireplace designs. Reasonably simple designs are available for most periods. Choose designs commensurate with talents of building crew. Dress mantel according to play. Fireplaces are made as individual units and are bolted, nailed, screwed, or loose-pin hinged to flat.

FIREPLACE EFFECTS. Equipment used to simulate fire in a fireplace. Wildly flickering lights, leaping flames of silk, and other such attempts usually result in distracting the audience. A simple, rotating, transparent cylinder operating from the heat of a lamp will usually provide an adequate flicker. Coal grates filled with wadded gelatine of all colors, painted broken lenses, or melted glass lighted from beneath are most effective. A small floodlight or baby spot with medium amber gelatine is sometimes used through fireplace opening to supplement the effect.

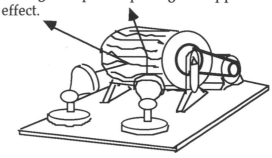

FIREPLACE EFFECT

FIREPLACE LOGS. Simulated logs that glow when lighted. Use chicken wire frames covered with flameproofed cheesecloth or scrim grained to resemble logs. Two or three lamps and a rotating cylinder built inside the logs complete the effect. Assembled log units are also available through window display stores, mail order houses, and some supply houses.

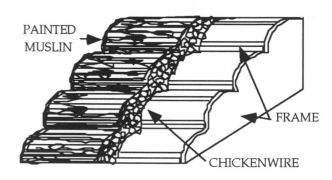

PAINTED MUSLIN
FRAME
CHICKENWIRE

FIREPLACE LOGS

FIREPROOFING. See FLAMEPROOFING.

FIRE UP (light 'em up, strike it) (Command verb). Order to start or light the light source in followspots.

FIRST BORDER (concert border). Older term for first border lights upstage of the act curtain. See also LIGHTING STAGE, PROSCENIUM.

FIRST RUN. The original production of a show.

FIVE PLY. Denotes five separate layers of wood in plywood, often used as a generic term for 3/4" plywood, though it is possible to have seven ply in 3/4".

FIXTURE (instrument, light, luminaire, unit). See LIGHTING INSTRUMENTS.

FLAG (ribbon, trim mark). A ribbon or piece of cloth inserted in the lay of the rope to identify a trim mark showing the tieoff point for a predetermined height of a flown piece of scenery. "Flag" is used either as a noun (the ribbon or marker) or as a verb (the marking of a line).

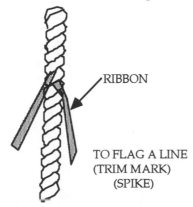

RIBBON

TO FLAG A LINE
(TRIM MARK)
(SPIKE)

FLAKE GLUE. See GLUES.

FLAKING FLAT (gatoring). A flat from which paint is chipping. Wash or recover flat. See **Flat recovering** and **Flat washing** under COVERING FLATS.

FLAMEPROOFING. Be aware that this is a misnomer; in truth, the term means the application of flame retardants; almost anything backstage will burn with enough heat and enough time subjected to that heat. Fire laws require all scenery on stage to be flameproofed. Flats can be sprayed or brushed with solution, or solution can be added as liquid part of prime coat (size coat). Draperies and curtains can be sprayed or sent out for commercial flameproofing. A homemade fireproofing solution is 2 pounds of ammonium sulfimate dissolved in 1 gallon of warm water; a second solution is 1 pound borax to 1 pound sal ammoniac to 3 quarts of water. Many prepared flameproofing solutions are available through theatrical supply houses. A piece of fabric should be tested first, since discoloration sometimes results.

FLANGE. See under PIPE FITTINGS.

FLASH BOX. See under SMOKE EFFECTS.

FLASH POWDER. Used for smoke and flash effects where legal. Available in slow, medium, and fast speeds. Check with local fire department. See also PYROTECHNICS.

FLAT. See also COVERING FLATS; FASTENING FLATS; HANDLING FLATS; SCENERY, SHIFTING. A unit of scenery, varying in width from 1' to 6' and varying in height from 8' to 30', covered with fabric suitable for painting (see **Materials** under COVERING FLATS). Flats are made with the best grades of white pine, spruce, or other LUMBER available. Variations in construction practices exist between professional and nonprofessional technicians, primarily because professional scenery is built for a specific show, while nonprofessional scenery is built as stock scenery to serve in many shows over a period of years. A set made of flats is known as a HARD SET.

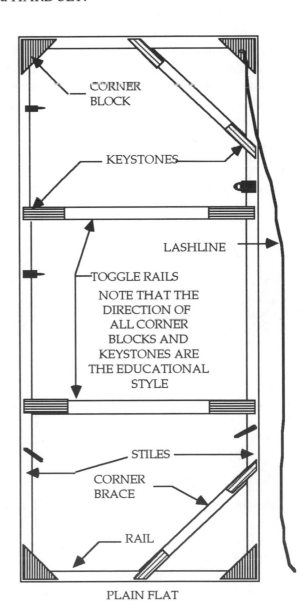

CORNER
BLOCK

KEYSTONES

LASHLINE

TOGGLE RAILS
NOTE THAT THE
DIRECTION OF
ALL CORNER
BLOCKS AND
KEYSTONES ARE
THE EDUCATIONAL
STYLE

STILES

CORNER
BRACE

RAIL

PLAIN FLAT

Components

Two stiles (uprights). Vertical side pieces.

Two rails (end pieces). Top and bottom pieces.

One or more toggles. Cross members located between the two end rails. Toggles should be not more than 6' or less than 4' apart.

Corner braces. Short diagonal braces used to keep the frame square.

Corner blocks. Reinforcing triangles made of 1/4" plywood used on the corners of flats to fasten stiles and rails. Usually made by cutting 9", 10", or 12" squares through the diagonal.

Keystones (straps). 1/4" plywood used to reinforce joints between toggle rails and stiles. A keystone in professional theatre is shaped like a truncated trapezoid, 8" long and 3" wide on one end and 4" wide on the other. In nonprofessional theatre, straps are 2 1/2" x 8" rectangles. Keystones or straps should cover joints of all cross members and corner braces.

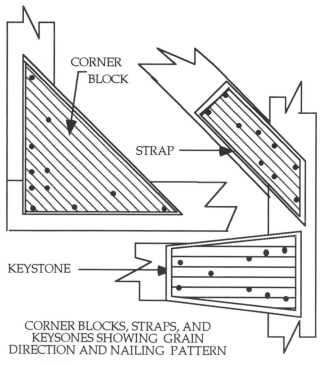

CORNER BLOCKS, STRAPS, AND KEYSONES SHOWING GRAIN DIRECTION AND NAILING PATTERN

Professional flat construction. All stiles, toggles, and rails are made of 1" x 3" net (not 2-1/2") lumber for flats up to and including 16' in height and often 5/4" x 3" net stock for taller flats. Edges of corner blocks and keystones are beveled; joints are sometimes mortised and tenoned as illustrated; corner blocks and keystones are placed 1/4" from outside edges of stiles and rails and usually fastened with narrow or wide crown staples (if nails are used, see nailing pattern illustrated). Standard width of older professional flats was 5' 9", but today they are often wider but not too wide to fit into a covered truck.

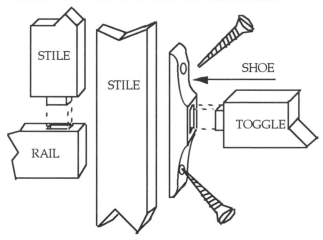

PROFESSIONAL-STYLE CONSTRUCTION USING MORTISE AND TENNONS

Nonprofessional flat construction. Lumber specifications remain as above except the 1" x 3" (actually 2 1/2") lumber is used. Butt joints with corrugated fasteners (no. 5, 5/8") are used. Corner blocks and rectangular keystones are placed 3/4" from outside edge of stiles and rails to allow flats to be joined at right angles. Staples are often used instead of clout nails; if clout nails are used, they are driven home and turned back into the wood with a clinch plate. Outside grain of corner blocks and keystones is perpendicular to the joints. Standard stock widths of flats are usually from 1' to 6' on 12" modules.

Window flat. Construction same as for plain flat except for placement of toggles: height of window from floor (usually 30" to 36") determines location of lower toggle, and overall height of window (usually 7') determines location of upper toggle. Width of window is determined by placement of inner stiles; if removable casements are to be used, a clearance of at least 3" is recommended in both height and width so as to allow casements to slide in and out without undue strain; inside casement dimensions are 3' wide by 4' to 4' 6" high, and dimensions for openings to accommodate casements are 3' 3" wide by 4' 3" or 4' 9" high.

Door flat. Constructed similarly, except for the lower rail, which is replaced at the opening by a sill iron (see under STRAP IRON); door openings are 3' wide by 7' high for single doors and 3' or 4' wide by 7' to 9' high for double doors. If casements are to be used, a minimum of a 3" clearance is recommended, making door openings 3' 3" x 7' 3" for a single door. If legs of a door

flat are 1' or less in width, a single square block of plywood can be used instead of two corner blocks to join stile, inner stile, and lower rail. On very narrow legged door flats, solid wood can be used as the stile. All openings should be centered widthwise in flats.

Hardcover flat (Hollywood flat, high-tech flat). Sections of 1" square steel tube (1 1/2" tube in really large applications) are welded together with a mig welder to form the frame. Usually, 1/4" plywood or lauan is affixed on the face with PL 400

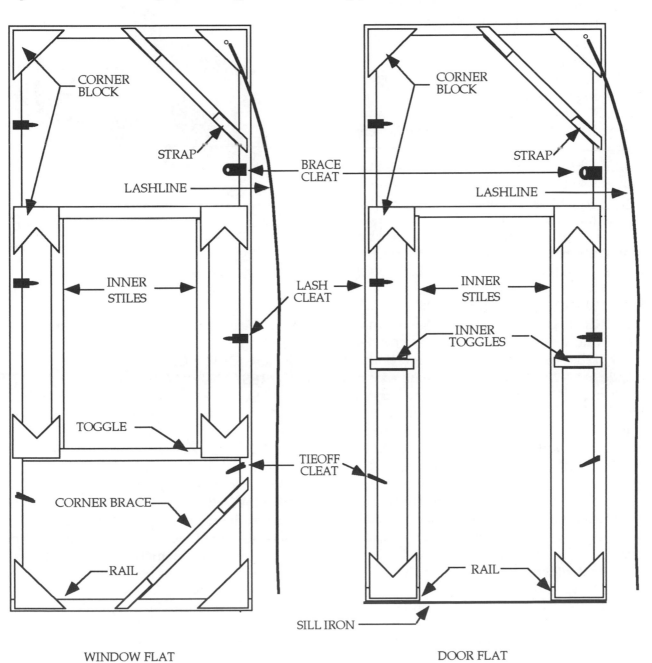

WINDOW FLAT   DOOR FLAT

71

flooring adhesive and tee nails. Hardcover flats are built in manageable sizes to get through doorways and into trucks. Some of these flats are quite large and heavy, with maximum size near 6 1/2' x 24'. The treatment on the plywood can be white shellac with spackle, latex paint, wallpaper, or any other material the SCENE DESIGNER specifies.

FLAT PAINT. A paint that absorbs light, as opposed to a glossy paint, which reflects light. All scene paint is flat paint.

FLECK. See under PAINTING TECHNIQUES.

FLEXIBLE SCENERY OR LIGHTING. Adaptable and readily changed, in contrast to permanent installations.

FLIES (fly loft). The space above the stage used for flying scenery.

FLIPPER. Any narrow flat or piece of lumber, hinged, usually at a 90° angle to another unit or flat.

FLOAT A FLAT. See under HANDLING FLATS.

FLOCK. A substance giving a napped effect, usually sprayed on an object. Often applied to Christmas trees to give a fuller effect. It is also handy on props to hide defects and add body.

FLOODLIGHT (bunch light, olivette, scoop). See under LIGHTING INSTRUMENTS, GENERAL.

FLOORBLOCK. See under BLOCK.

FLOORCLOTH (groundcloth). A padding for the acting area, usually canvas, often painted as part of the scenic decor. Canvas floorcloths are made of 10- to 12-ounce duck, hemmed with a 2" hem on all four sides. If seaming is necessary, run seams parallel with front of stage. Floorcloths should be at least 4' wider than the acting area and 2' to 4' deeper. Stretch and tack to floor with no. 4 carpet tacks or 1/2" staples every 2" to 4". Floorcloths to be removed during scene changes should be grommeted with no. 2 or 2 1/2 grommets at 8" to 12" intervals and held in position with 3/4" roundhead wood screws leaving as little showing as possible to catch the grommet. Floorcloths are best painted with latex or casein paints.

FLOOR IRON. See **Foot iron** under STRAP IRON.

FLOOR PLAN (ground plan). A working draw-ing indicating exact outline of setting on floor. See under DRAWINGS; see also SIGHTLINES.

FLOOR PLATE. A small metal plate with a ring, used for tying guy lines, cycs, or scenery to the floor.

FLOOR PLUG. See under PLUGS, ELECTRICAL.

FLOOR POCKET. An electrical receptacle recessed in the stage floor and protected with a metal cover. See also PLUGS, ELECTRICAL.

FLOOR POCKET WITH PIN
CONNECTORS

FLOWN SCENERY. Scenery raised into the flies by means of ropes or a counterweight system. See also RIGGING.

FLUORESCENT PAINT. See under PAINTS, MISCELLANEOUS; ULTRAVIOLET LIGHT.

FLUSH. Even, level, or forming a continuous surface.

FLUTING. A groove, crimp, or wrinkle, usually refers to a COLUMN or PEDESTAL.

FLUX. A measure of light in units of LUMENS.

FLUX, SOLDER. A greasy substance used to prevent oxidizing during the soldering process, thereby aiding the flow and bonding of solder. Since acid fluxes sometimes tend to corrode, paste and stick fluxes are generally considered superior. See also SOLDER.

FLY. To elevate scenery by means of pulleys, ropes, or a counterweight system. See also **flying scenery** under SCENERY, SHIFTING; RIGGING.

FLY GALLERY (fly floor, pin rail, rail)

In a counterweight house, the fly gallery is a platform located above floor level usually on the counterweight side of the stage. In some counterweight houses rope locks are available on the fly gallery as well as on the stage floor. The fly gallery is for tying lines, loading weights (see also LOADING PLATFORM), and handling lines during a performance.

In a hemp house, the fly gallery is a platform located above floor level on either side or on both sides of the stage. It contains one or two pin rails for tying off sets of lines, loading sandbags, and generally running the rigging of a performance.

FLYING SCENERY. See under SCENERY, SHIFTING.

FLYING SYSTEM. See under RIGGING SYSTEMS.

FLYMAN. A stagehand who handles rigging during a performance.

FOCAL LENGTH. Distance from the center of a lens or reflector to its focal point. See also LENSES; REFLECTORS.

FOCAL POINT (nodal point). The point at which rays of light from a lens converge. See also LENSES; REFLECTORS.

FOCUS LIGHTS

To set positions of spotlights and other lighting equipment.

To aim the lighting instruments at a given object or area.

To adjust the distance between lamp and lens or adjust shutters, thereby changing the size or shape of the area covered by light.

FOG EFFECT. A scrim or gauze drop, lighted evenly with low-intensity front light, together with wisps of smoke from either dry ice or a fog machine (see SMOKE EFFECTS), will provide a convincing effect. For localized fog that clings to the floor, use dry ice; for fog that rises, use a fog machine.

FOH. Front of the house. See also ANTEPROSCENIUM; AUDITORIUM.

FOLD. See TWOFOLD; THREEFOLD.

FOLDBACK. See under SOUND EQUIPMENT.

FOLDING JACK. Jack hinged to back of FLATS so that it folds against flat for scene change.

FOLIAGE BORDER. See TREE LEAVES.

FOLLOW

To focus a spotlight on a performer as that performer moves about.

To increase and decrease light intensity on stage areas, synchronized with the movement of the performer. Most effective if subtly done.

FOLLOWER. See AUTOFOLLOW.

FOLLOWSPOT. A spotlight mounted on a swivel so that it can follow a performer. Followspots are used for musicals, vaudeville, opera, ice shows, etc. Followspots can have incandescent lamps, arcs, encapsulated arcs, and quartz lamps with throws up to 600' or more. The followspot can change the shape of its beam with IRIS and DOUSER, focus with a TROMBONE, and change color with a BOOMERANG. See also **Arc light** under LIGHTING INSTRUMENTS, SPECIFIC.

FOOD ON STAGE (props). Most food used as properties on stage consists of bread or soft fruits cut in required shapes. Sticky or overly sweet foods and BEVERAGES are usually avoided. In some productions, especially with audiences seated close by, actual food is used, though again foods that impede speech or line pickup are avoided.

FOOT A FLAT. To place a foot against the lower rail of a flat to prevent slipping when raising or lowering a flat. See also HANDLING FLATS.

FOOTCANDLE. See also ILLUMINATION; LUMEN. A unit of illumination equal to 1 lumen per square foot. Light produced by 1 standard candle at a distance of 1'. If the candlepower of a given lamp is known, footcandles at a given distance can be computed from the following equation:

Footcandles = Candlepower/Distance in feet, squared.

For example, illumination at a distance of 10' from a 150-candlepower lamp = 150/10 x 10 = 150/100 = 1.5 footcandles.

FOOT IRON (flat iron, floor iron). See under STRAP IRON.

FOOTLIGHTS. A trough of lights on the floor or embedded in the floor immediately in front of the curtain and at the edge of the apron. See under LIGHTING INSTRUMENTS, GENERAL.

FORCED PERSPECTIVE. See PERSPECTIVE, FORCED.

FORESTAGE. See under APRON.

FORM. One of the four aspects of visual manifestation, the other three being line, color, and texture.

FORMAL SETTING. A formal, permanent background not enclosing the stage. Originated in the sixteenth century when settings were permanent and all plays were staged in front of them. Modifications of formal settings are still popular, appearing as arches, set pieces, or platforms backed by draperies.

FORM NAIL (scaffold, duplex, double headed). See **Double-headed nail** under NAILS; FASTENING FLATS.

FORMULA

　　Math. A mathematical method of solving a particular problem.

　　Lighting. A predetermined method of lighting individual AREAS. See LIGHTING STAGE, ARENA; LIGHTING STAGE, PROSCENIUM; LIGHTING STAGE, THRUST.

FORWARD. Stage direction meaning downstage, toward the footlights.

FOUL (hung up). Scenery or lights or objects in the flys becoming entangled. See also FREE.

FOULING POLE. A long pole or stick usually of fir and 1 1/4" to 1 1/2" in diameter used to free fouled scenery in the flies. A stage brace may serve in the absence of a fouling pole.

FOURFOLD. Four flats hinged on face with a tumbler in the middle, allowing all four flats to fold together compactly. See illustration under THREEFOLD.

FOURTH WALL. In a realistic setting, the proscenium opening is considered the invisible fourth wall.

FOUR-WIRE THREE-PHASE. See under CIRCUIT, ELECTRICAL.

FOYER. The area encountered immediately upon entering a theatre, before the lobby.

FRAME (verb). To put the stiles and rails of a flat together. To put together the framework of any piece of scenery.

FRAME, COLOR (gel frame). See COLOR FRAME.

FRAME, PAINT. A large frame of wood or metal, sometimes counterweighted, used to hold scenery or drops while being painted. See also BOOMERANG.

FRAMED DROP. See under DROPS.

FREE. Refers to scenery that is not fouled by other scenery but is free to be moved. See also FOUL.

FREEZE ON-OFF. A phenomenon occurring with SCR dimmers in which a malfunction causes a light to stay on or off depending on the gate position. In some early dimmers, disconnecting the instrument from the dimmer was the only solution.

FRESNEL (fresnel light) (pronounced Fra nel´). A spotlight providing a soft diffused light. The lens was invented by Augustin-Jean Fresnel (1788-1827) for use in lighthouses. See **Fresnel lens** under LENSES; **Fresnel spotlight** under LIGHTING INSTRUMENTS, SPECIFIC.

FRICTION HINGE. See under HINGES.

FRONT ELEVATION (front el). See under DRAWINGS.

FROST. Translucent color media used to diffuse light. Useful in blending area lights and softening harsh lines of a beam. **Star frost:** frost color media with center cut out in irregular pattern, used to maintain concentration of light in center but to soften edges by diffusing through frost. The same effect can be achieved by smearing a drop of oil on the rough side of frost GELATINE, causing this portion to become transparent.

FROSTED BULB, LAMP. A lamp with translucent bulb giving a diffused light.

FROSTED LIGHT (frosted spot). A lighting instrument using frost color media to diffuse the light.

FULL. Refers to the maximum intensity of lighting instruments or sound equipment.

FULLNESS. Folds in costumes or draperies. Draperies should have a fullness of at least half the width, though double width gives a more luxurious appearance. See also PLEATS.

FULL UP. A light or grouping of lights at maximum intensity.

FUNNEL. See **Top hat** under LIGHT SPILL CONTROL.

FURNITURE (props). Furniture to be made part of permanent stock should be made of harder wood than that used for flat construction. Hardwoods such as maple and oak are more difficult

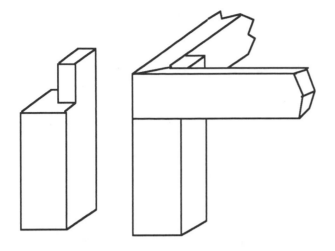

RABBETING IN FURNITURE CONSTRUCTION

to work and often too expensive to buy, while semihardwoods (fir, ash, Philippine mahogany, and alder) are easier to machine, less expensive, and lighter weight. Plywood (3/4") is adequate for table tops, desk tops, seats, and benches. Many books on period furniture provide pictures of styles that can be easily duplicated or modified to simplify construction. Cabinet or furniture manufacturers often make different types of legs for chairs, tables, and davenports, which can be purchased in sets and applied to frames built in theatre shops. Authenticity can thus be provided at a nominal fee. Frames should be put together with wood screws and glue. Wherever possible, legs should be notched or rabbeted so that a portion of the frame rests on the legs. Foam makes excellent padding for chairs, chaise lounges, and sofas; a bandsaw or electric knife will cut and shape the foam readily. Foam can be glued in place (see GLUE) and can be upholstered with appropriate materials. Colored upholstery tacks, gimp tacks, and gimp tape along with staples make upholstering

relatively easy. See also LUMBER; PAINTING FURNITURE.

FUSE. An electrical conductor in a circuit that melts with heat and breaks circuit if a current greater than rated load is introduced. Fuses up to 30-amp capacities are available in screw type and in automotive types. Larger capacities are cartridge type. All electrical circuits should be protected by fuses of a capacity no greater than that of the dimmer. Fuses larger than those specified may burn out dimmers or expensive equipment and lead to serious electrical fires. Fuses are wired in series with the load. Must be replaced when blown. See CIRCUIT BREAKERS; CIRCUIT, ELECTRICAL; SHORT CIRCUIT.

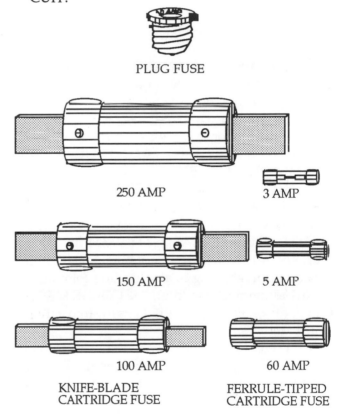

PLUG FUSE

250 AMP   3 AMP

150 AMP   5 AMP

100 AMP   60 AMP

KNIFE-BLADE   FERRULE-TIPPED
CARTRIDGE FUSE   CARTRIDGE FUSE

G

GAFFER. Professional term for stage crew department head or foreman.

GAIN. Volume control on an amplifier. See also SOUND EQUIPMENT.

GALLERY. The highest balcony in a theatre or the occupants thereof.

GALLERY, FLY. See FLY GALLERY.

GANG

To control or connect several electrical units together for group operation.

To hook together two or more electrical units on one circuit.

To operate together two or more dimmers or channels on LIGHTING CONTROL. See also DIMMERS, MASTER.

GATORBOARD. See SCENERY PANELS.

GAUGE. See METAL GAUGES; WIRE; WIRE, ELECTRICAL.

GAUZE, THEATRICAL. See SCRIM.

GEL (noun). Abbreviation of GELATINE. A generic term referring to any lighting color media (including plastic media). See COLOR MEDIA.

GEL (verb). Put color with its frame into lighting instruments.

GELATINE (gel). Thin, transparent sheets made of animal or grain jelly and dye and used as color media for stage lights. Gelatine comes in sheets approximately 20" x 24" and in nearly 100 different shades and tints. All gelatines will fade after continuous use, sometimes within a few hours or, when used with certain quartz lights, will burn within a few seconds. See COLOR MEDIA; DICHROIC FILTER.

GENERAL ILLUMINATION. Refers to light spread over the stage as opposed to specific light for a given purpose. See LIGHTING INSTRUMENTS, GENERAL.

GENERAL LIGHTS. Footlights, border lights, strip lights, etc., used for toning, blending, and establishing basic color mood for a play. See LIGHTING INSTRUMENTS, GENERAL.

GENERIC TERMS. The following are the major terms. GEL for COLOR MEDIA, LEKOLIGHT for any ELLIPSOIDAL REFLECTOR SPOTLIGHT, BATTEN for a 1" x 3" piece of lumber, SKILSAW for any portable circular saw.

GENIE LIFT. A trade name for a pneumatic lift used to raise people in a telescoping device, used also as an air-operated lighting tower or boom.

GET AWAY. See CARRY OFF.

GHOST LIGHT (night light). A portable, naked bulb mounted in a wire cage on a light standard placed center stage after rehearsals and performances, and used as a safety light to help prevent accidents.

GHOST LOAD (phantom load). A lamp or a resistance in an unseen or obscure place on stage which can be connected in parallel with a stage light in order to load up the dimmer for complete dimouts. Usually only resistance dimmers need ghost loads, and they need them only if the load they control is less than the rated minimum load of the dimmer. On occasion early SCR dimmers that controlled low wattages such as flame type flicker lamps also needed to be ghost-loaded. In the case of SCRs the problem is not resistance but rather the inability of the SCR to detect a load at all. See also **Resistance**, and **Silicon controlled rectifiers** under DIMMER.

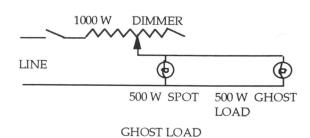

GHOST LOAD

GILDING PAINTS. See under PAINTS, MISCELLANEOUS.

GIMP TACKS. Small roundhead tacks used for furniture upholstering in places where tacks would show. Available in hardware stores and upholstery shops. No. 6 is the most useful size. See GIMP TAPE.

GIMP TAPE. A special decorative tape usually about 1/2" wide, available in a variety of colors. Used to reinforce and decorate material to be gimp tacked.

GLARE (bounce light). A light reflection too bright for comfortable vision. Glare is also caused by too light a background or too great a contrast of color in background.

GLASS. Glass in stage windows is simulated with fiberglass screen, dyed scrim or cheesecloth , or nonglare acrylic clear plastic. Plastics that cause glare, glass, cellophane, and other highly reflective materials are not used because of problems with reflection. Fiberglass screening is very flexible, resists creasing, and can be restretched and used many times. Windows to be broken on stage can be made of sugar and water, cooked and poured onto a form of correct size. A pane of sugar glass can be made with 2/3 cup water to 1/2 cup sugar cooked at 325° on a candy thermometer and poured on a greased Formica sheet. Crystallization occurs within a relatively short period, causing translucency. Casting resin, a polyester resin sold in hardware stores and marine supply houses, also makes excellent windows for breaking. Approximately 4 ounces of resin poured on a sheet of mylar (a releasing agent used for casting resins) will make a 10" x 12" pane of glass. See also WINDOWS.

GLASS, CRASH. A box filled with scraps of glass and dropped on cue gives an offstage sound of crashing glass. Small scraps of stainless steel, available at sheet metal shops, can be added to glass in crash boxes. Crash boxes should be screened on top to avoid scattering contents. See CRASH BOX.

GLASS, STAINED. See **Stained glass windows** under WINDOWS.

GLAZE. See under PAINTING TECHNIQUES.

GLIDES (domes of silence, chair glides). Small, smooth domes attached under legs of furniture or small platforms and set pieces to facilitate sliding and shifting. Larger platforms require CASTERS.

GLITCH (surge). See **Computer terminology** under LIGHTING CONTROL.

GLITTER (sequins, sparkle). Small particles of metal, metal foil, glass, or plastic, used on costumes or props to give a rich appearance. On props and scenery, glitter can be sprinkled on a wet coat of glue or size water.

GLOSS. See **Glaze** under PAINTING TECHNIQUES.

GLUE. Adhesives used as paint binders and for scenery and property construction. Animal, white flake, amber flake, ground gelatine, and flexible rubber (fish) are the most popular types of glues used with dry pigments. Polyvinyl alcohol is a water-soluble synthetic resin used as a binder for scene paint, replacing animal glues. This resin has excellent storage stability in solution but can ball up when painted over standard flameproofing. Dextrine is another dry glue and is a standard binder for bronzing powders. All of these powder glues need heating to become clear. Some confusion about glue and adhesive exists. Glue is is usually considered organically based material and adhesive is a man-made material. In reality, the terms are often used interchangeably.

Heating-type glues

Animal and gelatine glues. Preparation of common dry, animal and gelatine glues. Place glue in bucket and add equal amount of water; allow to soak overnight. The resulting semihard, gelatinous mass, when melted in a double boiler or glue pot, is ready to use as a full strength glue. *Warning:* Always use when hot; always heat in a double boiler; add water to replace what has evaporated over sustained heating periods. Burning glue is not a smell easily forgotten.

These proportions given here are approximate and the glue should always be tested before being used. See also PAINT MIXING.

Covering. Add 1/4 glue to 3/4 water to make glue water; then add 1 cup whiting to 4 cups of the glue water.

Dutchman. 2 to 3 cups of glue to 10 quarts of paint mix.

Furniture repair. From 1 part glue to 1 part water to full-strength glue.

Glue dope (alternative mixture for covering). 1 part melted glue, 1 part Danish whiting, 1 part **wheat paste** (see below). Dilute with hot water to spread easily, but maintain body.

Hot melt glue. A plastic adhesive used in GLUE GUNS. This hot melt glue does not form the strongest of bonds, but it has the double advantage of sticking to most surfaces and setting usually within a minute; and it has the disadvantage of burning fingers. Invaluable in prop departments. Comes in clear, regular, and white sticks.

Painting. 1 to 2 cups of glue to 10 quarts of paint mix. Flexible rubber (fish) glue is used in the same proportions for painting drops.

Papier-mâché. 3 to 4 cups of glue per 10-quart bucket of water.

Patching. Same as for **Dutchman.**

Size water. 2 cups of glue per 10-quart bucket of water.

Sizing. 2 cups of glue per 10-quart bucket of water. Prepared cold-water size from paint stores is also very good.

Nonheating-type glues

Caulking-gun adhesives. Used often in the building trades for adhering panels to frames or walls. There are many different types from which to choose. A caulking gun allows ease of application.

Clear latex. Often used as a binder for dry pigments, it has the advantage of not rubbing off and the disadvantage of higher cost and higher gloss than the fish and animal glues.

Contact cement. Used for gluing laminate plastics, veneers, etc.

Duco cement. Available in tubes for small jobs. Very good for jewels, sequins, etc.

Epoxy glues. A two-part glue that must be mixed; forms a very hard and strong bond. Epoxy will bond wood to metal and glass.

Mastic no. 11. Excellent bonding material for rigid foams.

Rubber cement. Very good for paper and cloth. Works well on gluing back edges on cutout drops.

Silicone adhesives. Very strong, used in electrics and props.

Spray adhesive. Good adhesive qualities for papers, foam rubbers, cloth, and some plastic materials.

Wheat paste. Old standby for hanging wallpaper, making papier-mâché, and using in dilute form for sizing of muslin and canvas for flats.

White glue. Flexible (Sobo): used with fabrics and anything that needs to bend. Works well on gluing back edges for cutout drops. Nonflexible (Elmers, Weldwood, Gluebird, etc.): these glues are recommended for furniture repair or construction and for flat covering. For covering flats, thin the glue 10 to 15 percent with water. Any water-soluble glue can be used as a binder for small quantities of scene paint.

GLUE BURN. A stain caused by glue. If glue spills on flats or if glue content of paint is too high, a glue burn will result. For covering glue burns see under STAINS.

GLUE GUN. An electric, gun-shaped tool that heats a hot melt glue stick and applies it; a mainstay in any prop shop. Sticks of hot glue come in clear, regular, and white sticks. Can also be used for applying glue as a decorative filigree, caulking, or embossing on props and furniture.

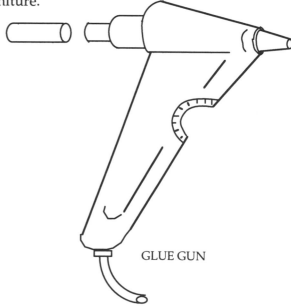

GLUE GUN

GO (Command verb). Do the cue now. This word is generally preferred to all others as a final cue. Stage managers give warnings 10 to 30 seconds before saying, "Go."

GOBO (pattern, mat, cookie). A cutout design placed in the gate of an ellipsoidal reflector spotlight to shine a pattern or image on an object or screen. A wide variety of patterns are available from theatre supply houses. Highly heat resistant patterns for AUTOMATED LIGHTS are made of glass with thin metal designs and sometimes with color added.

GOBOS (GREAT AMERICAN MARKET)

GOBO HOLDER

In some spotlights the gobo must be put into a special carrier that is then put into the slot.

A slot placed near the shutter position (the

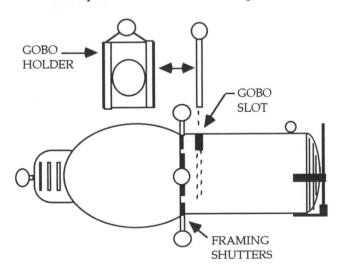

LOCATION OF GOBO SLOT IN
ELLIPSOIDAL SPOTLIGHT

focal point) in an ellipsoidal spotlight, designed to receive a pattern slide for a background projection. *Warning:* Since this is the hottest part of a spotlight, any gobo designed for this position must be capable of withstanding great heat up to 1000°F.

GOLD PAINT. See **Gilding paints** under PAINTS, MISCELLANEOUS.

GONGS (sound effect). Gongs can be made by suspending a pipe, wrecking bar, circular saw blade, cymbals, or brake drum, etc., and using a partially padded wooden or rubber mallet for a striker. See also CHIMES.

GOUGE. A chisel with a concave blade, used to cut grooves and hollows.

GOVERNOR. A device used to govern the speed of a motor. Usually found on spring-driven mechanisms such as windup phonographs and sciopticons. Governors have been replaced by electric motors of fixed gear ratios for given speeds or by motors equipped with rheostats for variable speed. SCRs (see under DIMMERS) will control the speed of most electrical motors.

GRAIN. See under PAINTING TECHNIQUES.

GRAND DRAPE. Draperies separating stage from auditorium. See CURTAINS.

GRAND MASTER DIMMER. See DIMMERS, MASTER.

GRAND VALANCE (teaser). The first drapery border in front of the main act curtain, generally made of the same material and often used to vary the height of the proscenium arch.

GRAPHITE. A carbon product with a variety of theatrical uses. Used as a lubricant for locks, ratchets, etc. Used as carbons or electrodes in arc lights. Simulates a gun-metal finish when rubbed on the surface of props or scenery. *Warning:* Since graphite will rub off, props treated in this way should not be handled. See also SILICONE LUB.

GREENFIELD. A flexible armored steel conduit into which electrical wires are pulled. See also BX.

GREEN ROOM. Traditional waiting room or reception room of a theatre, located near the stage and serving as a meeting place for guests or a place where actors can spend free moments between cues. An intercom system between stage and green room will prevent many missed cues.

GRID (gridiron). Structural framework of parallel beams located near the top of the stage house and supporting sheaves, loft blocks, head blocks, cable, and rope necessary for flying scenery and lights. See illustration under COUNTERWEIGHT SYSTEM; see also RIGGING.

GRIP. A stagehand assisting the carpenter in shifting, setting and striking scenery. See also STAGE CREW.

GROMMET. Metal eyelets placed at 6" to 12" intervals in the top webbing of drapes and drops, used for tying to pipe battens (see **Tie line** illustration under KNOTS). Setting dies for grommets are reasonably priced and easily used. No. 2 or 2 1/2 grommets are adequate for most drops. Projection screens are usually grommeted on four sides.

GROUND

A conductor directly connected to a water pipe or other suitable connector in the earth.

The third uninsulated wire in an electrical wire, which connects to ground in an outlet, thence to the ground in the panel.

GROUNDCLOTH. See FLOORCLOTH.

GROUND GLUE. See GLUES.

GROUND PLAN. See **Floor plan** under DRAWINGS.

GROUNDROW (profile piece). A low silhouette or painted cutout representing hills, mountains, bushes, distant horizons, etc., and designed to stand independently in the background. **Construction**: If design does not include **Rear elevations** (see under DRAWINGS) showing construction, put carbon paper face up under drawing and trace contour; turn drawing over and lay out 1" x 3" framework to full scale as for building a flat, keeping frame as close to contour as is feasible. Parts of frame supporting 1/4" plywood contour are rabbeted 1/4" x 1 1/2" to receive plywood. Put frame together on back side with corrugated fasteners, corner blocks and keystones; turn frame over, and fit 1/4" three-ply into the rabbeted edges of the frame; lay the final contour on 1/4" plywood and cut with bandsaw, sabre saw, or keyhole saw; glue contour; and screw in place with 3/4" (no. 8) wood screws. Frame for the groundrow is covered like a flat (see COVERING FLATS) and trimmed to contour. If the groundrow is too tall for transporting, it is divided in the middle with additional stiles and hinged on the face to fold down. Groundrows can be made more quickly and economically by using standard jogs or flats and plugs. Plugs of appropriate sizes are battened to the jog or flat; contour is cut in 3/4" plywood, which is fastened to sides of flat and plugs with keystones and 3/4" (no. 8) wood screws; dutchman the cracks. This type of groundrow is disassembled after show and returned to stock.

GRUNT (bellylugger). A professional colloquial term of derision for a stagehand who is doing very heavy work. Often used to imply no brains, only brawn.

GUNS (prop). Guns to be used on stage should be as small a caliber as feasible (a 22- or 32-caliber gun is preferable). Never fire a blank directly at an actor; stage the action so that the shot can be fired upstage of the actor. Serious

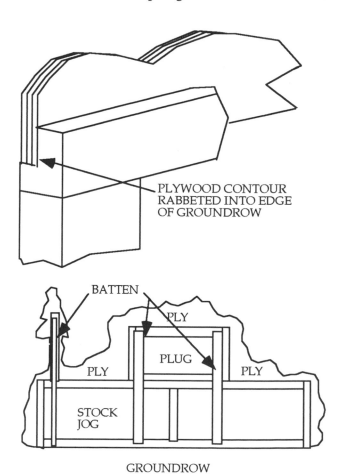

PLYWOOD CONTOUR RABBETED INTO EDGE OF GROUNDROW

BATTEN

PLY

PLUG

PLY

PLY

STOCK JOG

GROUNDROW

powder burns may result from close firing of blanks. Starter guns used at athletic events are generally reliable and more readily available than real revolvers. Guns should be under the care of a single prop person who loads and keeps revolver under personal control until the gun is needed.

GUN SHOT (sound effects). Guns to be used as sound effects offstage should always have blank cartridges, should be handled with care, and should always be pointed down or away from people, costumes, draperies, and scenery when fired. Always inspect cartridges to be used before each show making sure the end of each cartridge is a paper wad rather than a bullet. Serious accidents have resulted when there has been no preliminary inspection. Metal ashcans make excellent resonance chambers to increase the sound of guns. See also SLAPSTICK; SHOTSTICK.

GUTTER. See WIREWAY.

GUY LINE

A rope or wire tied from a pole or high piece of scenery to floor for purposes of steadying or strengthening.

Tension wires (guide lines) fastened from grid to floor on each side of lift curtains. Rings sewn to the edge of the curtain slide on the guy line, keeping curtain in place.

H

HACKSAW. See under SAWS.

HALATION. A halo of light around a spotlight's main beam. Frequently caused by a dirty or dusty lens. See also ABERRATIONS.

HALF-PLUG. A stage plug of half thickness. See also PLUGS, ELECTRICAL.

HALF-ROUND. Molding. Used as trim for doors, windows, baseboards, pictures, etc. Pine or softwood half-round is easier to apply than hardwood half-round. Available in many sizes, designated by diameter, of which the most useful are 1/2", 3/4", and 1 1/2". See also MOLDING.

HALVED JOINT. See **Half lap** under JOINT.

HAMMER. Driving tool. Four types of handles are available for hammers: wood, fiberglass, tubular steel, and solid steel, listed in the order of ease and comfort in handling, with the preference being wood.

Ball peen. Hammer with round head in place of claw, useful for metal work and machine shop work.

Claw, curved. For light work, cabinet work, and scenery construction, the curved claw hammer seems to have a better balance and is easier to use than the straight claw hammer. The most useful weights are the 13- and 16-ounce heads. Hammers with a curved claw make pulling small nails easier.

Claw, straight. Hammer with a straight claw helpful in digging into wood to a driven head. Most useful in wrecking scenery and removing corner blocks. Available in several sizes (16, 20, and 22 ounces).

Mallet. Hammer with wooden or rubber heads, used primarily for striking chisels.

Tack hammer. Hammer with magnetic end, useful for upholstering; 7 ounces is the best weight.

HANDLING FLATS. Illustrations will help explain some of the many ways of raising, lowering, and carrying flats.

Float a flat. To allow a plain flat to fall to the floor with only air resistance to cushion the fall. Place one foot against the bottom rail; check to make sure the floor is clear where the flat is to fall; release the flat. Floating relieves the structural members in flats of all strain or rack. Do not try to float flats with openings.

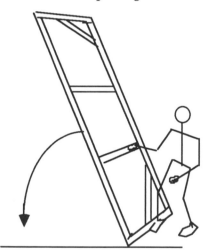

FLOATING A FLAT

Lift a flat, edge up. To raise a flat up from the floor. Raise one side so that flat rests on one stile. One person stands directly in front of the bottom rail with hands on the stile and one foot against the bottom corner; second person starts to lift from top rail and continues following down the stile until the flat is vertical. Person footing at bottom rail controls balance.

Lift a flat, walk up. To raise a heavy flat or wall from the floor. Two or more people foot the flat on the bottom rail; two or more people lift from top rail, transferring to stiles or toggle rails as flat is raised to vertical position. Those who foot can assist in raising by pulling on lash lines.

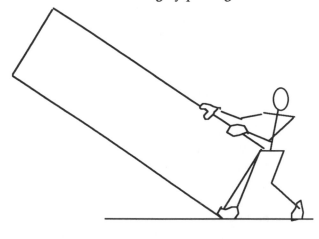

EDGE-UP, SINGLE PERSON

EDGE-UP LIFTING

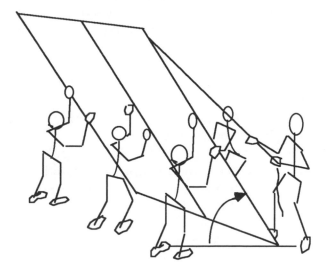

WALK-UP LIFTING

Run a flat. To carry a flat. One person can run most flats. Avoid smudge marks on face of the flat by carrying from the rear. Face in direction of travel; lift with low hand placed on the stile and balance with the other hand as high as possible. If two people are needed to run a heavy flat or a battened wall, the lead person lifts and balances while the tail person pushes and balances, allowing that end of the flat to drag.

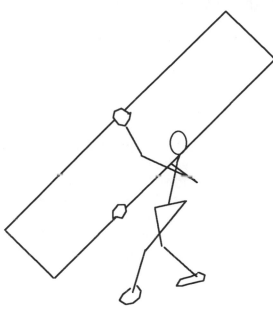

CARRYING A JOG

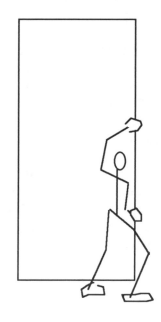

RUNNING A FLAT

HAND PROPS. All properties carried and handled by actors.

HANDRAIL. See BALUSTRADE; BANISTER; NEWEL POST.

HANDSAW. See SAWS.

HAND TOOL. Any tool operated by hand, as opposed to POWER TOOLS. See also TOOLS, HAND.

HANGER
>**Lights.** The pipe or yoke mounting for a SPOTLIGHT.
>**Rigging.** Anything in the FLIES.
>**Scenery.** Colloquial for a painted drop.

HANGER, WORKING. Anything that moves in the FLIES as part of a production.

HANGER IRON (hanging iron). See under STRAP IRON.

HANGING LIGHTS. Physically putting the lights up, cabling the lights, and connecting the control for the lights.

HANGING THE SHOW (the hang). Setting the scenery for a production. Expression originated in the days of wings and drops. See also SET-IN.

HARD LIGHT. A hard-edged light beam from a step or plano convex lens in a spotlight that produces sharp shadows, as opposed to SOFT LIGHT from a diffused source.

HARD SET. A framed set of scenery, which is acoustically reflective, as opposed to a soft set of draperies or drops, which is acoustically absorptive. Composed of flats, wings, and set pieces.

HARDWARE CLOTH (hog wire). A heavy, wire, galvanized fence material that usually has 1/4", 3/8", or 1/2" square holes in the material. Comes in 24", 30", 36", and 48" widths. The material is stiff enough to hold shapes well and is often used for irregular forms such as tree trunks.

HARDWARING FLATS. Applying standard lash and brace cleats to a flat. All flats in stock scenery should carry standard hardware. For description, see FASTENING FLATS: **Lashing.**

HARDWOOD. The wood of a number of broadleaf trees; maple, oak, walnut, and birch are perhaps the most commonly used hardwoods. See also LUMBER; SOFTWOOD.

HAVENS GRIP (Klein tool). A special tool that locks onto a wire rope so it cannot move.

HAZARDOUS WASTE. Most chemicals, solvents, cleaning fluids, thinners, dyes, coolants, and petroleum products are considered hazardous materials, and although it is unusual for a theatre to generate great quantities of these wastes, increasing use of plastics and solvents creates a potential problem. The Environmental Protection Agency (EPA) has developed rules concerning storage and disposition of such waste, and shop management should be aware of the problem and learn proper care. From time to time, directories are published by the state Offices for Hazardous Waste Management, listing regional locations of agencies accepting hazardous materials. Updated information may be obtained by calling the branch office of the EPA in your district. Usually these numbers are listed in the blue pages of the phone directory under U. S. Government Environmental Protection Agency. In many cases, state laws governing hazardous waste are more stringent than those of the federal government, so check locally first.

HAZE EFFECT. See FOG EFFECT; SCRIM.

HEAD (gaffer). A department head.

HEAD BLOCK. See under BLOCK.

HEAD CARPENTER. See **Master carpenter** under STAGE CREW.

HEADER (noun)
>Overhead masking, as part of a portal.
>Beam of an arch or a beam supported by two or more pillars or columns.
>Boxlike enclosure for curtains or draperies on windows (valance). The drapery header is usually suspended by picture hooks or loose-pin hinges and contains either a pole, a stretched wire for curtain hooks or rings, or a commercial traverse rod. See also DRAPERY, SET.

HEADROOM. See **Computer terminology** under LIGHTING CONTROL.

HEADS UP (Command verb). Warning given when letting in flown scenery.

HEARTWOOD. The wood nearest the center of a tree. Since heartwood is apt to be tough and hard, lumber milled from the outer part of the tree is more desirable for scene construction.

HEAT GUN. Hot to very hot blow dryer used to shrink tubing (to make a tight fit; see SHRINK TUBING) or to soften or form plastics. Available

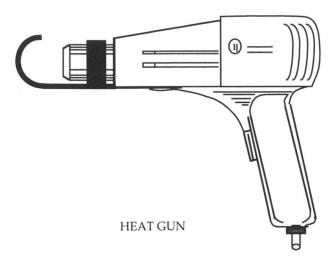

HEAT GUN

at electronic stores. *Warning:* This is not intended for, nor should it ever be used for, drying hair.

HEAT SINK. A mechanical device of metallic fins used to dissipate heat on units that generate heat.

HEAT UP (heat up time). Refers to the time it takes some dimmer controls to make lighting instruments incandescent. This is a major problem with some control units; e.g., if heat up is at a reading of 4 on a 0 to 10 calibrated POTENTI-OMETER, the electrician must bump the control to 4 to get a glow from the light and then start the count to have the light come up to set intensity in the proper time. On some manual control boards, this can become a major problem if each control or handle has a different reading. This was a major problem with SCR dimmers. See **Silicon controlled rectifier** under DIMMER.

HEAVY SHOW. Designation used when one or more of the components (scenery, lights, or costumes) are very large or complicated. Spec shows and Shakespeare productions are often in this category. The play *Our Town* is considered a light technical show because the major backstage components are minimal.

HEDGE. Exterior set piece. Made as a cutout and painted (see GROUNDROW) or made of chicken wire or Styrofoam and covered with colored cloth foliage. Three-dimensional paper hedges are available by the roll or piece in window display stores and can be draped over plugs or frames to create a realistic effect. See also TREE LEAVES.

HEMLOCK. A softwood of the evergreen variety. Wood is passable but not generally recommended for scene construction. See also LUMBER.

HEMP HOUSE. Theatre with a stage using rope rigging for supporting, raising, and lowering scenery. The term stems from the days when theatres were rigged with hemp rope because it was economical and available; manila rope is now used. See also RIGGING; ROPE.

HIGH HAT. See **Top hat** under LIGHT SPILL CONTROL.

HIGHLIGHTING. See **Computer terminology** under LIGHTING CONTROL.

HIGH-SPEED STEEL. A steel made exceptionally hard by adding a high percentage of tungsten. Drills made of high-speed steel will retain temper after becoming red hot and will therefore last longer than other types of drills.

HIGH-TECH SHOW. A show that uses one or more of the modern technologies such as AUTOMATED LIGHTS, CHAIN HOISTS, COMPUTERS, **hardcover flats** (see under FLATS), HYDRAULICS, PNEUMATICS, SCROLLERS, TRUSSES, WINCHES, etc.

HINGES. Fastening devices used for doors, screens, and folding flats (see also FASTENING FLATS). The most useful hinges in scene construction are the following:

  Backflap

   Loose-pin (unswaged). 1 1/2" x 3 1/2" or 2" x 4 1/2" (open dimensions). Used for returns or scenery to be taken apart. Available from scenery supply houses.

   Tight-pin (swaged). Same sizes as loose-pin hinges but hinge cannot be taken apart. Used for flats and doors. Available from scenery supply houses.

  Butt hinge. 1 1/2" wide by 2", 3", or 4" long (open). Used for screens, chests, doors, etc., and secured to the butting surfaces rather than to adjacent sides. Available in hardware stores.

  Friction hinge. Designed to introduce controlled friction in doors and casement windows which swing too freely. Sometimes used on stage doors to keep them opened or closed in position set by actors. Available in hardware stores.

  Piano hinge. A long narrow hinge designed to fasten the top of a grand piano to its sound box. Also used for doors and lids requiring rugged construction and concealed hinges. Available in 6' lengths in the following widths when open: 11/16", 1 1/4", 1 1/2".

Polyhinge. A plastic hinge extruded in continuous length and sold by the foot. Easily cut, nailed, screwed or stapled and considerably cheaper than the piano hinge.

Spring hinge. One-way spring hinges, 2" or 3", are used for screen doors or to keep scenery doors closed. Two-way spring hinges are used on swinging doors; 3" or 4" hinges should be used, depending on the weight of the doors.

Strap hinge. Long hinge of varying sizes; most useful are 1 1/2" x 8" and 2 1/2" x 12" (open). Used for hinging doors and particularly heavy scenery and for fastening door and window casements in place. Pin is often ground out and replaced by bolt or nail to make a loose-pin strap hinge, which is used to fasten platforms and wagons together.

Tee hinge. Used for hinging doors; 4" is most useful size.

HMI (hygerium metallic iodide). An encapsulated high-output arc light of the short-arc variety. Used predominantly for AUTOMATED LIGHTS, FOLLOWSPOTS, and PROJECTORS.

HOG RINGS. Small, round, unclosed rings made of heavy wire sharpened on both ends, used to attach fabrics to metal frameworks.

HOIST. See CHAIN HOIST; WINCH.

HOLE (in a flat). See **Flat patching** under COVERING FLATS.

HOLIDAY. Small spot inadvertently not covered by paint or glue.

HOLOGRAPHY. The science and art of recording radiating points of light (object wave) of something and reconstructing that wave with coherent light (laser) on a projection medium (polyester film, smoke). The film containing the optical information is called a hologram and the projected result is a holographic image.

HONEYCOMB. See under SCENERY PANELS.

HOOD. See **Top hat** under LIGHT SPILL CONTROL.

HOOKS. Fastening devices.

Brace hook. The top metal piece on a STAGE BRACE.

Cable hook. A wire hook on a light standard or ghost light, used to hold surplus cable.

Curtain pole hook. A hook set on the wall with wood screws and used to hold curtain poles

Lead hook (lead carrier). First hook on a traveler or traverse curtain rod. Since lead carriers receive all the strain in opening and closing draw curtains, they should be tied to the second and third hooks of the traveler to avoid failure in case of breakage. See also CARRIER.

Picture hook. 1/16" x 1/2" strap iron bent into a hook on one end and fastened to the back of a picture. Another piece of strap iron is bent into a hook socket and fastened to the flat. Pictures that do not have to be moved can be screwed to flats through their frames. Light-

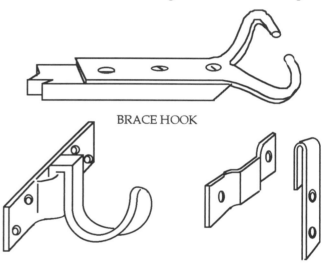

BRACE HOOK

CURTAIN POLE HOOK   PICTURE HOOK

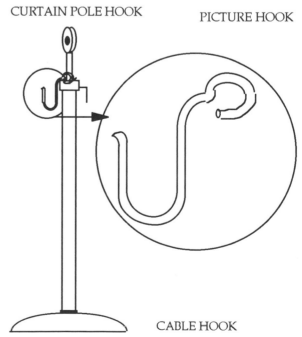

CABLE HOOK

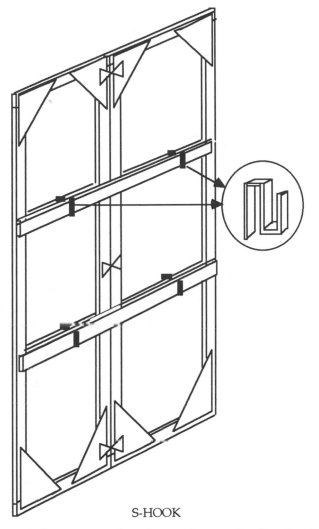

S-HOOK

weight pictures that do not have to be detached can be stapled or tacked through the muslin from behind.

S-hook (keeper hook, batten hook). A small S-shaped strap iron hook used as a quick means of placing a stiffener batten on the back of hinged flats. See illustration.

HORIZON. Use GROUNDROWS to break line of stage floor and cyclorama. Striplights or flood-lights behind the groundrows will add apparent depth.

HORSEPOWER. A unit of power. See MOTOR, ELECTRICAL; ELECTRICITY.

HORSE'S HOOVES (sound effect). Use record-ings or strike coconut shell halves on various surfaces in proper cadence. Variations can be made by striking on floor, sandboxes, gravel, etc.

HOT CIRCUIT. An electrical circuit carrying a current.

HOT LINE. See **Electrical** under LINE.

HOT SPOT. A stage area brighter or "hotter" than others due to uneven distribution of light. Solve this problem by refocusing lights.

HOT WIRE CUTTER. Usually high-resistance Nichrome wire in series with a ballast used to cut Styrofoam. If the wire is heavy enough to hold its shape while cutting, the Styrofoam can be cut in a predetermined shape in the same manner as ripping a board on a table saw.

HOUSE. The auditorium or audience.

HOUSE BOARD. A permanently connected con-trol panel for lights or sound. Usually not used by professional touring shows except for house lights because they carry their own control for lights and sound.

HOUSE LIGHTS. Lights used to illuminate the auditorium. Intensity should be adequate for reading programs, but never glaring. A reading of 10 footcandles is minimum for auditorium illumination.

HOUSING. Outer casing for lighting equipment.

HUE. Designation of color, e.g., red, blue, yellow. See COLOR.

HUM, 60 HERTZ (60-cycle hum). Noise in audio circuit usually caused by close proximity of 120-volt lines.

HYDRAULICS. Use of fluid to power various moving devices. Often controlled by computer. See CYLINDER.

HYDROCHLORIC ACID. Obsolete; formerly used with ammonia to form smoke. Hydrochlo-ric acid is a highly toxic acid. Substitute smoke machines, dry ice, low-pressure steam, etc. See SMOKE EFFECTS. For disposal of dangerous chemicals see HAZARDOUS WASTE.

I

ID. Inside diameter of a pipe or tube.

IDLER

A gear used to transfer power from one gear to another without changing speed or direction.

A floating tension pulley on the floor in a counterweight system. See COUNTER-WEIGHT SYSTEM.

A wheel used to apply pressure to a machine belt, thus maintaining tautness of the belt to prevent slipping.

ILLUMINATION. Surface light intensity expressed in FOOTCANDLES. The human eye adjusts to intensities from 1 to 10,000 footcandles, but degrees of brightness above 100 footcandles are not easily discernible. It is therefore seldom necessary to attempt to illuminate any stage with more than 100 footcandles. A standard light meter may be used to check proper intensity onstage or in the auditorium. See also HOUSE LIGHTS.

IMPROV. An improvisational show. A production that is not scripted.

IN. The set-in of a show as contrasted with the STRIKE or out.

> **Defining stage space:**
>
> **In one.** Space from left to right stage between fire curtain and TORMENTOR.
>
> **In two.** Space from left to right stage between tormentor and first wing.
>
> **In three.** Space from left to right stage between first wing and second wing.
>
> **In four.** Space from left to right stage between second wing and third wing.

INCANDESCENT LAMP. An electric light with a filament that reaches incandescence when an electric current is passed through it. See also LAMPS.

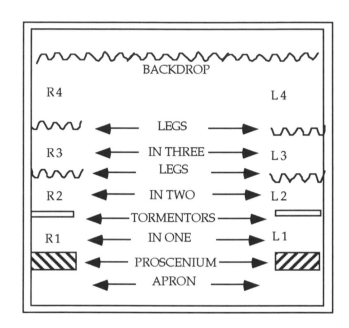

DEFINING STAGE SPACE

INDEPENDENT. A dimmer not controlled by a master, group master, preset, or scene master. Independent of all other controls.

INDEXING. Numeric placement or calibration to find "zero." Putting gobos in the proper place relative to other gobos being used at the same time is particularly necessary with groups of rotating GOBOS.

INDUCTANCE DIMMER. See **Inductor dimmer** under DIMMERS.

INFINITE PRESET. A preset light board with no limit on the number of scenes available. Computer boards are considered to be able to produce an infinite number of scenes; in reality they are limited only by the available memory. See also LIGHTING CONTROL.

INFRARED HEARING SYSTEM. A system using infrared light to transmit onstage sounds to lightweight wireless headphones for hearing-impaired people.

INNER ABOVE. Gallery above the inner stage of an Elizabethan theatre, with a balcony projecting over the audience. In stage directions for Elizabethan theatre, "above" refers to this position. See SHAKESPEAREAN STAGE.

INNER BELOW. A recess or alcove set behind the outer stage on the same level and separated from it by a curtain. See SHAKESPEAREAN STAGE.

INNER PROSCENIUM. See **False proscenium** under PROSCENIUM.

INNER STILE (vertical toggle). Vertical framings for openings in window or door flats. See FLAT.

INSERTING. See **Computer terminology** under LIGHTING CONTROL.

INSET. A small setting placed inside a larger setting. See **Set within a set** under SCENERY, SHIFTING.

INSTRUMENT. Lighting equipment, spotlights, floodlights, etc. are referred to as instruments. See LIGHTING INSTRUMENTS.

INSTRUMENT FUSE (board fuse). Small glass cartridge (automotive type) fuse usually rated at very low amperage, e.g., 1/8 A, 1/4 A, 1/2 A, etc.

INSULATION, ELECTRICAL. Covering made from nonconducting materials such as fabrics, plastics, rubber, etc., used on conductors to prevent short circuiting and to make them safe to handle. See also WIRE, ELECTRICAL.

INTELLABEAM. A brand name of a moving-mirror-type AUTOMATED LIGHT manufactured by High End Systems.

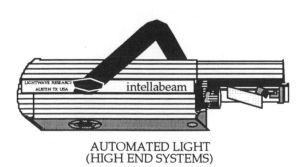

AUTOMATED LIGHT
(HIGH END SYSTEMS)

INTENSITY

Lights. Brightness of light on any given area or from any given instrument. Light intensity depends upon capacity of lamp, quality of lens and reflector, distance of throw, and color media used. Measured in footcandles.

Paint. Degree of purity or saturation of a color.

INTERCOMMUNICATION SYSTEM (abbr. intercom). Many stages require three intercom systems to enable stage managers to keep in touch with all aspects of a production. Matching components are necessary for quality reproduction and trouble-free operation.

Stage manager talk-back system (squawk box, bitch box). Allows communication with the FOH personnel in the lobby and box office and with backstage personnel in a variety of spaces; also allows direct paging of performers in dressing rooms, bathrooms, and green room.

Stage monitor system. Many theatres have a system that broadcasts all dialog from the stage into the various spaces. This is of great benefit to the performers and tends to prevent missed entrance cues. It also helps the stage manager and crew hear the show clearly for their warnings.

Headphone system. A battery/AC-operated headphone system between stage manager and crew is necessary for the warning and execution of cues. This system can be either wired or wireless and can incorporate open speakers along with the headphones. Often this system is used in conjunction with the CUING SYSTEM.

INTERCONNECTING PANELS. Allow the connecting of any control to any load. See PATCH PANEL.

INTERIOR. Any set representing an indoor scene.

INTERLOCK

A safety device on equipment that kills power when an electrical case is opened or will not allow case to be opened until power is off.

The ability of individual dimmers to connect (interlock) into mechanical mastering on older switchboards. See **Mechanical master** under DIMMERS, MASTER.

IONIC COLUMN. See under COLUMNS.

IRIS. An attachment for a spotlight that will vary the diameter of a light beam from closed to wide open. Primary use is to control beam size on an arc light or followspot. See **Arc light** under LIGHTING INSTRUMENTS, SPECIFIC.

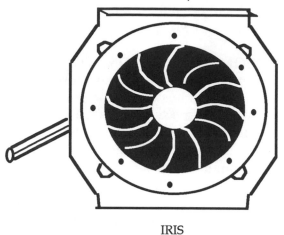

IRIS

IRON. See under STRAP IRON.

IRON-ON FABRICS. Handy method of repairing stage drapes if time is not available to sew up the cut or tear. Good only on small rents.

IRREGULAR PIECES. See BUSHES; GROUND-ROW; PLASTIC SETS; SET PIECES.

ISOMETRIC PROJECTION. See under DRAWINGS.

IVORY BLACK. Originally a black scene paint made by burning ivory in a closed vessel. See also PAINT AND PAINT COLORS.

IZENOUR SWITCHBOARD. A lighting control board invented in 1947 by George Izenour at Yale University, using thyratron tube dimmers. Now superseded by computer boards. See also DIMMERS.

J

JACK

    Scenery. A triangular brace hinged to a flat, groundrow, or set piece and used for rigid support.

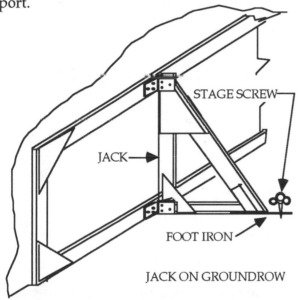

JACK ON GROUNDROW

    Shop. A tool that raises heavy objects with minimum effort.

    Sound. A female audio connector used in SOUND REINFORCEMENT SYSTEMS in place of standard electrical plugs.

JACKKNIFE STAGE. An irregularly shaped wagon pivoting from one corner. See under SCENERY, SHIFTING.

JAMB. One of two uprights in a DOOR or WINDOW casement.

J-BAR. See JOHNSON BAR.

J BOX (jay box). Junction box used by stage electricians for electrical wiring.

J HOOK. See **Cable hook** under HOOKS.

JIG. A guide or TEMPLATE used as an aid in cutting, drilling, fastening or bending material to ensure accuracy and uniformity in duplication.

JIGSAW. See under POWER TOOLS.

JOG

    Drawings. An offset in a **Floor plan**. See under DRAWINGS.

    Scenery. A narrow flat, usually under 30" in width.

JOINT. Place at which two pieces of lumber are fastened together. Types of joints most often used in scene construction include the following:

    Butt joint. Square end butted against side or end of another board. Commonly used in framing flats, usually overlaid with a 1/4" plywood corner block or keystone.

    Dado. A notch cut in the face of one piece of lumber to receive the end of another. Commonly used to give strength to the shelves of a bookcase.

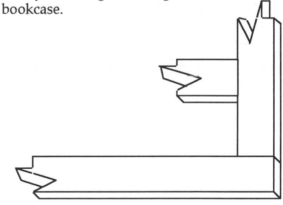

BUTT JOINTS

    Doweled. Aligned and matching holes drilled in two pieces of wood so dowel may be inserted and glued to further strengthen several kinds of joints: butt, miter, mortise and tenon, etc. Commonly used in furniture construction.

    Half lap. Overlapping lumber with half of each thickness cut away. Used for door construction and double-faced flat construction.

Full lap joint. Two pieces of lumber overlapping.

Miter joint. Ends of lumber cut to 45° angle and butted together. Used for moldings and frames. Stronger than **Butt joint.**

Mortise and tenon. A tongue (tenon) cut in one end of lumber and a slot (mortise) cut in side of another piece. Used for framing flats in professional scene construction. Requires special tools but is a strong joint.

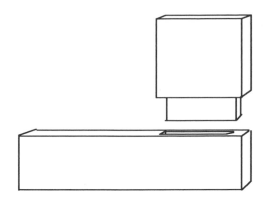

MORTISE AND TENON

Notched joint. A kind of halved joint used primarily for joining verticals and horizontals, e.g., window muntins.

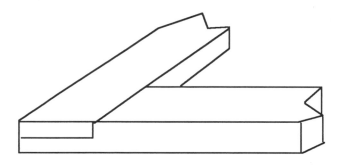

HALF LAP JOINT

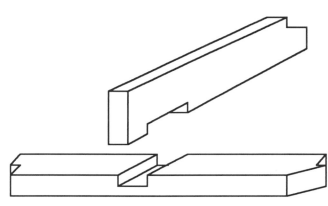

NOTCHED JOINT

Scarf joint. Used for joining lumber end to end to form long lengths. Ends of lumber are either tapered or cut diagonally through the 3" side over an 18" span and then glued and nailed together and reinforced with 1/4" plywood. Lumber may also be joined together for this purpose using an 18"-long diagonal cut through the 1" side; however, this is a weaker joint.

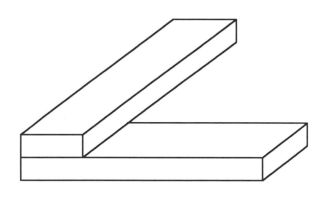

FULL LAP JOINT

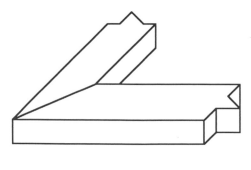

MITER JOINT

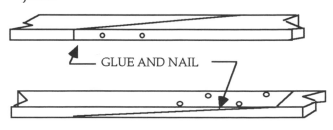

GLUE AND NAIL

SPLICE OR SCARF JOINTS

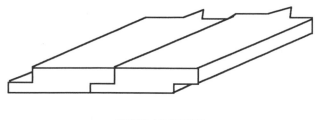

SHIPLAP JOINT

Shiplap joint. Overlapping lumber on the edge with half of each edge cut away. Sometimes used for platform tops but not as strong as plywood or **Tongue and groove.**

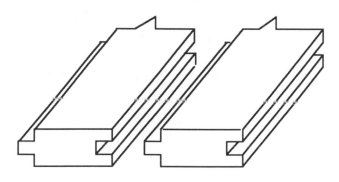

TONGUE AND GROOVE

Tongue and groove (T&G). Boards are bought at the lumber yard with a tongue milled on one edge and a groove milled on the other. Used primarily for flooring, T&G boards make good platform tops.

JOHNSON BAR (J-bar). A wheeled lever tool used for lifting the edges of heavy boxes or equipment. Often used to lift a box without wheels high enough to put a dolly underneath. See also BO-BAR.

JOINTER (planer). See under POWER TOOLS.

JOYSTICK (pan pot). A handle that controls several potentiometers and permits sound to be moved from one speaker to another around the auditorium with a single control. See also SOUND EQUIPMENT.

JUICE. Colloquialism for electricity, power, or the electric department.

JUICER. A colloquial term for stage electrician who works on the lights.

JUMPER. A cable with appropriate connectors used for a temporary connection between two circuits. May also serve as connectors in a PATCH PANEL.

JUNCTION BOX. See J BOX.

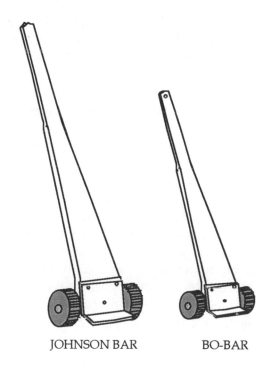

JOHNSON BAR   BO-BAR

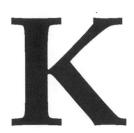

K

KEEPER HOOK. See **S-hook** under HOOKS.

KELVIN SCALE. A temperature scale used to designate color of light by the temperature at its source. Kelvins are the same as centigrade degrees but the starting point is absolute zero (-273° C). Zero degrees centigrade equals 273 kelvins; 100° C equals 373 K. Visible light begins at 600 K. The normal temperature range of gas-filled spotlight lamps is between 2,750 and 3,100 K and the normal range of tungsten halogen and quartz iodine lamps is between 3,000 and 3,400 K. The color of light within this range is compared with the color of sunlight from 40 minutes to 1 hour after sunrise. Warm colors are within the 1,800 to 3,500 K range. Temperatures ranging from 3,500 to 28,000 K progress in color from the palest blue to the blue of a clear daylight sky. See also COLOR TEMPERATURE.

KERF. That part of the wood that is removed by the action of a cutting saw. Depending upon the saw blade in use, kerf is usually 1/8".

KEYHOLE SAW. See under SAWS.

KEY LIGHT (key). The main source of light, establishing direction of illumination, mood, and atmosphere. Since spotlights are highly directional, they are used to provide the key light. See LIGHTING STAGE, PROSCENIUM; FILL LIGHT.

KEYPAD. See **Computer terminology** under LIGHTING CONTROL.

KEYSTONE. A three-ply plywood reinforcement for joints in scene construction. See also **Components** under FLAT.

KEYSTONING. The distortion of an image caused by misalignment of a projector with its reflective surface. When a projector is not in the OPTICAL AXIS of a screen, the image is dis-torted. This distortion often occurs because the projector is below the center of the screen, in which case the image appears larger on the top than on the bottom. The opposite is true if the projector is above the center of the screen. If the projector is to the left, the image is larger on the right side and smaller on the left. Solution is to align the axis. See also PROJECTED SCENERY.

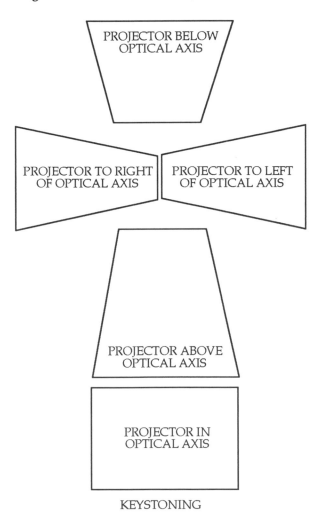

PROJECTOR BELOW OPTICAL AXIS

PROJECTOR TO RIGHT OF OPTICAL AXIS

PROJECTOR TO LEFT OF OPTICAL AXIS

PROJECTOR ABOVE OPTICAL AXIS

PROJECTOR IN OPTICAL AXIS

KEYSTONING

KEYWAY. A slot in a shaft cut to match a slot in the hub of a wheel or pulley. A small piece of metal, a key, is inserted in the aligned slots, locking wheel or pulley to shaft.

KICKING BLOCKS. Moving loft blocks overhead by loosening the bolts and moving (kicking) the block a few inches for more clearance. See also **Kick-up block** under BLOCK.

KILL (Command verb)

    Acting. To delete a line of the script.

    Lights. To turn off lights.

    Prop. To strike a prop from the scene.

KILOWATT (Abbr. kW). A unit of power equal to 1,000-watts. Spotlights are often identified by their kilowatt power: a 1,000-watt spotlight is called a 1 kW or an ace; a 1,500-watt spotlight is a 1 1/2 kW or an ace and a half; a 2,000-watt spotlight is a 2 kW or a deuce; a 3,000-watt spotlight is a 3 kW or a tray.

KILOWATT HOUR (abbr. kWh). Electricity is sold by the kilowatt hour, equal to 1,000-watts expended over a period of 1 hour.

KLIEGLIGHT. First theatre lighting word accepted in general dictionaries. A high intensity light using the arc between two carbon electrodes as a light source. Also a trade name for equipment manufactured by Kliegl Brothers. Sometimes used as a synonym for any bright light. See also GENERIC TERMS.

KLIEGSUN. Obsolete; trade name for a narrow-beam projector spot.

KNIFE

    Electrical work. A pocketknife with a sharp blade is used for cutting insulation and a dull blade is used for stripping wire. A combination knife with a screwdriver blade may also be useful.

    Paint. Knives with interchangeable blades are most useful: razor blades with handles, X-ACTO KNIVES, mat knives.

    Shop. Tool for cutting, stripping, and trimming.

KNIFE SWITCH. Obsolete. See under SWITCHES.

KNOCKER, DOOR (sound effect). Offstage door knockers are made of strap hinges. Hinge is fastened to door or offstage wall, and bolt is placed in one end to act as a handle. Ornate cutouts of plywood can be bolted to hinge for onstage use.

KNOTS. Ties for specific uses.

    Bow. Used to tie draperies and curtains to pipe battens.

    Bowline. Used on ceiling plates, sandbags, or whenever line passes through an eye or ring. The bowline will not slip and is easily untied.

    Clove hitch. Used for pipe or wooden battens or poles of any kind, must be terminated in a half hitch or it is worthless.

    Half hitch. A knot used as a binder for several other knots or hitches. A clove hitch must be terminated with a single or double half hitch or it will slip.

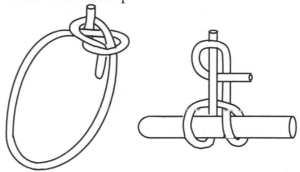

BOWLINE   CLOVE WITH A HALF HITCH

    Prusik knot. Pressure knot used to tie a sandbag to a set of lines.

    Safety hitch. Pressure knot used to tie a safety line around set of lines or on the two lines of the counterweight overhaul line. Knot may also be used to marry lines together.

    Sheet bend. Used to tie together two ropes of different sizes or materials.

    Square knot. Used to tie together two ropes of the same size and material.

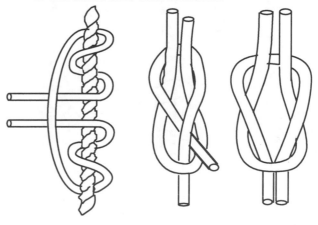

PRUSIK KNOT   SHEET BEND   SQUARE KNOT

Stopper hitch. Pressure knot used to tie lines together to attach another line or weight.

Sunday knot. A knot used to fasten two ends of a cable or wire rope together without putting a kink in the wire, used to attach a sandbag to a set of lines in professional theatre.

Tie-line knot. A simple loop knot used to fasten short ties to grommets in a drop.

Tie-off, pin rail. A figure-eight around a belaying pin with top half hitch and bottom half hitch taken to dress lines.

Tie-off, lash. Used as a final tie for lashing flats. The lash tie-off is part bowknot and can be untied quickly.

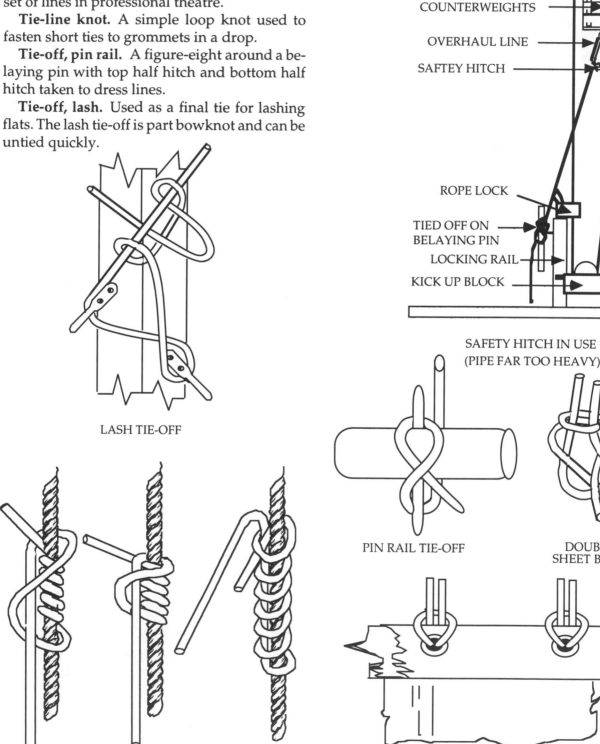

TURNBUCKLES

ARBOR

COUNTERWEIGHTS

OVERHAUL LINE

SAFTEY HITCH

ROPE LOCK

TIED OFF ON
BELAYING PIN

LOCKING RAIL

KICK UP BLOCK

LASH TIE-OFF

SAFETY HITCH IN USE
(PIPE FAR TOO HEAVY)

PIN RAIL TIE-OFF

DOUBLE
SHEET BEND

STOPPER HITCH

SAFETY

TIE-LINE KNOTS

Teamster's hitch (trimming hitch). Used as a cinching knot to obtain a mechanical advantage without using a pulley.

kW. See KILOWATT.

SUNDAY KNOT

SUNDAY

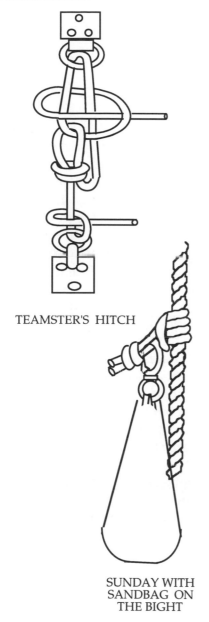

TEAMSTER'S HITCH

SUNDAY WITH
SANDBAG ON
THE BIGHT

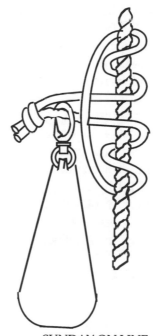

SUNDAY ON LINE
WITH PRUSIK KNOT
AND HOOK FOR SANDBAG

L

LACQUER. A quick-drying clear or opaque finish. See under PAINTS, MISCELLANEOUS.

LADDERS. Ladders are essential equipment in any theatre. Good wood ladders are usually preferred because they are not electrical conductors and they do not become slippery if liquid gets on them. Always purchase the best ladders available and make sure they are rated for heavy people, 250 pounds at least.

A-ladder. Ladder shaped like an "A" with straight extendable section in the center, most useful for work on light borders set for high prosceniums. A-ladders are available in heights from 20' to 40' and are often mounted on dollies. Check ladders periodically, tighten loose bolts, peen loosened rivets, and discard ladders that cannot be repaired. Broken ladders are dangerous. See also GENIE LIFT.

Extension ladder. Not often needed, but handy to have one at least 24'.

Step ladder. Most useful sizes are 6', 8', 10', 12', and 16'.

LADDERS, LIGHTING. A ladderlike pipe arrangement from which LIGHTING INSTRUMENTS are hung. The ladder is often suspended on two sets of lines from overhead. See also **Flying booms** under LIGHT MOUNTING DEVICES.

LAG, TIME. See TIME LAG.

LAG SCREW (lag bolt). See under SCREWS.

LAMPBLACK. See under PAINT AND PAINT COLORS.

LAMP DIP (colorine). Lacquer used to color light bulbs. Commercial lamp dips are available in many colors for lamps of lower wattages. Bulbs are dipped briefly while burning. Dipped bulbs are suitable for strip lights and older types of footlights and border lights. Heat generated by lamps of 100 watts or more causes flaking of lacquer. Boiling caustic soda will remove faded or chipped lamp dip, preparing lamp for recoloring. Most colors are now available in special factory colored lights that will not fade or chip. Available from theatre supply houses.

LAMPLIGHT EFFECT. Although lamplight is actually yellow, it is usually represented on the stage by amber colors. Practical lamps used as props should be electrified with concealed wire if stationary or with batteries if movable. Flashlight batteries and flashlight lamps are generally sufficient. Modern electric lamps should use 25- to 40-watt bulbs to avoid distracting intensities. Supplement area lighted by a lamp with overhead spotlights. Lamps to be turned on or off on cue should be on the same circuit as supplementary light so the electrician can control and synchronize area light as an actor fakes cue. See also LANTERNS.

LAMPS (lights, bulbs, globes, etc.)

Arc type. An encapsulated high-output arc light. Used predominantly for automated lights, projectors, and followspots. See HMI; XENON LAMP.

XENON ARC LAMP

Incandescent. Lamps for theatrical lighting equipment. Catalogue designations for lamps carry all pertinent information, including wattage, shape of bulb, maximum diameter, and base type. Lamp codes are as follows: first number indicates wattage; first letter, shape of bulb; second number, size of bulb diameter in eighths

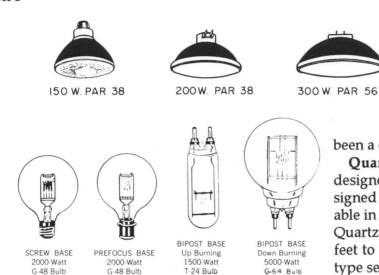

150 W. PAR 38   200W. PAR 38   300 W. PAR 56

150W. R40

500W. R40

SCREW BASE
2000-Watt
G-48 Bulb

PREFOCUS BASE
2000-Watt
G-48 Bulb

BIPOST BASE
Up Burning
1500-Watt
T-24 Bulb

BIPOST BASE
Down Burning
5000-Watt
G-64 Bulb

LAMPS

of an inch (T-20 is a tubular bulb 20/8" [2 1/2"] in diameter). Any number following is generally the manufacturer's code number. After coded designations, most catalogues list lamp base, volts, filament, approximate hours of life, lumens, etc. Lighting instruments are designed for lamps of a given size, shape, wattage, and lamp base, although in some cases sizes and wattages can be interchanged. Buy lamps according to the recommendations of manufacturers of lighting equipment. Burn lamps according to the position recommended on the bulb in order to realize the maximum rated hours of life. ANSI designations, three-letter codes identifying similar lamps made by different manufacturers, are the most common method of identification for quartz and halogen lamps. Lamps for theatre use tend to be appropriated from other industries; e.g., airplane landing lights were picked up by theatre for their high-intensity and long throw capabilities. This trend has

been a constant from the beginning.

Quartz iodine (QI). Used in instruments designed for quartz lamps or in adaptors designed to fit other types of instruments. Available in most wattages, from 300 to 3,000 watts. Quartz lamps are designed for throws from 25 feet to 125 feet and over, depending upon the type selected. The lamp is designed to burn in any position and has a long life. On occasion QI refers to a spotlight containing quartz lamps.

Tungsten-halogen (TH). Originally the quartz-halogen, the lamp no longer uses quartz but rather hard glass. The TH lamp is often still referred to by the quartz light designation. The TH has good uniformity of light output and an excellent life expectancy compared with other lamps. Conversion lamps designed to fit older units are available, converting older conventional spotlights to quartz lights. Available for ellipsoidal, fresnels, scoops, border lights, and followspots. *Warning:* Do not touch the glass envelope of the lamp with bare fingers; the oil of the skin will allow a hot spot to develop and will substantially shorten the lamp life. These lamps use ANSI designations.

Bases. Metal portion of lamp fitting into a socket. Most bases are available in the following sizes: candelabra, intermediate, medium (standard), and mogul. Medium (med.) and mogul (mog.) are the most commonly used for stage lighting instruments. Most bases, except screw, give positive orientation of filament to optical system.

Bipost base. Two pronged base used in spotlights and projectors; gives positive orientation of filament to optical system.

Mogul end prong. Used only on larger PAR lamps.

Prefocus base. Used in spotlights and projectors; gives positive orientation of filament to optical system.

Screw base. Used in some older spot-

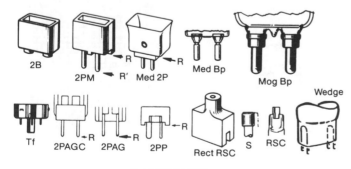

2B   2PM   R' Med 2P   Med Bp   Mog Bp   Wedge

Tf   2PAGC   2PAG   2PP   Rect RSC   S   RSC

LAMP BASES

lights, but primarily used in floodlights, border lights, footlights, and strip lights.

TH bases. A wide variety of specialty bases are in use for ANSI-designated tungsten-halogen lamps. See illustration.

Bulbs. Glass portion of lamp housing filament. Bulbs are available in many different shapes.

Globular (G-type). Generally used in older spotlights; available in 100- to 2,000-watt ratings. Generally of longer life than T-types.

Parabolic reflector spot, PAR. PAR is an abbreviation for a parabolic aluminized reflector, which is built into the bulb, thereby directionalizing the beam of light and increasing efficiency. Originally called Birdseye lamps after their inventor, Clarence Birdseye. PAR lamps are available in many sizes (size is measured by lamp diameter in eighths of an inch; the Par 38, 46, 56, and 64 are the most popular),150- to 1,000-watt capacities, and several beam widths (narrow spot, medium flood, and wide flood). Housings, available for all four sizes, include yokes and color media holders. PAR 200-, 300-, and 500-watt lamps require special sockets. See **PARcans** under LIGHTING IN-STRUMENTS, FIXED FOCUS.

Pear-shaped (PS). Often used in older strip lights, footlights, and border lights; 500- and 1,000-watt olivettes usually use PS lamps. Generally of longer life than T-type.

Reflector (R-type). Used in border lights, strip lights, and footlights. Available clear (in 75-, 150-, and 300-watt sizes) or in color (75- and 150-watt sizes).

Tubular (T-type). Used for spotlights and projectors; available in 300- to 10,000-watt capacities.

LANDING SCENERY. Lowering hanging scenery to the floor.

LANTERNS (props). Electrify lanterns with flashlight batteries and bulbs. Small flashlights or penlights can be used intact in certain types of lanterns or torches, but small batteries have a short life. Period lanterns can be made by perforating tin cans and attaching funnel or cardboard tops. A ring in the top serves as a handle for carrying.

LAP JOINT. See **Half lap** under JOINT.

LAP SEALER. A plastic material used to hide and sometimes glue joints in 3-dimensional units.

LASER. Light amplification by stimulated emission of radiation. A device that converts electromagnetic radiation of mixed frequency to a frequency of highly amplified, COHERENT, visible radiation.

LASER SIMULATOR (mock laser light). Very narrow beam light produced with dichroic filters for pure color and used for fast panning and tilting. The simulation light does not have the inherent dangers associated with the LASER. These instruments are often produced by the AUTOMATED LIGHT manufacturers.

LASH. To fasten flats together with a rope and lash cleats. See **Lashing** under FASTENING FLATS.

LASH CLEAT. See **Lashing** under FASTENING FLATS.

LASH EYE. See **Lashing** under FASTENING FLATS.

LASH LINE. See **Lashing** under FASTENING FLATS.

LATCH, RIM. A door latch commonly used on the stage. See under DOOR.

LATCHES. Catches devised to hold doors closed. Standard latches include cabinet, magnetic, friction, spring, and screen door latches. The standard rim latch is preferred.

LATHE. See under POWER TOOLS.

LAUAN. See MAHOGANY, PHILIPPINE.

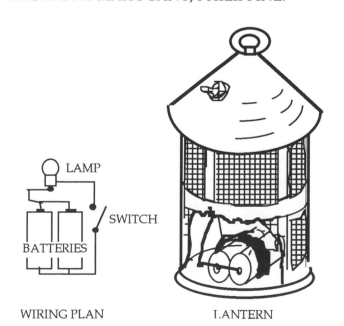

WIRING PLAN   LANTERN

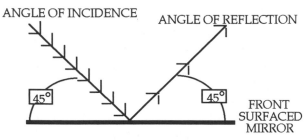

ANGLE OF INCIDENCE   ANGLE OF REFLECTION

45°   45°   FRONT
                                           SURFACED
                                           MIRROR

LAW OF REFLECTION

LAW OF REFLECTION. The angle of incidence equals the angle of reflection.

LAW OF SQUARES

Light intensity. The intensity of light decreases in inverse proportion to the square of the distance from the source. **Example:** If a source produces 32 footcandles at a 1' distance, the same source will produce 8 footcandles at a 2' distance (32 ftc/2' x 2'), and 2 footcandles at 4' (32 ftc/ 4' x 4').

Dimmer curve. Said to be square law when the specified readings on the control calibrations produce apparent corresponding readings in light intensity. The controller "zero" reading for a standard square law curve is typically about 12 1/2 volts.

LAY

Cable. Putting electrical cable or wire rope in a particular place or path.

Fabric. Gluing down fabric such as muslin or canvas very smoothly on a flat frame.

Rope. The direction that rope fibers rotate around a core.

LAYOUT (cartoon). To enlarge and transfer a design from a drawing or blueprint to full scale. Layout work is usually done by squaring drawing to scale and squaring flats or surface at 2' intervals to receive the transfer. Intersection points are plotted, and lines are filled in freehand. See illustrations on next page. See also **Cutout drop** under DROPS.

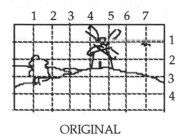

ORIGINAL

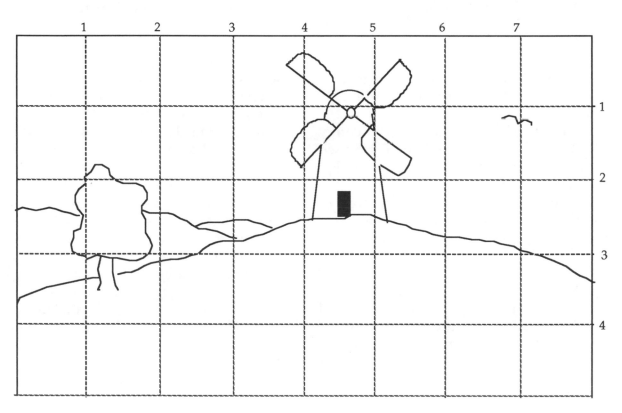

ENLARGEMENT

LCL (abbr. light center length). Used in lamp catalogues to indicate distance between the center of the lamp filament and the part of the base that seats on the socket.

LEAD BLOCK. See under BLOCK.

LEAD CARRIER (LEAD HOOK). The first rolling hook on each side of a traveler, which pulls the rest of the curtain open or closed. See also TRAVELER.

LEAD HOOK (LEAD CARRIER). See under HOOKS.

LEAF BORDERS. See TREE LEAVES.

LED. An acronym for light-emitting diode.

LEG

    Electrical. One side of an electrical line.

    Scenery

       Drop. The side masking of CYCLORAMA DRAPES.

       Flats. Parts of a door flat extending to the floor.

       Platforms. Supports for step units, platforms, etc.

       Touring. A particular section of a touring company's schedule.

LEG DROP. See under DROPS.

LEGITIMATE (Legit). A live production as opposed to a taped, movie, or television production.

LEG UP. To raise a platform, parallel, or ground-row by fastening temporary legs to last for the run of a play.

LEKOLIGHT (Leko). Trade name for a Century (now Strand) ellipsoidal spotlight. Often used as a generic term for any manufacturer's ellipsoidal reflector spotlight.

LENSES. Transparent glass or plastic ground or cast to change the direction of the light rays passing through. Lenses used in spotlights are generally made of crown glass, cast and polished but not corrected. Lenses are designated by diameter and focal length; thus, a 6" x 8" lens is 6 inches in diameter with an 8-inch focal length. Focal length (distance from the center of the lens to the point where rays converge) can be roughly determined by holding the lens in direct sun, adjusting until the sharpest point of light is determined, and measuring the distance from point to lens. Thicker lenses have shorter focal lengths. Range of focus in a spotlight is between lens and focal point. Short focal lengths are more desirable for short throws and long focal lengths for long throws. Combined focal length of two lenses used together is determined by the equation $(F1 \times F2) / (F1 + F2 - D) = F$, in which $F1$ = focal length of first lens, $F2$ = focal length of second lens, and D = distance between lenses in inches. **Example:** A lens with a 4" focal point used with a lens with a 6" focal point at a distance of 2" results in a combined focal length of $(4" \times 6") / (4" + 6" - 2") = 24" / 8" = 3"$. Adaptors designed to change the focal point of certain spotlights are available, though the use of zooms (variable focal length lenses) is a more practical solution if purchasing new equipment.

f number. In photographic equipment the amount of light allowed through the lens is a variable controlled by an iris. The f number describes the focal length of the lens divided by its effective diameter as controlled by the iris. A 6" x 12" spotlight lens would then be 12/6, or f 2, if the entire diameter of the lens is used.

Fast lens. A lens capable of transmitting a large amount of light. Generally speaking, a short focal length.

Slow lens. A lens capable of transmitting a small amount of light. Generally speaking, a long focal length.

Fresnel lens. See also **Fresnel spotlight** under LIGHTING INSTRUMENTS, SPECIFIC. Named for the French physicist Augustin-Jean Fresnel, and developed for stage use in the early 1930s. The lens is reduced in thickness by cutting out concentric rings and stepping them back toward the plane as illustrated, so that shorter focal lengths result without increasing the thickness of the glass. Thinner lenses reduce weight and reduce the danger of cracking through exposure to heat, thus making possible higher wattage spotlights in more compact housings. To eliminate the color aberration caused by the risers of a Fresnel lens, the plane

FRESNEL LENS

surface is given a slight waffle pattern to diffuse the light. Light from fresnel equipment is therefore soft-edged, diffused light, limiting the use of such equipment to the stage proper.

Objective lens. The lens or lenses in a projector used to focus a slide on a screen. The objective lens usually consists of two lenses mounted in a tube in fixed relation to each other but capable of moving closer to or away from the slide, thus sharpening focus.

Plano-convex lens (PC lens). Plane on one side and convex on the other, the plano-convex lens gives a sharp-edged light that is ideal for beam, booth, and balcony positions. See also **Plano-convex spotlight** under LIGHTING INSTRUMENT, SPECIFIC.

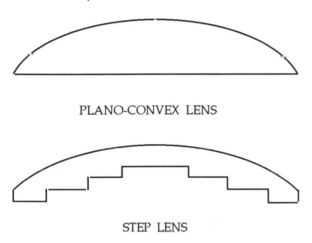

PLANO-CONVEX LENS

STEP LENS

Step lens. The reverse of the fresnel lens, the step lens has risers placed on the plane side of the lens, leaving convex side with its original curve. Step lenses (available with or without black risers to reduce color aberration and spill) are lightweight and heat resistant and produce a hard-edged light suitable for beam, booth, or balcony positions. Many ellipsoidal spotlights are equipped with step lenses, but a sharper focus is obtained with a double plano convex lens system.

Zoom lens. A system of lenses in which focal length can be changed either manually or electrically. The advantage is more flexibility in using spotlights. Lights may work equally well from the balcony rail or the first electric, depending on size of house and stage. See also ZOOM LENS.

LEVEL

Lights. Intensity of light, often referred to either by percentage or by calibrated scale reading.

Scenery. A platform or parallel or any raised acting area on stage is commonly referred to as a level.

Tool. A straight edge frame in which vials of liquid are placed to determine precise vertical and horizontal planes. A 24" level is the most useful in the shop.

LID. Colloquial for top of a platform, ceiling of a set, etc.

LIFT. Any telescoping tower or boom that lifts people or equipment. Lifts may be powered by handcrank, pneumatics, hydraulics, or electricity. See also GENIE LIFT.

LIFTING SCENERY. See HANDLING FLATS.

LIFT JACK. See under SCENERY, SHIFTING.

LIGHT BRIDGE. A narrow, metal catwalk placed in the first border or first electric position and used for mounting lighting instruments. Bridges are usually counterweighted and controlled by either motor or winch. With a light bridge, electricians have the advantage of being able to mount instruments from the floor, raise the bridge to prescribed height, and focus from the light bridge, eliminating much ladder-work.

LIGHT 'EM UP. See FIRE UP.

LIGHTENING HOLES (Swiss cheesing). Holes cut into large pieces of plywood or metal in order to lighten the weight of the item.

LIGHTING ACCESSORIES. See **C-clamp** and **Yoke clamp** under **CLAMP**; LIGHT SPILL CONTROL; LIGHT MOUNTING DEVICES; PLUGS, ELECTRICAL.

LIGHTING BACKINGS. Entrances and exits should always be lighted unless otherwise mentioned in the script. Small floods, spotlights, or PAR units are sufficient for most purposes, but larger spots or projector beams are necessary when an intense light is needed. Lighting from overhead is often achieved with a WIZARD. Avoid parallel lighting of backings that will show imperfections on the surface of flats. Use colors as dictated by motivation or by pattern chosen for stage lights. See also LIGHTING STAGE, PROSCENIUM; LIGHTING COLORS.

LIGHTING COLORS

Border lights (toning lights). In theory, the primary colors of light (red, blue, and green) in equal intensities will give a white light. However, perfect conditions for this are seldom found outside laboratories. Because of variables found on stage (impurities of color, yellow inherent in the incandescent lamp, reds appearing when lamps are used at low intensity, and variations in light transmission of media) and because of light loss due to density of pure colors (up to 95 percent), many technicians prefer to use the so-called dilute primaries. These colors include medium blue, medium green, and light red. Varying intensities of these three colors will produce a wide range of colors on stage. Secondary colors of magenta, blue green, and amber are sometimes used in border lights, but the spectral range of this combination is limited. The table below gives the code numbers for these colors as listed by four of the larger color media companies: Olesen Company's Dura brand, Lee Filters, Rosco Laboratories' Roscogel, and Strand Electric Company's Cinemoid. These companies make many hues of color media; these are just a few examples.

	Olesen	Lee	Rosco	Strand
Primaries				
Red	025	106	224	506
Blue	049	120	264	520
Green	071	139	274	539
Secondaries				
Magenta	039	113	237	513
Blue green	057	116	276	516
Amber	018	105	214	533
Dilute primaries				
Light red	024	164	221	*
Medium blue	055	118	257	518
Medium green	070	124	271	523

*No light red offered by Strand; use primary red.

Cyclorama colors. Sky cycs are best lighted with enough hanging floodlights, border lights, or scoops to cover the cyc completely in the colors necessary for the play, plus strip lights or floodlights on the floor to provide horizon light. Lights on the floor should be in at least two circuits, preferably three circuits, in order to provide sufficient color change for sunrises or sunsets. Horizon lights are placed close enough to the cyc to permit the use of primary or dilute primary colors. The table below gives the manufacturer code numbers for several colors that can be used in overhead floods. It is understood that many other combinations are satisfactory, and electricians will find through experience other effective colors to set mood, time, or season.

Scene and color	Olesen	Lee	Rosco	Strand
Daylight sky				
Daylight blue	053	117	251	540
Steel blue	047	141	254	541
Night sky				
Urban blue	055	120	264	520
Moonlight blue	056	116	258	516

For changing skies, three circuits of primaries or dilute primaries can also be used in overhead position if sufficient equipment is available.

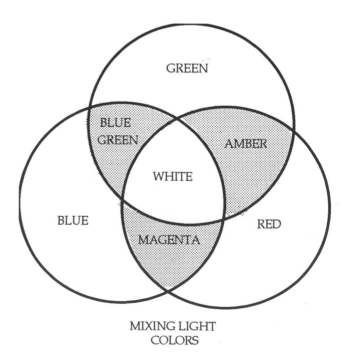

MIXING LIGHT
COLORS

Spotlight colors. Since the function of spotlights is to light actors, colors are chosen that will allow a high degree of light transmission. Colors suitable for area lighting include light pink, light amber, light straw, light blue, light lavender, light gray, and light chocolate. Darker shades of straw and amber tend to turn skin pigments yellow. Most flattering and youthful colors include pink, lavender, and light blue. It is present practice to use warm colors on one side and cool colors on the other, leaving a wide variety of combinations to the electrician's or lighting designer's choice. The chart below gives a few widely used combinations with their manufacturer code numbers.

Scene and color	Olesen	Lee	Rosco	Strand
Bright day				
Flesh pink	030	153	226	553
Light straw	009	103	205	550
Day				
Lavender	044	136	242	536
Light scarlet (bastard amber)	027	152	202	552
Dark day				
Gray	075	211	280	560
Chocolate	073	156	281	556
Warm				
Flesh pink	030	153	226	553
Light scarlet (bastard amber)	027	152	202	552
Night				
Light blue	053	118	250	518
Light scarlet (bastard amber)	027	152	202	552

LIGHTING CONTROL

Equipment. There are four major categories of boards: switchboards, light boards, control boards, and consoles. These boards can be further categorized as DIMMERS, numbered presets, or infinite presets.

Switchboard. The oldest type of board. Originally a group of knife switches; later resistance dimmers were added; and finally mechanical interlock mastering and submastering were integrated into the units. See DIMMERS; SWITCHBOARDS.

Light board (board). Control panels mechanically linked to the dimmers; see picture of Luxtrol board with autotransformers and older piano board with resistance dimmers. See DIMMERS; SWITCHBOARDS.

Preset. From two scene units to multiscene units, this board uses the submasters, faders, split faders, and masters to produce flexibility and movement from one scene to another. These boards are now made as control boards; previously, they were made as consoles.

MICRO-SET BOARD   (ELECTRO CONTROLS)

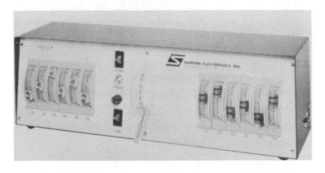

TWO SCENE CONTROL STATION (SKIRPAN)

Microprocessor (computer boards). These compact devices can be added to most electronic dimmers with an interface. Usually they consist of dimmers, memory, keypads, assorted faders, submasters, masters, and readouts or a CRT. The ability to create cues, record and save cues, play back cues, and be assigned to all kinds of control make the microprocessor a truly flexible device to work with. Many accessories are available: printers for hard copy, designer remotes, electrician's remote, self-diagnostic tests, special effects units, etc. Available in both control boards and consoles.

Control board (board). This is the remote control board, preset, or microprocessor that is not built into a piece of furniture or desk. The remote control board is usually smaller and

Console. This is a remote control unit preset or microprocessing device built into a desk-type unit and incorporating some of the following: controllers, keyboards, faders, memory units, and one or more monitors.

Control locations. The oldest locations are on downstage right or left near the proscenium wall, in an out-of-the-way space or room (even in the basement), or in the orchestra pit. Recent locations are in back of the audience on the main auditorium floor or in a special booth in the rear of the auditorium either on the main floor or on a balcony.

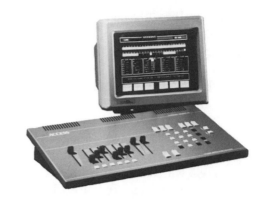

ACCESS (GREAT AMERICAN MARKET)
COMPACT CONTROL BOARD

AUTOCUE (SKIRPAN)

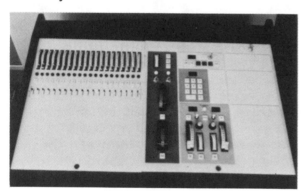

MEMO-Q CONTROL BOARD
(CENTURY STRAND)

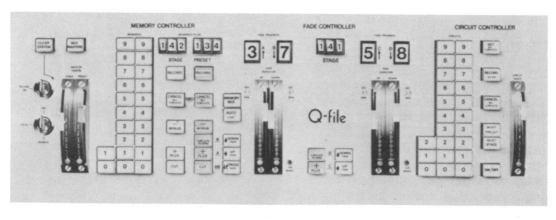

Q-FILE MEMORY SYSTEM CONTROL PANEL (KLIEGL)

Computer terminology. See also AUTO-MATED LIGHT CONTROL.

Address. Refers to a fixture, instrument, or luminaire.

Audio connectors. Inputs and outputs used to connect **MIDI interface;** see below.

Backup. An auxiliary that allows a takeover (usually manual) in case the primary system malfunctions completely. On some systems the backup is actually another microprocessor separate from the primary one.

Blind recording. A method of programming a board without actually seeing the lighting on a stage. Often used as a starting point and then modified during rehearsal.

Channel. An individual control unit. Often used to describe the size of a system e.g., 60 channels in use on a 120 channel system.

Clear. To erase a given unit of information.

Command. An order given by typing instructions on the keyboard or by hitting specific command keys on the keyboard.

Computer board (microprocessor). A lighting control system with a microprocessor at its heart. Usually associated with memory systems.

Contactor. Remote, electromagnetically controlled switch.

Controller. Usually a small potentiometer used to control one or more groupings of dimmers, controllers, or channels. Loosely it means the control of dimmers to some electricians.

Cross-fade. The process of simultaneously fading one cue out and another cue in.

Cross-fader. A device, often a dimmer, used to fade one cue out as a second cue fades in.

CRT. An acronym for cathode-ray tube.

Default. User or manufacturer settings for various functions to which the computer always returns unless changed.

Delay. Holding or stopping a cue movement for a prescribed effect. A concept often associated with a split fader.

Delete. Remove a given cue, group of cues, or parts within a cue.

Diagnostics. The ability of a computer board to self-test its many functions and controls.

Display (mimic, CRT, monitor, screen). A screen (cathod ray tube) on which information is viewed. See also SOUND EQUIPMENT; TV; VIDEO EQUIPMENT.

Error. Caused when the computer has a problem with the manner in which input is given or has an internal problem in reading the software. May also occur due to computer malfunction.

Fade profile (profile fade). The ability of some control boards or consoles to shape a fade up or down in a nonlinear manner. With this capability a designer may have fades that start slowly and speed up to a slam out, all done by the machine and thus able to be re-created for every performance. See **Real-time fades.**

Floppy disk (floppy). A record used to store and to retrieve data from a microprocessor board.

Glitch (surge). A power fluctuation that, in the case of computer or microprocessor light controls, may be the equivalent of a random command, causing control boards to act unpredictably. The use of a line or surge filter will often help alleviate glitches and power surges.

Headroom. The amount of space available left in memory. See **Memories available.**

Inserting. Adding additional cues within existing cues. See **Part.**

Keypad. A method of controlling computers by using a grouping of keys having both numbers and symbols on them.

Level wheel (wheel). A device that acts like a potentiometer with no stops. Used to raise or lower intensity of individual or groups of channels. Often used in prerecording or playback situations.

Library.

A method of storing switchboard information on either floppy disks or tapes. Not all electronic boards have this capability.

A predetermined value or a group of settings stored for instant recall.

Term can also be used in computers for a macro, a repeatable method of implementing a preference or command.

Live recording. Setting up a viewed lighting situation on stage and then recording it. See also **Blind recording.**

Locked. A method of protecting a recorded cue on a disk or tape from being wiped out or accidentally recorded over. A key switch is often used for this purpose. Floppy disks can also be locked so cues cannot be recorded over.

Manual override. The ability to switch to manual control at any time during a cue or even before a cue is a very necessary feature of any automated board.

Memories available. The number of cues available for use or, depending upon the system, the number of cues used up. Sometimes this is referred to in percentage of memory rather than number of cues.

Memory limit. Some light control systems are equipped with an override feature that allows the operator to delete certain portions of the memory of a cue temporarily. This may be used, for example, to turn off one instrument that has been accidentally knocked out of focus.

MIDI interface. A method of using music to control a lighting computer.

Mode. An operational function to give certain commands or view displays. Patch, master, submaster, and record are considered modes of operation.

Monitor. The viewing screen of a computer or TV.

Multiplexing. Sending the control signals from computer to dimmers by one or two cables rather than over individual dimmer control wires.

Optical dimming. Using a mechanical DOUSER remotely to increase or dim light intensity in an arc-type lamp.

Page (cue page, cue sheet). A series of cues shown on the display screen of an electronic board is referred to as a page.

Pages. Cues or scenes.

Part. A method of adding different components within a cue. In nondigital devices when cues or parts of cues were added the method was cue 1, cue 1a, cue 1b, cue 1c, cue 2, etc.; with digital devices it is cue 1, cue 1.1, cue 1.2, cue 1.3, cue 2, etc. Within the framework of any one cue or part of a cue, 3, 5, 10, or any number of parts may be added, depending upon the system.

Patch at level. A feature of some electronic control systems making it possible to balance the intensity of a dim instrument and a bright instrument before entering their control into a single channel. This works only if a dimmer-per-instrument technology is in use.

Preset. A system by which one series of dimmers, controllers or channels is assigned a given cue while another series is assigned another cue.

Preview (previewing cues). A method of viewing past or present cues without actually changing existing intensities on stage at the moment; e.g., when preset 5 is in progress on stage, the operator can view preset 3 to see what was wrong with that cue, without changing the stage lighting at the moment.

Programmable patch. Electronic patching featured in certain computer boards allowing various dimmers to be patched to any control channel. See **Patch at level.**

Rate wheel. See **Level wheel.**

Real-time fades. The ability of a board to let an operator do a manually controlled fade, record it, and play it back within a production upon demand. The advantage of this capability is that not only the time but the nonlinear qualities of any fade or cross-fade can be stored.

Record. To store a given unit of information for future use.

Repeatability. Ability to repeat a given set of cues (pages) on command.

Reverse video (highlighting). A shaded area used to show a particular piece of information on the display screen. Varies slightly with manufacturer.

Sequencing (sequence mode). A method of assigning cue numbers to faders. May be accomplished manually or automatically depending upon system.

Split fader. Two submaster dimmers allowing simultaneous fading up of one cue and down of another at different speeds, even permitting a lag or hold in either cue.

Step. The moving from one part of a cue to another or from one cue to another. Often used describing parts of a sequential cue.

Symbols. Some typical symbols found on keyboards:

+ "Plus" or "and" symbol, e.g., channel 3 + 5 + 8 at (intensity, level of) 5.

@ "At," e.g., channel 70 @ (level of) 80.

F Full intensity, e.g., channel 2 F.

* "Execute." Command to do it now.

> "Through," indicating a range, e.g., channels 3 > 8 at (level of) 5.

↑ Raise intensity level.

↓ Lower intensity level.

X C Erase or clear.

Timed fade. A fade up or down at a predetermined speed set on the control board timer. Calibrated in both seconds and minutes, these timers are features of most computer boards. Timed fades can be programmed to happen with parts of a second or many seconds, some up to many minutes.

Tracking control. The ability to retain a previous cue in memory while other cues are implemented even though the cue has not recently been used.

VDU. An acronym for visual display unit. See also **CRT, Display, Monitor** above.

LIGHTING INSTRUMENTS (fixture, instrument, light, luminaire, unit). Lighting equipment falls into three broad classifications: FIXED FOCUS, GENERAL, and SPECIFIC. Fixed focus includes instruments that do not quite fit into the other two categories. General equipment includes instruments designed to flood the stage for toning, blending, and fill light. Specific lights are spotlights or lensed instruments designed to illuminate given areas. There are also several types of lights called general fixed-focus lights, which do not include lenses but are sufficiently directional to be used as specific lights. See also AUTOMATED LIGHTS.

LIGHTING INSTRUMENTS, FIXED FOCUS

Beam projector. Widely used for sunlight or moonlight through windows or in any situation where a strong directional light is needed. In one type a large parabolic reflector located behind the lamp features a small spherical reflector in front of the lamp that directs all forward light back into the large reflector, thus eliminating all direct light and using only controlled reflected beams; this unit produces a dark hole in the center of the beam. A second type utilizes a metal louvre in front of the lamp to control spill from the direct light of the filament. A third type uses a lens in a metal louvre in front of the lamp to control spill and to remove the dark hole of the first type. A focusing device permits some

adjustment, but the beam projector is essentially a narrow-beam light with a spread of approximately 6' to 8' at a throw of 20'. Available in 10", 14", and 18" sizes with 250- to 2,000-watt lamps.

PARcan. Simply a tin can–type mounting device holding a PAR-type lamp comprising its own reflector, light source, and lens. The PARcan has clips on the front to hold color media and can be either a flimsy or a very solid,

15" KLIEGSUN PROJECTOR SPOT (KLIEGL)   10" BEAM-LIGHT PROJECTOR SPOT (CENTURY)

well-built unit depending upon manufacturer. PARcans are often used in rock shows and industrial shows, and it is not uncommon to see them chrome-plated with autopanning and color change mechanisms; this of course makes them very expensive.

PAR lamp. Mounted in a frame or in clamp on units, high intensity, low wattage, and long lamp life, PAR-type lamps are their own reflector, light source and lens, making PAR lamps highly efficient, inexpensive substitutes for

PAR-38 HOUSING (ARIEL DAVIS)

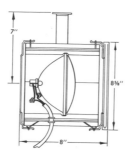

PAR-56 PARLITER (ARIEL DAVIS)

OPEN TROUGH BORDER LIGHTS

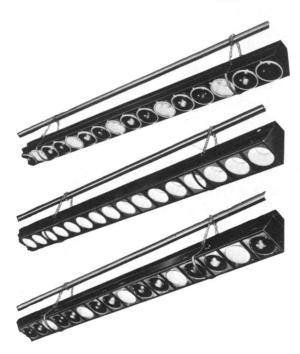

spotlights. Special clip-on louvres with color media clips are available. The potential of PAR lamps can be appreciated when it is realized that the intensity of a PAR 150-watt lamp is almost equal to the intensity of an older 500-watt Fresnel spotlight. See also under LAMPS.

LIGHTING INSTRUMENTS, GENERAL

General lights are nonlensed instruments, sometimes capable of being focused or framed (see **Barndoor** under LIGHT SPILL CONTROL), to provide fill, base, and toning to the stage area. General lights consist of a lamp and a reflector. A good floodlight should have the following features: reasonable compactness; ample ventilation with no light leaks through ventilating holes; a sturdy, positive lock hanger for mounting; and ready accessibility to the inside for relamping and cleaning reflector. Housings should be strong and lightweight and equipped with clips or slides for holding color frames, as well as yokes and clamps for mounting on pipe battens or standards.

Border lights (toning lights, X-rays). Should extend approximately two-thirds to entire width of the proscenium and should be divided into three or four circuits for proper color control (see LIGHTING COLORS). Modern lighting methods use the downstage borders for the acting area, the last border for cyc. Three basic types of border lights available are **open trough,** consisting of a long open reflector behind colored lamps, oldest and least-expensive type; **compartmentalized,** with each lamp enclosed in a separate compartment provided with a gelatine frame (reflectors of various kinds are

COMPARTMENTALIZED BORDER LIGHTS USING ROUNDELS ON TOP & BOTTOM UNITS (KLIEGL)

often used in this type to increase efficiency); **roundel** (or rondel), border lights with reflectors behind each light and a heat-resistant glass color filter known as the roundel. Roundel filters are available in many colors and have the advantage of being nonfade. **Pear-shaped** or **Reflector lamps** (see under LAMPS: **Bulbs**), 150 to 300 watts, mounted on 6" centers provide adequate light for prosceniums up to 30 feet. **Tungsten halogen** border lights of exceptional intensity are very popular but the heat they generate burns up standard color media, making special strip glass color filters mandatory. Border lights can be improvised by using two or three 500- to 1,000-watt hanging floodlights (scoops) for each color circuit, if the lights are placed to provide even distribution of light.

Floodlight. Available in parabolic and ellipsoidal scoops; also, the olivette can still be found. Olivettes consist of a metal box painted white or silver inside; grooves on the front to hold gelatine frames; mogul base receptacle designed to accommodate a 300-, 500-, 1,000-, or 1,500-watt lamp; and a swivel connection to a telescoping floor stand or clamps or chains to hang the unit from a pipe batten. Scoops include spun aluminum parabolic reflectors and ellipsoidal reflector floods (ERF), which increase efficiency, especially with quartz lamps. Some of the ERFs can be focused from narrow to wide flood. Floodlights are used for cyc lighting and concentration of light from a given source, as through windows. Scoops (see below) have generally replaced hanging floods.

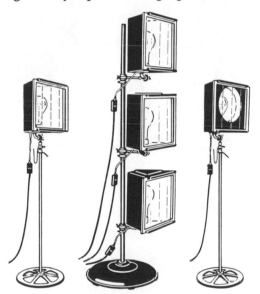

FLOODLIGHTS (OBSOLETE)

DOUBLE SEALED-BEAM QUARTZ-LIGHT
(KLIEGL BROS)

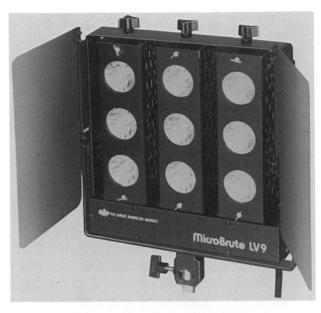

MICRO BRUTE 9-VOLT 1225 HR LAMP LIFE
(GREAT AMERICAN MARKET)

HANGING FLOODLIGHTS (OBSOLETE)

Footlights. A trough of lights on the floor or embedded in the floor immediately in front of the curtain. Footlights are similar to border lights and in some cases can be used interchangeably. Types include open trough, compartmentalized, roundel, and quartz (see **Border lights**, above). There are many schools of thought concerning footlights: some advocate three color circuits, some a nearly continuous line of clear light; some discard footlights altogether. In general, a small proscenium opening has less need of footlights than a large opening, and colored footlights are a matter of individual taste. If colors are to be used, the best results are usually obtained with three color circuits with the lamps as close together as possible, extending two-thirds the width of the proscenium. Lights mounted closely together tend to give less defined shadows on back walls and therefore can be used at greater intensity. Most footlights are designed for low wattage lights placed

111

on 4" to 6" centers. Open trough and compartmentalized footlights are usually designed for 40- to 100-watt lamps, while roundels are designed for 100- to 200-watt lamps. Tungsten halogen footlights are always compartmentalized, using 300- to 500-watt lamps and strip glass color filters. Disappearing footlights and recessed footlights are available in addition to portable types. Footlights have the advantage (because of the low angle) of tending to erase wrinkles from faces, and since youthful characters are often played by middle-aged actors, this can be of crucial concern. Dimmer readings for footlights should be set by bringing dimmer up to the point where multiple shadows of actors barely appear on the backwall, then taking dimmer down one point.

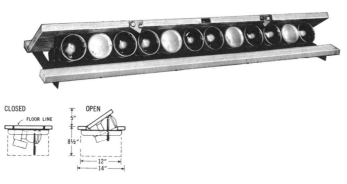

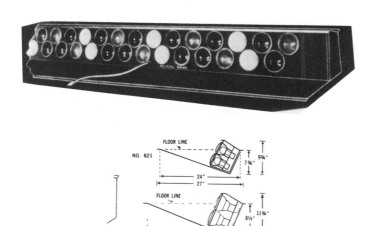

ROUNDEL DISAPPEARING FOOTLIGHTS
(KLIEGL BROS)

DOUBLE-ROW ROUNDEL FOOTLIGHTS
(KLIEGL BROS)

Scoop. Spun aluminum parabolic or ellipsoidal reflectors with no outside housings, light in weight, and particularly adaptable as hanging floodlights for lighting cycloramas. Scoops are designed with 250- to 400-watt lamps for 10" scoops (see WIZARD), 300- to 500-watt lamps for 14" scoops, and 750- to 1,500-watt lamps for 18" scoops; they are equipped with either C-clamps for batten mounting or swivel attachments for a telescoping floor stand. Scoop reflectors offer greater concentration of light than older style floodlights.

14" SCOOP   18" SCOOP
(ARIEL DAVIS)   (CENTURY STRAND)

Strip light. Older strip lights consist of an open trough with low-wattage colored lamps. Improved types are similar to border lights, with three color circuits. Strip lights were formerly hung on the offstage side of doors for a low, diffused backing light (see also WIZARD). They are now called cyc strips and used between groundrows on the floor below the cyc for horizon lighting, and should be placed sufficiently far from the surface to be lighted to have thorough color mixing from each unit. Hanging strip lights are also used for cyc lighting.

X-rays. A professional term for border lights still in use even though the original equipment is not. Obsolete. Large, compartmentalized border lights, using 300- to 1,000-watt lamps and equipped with gelatine frames.

LIGHTING INSTRUMENTS, SPECIFIC

Specific lights are spotlights or lensed instruments, capable of being focused or framed to provide accents or highlights to any given stage area. Conventional spotlights consist of a lamp, a spherical reflector, and a lens. A good spotlight should have the following qualifications: reasonable compactness; ample ventilation with no light leaks through ventilating holes or focusing slot; a sturdy, positive lock hanger for mounting; ready accessibility to the inside for relamping and cleaning lens and reflector; a color-corrected lens free from ABERRATION; and easy focus or shutter control from wide to narrow beam at recommended throw. Housings should be strong and lightweight and equipped with clips or slides for holding gelatine frames, as well as yokes and clamps for mounting on pipe battens or standards. For a less detailed discussion, see SPOTLIGHTS.

GROUNDROW STRIP (CENTURY)

BACKING STRIP (CENTURY)

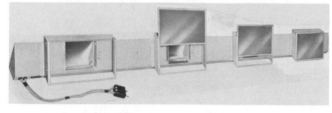

QUARTZ STRIPLIGHTS WITH GLASS MEDIA
(KLIEGL BROS)

Arc light (abbr. arc). A high-intensity light created by an arc between two electrodes or by an encapsulated arc. Used extensively as followspots in musicals, extravaganzas, ice follies, vaudeville, aqua follies, etc. Since arc lights require an attendant and cannot be dimmed except by iris, they are seldom used in dramatic productions. Arc lights are designed to be used on standard 120- or 220-volt AC circuits, having built-in transformers and rectifiers to change the AC to DC, reducing voltage and increasing amperage at electrodes. Each light is equipped with an iris, douser (cutoff), trombone (for variable diameter), and color boomerang. Can be designed for throws up to 400'. Cannot be dimmed by a dimmer, but an auxiliary device called a fader will give a smooth fadeout. On older units an iris placed in front of the color boomerang will fade an arc light. Since this position is well ahead of the focal point of the optical system, dimming is smooth and imperceptible, though at the last the douser must be closed. Much older forms of arc lights operate

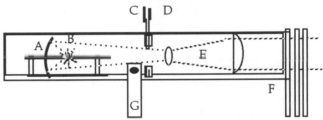

A	REFLECTOR	E	OBJECTIVE LENS
B	CARBON ELECTRODE		SYSTEM
C	DOUSER	F	COLOR BOOMERANG
D	IRIS	G	ADJUSTABLE STAND

CROSS SECTION OF ARC LIGHT

TROUPER (STRONG ELECTRIC)

SUPER TROUPER (STRONG ELECTRIC)

on DC and range from 25- to 125-A capacity. The arc is being superseded by the encapsulated arc. See also chart under SPOTLIGHTS.

Baby spot. Developed as a compact spotlight, this spotlight uses a plano-convex lens and a small spherical reflector. Fresnel spotlights have largely replaced baby spotlights in most manufacturers' catalogues, but some small theatres still use baby spots as area lights from first pipe. Baby spots are designed to use 100-, 250-, or

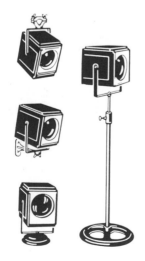

BABY SPOTLIGHTS

400-watt lamps and have an effective throw up to approximately 15' and a good focusing device from narrow beam (4' in diameter) to wide beam (10' in diameter) in a 10' throw. The lens of a baby spot is generally 4" in diameter. Larger theatres now use the small 3" ellipsoidal spots where once baby spots were used. See also chart under SPOTLIGHT.

Ellipsoidal spotlight (ERS, leko). Ellipsoidal spotlights combine reflector, lamps, shutter, and lenses to increase intensity and to frame light to a given pattern. Ellipsoidal reflectors direct light rays to a conjugate focal point (the location of a framing device consisting of four to eight shutters that can be moved in or out or swiveled) to frame aperture to any desired pat-

VARIABLE FOCUS LEKOLITE 500-WATT
(CENTURY STRAND)

tern. Because of this control feature, ellipsoidal spotlights are particularly valuable as FOH lighting units, where beams must be cut to proscenium edge. The lens system consists of either two plano convex lenses or one step lens, focused on the gate, where a framing device and a GOBO slot project a hard-line image to the stage. Ellipsoidal spotlights are available in many sizes, including 300, 500, 750, 1,000, 1,500, and 2,000 watts, with a 4 1/2", 6", 8", 10", and 12" lens encompassing throws of 15' with a 15'-diameter spread to a throw of 100' with a 14' spread, and almost all points in between. Fixed-focus units are referred to by lens size, 6 x 6, 6 x 9, 6 x12 (lens diameter x focal length), etc., or by the field angle, 30°, 15°, 8°, etc., with the narrower field angles similar to the longer focal length. The variable focus (zoom) unit is becoming very popular because it can be used in a variety of situations where once two or three lens barrels would have been necessary; a field angle between 15° and 30° is not unusual.

Common usage has units of 25' to 35' throw with 15'- to 30'- diameter spreads hung from the onstage electrics. More and more in professional theatre the ERS is supplanting the fresnel. Manufacturing representatives should be consulted in determining the correct instrument for size of stage, size of beam, length of throw, and footcandles delivered. See also chart under SPOTLIGHTS; **Ellipsoidal** under REFLECTORS.

ELLIPSOIDAL 1,000 WATT SPOTLIGHT (STRAND)

PROFILE SPOTLIGHT (STRAND)

ELLIPSOIDAL 250-750 WATT (KLIEGL)

FRAMING PARLITER (ARIEL DAVIS)

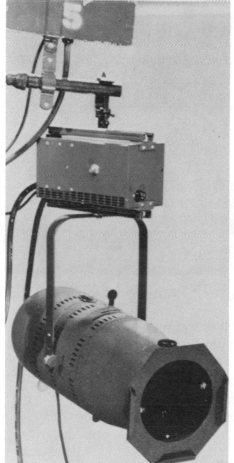

TH 8" ELLIPSOIDAL, 1,000 WATT WITH DIMMER PER LIGHT (KLIEGL)

3 1/2" ERS (KLIEGL)

DIE-CAST LEKOLITE (CENTURY)

ELLIPSOIDAL SPOT (STAGECRAFT IND.)

ELLIPSOIDAL 1,000-2,000 WATT (KLIEGL)

LEKOLITE (CENTURY)

QI ELLIPSOIDAL (KLIEGL)

Embryo spot (inkies). A tiny spotlight very useful on the stage in small quarters such as telephone booths, fireplaces, under platforms, etc. Embryo spots are usually designed for 100- to 150-watt lamps, small spherical reflectors, and a 3" fresnel lens; they provide efficient, diffused light up to a 10' throw. These units are also handy in control rooms for colored, directional lighting on key equipment.

Followspot. Since arc lights require an attendant, cannot be dimmed from control board, and are very expensive, they are seldom used in dramatic productions, thus necessitating the incandescent unit followspot. The newer followspots have quartz lamps, HMI lamps with iris, douser (stripper), trombone (for variable diameter), and boomerang. Since these followspots are substantially smaller than the arc light type, they are often used from high-angle positions in FOH catwalks, thus removing the backwall shadow problem, and they may be dimmed.

Fresnel spotlight. The fresnel spotlight combines spherical reflector, lamp, and lens to increase intensity and gives a soft-edged, diffused light. Since it is diffused light, it should be used behind the proscenium on first pipe, tormentor, or other onstage locations. Fresnel spotlights are available in many sizes: 3" (inky), 6", 8", 10", and 12" with lamps from 100- to 2,000-watts. Recommended distances of throw correspond to those for plano convex spotlights. See **Fresnel lens** under LENSES; also chart under SPOTLIGHTS.

FRESNEL 500 WATT
(STRAND)

FRESNEL 1,000 WATT
(STRAND)

FRESNELITE 500 WATT
(CENTURY)

FRESNELITE 2,000 WATT
(CENTURY)

QI 400-WATT FRESNEL
(PACKAGED LIGHTING)

OVAL BEAM FRESNEL
(KLEIGL)

Oval beam. Obsolete; a spotlight with a special fresnel lens, designed to provide a controlled oval beam with a ratio of approximately 3 to 2. Vertical and horizontal placement can be varied by rotating the lens in the instrument. Particularly useful in lighting the corners of sets and narrow parts of the stage.

Pin spot. A spotlight set as a special-purpose light with focus narrowed to cover a small area.

QI 6" FRESNEL
(KLIEGL)

12" FRESNEL 2,000 WATT
(KLIEGL)

Top hats and funnels (see under LIGHT SPILL CONTROL) are used to lessen light spill.

Plano-convex spotlight (PC). A great variety of spotlights differing only in lamp capacity, lens size, and design fall into the classification of plano-convex lights. These units usually have spherical reflector, lamp, and lens on a movable base, however, some older units have no reflector at all. Since **plano-convex lenses** (see under LENSES) produce a sharp-edged light, spotlights in this category are not limited in location. The PC is inefficient in comparison with ellipsoidal and fresnel spotlights. Among spotlights found in this category are the following: 250-to 400-watt units with 4" lenses (baby spot) and 500- to 3,000-watt units with 6" to 10" lenses and throws to 60' (not very efficient). See also chart under SPOTLIGHTS.

PLANO-CONVEX 2,000-WATT (KLIEGL)

LIGHTING STAGE, ARENA

Plan for arena lighting. To establish a plan for lighting arena theatres, divide stage proper into acting areas coinciding with proscenium lighting practice. Size of each area (usually between 10' and 16' in diameter) is determined by spread of spotlight used and distance of throw to stage. Number of areas on stage will be determined by size and shape of stage (usually four, six, or nine areas). Since actors are viewed from all sides, it is necessary to focus three or four lights on each area. It is possible to light a stage from pipe standards on each corner of area, but better lighting will result if lights are placed on pipe grid or false ceiling above arena. A rectangular stage can be minimally lighted from a grid of four pipes, somewhat longer than length of stage if outside pipes are located at approxi-

mately 60° angles from edges of acting area and inside pipes are equally spaced (see diagram). Location of spotlights on grid can be determined by enclosing each acting area in an imaginary equilateral triangle or square and placing a spotlight on or near each of the three or four angles. Additional spotlights, preferably sharp-focus framing type, are provided to light each entrance. It is advisable to use two lights on each entrance, one focused into acting area from entrance and the other focused into entrance from acting area. Steep-angle lighting is necessary on arena stages to light actors in fringe areas without spilling into the eyes of the audience. Beige-colored floorcloths or carpets will reflect light, helping to compensate for steep-angle lighting. Light-colored scatter rugs in key positions are also helpful.

PIPE BATTENS ——→
←—— ON CEILING

ACTING AREAS

LIGHTPLAN FOR ARENA SHOWING MINIMUM LIGHTS USED FOR ACTING AREAS 2 AND 3 AND ENTRANCE 5 ONLY

Color for arena lighting. The customary warm and cool color combinations used in proscenium lighting are not practicable on arena stages, where each area is lighted with three or four lights. It is therefore advisable to use clear or the same color light for area lighting and provide over all toning with special color circuits. Usually a circuit of light blue and one of

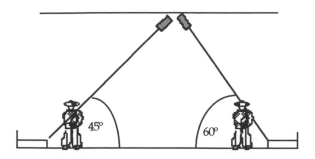

LIGHTING ANGLE FOR ARENA

pink will suffice, but secondary colors or dilute primary colors may be used. Permanent color lights (100-watt PAR-38 or 150-watt R-40) serve adequately for these circuits on smaller stages. Color circuits are mounted on inside pipes and focused to blend in center and cross to far side of stage.

Equipment for arena lighting. Since one of the greatest physical problems of arena lighting is preventing light from spilling into the eyes of the audience, plano-convex lenses on spotlights provide best results. Diffused light from fresnel lenses or PAR lamps is difficult to control unless long funnels are provided or light is directed through holes in a false ceiling, which will provide adequate cutoff. It is possible to use diffused light from offstage sides focused into acting areas if sharp-edged light (or controlled light) is used from onstage positions focused to outer fringe areas. Since throw to small arena stages is seldom over 16', baby spotlights or PAR-38 units provide minimal light. Stages requiring a longer throw will obviously need larger spotlights, but because of the number of lights required for effective lighting, it is desirable to use low-wattage units.

Control for arena lighting. The elaborate control of lights necessary for proscenium stages is not always required for arena lighting, but choice of plays should not be limited by inadequate light control. Sufficient control should be provided for each acting area, each entrance, each color circuit, and a minimum of six extra dimmers for special lights. An alternative plan calls for one or two high-capacity dimmers to handle all lights considered general lights in a given production, plus lower-capacity dimmers to which color circuits and any

special areas may be plugged through an interconnecting or plugging panel. Since blackouts are used in place of a curtain, master switches must be of sufficient capacity and strong enough in construction to withstand continual operation with lights at full capacity, or the board must be equipped with a special blackout switch. Control should be provided for each acting area, each entrance, and each color wash, extra dimmers for special lights.

LIGHTING STAGE, PROSCENIUM

Plan for proscenium lighting. Basic principles of stage lighting are simple in concept but often complex in execution. The stage, in theory, is divided into areas, usually between six and fifteen as determined by size of proscenium opening and shape of the set. Lighting positions in FOH are booth, balcony, overhead pipes (beams, catwalks), and side pipes (portals). Onstage positions include footlights, sidelights (booms, trees, etc.), overhead lights from electric pipes, backlighting, and cyc lights.

McCandless method. In a widely used method developed in the 1930s by Stanley McCandless of Yale University, each area downstage is lighted by two spotlights from FOH beam position and each area upstage is lighted by two spotlights from electric pipe po-

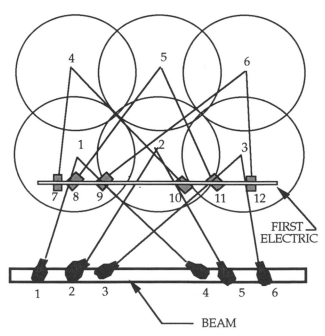

BASIC PROSCENIUM AREA LIGHTING

sitions. Ideally, spotlights should be mounted to form a 45° to 60° angle with the stage floor and a 60° to 90° angle with each other (physical limitations of most stages force adjustments, and the ideal is seldom obtainable). Area lighting such as this provides a basic formula with which to work. Each area should be well blended with adjacent areas, and each area should have individual dimmer control. As an aid to providing a three-dimensional quality, the McCandless method establishes a warm and a cool side of the stage and places warm colored gelatines in all spotlights focused from one side of the stage and cool-colored gelatines in all spotlights focused from the other side. In adhering to this practice, however, excessive contrasts of colors should be avoided.

Double McCandless. First set of lights has warm colors stage left and cool colors stage right; second set covers the same area with cool colors stage left and warm colors stage right.

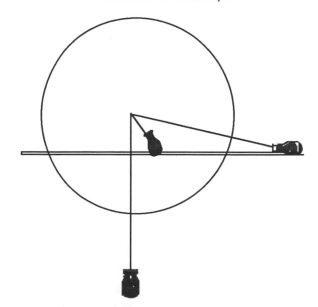

POOL WITH CROSSLIGHT AND WASH

Color control by area. Spotlights are set as for **double McCandless** (see above), with one circuit in cool color and the other circuit in warm color. The use of more saturated colors gives a wider range of color control for each area.

Motivated light. Realistic plays require light from a realistic source such as a lamp, window, fireplace, etc. An interior night scene can derive its light from a lamp, overhead fixture, fireplace, or moonlight through a window. If, for example, a practical fireplace is stage left, warm colors

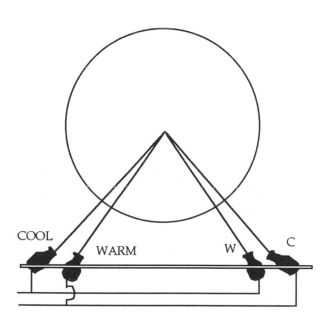

DOUBLE McCANDLESS

Pool with crosslight and wash. Spotlights covering each area are in as close to straight-down position as possible with extreme crosslights from first pipe or tormentor; beam or balcony spotlights are used as a wash to fill and color.

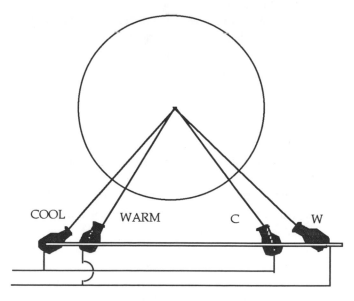

COLOR CONTROL BY AREA

could be placed in all spotlights focused from stage left position and cool colors in all spotlights focused from stage right position. The stage left area could be higher in intensity than the other areas and further strengthened by a small spotlight or floodlight placed inside the fireplace. Crosslighting of this nature is highly desirable and should be planned for windows, doors, wings, and tormentor positions. Artistry in lighting is attained by the lighting designer's choices of motivated sources, colors in spotlights, intensities of areas on stage, angles of lighting, random or gimmick light, and use of color washes.

Random light (gimmick light). Light for lighting's sake. Many episodic or nonrealistic plays do not need motivated light. In such plays lights are placed and used according to the lighting designer's judgment to provide dramatic value, emphasis, mood, etc.

LIGHTING STAGE, THRUST. Divide stage proper into acting areas coinciding with proscenium lighting practice. Size of each area, usually between 8' and 12' in diameter, is determined by spread of spotlights used and distance of throw to stage. Number of areas on stage will be determined by size and shape of stage, usually nine to fifteen areas. Since most of the actors are viewed from all sides, it is necessary to focus a minimum of three lights on each area. Light stage by placing a pipe grid above thrust. A rectangular stage can be well lighted from a grid of three pipes, somewhat longer than length of stage if outside pipes are located at approximately 45° angles in front and on the nearest edge of side; use 60° angle on farther edge of side (see diagram). Location of spotlights on grid is 90° between each spotlight, one front and one on each side. Steep-angle lighting is necessary on farther edge of side to light actors without spilling into the eyes of the audience. Lighting angles over the thrust should be duplicated upstage in the nonthrust areas so the eye cannot tell a difference.

Color for thrust lighting. As with the arena, the customary warm and cool color combinations used in proscenium lighting are not practicable. It is therefore advisable to use one color of light for area lighting and provide overall toning with special color washes. Usually color washes of primaries will suffice, but secondary colors or dilute primary colors may be used. Color washes are mounted on inside pipes much the same as arena lights.

Equipment for thrust lighting. As with arena lighting the prevention of light spilling into the eyes of the audience is of paramount concern, ellipsoidal spotlights provide best results. It is possible to use diffused light, for color wash, from directly overhead into acting areas. Since lighting throws for these stages can be both medium and short distance, the variable-focus (zoom) ellipsoidal is a most effective spotlight. Stages requiring a longer throw will obviously need larger, long-throw spotlights.

Control for thrust lighting. The control of lights necessary for thrust stages is similar to that needed for proscenium stages. Control should be provided for each acting area, each entrance, each color wash, and extra dimmers for special lights. Since blackouts are used in place of a curtain, blackout switches are an advantage.

LIGHT MOUNTING DEVICES. Made of pipe, wood, or structural steel and designed for mounting spotlights.

Boomerang (light tower). Located downstage right and left; used to support spotlights and special equipment.

Flying boom. A pipe hung from overhead to which lighting instruments are attached.

Ladder. Two vertical pipes with rungs between, suspended from the grid or hung from a pipe. Allow clearance under the lowest spotlight for passageway.

Light standard (boom). A weighted base with a pipe upright on which side arms are mounted and lighting instruments hung. A portable or traveling light standard is one with casters mounted on the base and usually, a telescoping upright pipe with a single light mounted on the top.

Trees. Vertical pipes with side arms, suspended from the grid or hung from a pipe.

LIGHTNING EFFECT. Photographic flashbulbs are ideal for single, intense flashes. High-intensity photographic lamps with a 4- to 6-hour life

are adequate for repeated flashes. Cyc strip
lights with 500-watt TH lamps give good distant
lightning effects. The time lag involved in heating and cooling filaments of high wattage lamps
is generally undesirable for lightning effects. A
jagged streak of lightning can be projected on
sky cyc with a **Linnebach projector** (see under
PROJECTORS). The streak is cut in a piece of
cardboard large enough to cover the opening of
the projector. The greater the distance between
lamp and cutout, the sharper the lines of the
streak. A quick flick of the switch produces an
effective streak across the cyc.

LIGHT PALETTE. Trade name for top-of-the-
line Strand computer board.

LIGHT PLOT. Lighting designer's layout, showing areas on the stage and mounting positions of
all instruments used to light the production.
Templates (1/4" and 1/2" scale) of different
types of lighting instruments are available and
are most useful in making accurate, easily read
light plots. Legends should include type of instrument, wattage, color number of media, circuit number, dimmer number, and space for
comments, e.g., pin spot to center left, barndoor,
wash light, framed to door, etc. See lighting
diagrams under LIGHTING STAGE, ARENA;
LIGHTING STAGE, PROSCENIUM

LIGHT, SIGNAL. See SIGNAL LIGHT.

LIGHT SPILL. Light straying from the main
beam of an instrument, falling on parts of the
stage where it is not wanted.

LIGHT SPILL CONTROL. The devices illustrated on the right side are designed to control
the beam spread of light, to frame given areas,
and to keep light from spilling on stage into
areas where it is not wanted. Of these, all but the
barndoor are used on spotlights.

    Barndoor (blinder, shutter). A commercial
product made of metal that shutters the light
either with two shutters (two-way) or with four
shutters.

    Funnel. A conical metal device that contracts
the beam of light.

    Louvre (spill ring). Series of concentric
metal rings or parallel slats.

    Top hat (hood, Ted Lewis). Sheet metal
shield resembling (and sometimes made of)
stovepipe and painted black.

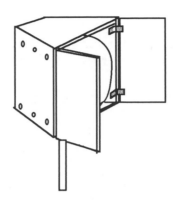

2 WAY BARN DOOR
ON OLIVETTE

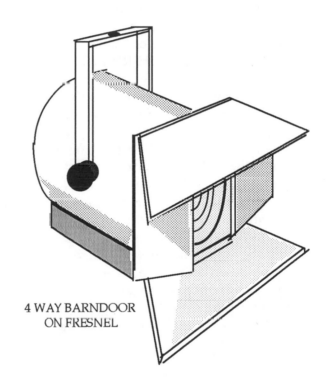

4 WAY BARNDOOR
ON FRESNEL

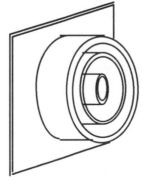

LOUVRE

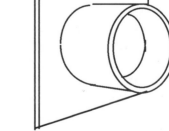

TOP HAT

LIMELIGHT (calcium light). An intense white light, once popular for stage use, created by directing an oxyhydrogen flame against lime.

LINE (noun)

Drawing. One of four aspects of visual manifestation, the other three being form, color, and texture.

Electrical. Source of power; the "line" side of a circuit, as opposed to the "load" side. See also CIRCUITS, ELECTRICAL.

Feed line. Conductor delivering power to equipment.

Hot line (live line, live wire). An electrical circuit carrying a potential and usually terminating in a receptacle or panel. A leg of a line as opposed to the ground or neutral wire.

Rigging. Any line or set of lines from the grid. See also COUNTERWEIGHT SYSTEM; RIGGING.

Messenger. A rope that is rigged to take various items aloft or bring them down from the flies; in particular the line that hoists a sunday (see under KNOTS) up a set of lines in a HEMP HOUSE to attach a sandbag. See drawing for BULL LINE.

Overhaul line (hand line). Line used to operate individual sets in a COUNTERWEIGHT SYSTEM. Overhaul lines are strung from the top of counterweights, to head blocks in grid, down through locks on pin rail, to floor, where they pass through tension idlers and back to lower part of counterweights. Ship-grade Manila line is the best to use for the overhaul line. Average size is 1/2" or 5/8".

Safety line. A line or tail used to tie to a set of lines or overhaul line and made fast to a belaying pin so the tied set cannot move.

Spot line. A single line from the grid over an exact location on the stage floor, to fly a special effect or other special piece of equipment; often used for cable pickup to keep deck clear.

Stage. A rope or steel cable used in sets of two or more for flying scenery. Lines are designated according to position by short, center, and long or short, short center, long center, and long.

Stop line (check line). A rope tied to off-stage edge of a draw curtain to prevent it from being pulled too far.

Scenery

Lash line. No. 8 sash cord (1/4") used to lash flats together. Line is fastened to a lash eye or through a hole in a corner block (usually on the top right side of the flat) and cut the same length as the flat. *Warning:* Lash lines cut longer than the flat are hazardous when gripping flats.

Tie line. 1 1/2' or 2' lengths of 1/8" cord used to tie curtains and draperies to battens. See illustration under KNOTS.

LINE (verb). To paint a narrow line with a straight edge, e.g., as a shadow or highlight on a molding or panel.

LINEAR FOOT. A measurement of length only, without reference to thickness and width. See also BOARD FOOT.

LINER. See PAINTBRUSHES.

LINNEBACH PROJECTOR. See under PROJECTORS.

LINTEL. A horizontal piece of wood or stone over a door, window, or arch.

LIQUOR. See BEVERAGES.

LIVE STACK. See under STACK.

LIVE WEIGHT. The weight of a moving body as opposed to that of an inert body. Platforms should be built to withstand live weight, approximately twice the thrust of dead weight.

LOAD, ELECTRICAL. The current or amperage used in a circuit. Electrical plugs are often marked "load" (male plug) and "line" (female plug). Load is electrical equipment to be connected to the line. See also CIRCUITS, ELECTRICAL.

LOADING PLATFORM (loading floor). A catwalk located near the grid, running perpendicular to the footlights and used for loading counterweights on arbors to counterbalance flown scenery.

LOAD OUT. See OUT and STRIKE A SET.

LOBBY. The area immediately outside the auditorium where the audience spends intermission.

LOBSTERSCOPE. A disk attachment for a spotlight, used to produce a flicker of light. The disk is irregularly perforated and is made to revolve in front of the spotlight. Control is either electrical or by clock mechanism. The effect is most effective for slow-motion effects.

LOCK. See under DOOR.

LOCK, ROPE. Lever devices used to lock overhaul lines (hand lines) of a counterweight system to hold flown scenery in any given position. Do not trust rope locks to hold loads that are seriously out of balance. See illustration under RIGGING SYSTEMS.

LOFT

Space between grid and roof of stage house. Sometimes refers to the FLIES.

LOFT BLOCK. A sheave or pulley used on the grid for each line. See also GRID.

LOGS, FIREPLACE. See FIREPLACE LOGS.

LONG LINE. Longest line in a set of lines strung from the grid. See also COUNTERWEIGHT SYSTEM.

LOOSE-PIN HINGE. See **Backflap** under HINGES.

LOUDSPEAKER. See **Speakers** under SOUND EQUIPMENT.

LOUVRE

A series of concentric metal rings or parallel slats used to direct a beam of light and control spill. See illustration under LIGHT SPILL CONTROL.

Metal slats used in SMOKE VENTS at the top of the stage.

LUMBER (used for scenery). See also FURNITURE. Sugar pine, white pine, ponderosa pine, spruce, fir, cedar, and basswood (listed in order of preference) are used for scenery construction. Lumber unsuited to scene construction includes all hardwoods and extremely soft woods such as redwood, balsa, etc. Lumber is sold by the BOARD FOOT (1 square foot by 1 inch thick), and prices are often quoted by the thousand board feet (1M). *Warning:* Lumber that is unevenly or carelessly stacked will become warped; green lumber should be stacked straight, with spacing boards between layers to allow air circulation; seasoned lumber should be stacked straight and without bends. Lumber

is graded by letter, by number, or by description, depending upon the type and uses. Other grades, including common 1, 2, and 3, run from low-fair to very poor. Bottom grades are used primarily for very rough work and crating. The following is a partial guide to grading:

Top grade	Good grade	Fair grade	Poor grade
A	B	C	D or 1 common
1 Construction	2 Standard	3 Utility	4 Economy

Milled lumber. Lumber cut to thickness and planed smooth at the mill. Milled lumber, unless specified "net," is under dimension by approximately 1/4 " to 3/8 " in both thickness and width. Milled lumber is usually designated S-4-S (smooth on four sides).

Rough lumber. Lumber unplaned at the mill.

LUMEN. A standard unit of measurement of the rate of flow of light energy. The flow of light through 1 square foot of a sphere having a radius of 1 foot and a light source in the center of 1 candle-power. One lumen of light evenly applied to 1 square foot produces 1 foot-candle (measurement of intensity). Expressed in equation form:

Foot-candle = Lumen / area (in square feet).

LUMINAIRE (fixture, instrument, light, unit). Describes a complete lighting instrument: lamp, socket, housing, reflector, lenses, mounting device, and plug. Often used to refer to AUTOMATED LIGHTS. See LIGHTING INSTRUMENTS.

LUMINESCENCE. Ability of some materials to give off light when stimulated by an outside source such as ULTRAVIOLET LIGHT.

M

MACBETH TRAP. See under TRAP.

MACHINE. Obsolete: term for revolving stages, traps, crane-type lifts, sound and lighting effects in various types of Greek, Roman, Medieval, Italian, Renaissance, and Elizabethan theatres.

MACHINE BOLT. See under BOLTS.

MAGIC LANTERN. Obsolete; devises used to project transparent slides on a screen. Many of the same principles are still used for projecting scenery in the theatre. See PROJECTED SCENERY; PROJECTORS.

MAGNETIC AMPLIFIER. Obsolete. See under DIMMERS.

MAGNETIC CLAMP. Electromagnet in floor and a large steel base on moving scenic unit; when powered, magnet secures the unit firmly.

MAGNETIC TAPE. A plastic based tape coated with iron oxide and used for audio, video, digital recordings, and playback. Two plastics popular for tape are acetate, which breaks before it stretches, and Mylar, which stretches before it breaks; the former is usually more desirable for stage use because it does not stretch with repeated use.

MAHOGANY, PHILIPPINE (lauan). A reddish brown-blond, tropical wood often used for inexpensive furniture construction and door skins. This wood is easily worked and also, reasonably priced in many sections of the country. See also FURNITURE.

MAILING TUBE. Cardboard tubes of various diameters, useful for making pipes, columns, poles, etc., for scenic effects. Large columns may be made from cardboard tubes used in heavy construction as concrete forms. Contact local construction companies.

MAIN CURTAIN (grand drape). Drapery separating stage from auditorium. See CURTAIN.

MAKE FAST. To tie off a set of lines.

MALE PLUG. See under PLUGS, ELECTRICAL.

MALLET. See under HAMMERS.

MANTEL (mantelpiece). The decorative framing around a FIREPLACE opening including the shelf, if any.

MANUAL SHIFTING. See under SCENERY, SHIFTING.

MAPLE. A hardwood commonly used in the furniture construction industry, and characterized by its finish color of light red or yellow. Because of its hardness, it is seldom used for constructing furniture in theatre shops.

MARBLED EFFECT. Marbled wallpapers are available in many colors and may be used very successfully for covering columns, tables, fireplaces, etc. Apply with wallpaper paste or wheat paste. See also **Marble** under PAINTING TECHNIQUES.

MARK IT (Command verb). To write down a dimmer reading of light intensity or a potentiometer reading of sound effect or music volume.

MARRY. To hold together by hand the lines of a set, "marry them temporarily," while trimming or FEELING THEM UP. Trimming a set of lines by adjusting each line separately and then "marrying them" by bringing them together by hand, trim block, sunday, or tie. Usually associated with leveling or trimming a set of lines.

MASK. To obscure from view of audience.

MASKING. Backings of flats, groundrows, draperies, etc., used to hide from audience view areas of the stage not wanted in the scene.

MASONITE. Trade name for a compressed paper pulp sheet, impregnated with resin and formed under high pressure. This sheet stock is glossy smooth on one side and fabric textured on the other. Either side will take paint well, although the textured side is more porous and therefore requires more paint to cover. Masonite is used as floor covering, facings, thicknesses, doors, scrolls, furniture, etc. Available in standard 4' x 8' sheets and thicknesses of 1/8", 3/16", 1/4", etc. Thin sheets bend reasonably well to make thicknesses for arches. Masonite is stocked in either tempered or untempered sheets, the latter is usually adequate for average use and is a little less expensive. See also SCENERY PANELS.

MASTER, PROPERTIES. See under STAGE CREW.

MASTER CARPENTER. See under STAGE CREW.

MASTER DIMMER. See DIMMER, MASTER.

MASTER ELECTRICIAN. See under STAGE CREW.

MASTIC NO. 11. A glue for foams made by Dow Chemical. See GLUE.

MATTING. See PADDING.

MECHANICAL ADVANTAGE. Ratio of force exerted to work accomplished. Probably the most common applications in theatre are levers. See BLOCK AND TACKLE.

MECHANICAL INTERLOCK. See under DIMMER, MASTER.

MEDIA, COLOR. See COLOR MEDIA; LIGHTING COLORS; GELATINES.

MEDIUM. See under COLOR MEDIA; PAINTS AND PAINT COLORS.

MEDIUM BASE LAMP. See **Bases** under LAMPS.

MELODRAMATIC STAGING (nineteenth century). Melodramas are best staged according to the customs of the time in which the play is set, with wings, drops, set pieces, roll curtains.

MEMORIES AVAILABLE. See **Computer terminology** under LIGHTING CONTROL.

MEMORY LIMIT. See **Computer terminology** under LIGHTING CONTROL.

MERCURY SWITCH. See under SWITCHES.

MERCURY VAPOR LAMP. Light is produced by passing an electrical current through vaporized mercury, which results in an ultraviolet light plus visible light in the blue-green range.

METAL-FRAMED SCENERY. Sometimes considered high-tech scenery. See **High-tech** under

FLATS. As the name implies, this is scenery that is framed or backed by either steel or aluminum metal tubing.

METAL GAUGES. Numbers designating the thickness of sheet metal.

GAUGE	THICKNESS IN INCHES	GAUGE	THICKNESS IN INCHES
30	.012	21	.034
29	.014	20	.037
28	.015	19	.043
27	.017	18	.049
26	.018	17	.055
25	.021	16	.061
24	.025	15	.069
23	.028	14	.077
22	.031	13	.092

METALLIC PAINT. See **Aluminum paint** and **Gilding paints** under PAINTS, MISCELLANEOUS.

METER. Device used to measure levels of volts, decibels, amperes, etc.

METHOCEL. A water-soluble gum used as a binder for paints and dye.

MICKEY MOUSE. Colloquial term meaning substandard.

MICROPHONE. See under SOUND EQUIPMENT.

MICROPROCESSOR. See LIGHTING CONTROL.

MIDI. An acronym for musical instrument digital interface. Sometimes used for cueing AUTOMATED LIGHT CONTROL and COMPUTERS.

MIDRANGE SPEAKER (squawker). See SOUND EQUIPMENT.

MIL. A measurement in thousandths of an inch. The thickness of this page is approximately 3 1/2 mils, or 0.0035".

MINI PALLETTE. Trade name for a compact computer console manufactured by Strand.

MIRROR (hot and cold). See DICHROIC FILTERS.

MIRROR (props). Real mirrors are seldom used on stage without treatment to reduce reflection. Substitutes of sheet metal or aluminum painted plywood are less distracting. Galvanized screen or plastic screen placed over silvered plywood adds a more realistic depth. If real mirrors are used, surface should be soaped or covered with egg white to reduce reflection.

MIRROR IMAGE. A reverse image of a drawing, as the original would appear in a mirror.

MITER BOX. A guiding device for a handsaw, used to cut accurate angles. Miter boxes are essential for accurate work in the shop.

MIXER. See SOUND EQUIPMENT.

MOB SCENE (sound effect). Recordings in background plus all available offstage personnel, cued by stage manager.

MODE. See **Computer terminology** under LIGHTING CONTROL.

MODEL. Scaled miniature of a stage setting. Models may clarify complicated DRAWINGS, aid in proper proportioning, and assist technicians in carrying out DESIGNS. Even crude paper or cardboard models will be helpful. A front elevation, correctly drawn, can be cut and bent to form a model. Useful materials for models include balsa wood, illustration board, Styrofoam, quick-drying glue, etc. A common scale for models is 1/2" = 1'.

MODELING. Achieving a three dimensional effect through use of lights of two different colors coming from two different sources. See LIGHTING STAGE, PROSCENIUM.

MODULE. A standard size chosen for convenience, often in reference to scenery.

MOGUL BASE. See **Bases** under LAMPS.

MOL (maximum overall length). Abbreviation used in lighting catalogues indicating total length of LAMP from base to tip (base to base in double-ended lamps).

MOLD, PLASTER OF PARIS. A hollow form used for casting. Papier-mâché and CELASTIC are often used in plaster of paris molds to form objects too difficult to carve or otherwise fashion, and objects subject to breakage through stage use. Molds may be made around clay replicas or around original objects if they are properly greased for releasing (see below).

Directions. Sift plaster of paris into a shallow pan of water until powder no longer sinks. Stir solution thoroughly with hand submerged to guard against formation of bubbles. After solu-

tion has become thick, bounce pan a few times to release bubbles that may have formed (bubbles will cause imperfections and blemishes in finished casts). The thickening solution is then ready to pour on the greased replica or article to be molded. A thin covering is followed by successive layers until an overall thickness of at least 1/2" is attained. Allow a completed mold to set for one or two hours or until plaster is absolutely cold. Round or undercut articles require a split mold. To make a split mold, determine the exact center of the undercut and place a fishline around the article, holding it in place with masking tape. Follow procedure above and when plaster of paris starts to set (becomes shiny) gently pull fishline up through plaster, dividing mold in half. Again, allow mold to dry thoroughly before removing. Articles used to make the mold should be well greased with shortening, cold cream, Vaseline, car grease, or heavy oil.

MOLDING (trim, facing). Decorative trim either painted or applied, used to "dress" doors, windows, settings, etc., and make them appear more authentic. Obviously, molding should be designed to fit the period and location of the play. Painted moldings are often used for the backwall of a set or for flats that must fold, but many designers prefer applied moldings where

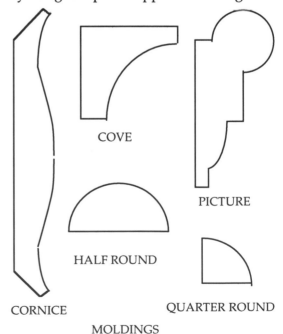

COVE

PICTURE

HALF ROUND

CORNICE

QUARTER ROUND

MOLDINGS

feasible (even if they have to be removed for folding) because of their natural shadow lines and relief. If a circular saw is part of shop equipment, applied moldings may be improvised at considerable savings by cutting from scrap lumber. If molding is to be bought, most lumber yards carry a wide variety, sold by the linear foot. White pine moldings are easy to work and tend not to split as readily as those made from harder woods. If lower part of the flat is painted woodwork color, 3/4" x 3/4" molding is adequate for the top line of baseboard or wainscoting. If scenery is to be griped molding should be secured to flats with 1 1/2" flathead woodscrews. Some of the most common types of moldings include the following.

Cornice molding (contour, cornicing cove). Ornamental molding placed on the wall near ceiling. Useful in suggesting a lower ceiling, breaking the monotony of a great expanse of wall, or suggesting period. Molding applied 6" to 24" below the tops of flats and painted wood color above gives a realistic shadow. Heavier three-dimensional cornices are built on a block frame and either bolted to flats or hung from the top of the set with strap iron brackets.

Cove molding. Used for baseboards and cornices.

Facing. Molding or trim around a door, window, or other opening. Usually made of stock lumber 1" x 3" or 1" x 6" applied with 1 1/2" (no.8) flathead woodscrews. Wider facings can be made of beaverboard or plywood with molding attached to outer edge or by applying molding to the flat at the prescribed width and painting the space from opening to molding as woodwork. Facing used on folding flats should either be painted with appropriate highlights and shadows or made detachable, so that flats may be folded together without damage.

Half round. Used for nosings for stairs and for handrails.

Picture molding. Used for frames, pictures, doors, etc.

Quarter round. Used for baseboards, handrails, cornices and fills.

MONAURAL (mono). A single channel of sound. See SOUND EFFECTS.

MONEY (props). Real money should never be used on stage. Substitute stage money or play money.

MONITOR. See SOUND EQUIPMENT; VIDEO.

MONOCHROMATIC. One color (HUE), varying intensity (CHROMA).

MONTAGE. In motion pictures, the practice of fading or blending from one scene to another. Montage effects may be achieved on stage through the use of PROJECTED SCENERY or by simultaneous staging with blackouts and dim ups on separate areas.

MOOD. See ATMOSPHERE.

MOONLIGHT EFFECT. Moonlight scenes are usually lighted with a blue or blue-green overall coverage (see COLOR MEDIA) with a white or light straw spot highlighting the acting area. Sometimes a perforated tin plate (STRAINER) is made to fit a spotlight frame and is used as a filter to reduce concentration of light but maintain brilliancy for highlighted areas. Always check costume and makeup colors under blue or green light before making final decisions.

MOPBOARD. See BASEBOARD.

MORTISE AND TENON. See under JOINTS.

MORTISE LOCK. See under DOOR.

MOTIF. Central or controlling idea. Scene designers often look for the central idea of a play to supply a motif for their setting. Such a motif might be supplied by a centrally placed picture of a dominating force in the play; an abstract design suggesting the theme; dark, somber, foreboding colors; etc.

MOTION CONTROL. See CHAIN HOIST CONTROL.

MOTIVATED LIGHT. Light originating from a source such as a fireplace, window, or lamp onstage. See under LIGHTING STAGE, PROSCENIUM.

MOTOR, ELECTRICAL. Power tools require varying sizes of motors for maximum efficiency (for a description of such tools see POWER TOOLS). Following is a partial list of motor requirements:

Equipment	Horsepower
Bandsaw	1/2 to 1 minimum
Blower	1/4 to 1/2 depending on size
Circular saw	1 to 2 depending on size
Drill press	1/2 minimum

Grindstone   1/4 to 1/3
Lathe   1/2 to 3/4 depending on
              size
Revolving   2 to 10 with gearbox
stage

For fusing to protect motors, 1 horsepower is equal to approximately 746 watts, about 6.2 amps, at 120 volts.

MOTORIZED RIGGING. See RIGGING.

MOUNTING. Any device used for attaching

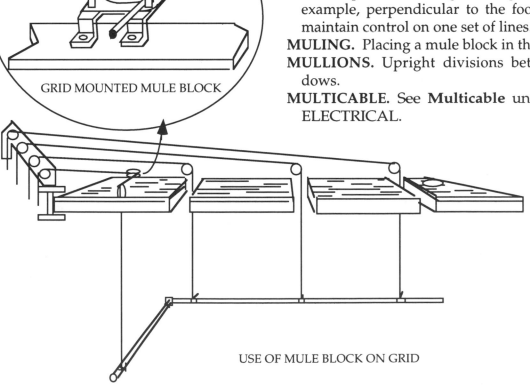

UNDERHUNG MULE BLOCK

GRID MOUNTED MULE BLOCK

USE OF MULE BLOCK ON GRID

equipment, e.g., spotlight mountings, motor mountings, speaker mountings. Control of noise and vibrations is often essential in theatre and mounting turntables, speakers, motors, special effects motors, etc., on rubber stoppers or corks will usually deaden unwanted noise and vibration.

MOUSING. Wrapping the mouth of an open hook with wire or line to ensure that nothing on the hook can come off.

MOVABLE SCENERY. See SCENERY, SHIFT-ING.

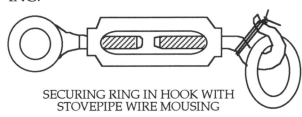

SECURING RING IN HOOK WITH
STOVEPIPE WIRE MOUSING

MOVING LIGHTS. See AUTOMATED LIGHTS; PAN AND TILT LIGHTS.

MOVING PROJECTION. See PROJECTED SCENERY.

MOVING SCENERY. See HANDLING FLATS.

MULE BLOCK. A sheave or block used to change the horizontal direction of a line. Mule blocks make it possible to hang masking draperies, for example, perpendicular to the footlights and maintain control on one set of lines.

MULING. Placing a mule block in the rigging.

MULLIONS. Upright divisions between windows.

MULTICABLE. See **Multicable** under WIRE, ELECTRICAL.

MULTIMETER. A piece of test equipment that measures several values. See VOM.

MULTIPLE PIN CONNECTOR. See under PLUGS, ELECTRICAL.

MULTIPLE-SET SHOW. A play with more than one setting. See SCENERY, SHIFTING.

MULTIPLEXING. The ability to send various signals at the same time over a pair of wires.

MUNSELL SCALE. A color wheel based on 10 colors. Albert H. Munsell (American, 1858–1918) first published his ideas on a color tree in 1898, using the following ten colors: 1 red; 2 yellow-red; 3 yellow; 4 green-yellow; 5 green; 6 blue-green; 7 blue; 8 purple-blue; 9 purple; 10 red-purple.

MUSLIN. See DRAPERY, SET; **Muslin** under COVERING FLATS: **Materials.**

N

NAILING BLOCK. Used when constructing flats to hold the parts of a flat on a template table to ensure consistency in spacing.

NAILS. Nail sizes are designated by numbers plus the suffix "penny," originally referring to cost per hundred nails. The penny abbreviation "d" is from Latin "denarius," an ancient Roman coin, at one time approximating the British penny in value. See table for lengths and approximate number of nails per pound. Used for both temporary and permanent fastening, nails are available in many classifications. Rule of thumb regarding choice of nail length is that a nail should be about three times as long as the thickness of board in which it is to be used. Thus a 1" board (actually measuring about 3/4" in thickness) requires a 2 1/4" to 2 1/2" nail (sevenpenny or eightpenny). Following is a list of the types most useful in theatre.

Box nail. Thin shank with a head. Most useful in all kinds of scene construction. Thin shank is less apt to split wood than common nail.

NAIL SIZE	LENGTH IN INCHES	NAILS PER POUND
2d	1	876
3d	1 1/4	568
4d	1 1/2	316
5d	1 3/4	271
6d	2	181
7d	2 1/4	161
8d	2 1/2	106
9d	2 3/4	96
	3	69
10d	3 1/4	63
12d	3 1/2	49
16d	4	31
20d	4 1/2	24
30d	5	18
40d		

Clout nail (cut nail). Blunt, wedge-shaped nail made of malleable metal and used in flat construction to hold corner blocks and keystones in place. 1 1/4" clout nails are used because they are long enough to clinch on the underside of the batten, holding plywood secure. In many shops, power staple guns and 7/8" staples, both narrow and wide crown, with rosin coatings are preferred to nails because they are so much easier and faster to use.

Common nail. Thick shank with a head. Used for framing and rough construction work.

Double-headed nail (form nail, scaffold nail). Designed for temporary use. Allows the lower head to hold the wood together while upper head allows easy withdrawal. These nails in sixpenny and eightpenny sizes are ideal for fastening scenery together for the single-set play remaining on stage until strike night. The double-headed nail is most useful for nailing sets together that have a relatively short run.

Finish nail (finishing nail). Thin shank and small head. Used in cabinet work and elsewhere where concealing nail heads is important.

Tee nail. A T-shaped nail used in air nailers.

NATIONAL ELECTRICAL CODE (NEC, code). Produced by the National Fire Protection Association. Regulations governing wiring practices. Copies available in book form or CD ROM.

NATIONAL UNDERWRITERS CODE (fire code). Produced by the National Fire Protection Association. Often the model for fire laws and regulations in local communities.

NEC. See NATIONAL ELECTRICAL CODE.

NEON. An inert gaseous element used in electric light bulbs or tubes in place of a filament. Neon tubes give light in a continuous line and are often used for special effects on stage.

NETTING. See BOBBINET; SCRIM.

NEUTRAL COLOR. See COLOR.

NEUTRAL WIRE. Common wire. See also CIRCUITS, ELECTRICAL.

NEWEL POST. A post supporting handrail at top and bottom of a flight of stairs. Elaborate newel posts are often available at wrecking yards or demolition companies for a nominal fee. Simple posts can be made by nailing 6" boards together and applying appropriate panels of molding as dressing. Newel posts are fastened to stairs with loose pin hinges or angle irons. Height of a newel post varies with style and design but is often about 36", with the handrail about 32" from the top of each riser. See also STEPS.

NICHROME WIRE. High resistance wire used in resistance dimmers, heaters, stove elements, and hot wire cutters for plastic foam.

NICOPRESS. A crimping tool used in conjunction with a sleeve to fasten two like cables together forming a loop or a union. The cables are inserted in a sleeve, which is then crimped by the Nicopress. This is a much faster method than using wire rope clamps. Manufactured in several sizes, the Nicopress tool will usually handle two or three sleeve sizes, the most useful in the theatre are 1/16", 1/8", and 3/16". The tool is expensive but time saved with its use may make it worth the cost.

NONCONDUCTOR. Any material that will not conduct electricity. The best nonconductors include glass, porcelain, Bakelite, and rubber. Used as insulators and fronts for panel boards for electrical equipment.

NONDIM CIRCUIT (hotline). A circuit supplying electrical power through a switch for on-off control rather than dimming control. Most light control boards provide several nondim circuits for special effects such as stage appliances, electrically triggered flash or smoke effects, signal systems.

NOSING, STEP. A lip or overhang on the tread of a step. For applied nosing, 1 1/2" half round is ideal.

NUTS. See BOLTS; TEE-NUT; WING NUT.

NYLON. A tough, strong, elastic thermoplastic available in sheets, rods, tubes, and fibers. Nylon has many uses in the theatre: ropes, paintbrushes, fabrics, weight-bearing surfaces, etc.

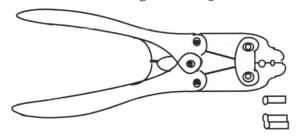

NICOPRESS TOOL AND SLEEVES

O

OAK. Hardwood, particularly strong and heavy, well suited to furniture construction but not generally used in theatre shops because of excessive weight and hardness.

OBJECTIVE LENS (dutchman). See under LENSES.

OBLIQUE DRAWINGS. See DRAWINGS.

OD. Outside diameter of a rod, tube, or pipe.

OFFSET. An alcove in a set or a deviation from straight line of a wall.

Offsets are used to break up lines of a set and add interest to a design or to permit lashing or fastening of flats without showing unsightly joining cracks.

OFFSET SCREWDRIVER. A screwdriver with the leverage handle at right angle to the bit.

OFFSTAGE. Any part of the stage outside confines of the setting or acting area. See also AREAS; STAGE DIRECTIONS.

OHM. Electrical unit measuring resistance. See ELECTRICITY.

OHM'S LAW. See ELECTRICITY.

OIL STAIN ON FLATS. See **Oil stain** under STAINS.

OLEO (olio). A roll curtain used as a show curtain or one on which advertisements are placed. See **Roll curtain** under CURTAIN; ENTR'ACTE.

OLIVETTE. See **Floodlight** under LIGHTING INSTRUMENTS, GENERAL.

OMNIDIRECTIONAL (omni). See **Microphones** under SOUND EQUIPMENT.

ONSTAGE

(Command verb). Used to order cast or crew onto the stage proper. See also PLACES.

Defines the area of the stage visible to the audience.

Acting area seen by the audience.

OP. Opposite prompter. Because prompters usually sit stage right, where control of curtain is located, this is known as the prompt side and OP generally refers to stage left. A stage direction found in acting editions of old plays. The term tends to be used primarily in professional theatre in modern times. See also STAGE DIRECTIONS.

OPAQUE SCENERY. To cover cracks, small holes, or tears or to paint scenery on the back to prevent light leaks from being seen by the audience. Back painting with a dark paint also minimizes light reflection.

OPENING (opening night). First public performance of a production.

OPERATING LIGHT (board lite). A work light often dimmer controlled, colored, and focused on a specific area in a CONTROL ROOM.

OPERATING LINE. See **Overhaul line** under LINE; illustration under RIGGING SYSTEMS: **T-track counterweight.**

OPERATOR. The person who operates a light or sound control board or console.

OPERATORS. Motion picture projectionists, members of IATSE, the theatre union of technicians. See UNIONS.

OPTICAL AXIS. An imaginary line running perpendicular to the major components of a lensed instrument, e.g., a spotlight or a projector. If one part of the major components is not in alignment, HALATION and ABERRATION will occur.

ORCHESTRA. Orchestra refers to the entire front lower floor of the auditorium. Originally the circular arena of a Greek theatre in which the chorus performed.

ORCHESTRA PIT (pit). Sunken area immediately in front of the stage intended to accommodate an orchestra. Many larger theatres have hydraulic orchestra lifts in the pit, permitting pit level to be brought up to stage height, where it can be used as an apron if an orchestra is not needed. Smaller theatres not anticipating extensive use of orchestras often have covers built for the pit, providing similar extensions of acting areas when needed. Space demands for an orchestra include 10 square feet for average musician; 20 square feet for harp; 50 square feet for average piano; 50 square feet for tympani.

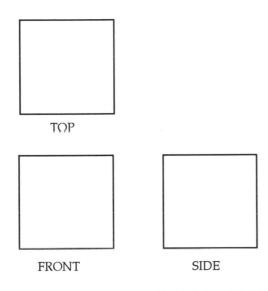

TOP

FRONT   SIDE

ORTHOGRAPHIC PROJECTION OF A CUBE

ORTHOGRAPHIC PROJECTION (orthog). A method of pictorial drawing showing top, front, and side views.

OSNABURG. Trade name for a fabric resembling a combination of burlap and muslin. Osnaburg dyes well and drapes reasonably well in short lengths but is not suitable for covering flats.

OUT. The strike of a show as contrasted to the "in," or set-in.

OUTER STAGE. That part of the Elizabethan stage projecting into the court. See SHAKE-SPEAREAN STAGE.

OUT FRONT. Auditorium or part of the theatre given over to the audience.

OUTLET (receptacle). A permanent electrical installation to which equipment may be attached. The line (outlet) as opposed to the load (equipment), which is plugged into the outlet.

OUTPUT. Power delivered by an amplifier, expressed in watts. See **Amplifiers** under SOUND EQUIPMENT.

OUTRIGGER.

Scenery shifting. A freestanding section of scenery that has casters mounted on back so it may be rolled away during scene changes. The set must be in a freestanding configuration or when it is mounted on an outrigger it will fall over. There are obvious advantages to using the outrigger for heavy scenery, but problems arise when doors with thresholds are used because of the 1/2" to 3/4" clearance from the floor required by casters. For further discussion of shifting scenery, see SCENERY, SHIFTING.

Truss. A triangular frame that helps stabilize a truss tower by extending support out from a unit. See also TRUSS.

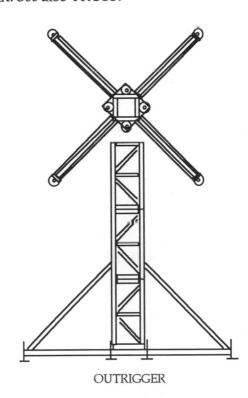

OUTRIGGER

OVAL BEAM. Obsolete; a fresnel spotlight with a special lens designed to provide a controlled oval beam. A very useful instrument that, unfortunately, is no longer available. See LIGHTING INSTRUMENTS, SPECIFIC.

OVERALL DIMENSION. Same as outside dimension as opposed to inside dimension. See OD.

OVERCOAT. The final coat of paint to be applied to scenery by any of the various methods of application, e.g., dry brush, feather dust, spatter, spray, etc. See PAINTING TECHNIQUES.

OVERHAUL LINE (hand line). See under LINE; see also illustration under RIGGING SYSTEMS: **T-track counterweight.**

OVERLOAD A CIRCUIT. To put a load on a circuit in excess of its capacity. Always protect dimmers and circuits from overloads and potentially expensive burnouts by fusing to the correct capacity. See AMP for determining capacities.

OVERSIZE WINDOWS. See **Flats** under PLUG.

OZITE PADDING. A type of rug padding sometimes used for deadening sound on platforms. Rug padding of the pressed-jute type used on platforms should be covered with muslin or canvas to prevent scuffing.

P

PA. See PUBLIC ADDRESS SYSTEM.

PACK. See STACK.

PADDING. Padding is generally placed on platforms and stairs to deaden sound. Effective padding can be old carpeting, rug pads, jute pads, cocoa matting, cardboard, ozite padding, etc. Jute padding (an inexpensive rug padding made from an East Indian plant fiber) is ideal for covering platforms, steps, and ramps. It is best to cover padding with tarpaulin, canvas, or heavy muslin to provide a uniform texture for painting.

PADDLE BOARDS. Boards or frames of various designs, loose pin hinged to wagons, and used as handles to move or guide wagons into place.

PAGE (cue page, cue sheet). A series of cues shown on the display screen of an electronic switchboard and referred to as a page.

PAGING CURTAIN. Walking a draw or tab curtain closed with stagehands on each leading edge (being careful not to be seen by audience) to ensure closure. Moving the downstage overlap part of curtain downstage and the other upstage to allow principals access to apron for bows.

PAINT AND PAINT COLORS. Although dry pigment systems still offer the largest dollar savings, the extra room, equipment, and specialized knowledge they require for use has made them far less popular than canned paints. Casein has largely replaced the dry pigment even in professional theatre, and the vinyl and latex paints are most popular with the nonprofessional theatre. See also ANILINE DYES.

Dry pigments. Catalogues from various supply houses list between forty and eighty different colors, including dye colors, dry colors, pulp colors, and metallic powders. Scene paint is sold in powder form by the pound. Among the many choices, usually several neutral colors (white and black), a basic earth palette (low intensity), and several chrome colors (medium and high intensity) are used more frequently than others. The table on page 136 may be used as a guide for a basic palette. For those preferring to work with a color wheel palette, the illustration under COLOR WHEEL provides the names of scene paints most closely related.

Acrylic latex (latex paint, rubber base paint). Premixed pints, quarts, gallons using latex as a binder. Rubber based paints in flat or semigloss are water repellent and can be used for outdoor scenery and floorcloths; can cover most stains to check bleeding. Must be diluted with water for spraying. Very useful for furniture and props. Clear latex, in flat or gloss, can be used as a medium for dry pigment or as a glaze. Available in twenty to twenty-five colors. Brushes and equipment may be cleaned with water.

Acrylic polymer. Used for studio art; the cost usually keeps it from being used in large applications. Very useful for specialized work because it adheres to most surfaces. Available in 2-ounce to gallon quantities.

Acrylic vinyl. Premixed paint using vinyl as a binder. Water resistant when dry. Twenty to twenty-five colors. Available in flat, gloss, clear, opaque, and colors, in gallon containers. 30-minute drying time is a major advantage of these paints. Clean up is with water.

Casein (Casein-Fresco color). Casein paints have largely replaced dry pigment for scene painting. Premixed with casein as a binder,

Paint	Price	Intensity	Uses
Whiting	Lowest		Sizing, ground coats; mixed with others to lighten value.
Zinc white	Medium		
Drop black	Medium		Black background; shadowing; mixed with others to darken value.
Ivory black	Medium		
Yellow ochre	Low	Low	Sizing; ground coats; general for dull yellow
Raw umber	Medium	Low	Ground coats; lowers value of other colors.
Burnt umber	Medium	Low	Ground coats; general for rich brown.
Raw sienna	Medium	Low	Ground coats; general for grayed brown.
Burnt sienna	Medium	Low	Ground coats; general for red-brown.
Venetian red	Low	Low	Brick red; general for dull red.
Vandyke brown	Medium	Low	Plain brown; base coats; woodwork, etc.
Cobalt blue	High	Medium	General for blue, sky, etc.
Ultramarine blue	High	Very high	Shadowing; general or intense blue; increases intensity of other blues.
Chrome green	Medium	Medium	Foliage; backgrounds; general.
Hanover green	Medium	Medium	Bright warm green for grass, trees.
Chrome yellow	Medium	High	Highlighting; mixed with others to increase intensity.
French orange mineral	High	High	Intense red-orange hue.
Chelsea vermillion	High	High	Intense rich red hue.

available in a thick paste which is thinned with water, about 2 quarts per gallon, to painting consistency. Water repellent and therefore suitable for outdoor use, floorcloths, etc.. May be mixed with aniline dye, vinyl paints, and latex for a variety of color combinations. May be used with any of the applicators and thins out sufficiently to be used even for transparencies. Available in twenty to thirty stock colors including brilliant, high-intensity colors. Water washup.

Lamp black. A carbon pigment sometimes used as a substitute for ivory black or drop black. Lamp black requires a "wetting" agent of alcohol or detergent to make it soluble in water.

Poster paint. Powder paints premixed with binders and available in 1 pound boxes at book-stores and art supply houses. Poster paints are more expensive than bulk scene paint but require no glue binder and are available in a wide range of colors. Poster paints can be mixed with scene paint to change value or intensity.

PAINT BINDERS. These include various animal products (gelatine, brown, white flake), clear vinyl, clear latex, dextrine, Methocel and starch. See also GLUES.

PAINTBRUSHES. Good brushes are expensive and should be given proper care. Always clean brushes after using in scene paint by washing thoroughly in warm water. Avoid excessively hot water and avoid running water full force into bristles. Hang brushes, bristles down, to dry. Natural hog bristle and nylon bristle brushes are very popular. Brushes used in oil paints should be cleaned in an appropriate SOLVENT. The most commonly used sizes of paintbrushes are as follows.

1/4 to 1 inch. Liners for highlighting, shadowing, and for freehand designs.

1 to 2 inches. Used for bold lining, small foliage, small patterns, painting furniture and woodwork, gluing muslin to flats.

2 1/2 to 3 inches. Used for large foliage brushes.

3 to 4 inches. General brushes, texturing brushes; used for spattering, stippling, scumbling, and dry brushing. See under PAINTING TECHNIQUES.

5 to 6 inches. Sizing, prime, and base coat-ing brushes.

PAINT FRAMES

Descending wall frame. A vertical frame that lowers into a pit or basement and allows the artists to work at floor level; the frame raises and lowers via winch and/or counterweight.

Wall frame. A stationary vertical frame; artist climbs to various levels to work from a rolling boomerang. Flying catwalks are sometimes used instead of the boomerang; they are operated by winch and/or counterbalance. The catwalk flies from floor level to the top of the paint frame.

Floor frame. Drops and flats lay on floor and artists walk across painting. By far the most difficult of all methods, requiring much experience. Biggest problem is need to get away far enough to view the overall picture.

PAINTING FURNITURE

Solid color. If furniture is to be painted with scene paints, extra glue should be added to protect costumes from being stained by rubbing against the furniture. Costumes are further protected if scene paint is covered by a thin coat of shellac. Since shellac darkens scene paint by many shades, make test samples first to determine the correct shade. Many prefer latex paints for furniture because they dry quickly, brushes can be washed in water, and the final product is waterproof and will not rub off. If a tough coat of clear, glossy, or satin finish is required for the furniture, VARATHANE may be used to cover any undercoat. It is also available in a variety of colors.

Stain. Various stains can be imitated for stage furniture by thinning shellac half and half with alcohol and adding a little pigment of desired color. Brush the solution on and wipe to desired shading.

PAINTING SCENERY. Scenery is always sized first with a thin flat coat or commercial wheat paste sizing to shrink the muslin or canvas. Casein paints do not shrink muslin well. On previously painted flats, a prime coat is brushed on to give a uniform base color and to act as a filler for the cloth. Use a full brush in a crisscross pattern. Avoid scrubbing of flats with dry pigment, which will cause undercoats to bleed through; also avoid puddling or dripping. Since other coats should follow sizing and/or priming, it is not necessary to have a finished, blemish-free surface. Base coat is the predominate color for the finished product and is the base for all other texturing. Often a prime coat is not necessary with the latex, casein, and vinyl paints, because these paints can be very opaque. See also PAINTING TECHNIQUES; **Choice of color** under DESIGN; STENCIL.

PAINTING TECHNIQUES. Various methods of applying paint over base-coated scenery in order to simulate texture. For all the techniques described below, make two or more applications, using different colors to attain the overall effect desired.

Dry brush (crosshatch). Draw bristles of a partially filled brush lightly over surface. Work diagonally, first one way, and then the other, over small areas at a time, achieving a crosshatch, shading effect. Apply several coats of different color.

Feather dust. Dip feather duster in paint and lightly flog surface. Stippling with a feather duster gives interesting texture to walls and floors. Foliage borders can also be painted in this manner.

Glaze. Dry-brush a previous application with hot water or a transparent dye color, achieving a better blending of colors. *Warning*: water allowed to drip on scenery may leave a permanent stain; dye paints will bleed through successive coats.

Glazed woodwork. Apply clear shellac or double-strength size water to painted wood-

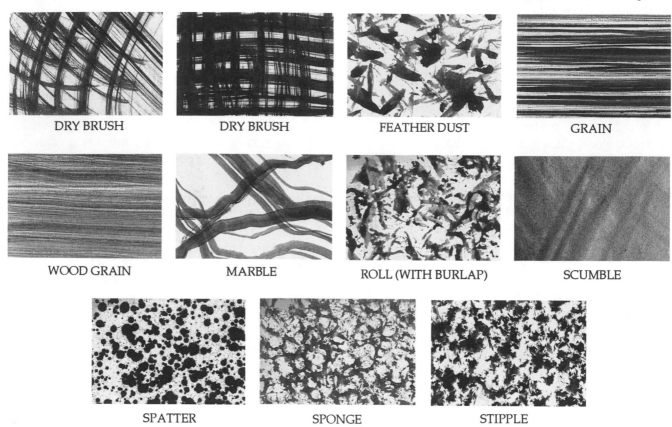

| DRY BRUSH | DRY BRUSH | FEATHER DUST | GRAIN |

| WOOD GRAIN | MARBLE | ROLL (WITH BURLAP) | SCUMBLE |

| SPATTER | SPONGE | STIPPLE |

PAINTING TECHNIQUES

work to give a glossy, varnished appearance. Both glue and shellac darken paint by many shades. Test samples first. An alternative method of obtaining a glazed woodwork effect is to apply clear latex wood finish diluted with water to desired gloss.

Grain. Same method as dry brush, using straight strokes instead of crisscross strokes. Apply several coats of different colors. Can be used to give effect of wood.

Marble. Dry-brush randomly with small brush or feather on fairly wet base color.

Puddle. Pour small amounts of two or three colors on flats and mix with a brush or spray water on wet paint to allow the colors to blend.

Roll. Dip cloth in paint, wring partially dry and roll on flats. Apply several coats of different colors. Effect is similar to that of marble. Different cloths (muslin, burlap, velour) give different results.

Scumble. Similar to dry brush techniques, with two brushes and two different colors ap-

plied alternately in a wet blend. The effect is more subtle than that of dry brush.

Spatter (fleck). Shake drops of paint from a partially filled brush onto flats. Apply several coats of different colors.

Sponge. Dip sponge in paint and squeeze out surplus. Daub flats in random pattern. Apply several coats of different colors. Use natural sponges for this technique. Rubber and plastic sponges are unsatisfactory, except for pattern use.

Spray. Use garden spray gun of tank type. Filter paint through cheesecloth into spray tank. Spray with rotating motion, avoiding pattern. Do not try for overall coverage; effect should be a more subtle rendition of spatter. Apply several coats of different colors.

Stipple. Daub ends of bristles of partially filled brush on flat. Apply coats of different colors.

Wet blend. See **Puddle,** above.

Wood grain. See **Grain** and **Dry brush,** above.

138

PAINT MIXING, DRY PIGMENT. No set formula exists for mixing scene paints because of the different characteristics of each pigment. However, the following formula can be used as a starting point: two parts pigment to three parts size water (2 cups full strength GLUE to 10 quarts of **hot** water) by volume. **Scene paint must have glue as a binder** to prevent it from being rubbed off. Since wet scene paint is many times darker than it is when dry, pigments should be mixed dry to shade desired. One quart of scene paint will brush paint approximately 60 square feet of new muslin (5' x 12'), depending upon the texture and condition of material. Scene paint will decompose within a few days if left mixed in cans or buckets. To make paint smell better add a tablespoon of oil of wintergreen to each bucket of paint. All paint should be tested on small pieces of wood or muslin before using. Force-dry samples with a hair dryer. Stem pipes, radiators, and hot water pipes make ideal testing surfaces for paints because they dry quickly. Check samples for the following problems:

Insufficient pigment. Paint is watery and does not cover surface. Add more pigment.

Too much pigment. Paint is gummy and tacky. Add more size water. Scene paint should be approximately as thick as latex paint and should flow smoothly from brush.

Insufficient glue. Paint rubs off. Add more hot glue (full strength) to hot paint. If glue is added to cold paint, it congeals in a mass and will not mix.

Too much glue. Sample appears to have a semiglossy often glittery surface. Paint is too sticky. Too much glue in paint results in eventual cracking (gatoring) and possible flaking. Add more hot water and if needed, pigment.

PAINTS, MISCELLANEOUS. The paints listed below are not generally used for scene painting but are useful for other purposes, as indicated.

Aluminum paint. A silvery paint used primarily for silvering props for the stage. It can be mixed with solvent that comes with it in a separate container, with shellac, with glue sizing, or with clear latex wood finish, according to need. To suggest silver finish and reduce reflection, add aluminum paint sparingly to pale blue scene paint.

Fluorescent paint. Designed to glow under ULTRAVIOLET LIGHT. Useful for props, costumes, outlines of scenery, etc. Fluorescent paints are available in spray cans, brushing lacquer, and crayons; fluorescent ribbons, and other materials can also be purchased. Available in a wide variety of colors from theatrical supply houses.

Gilding paint. Metallic powders can be used for gilding when mixed with one of the following binders: a lacquer vehicle used commercially for this purpose, shellac, dextrine, sizing, or clear latex wood finish. Large surfaces can be given a golden finish by mixing bronzing powder into yellow ochre scene paint and brushing the surface. Props to be handled should use the commercial vehicle, shellac, or clear latex wood finish as a binder. The last is a flexible binder, particularly good for painting draperies, drops, costumes, etc. Since latex is water soluble until dry, water can be used for thinning the paint and washing brushes.

Heat-resistant paint. Specially formulated to withstand high heat. Often sold as barbecue, auto engine, or stovepipe paints.

Lacquer. A quick-drying form of varnish available in paint stores in either brushing lacquers or spray cans. Useful for props and furniture. Do not use lacquers on Styrofoam or most other plastics.

Phosphorescent paint. Glows in the dark after being exposed to light. Useful in small amounts for spike marks or landmarks to guide actors and crew in blackouts. Phosphorescent paints are available in many paint stores and art supply houses.

Shellac. A purified lac resin used in varnishes. Used for painting furniture or props to be handled. Good as a binder for aluminum or bronzing powders. Use diluted to check bleeding of undercoats and to cover stains on flats before painting. Orange shellac is usually satisfactory and somewhat less expensive than white shellac. Use wood alcohol or shellac thinner as a solvent for diluting shellac and for cleaning brushes. *Warning:* Shellac tends to stiffen material and destroys the elasticity of canvas and muslin threads, causing material to wrinkle slightly and to fail to shrink at the same rate as the unshellacked portion of the flat.

Varnish. Clear or colored finishes for wood, furniture, props, etc. Urethane plastic varnishes are very popular. Mineral spirit cleanup. See also VARATHANE; VARNISH.

PALETTE

Artist's. A board on which colors are mixed for a particular painting or rendition. A rolling palette is larger version of the artist's palette mounted on casters and often having space for buckets, cans, brushes, and layout materials.

Colors. A particular range of colors used in a paint shop or for a given design.

PALINGS (pales). The verticals of a picket fence; loosely, the balusters in any balustrade.

PAN AND TILT LIGHTS (autopan, wiggle lights). Automated remote control powerheads designed to hold spotlights that pan (usually up to 270°) and tilt 90°. These lights may be programmed to work automatically or can be controlled by an operator. Often the units include a SCROLLER. Sometimes shows use this type of

PAN AND TILT LIGHT, LIGHT WIZ
(GREAT AMERICAN MARKET)

unit because they give the feeling of AUTO-MATED LIGHTS without the higher price.

PANA-VISE. A lightweight table vise used for working on electrical equipment.

PANEL, PLUGGING. See PATCH PANEL.

PANELING. A compartment with margins either apparently or actually on a different plane. Paneling usually consists of rectangular moldings applied to flats. Rectangles can be nailed or screwed to toggles or, when there is no support for nails, can be tacked or stapled through covering from behind. Lightweight panels can be stapled to muslin from behind. See also SCENERY PANELS.

PANEL LIGHT. A light used to illuminate a work area such as on a light board or sound board or in a stage manager's booth.

PANIC BAR. Lock designed to open exit door when release is pushed. Panic bars are required by fire laws on all exit doors in public buildings.

PAPIER-MACHE. Fibrous paper with a glue binder used in molds or on forms to make props, capitals, trees, etc. For general use, there are two types of papier-mâché, **Paper strips** and **Pulp mâché**. Although papier-mâché has been largely superseded by fiberglass and foam plastics, in theatre it is still used because of its low cost. See also CELASTIC.

Paper strips. Tear newspaper in 1" to 2" strips and dip in glue water (3 to 4 cups GLUE per 10-gallon bucket of water); draw between fingers to remove excess glue and lay on a chicken-wire form. Successive layers are built up to 1/16" to 1/8" thickness, crisscrossing each layer to give greater strength. Paper strip mâché is most useful for logs, TREES, stumps, etc. A final coat of burlap dipped in glue water and shaped in ridges resembling bark will add strength as well as texture to final product.

Pulp mâché. Prepared by boiling a fibrous paper, such as paper towels, until reduced to a pulp. Squeeze out water and add glue water (as above). Mash is then ready to press into molds of PLASTER OF PARIS (see also MOLD, PLASTER OF PARIS). Grease mold well before applying mâché and do not allow mâché to attain greater thickness than 1/2" to 3/4" in any one place. Greater thicknesses will not dry internally. Allow at least 12 hours for drying before removing from mold. Mâché can also be molded freehand on a frame of wood or wire mesh to form plaques, coats of arms, ornate capitals for columns, etc.

PARABOLIC REFLECTOR. See under REFLECTORS.

PARALLEL. A platform support designed to fold like a parallelogram. The top is made separately and can be detached for storage. Parallels are made of 1" x 3" lumber, with standard corner blocks and keystones reinforcing all joints, as illustrated. Place 2" backflap hinges on all corners as shown, allowing a 1" clearance between top of parallel and top of upper hinges. Two 3/4" (no. 8) flathead screws and one 1/4" x1 1/4" stove bolt are used in each half of hinge. Parallel tops are made of 3/4" plywood with 1" x 3" battens chamfered and screwed to the underside of the plywood and fitted snugly to end and center supports. Pad and cover the tops as in PADDING.

Continental parallel. Designed to collapse in the center, as illustrated, requiring less storage space.

CONTINENTAL PARALLEL

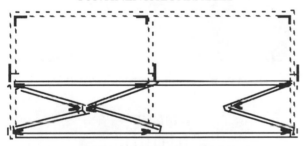

PLAN VIEW SHOWING HINGING
AND FOLDING PATTERN

Road parallel. Designed to fold as a standard parallel but with the end pieces set back 2" for ease in construction and easy access to hinges for repair when in the open position. Because the end support is 2" inside the ends of side frames, detachable facings are necessary.

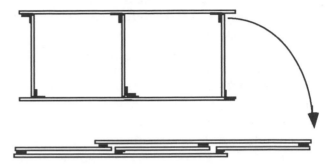

HINGE POSITIONS FOR ROAD SHOW PARALLEL

Standard parallel. End pieces are flush with the ends of the sides, forming a true box when in the open position. The major advantage of this unit is that it can carry the facings on the end and side pieces; the disadvantage is that in the open position one cannot repair hinges easily. See also RAMP; STOCK SCENERY.

PARALLEL CIRCUIT. See under CIRCUIT, ELECTRICAL.

PARAMETERS (ATTRIBUTES). Functions of a COMPUTER or AUTOMATED LIGHT.

PARCAN. See under LIGHTING INSTRUMENTS, FIXED FOCUS.

PARCHMENT PAPER. Used for scrolls. Certain lampshade manufacturers are able to supply

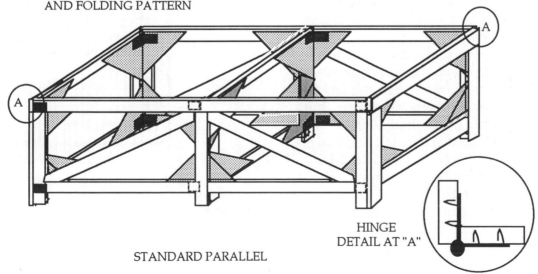

STANDARD PARALLEL

HINGE
DETAIL AT "A"

heavyweight parchment paper. Larger book-stores carry some grades of parchment, and smaller stores may be able to supply it through ordering houses. Lightweight butcher paper, rice paper, or onionskin paper can be used as a substitute for parchment.

PAR LAMPS. See **Parabolic reflector spot** under LAMPS: **Bulbs**; LIGHTING INSTRUMENTS, FIXED FOCUS.

PARQUET

An inlaid floor.

Once part of the auditorium now known as the orchestra.

PART

Acting. A role in a production.

Lights. See **Computer Terminology** under LIGHTING CONTROL.

PASTE. See WHEAT PASTE.

PASTEL

A tint of color obtained by mixing pigment with whiting.

A kind of crayon made by mixing ground paints with gum water. Pastels are also available in pencils and are useful in making color rendi-tions of settings or costumes.

PATCH AT LEVEL. See **Computer Terminology** under LIGHTING CONTROL.

PATCH BAY. See under SOUND EQUIPMENT.

PATCHCORD. See ADAPTOR.

PATCHING FLATS. See **Patching** under COV-ERING FLATS.

PATCH PANEL (patch, plugging panel, intercon-necting panel, cross-connecting panel). Panel used for interconnecting dimmers and outlets. A plugging panel of some type is absolutely necessary if lighting equipment and switch-boards are to be flexible.

Portable switchboards and control board (piano board, Davis, etc.). Incorporate patch panel into board by providing plug outlets for each dimmer. Cables from lights are thus plugged directly into the desired dimmer.

Telephone type. One of the most common of the older patch panels resembles an old-fash-ioned telephone switchboard, with each dim-mer connected to a receptacle and each outlet on stage connected to a male plug. By using patch-cords, any dimmer can be plugged to control any given outlet.

TELEPHONE TYPE PATCH
(STAGECRAFT INDUSTRIES)

TELEPHONE TYPE PATCH (STRAND)

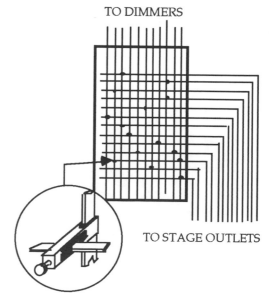

TO DIMMERS

TO STAGE OUTLETS

BUS-BAR INTERCONNECTING PANEL

Interconnecting panel. See **Slider patch**. See also QUICK-CONNECT.

Programmable patch. Electronic patching featured in certain computer boards allowing various dimmers to be patched to any control channel. As simple as assigning circuit number to a dimmer number via a keypad. See **Computer terminology** under LIGHTING CONTROL.

Rotary switch. Popular in public schools because of its safety factor. The rotary switch is placed in line between outlet and dimmers. Each dimmer is connected to its individual contact switch. By rotating selector to chosen dimmer number, any outlet can be connected with any dimmer.

Slider patch (bus bar type, interconnecting panel). A compact patch panel consisting of a permanent installation of vertical and horizontal bus bars with a sliding pin or interconnecting device usually on the load bus bar. Each vertical bar is wired directly to dimmer, and each horizontal bar directly to stage outlet or vice versa depending upon the manufacturer. By moving pin or slider to desired dimmer bar and plugging in, any outlet or any number of outlets can be put on any dimmer. Slider-type panels are custom-made for theatres. A common type of slider patch consists of vertical and horizontal bus bars with a sliding pin on each horizontal bar, spring-loaded so that it can be pushed in, slid to desired location, and released. Each slider represents one stage load with a capacity of 20 amps. Each bus bar represents one dimmer or other power source and has a maximum capacity of 40 amps. Commercially available from a variety of theatre lighting companys. Contact can be made and changed during play, resulting in greater flexibility of dimmers; however, because hot patching can produce arcs, it is advisable to patch cold (power off).

PATTERN. A full-scale model of design to be duplicated. Patterns can be made of paper, cardboard, beaverboard, or plywood. If a design is to be repeated, one-half is laid out, cut, and turned over, to be used as pattern for the other half. See also TEMPLATE .

PAY OUT (feed line). To allow a rope to pass through the hands, thus preventing tangling. If weight is involved in pay out, take a single or

SLIDER PATCH (CENTURY)

ROTOLECTOR ROTARY PATCH FOR SELECTING ANY OF 24 DIMMERS FROM THE STAGE CIRCUIT THAT IS CONNECTED TO THE ROTOLECTOR (KLEIGL)

double SNUB around a pin on the rail in order to control speed and avoid rope burns. It is advisable to wear gloves when handling lines.

PC. See **Plano-convex lens** under LENSES; **Plano-convex spotlight** under LIGHTING INSTRUMENTS, SPECIFIC.

PEDESTAL

The base of a column.

A short column supporting a statue, bust, or vase. Pedestals can be made from mailing tubes or cardboard rug cores for the main column, with wooden bases and capitals. For a realistic effect, fluted cardboard, available in window display houses, can be wrapped around columns.

PEDIMENT. An ornamental triangular piece over a window, door, or front of a building. Pediments are built as frames and applied to flats or are backed with plywood, beaverboard, or muslin.

PEG. A stage screw. See under SCREWS.

PENNY (abbr. d). Used as a suffix designating the size of NAILS.

PENTHOUSE THEATRE. See **Arena** under STAGE.

PERFORMANCE

A public display of a creative endeavor.

Brand name of a Kliegl Brothers lighting computer.

PERFORMER. Brand name of Kliegl Brothers compact lighting computer.

PERIAKTOS. Ancient Greek forerunner of the modern revolving stage. A three-sided revolving piece painted with scenery and located on each side of the stage.

PERIOD. A style or historical time. Often named after an important figure of the day (e.g., Louis XIV) or referred to by the century or certain of the years therein (e.g., Roaring Twenties).

PERIOD PLAYS. Plays set in any time other than the present. Authenticity of design, furniture, props, style of acting, and costumes makes a period play more convincing.

PERMANENT SET. See under SET.

PERSPECTIVE, FORCED. Perspective attained on stage by making portions of scenery in the background smaller than those in the foreground. Professional scenery is designed and built with downstage flats taller than upstage flats if forced perspective is desired. When the same effect is desired with stock scenery, triangular pieces are added to the tops of flats so that height will appear to decrease toward the backwall of the set. Do not cut or mutilate stock scenery for this or any other reason. Additions of this nature should be battened in place with 1 1/2" (no. 8) flathead wood screws and battens so that stock scenery can be reclaimed without damage.

PERSPECTIVE DRAWING. See under DRAWINGS.

PHANTOM LOAD. See GHOST LOAD.

PHASE. A unit of electrical time based on the rotation of AC generators. Theatre is usually

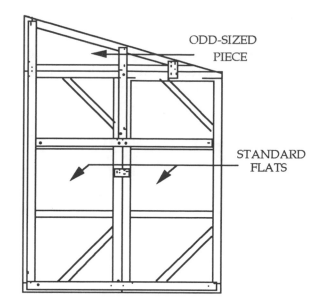

WALL IN FORCED PERSPECTIVE

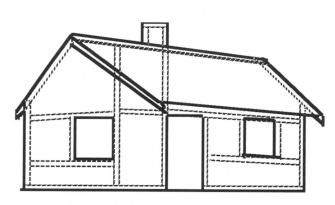

HOUSE UNIT IN PERSPECTIVE
USING FLAT CONSTRUCTION

concerned with single or three phase power. See ELECTRICITY.

PHONOGRAPH (phono, turntable). See under SOUND EQUIPMENT.

PHOSPHORESCENCE. Emission of light without heat from a material that glows in the dark for a limited time after being activated by a light source.

PHOSPHORESCENT PAINT. See under PAINTS, MISCELLANEOUS.

PHOTOMETER. An instrument that measures light intensity. Sometimes used on the stage for setting lights in order to discover hot or cold spots.

PIANO BOARD. See under SWITCHBOARDS.

PIANO WIRE. See under WIRE.

PICKET. Upright pointed stake used in making fences. Standard 1" x 3" battens are ideal size for pickets.

PICTURE FRAME STAGE. Proscenium stage, originating in the eighteenth century.

PICTURE HOOK. See under HOOKS.

PIGMENT. Usually a ground mineral or metal that is the base of most paints. See PAINT AND PAINT COLORS.

PIGTAIL. See ADAPTOR.

PILASTER (wall pier). A rectangular column with base and capital. Made of 1/4" plywood with desired thickness, usually 1" to 6" lumber nailed on. Molding is generally added for base and capital. Pilasters are sometimes used to cover cracks between flats which for one reason or another cannot be dutchmanned.

PILE. A nap on fabric having long fibres standing above the woven material. Pile fabrics (velvet, velour) have a rich depth visually. See also DRAPERY, STAGE.

PILE ON. To override one dimmer control with a second control. With electronic boards using presets, it is sometimes necessary to increase the intensity of one or two lights. This can be accomplished by piling on. Pile on cannot be used to decrease intensity below dimmer reading on preset.

PILLAR. See COLUMNS.

PILOT BIT. See **Center bit** under BITS.

PILOT HOLE. Small hole drilled in a certain location to prevent a larger drill from "creeping" off center.

PILOT LIGHT

A dim light used by stage managers or electricians for reading cue sheets. Such lights must be masked from stage by tin shields and are sometimes dimmed with blue gelatine.

A small light on a panel, radio, amplifier, dimmer, etc., indicating when equipment is on or off. Replacements are available at radio repair shops and stores. Check voltage on lamp.

PIN, BELAYING. See BELAYING PIN.

PINCH BAR. See CROWBAR.

PIN CONNECTOR. See under PLUGS, ELECTRICAL.

PINE. A softwood falling into general classifications of white pine and yellow pine. White pine is strong, lightweight, and easily worked and is therefore the best lumber for scene construction. See also LUMBER.

PIN HINGE. See **Backflap** under HINGES.

PIN RAIL. A rail in which belaying pins are set for tying lines. Pin rails are located on the side of the stage where lines from the grid are brought to the floor. They may be on stage level, halfway between stage and grid, or in both places or on both sides. See also RIGGING SYSTEMS.

PINS

Clevis pin. A straight pinning unit with a head and a pivot designed so the pin will not fall out. Often used in trusses instead of bolts.

Hitch pin. Originally used on farm equipment, hitch pins are now used in rigging and trusses. Must use an R CLIP to prevent it from vibrating out.

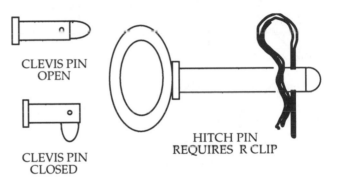

CLEVIS PIN OPEN

CLEVIS PIN CLOSED

HITCH PIN REQUIRES R CLIP

PIN SPOT. See under LIGHTING INSTRUMENTS, SPECIFIC.

PIN WIRE. See under WIRE.

PIPE. Galvanized or black iron water pipe is available in many sizes at plumbing and hardware stores. Pipe is measured by inside diameter and is usually sold in 21' lengths. Black pipe is best for theatre use. Standard C-clamps for spotlights and floodlights are threaded for 1/2" pipe and pipe fittings and are designed to clamp onto 1 1/4" or 1 1/2" pipes used as battens in flying systems. See also TAP AND DIE SETS.

PIPE BATTEN. See under BATTEN.

PIPE CLAMP. See under CLAMPS.

PIPE EXTENSION. A pipe that is smaller in diameter than the pipe batten and that can be telescoped into the batten and then kept in place with a small wooden wedge and gaffers tape (see under TAPE) over the joint; this is for relatively light loads only. Another method is to use a short pipe coupled on the end of a pipe batten. A smaller pipe screwed into a bell reducer also works. All of these methods are for temporary use only. A safety hitch (see under KNOTS) is tied on the long or short line to the extension pipe using a clove hitch and half hitches, forming what is called a becket or BRIDLE. This line should be near 45° to 60° from the vertical to support the extension from sagging or bending. Often a horizontal line is tied across the vertical flying lines of the batten to help keep everything in proper position.

Union. Double coupling with a special fitting making it possible to join two pipes without having to turn either one. The union consists of a fitting for each pipe and a nut that draws the two fittings together.

PIPE WEIGHT. The balancing of a counter-weight arbor and the empty pipe on an individual set of lines at the midway point between floor and grid. Often an empty arbor will do, but on occasion or with specific pipes such as electrics, it is necessary to add weight to the arbor,

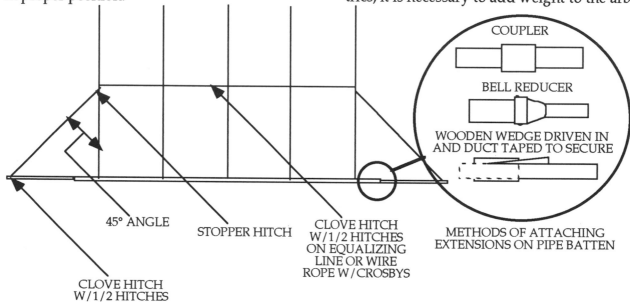

45° ANGLE STOPPER HITCH CLOVE HITCH W/1/2 HITCHES ON EQUALIZING LINE OR WIRE ROPE W/CROSBYS

COUPLER

BELL REDUCER

WOODEN WEDGE DRIVEN IN AND DUCT TAPED TO SECURE

METHODS OF ATTACHING EXTENSIONS ON PIPE BATTEN

CLOVE HITCH W/1/2 HITCHES

PIPE EXTENSIONS ON A SET OF LINES

PIPE FITTINGS. Attachments for fastening and joining pipe.

    Coupling (sleeves). Short length of pipe threaded on the inside and used to join other lengths of pipe.

    Elbow. Angles of 45° or 90°, threaded on the inside.

    Flange. A round plate with a threaded hole in the center to receive pipe. Available in standard pipe sizes and used to fasten pipes to floor, wooden bases, walls, etc.

    Nipple. Short length of pipe threaded at each end and used to join two pipe fittings in close connection. Nipples vary in length from about 1" (close nipple) to 3" (long nipple).

    Sleeve. See **Coupling** (above).

    Tee. A coupling device with which three pipes can be joined in the shape of a T.

and when this is done usually the top BRICK (counterweight) is painted to identify it as the "pipe weight" brick. Thus the commands to the loading platform when striking a set, "Go to pipe weight," or when loading, "Add [number] bricks above pipe weight."

PISTOL. See GUNS.

PIT. See ORCHESTRA PIT.

PITCH

    Lumber. Wood that is improperly seasoned or dried continues to bleed pitch or resin. For covering pitch stains, see **Pitch** under STAINS.

    Sound. Used to describe the high or low frequency of sound.

    Stage. Angle of RAKE STAGE.

PIVOT STAGE. See **Jackknife stage** under SCENERY, SHIFTING.

PLACES (Command verb). Order given by the

stage manager, alerting cast and crew that curtain is going up and that each member is to go to his proper place.

PLAN. Generally refers to floor plan but is sometimes loosely used to include all DRAWINGS.

PLANE. A carpenter's tool for smoothing wood surfaces. Sureforms (rasplanes), utilizing self-cleaning cutting edges in a steel blade, are useful in shop.

PLANER (joiner). A machine for smoothing or planing wood, not usually a part of the equipment of a small shop.

PLANO-CONVEX LENS. See under LENSES.

PLANO-CONVEX SPOTLIGHT. See under LIGHTING INSTRUMENTS, SPECIFIC.

PLANT. A member or members of the cast seated in the audience and speaking lines to give the impression of audience participation.

PLASTER BANDAGE. Gauze impregnated with plaster of paris used originally for casts for broken bones. Very useful in making molds to cast various plastics because the gauze adds a great deal of strength to the mold. Purchase at medical supply houses.

PLASTER CYC. A permanent backwall of a theatre, plastered and painted white and used as a sky cyc. Excellent for projections or for sky, but tends to eliminate stacking space and will scratch, chip, or mar over a period of time. Sand-floated plaster with a coarse grade of sand is best for plaster cycs.

PLASTER EFFECT. A rough plaster effect can be achieved by mixing cornmeal or sawdust in the paint. Achieved also by **Spattering** or **Stippling**; see under PAINTING TECHNIQUES.

PLASTERLINE. The upstage side of the proscenium wall.

PLASTER OF PARIS. A white powder formed by calcining gypsum. When mixed with water, plaster of paris forms a quick-drying paste ideal for making MOLDS. Plaster of paris is inexpensive and is sold by the pound at paint and hardware stores.

PLASTICITY

　　Acting. In a performer, the fluidity of motion.

　　Stage. The use of lighting and settings to produce a three-dimensional feeling.

PLASTICS. Many plastics are made by polymerization, a process that links together identical molecules to produce a plastic substance. These plastics are sometimes referred to as polymers. Although most plastics will either burn, melt, release toxic fumes, or all three when subjected to fire, the ease with which they are formed and machined makes them intriguing materials for theatrical uses. Check with fire codes or inspectors before using. Following is a list of some of the many useful kinds of plastics, a few of the ways they may be used, and some of their characteristics.

　　Acetate. Clear transparent sheets of plastic used as slides for low temperature, DIRECT BEAM projectors. Colored, felt-tip pens may be used on either acetate or glass slides. Acetate sheets come in standard sizes of 20" x 50" and vary in thickness from 0.2 mils (0.002") to 125 mils (1/8"). *Warning*: Acetate is a thermoplastic and starts to distort at temperatures of about 130° F; it melts at about 220° F. See also PROJECTOR SLIDES. Fire: ease of ignition, MODERATE; non-self-extinguishing.

　　Acrylic (acrylite, Lucite, Plexiglas). Available in sheets, tubes, bars, rods, clear or colored. Clear or translucent plastic sheets suitable for furniture, objects of art, etc. Acrylics can be cut with standard shop saws (generally, the finer the teeth, the smoother the cut), drilled with metal bits, and turned in a lathe. Slow speeds should be used with power tools to avoid friction heat, which melts the plastic. Use of sandpaper or emery cloth will result in a frosted or translucent effect and a wet rouge cloth will maintain the clear transparency. For a transparent floor, a 1/2" thickness will show little weight deflection if joists are on 2' centers. Stock sheet sizes are 4' x 6', but standard sizes of 4' x 8', 5' x 6', and 5' x 8' are usually available. Available in 1/8", 1/4", 3/8", 1/2", 5/8", 3/4", 1", and 1 1/2" thicknesses. Acrylic surfaces scratch easily; lightweight oil or a thin wax will help to conceal scratches. Acrylic is THERMOFORMING, machines easily, and has a variety of uses from weight-bearing furniture to sets. Casting resin also available. Fire: ease of ignition, READILY; non-self-extinguishing.

　　Acrylic modeling paste. Acrylic resin emulsion compounded with marble dust to form a paste that can be used in a variety of ways in theatre: paint it on sculptured objects made of Styrofoam or urethane to form a tough skin, resisting shock and breakage; build up wear-resistant, decorative filigrees or designs on furniture and props; use as a texturing compound for different surfaces (build up successive layers of 1/8" thicknesses, allowing drying time between each layer, and carve, sculpt or cut with knives, saws, or chisels into plaques, jewelry, etc). Acrylic modeling paste drys within 45 minutes to an hour and can be molded during this drying cycle. Clean tools and brushes in water before they dry. Available from art suppliers.

Casting resins. Most plastics are formed and cured by heat and pressure, but **unsaturated polyester** casting resins are mixed with a catalyst and poured into a mold to cure at room temperature. Curing time is determined by amount of catalyst used (usually 4 to 6 drops per ounce of resin) and may vary from 1 to several hours. Plastic manufacturers and distributors of casting resins sometimes sell polystyrene molds of various ornamental designs which require no releasing agents. However, other molds must use a wax releasing agent, or, as is the case of casting sheets of breakable window "glass," the resin may be poured on Mylar film, from which it is easily separated. Since these resins cure from within, thickness of the casting is of relatively little importance, though with great thicknesses, tremendous heat builds up and warping can occur. When ordering casting resin, specify intended use for either casting or molding. These are usually two different resins. One gallon contains 230 cubic inches.

Celastic. Colloidal filled fabric. Looks a little like felt, may be cut with scissors and sewn on machine, adheres to itself with a solvent, and hardens with an activator. Used for props, jewelry, and costumes.

Cellulose acetate (Celanese, Vupa). Available in sheets, for THERMOFORMING, as a glass substitute, and in roll stock for costuming, sewing, and props. Fire: ease of ignition, READILY; non-self-extinguishing.

Cellulose acetate butyrate (Tenite). Available in clear sheets and colored adhesives. Cuts well using power tools at slow speeds. Uses include THERMOFORMING, glass substitute, making armor, props and jewelry. Fire: ease of ignition, MODERATE; non-self-extinguishing.

Epoxy (auto putty, Devcon Steel). Putty type material. Some kinds need hardener, used for props, molds, and models, very hard when dry. Fire: ease of ignition, READILY; non-self-extinguishing.

Fluorocarbons (Teflon, Fluon, Tetron). Sheet rod tape, usually bonded to base material. No adhesives used for superslick surfaces.

Foam, Ethafoam rod. Expanded **Polyethylene** foam rod in flexible form. Ethafoam rod has a wide variety of uses including molding for curved walls and columns; scrolls for wrought iron railings and grills; trim on capitals; ornamental appliqués on picture frames or shields; piping for furniture upholstering. Ethafoam is used commercially as an expansion seal in construction work and is sold at reasonable prices. Standard diameters include 1/4", 3/8", 1/2", 5/8", 3/4", and 1". Fire: ease of ignition, READILY; non-self-extinguishing.

Foam, flexible. Resembling foam rubber, flexible **Polyurethane** foam has many uses in upholstering, padding, deadening vibrations and noises, making moldings and trims for curved scenery and columns, and making props. It may be cut with a sharp knife or a bandsaw but it is too flexible to risk cutting on a table saw. Flexible foams are generally more expensive than rigid foams. Standard sheets are 3' x 6' x 1" but 4' x 8' sheets are available on special order in thicknesses up to 1'.

Foam, Insta-Foam. A rigid **Polyurethane** foam in liquid form in a pressurized, disposable container. Two different nozzles are available in this package, one for spraying foam for texture and the other for pouring. Like other forms of urethane, Insta-Foam is flame resistant, non-toxic, and adheres well to most surfaces, including cloth and paper. Available in 1, 10, 25, and 50 cubic foot containers. Fire: ease of ignition, READILY; non-self-extinguishing.

Foam, rigid . This form of plastic is useful as a material for carving busts, statues, capitals, plaques, etc. Because of its density, rigid **Poly-**

urethane carves more easily with a sharp or an electric knife and does not tend to chip or mash as is the tendency with other foams. Finished products treated with **Acrylic modeling paste** (see above) are rigid and durable and may be painted with most kinds of paint. Urethane sandwiched between 1/4" plywood or 1/8" Masonite will make lightweight steps, stepping stones or cube furniture. Available in 4' x 8' sheets in a variety of thicknesses up to 12".

Foam, Styrofoam. A white, porous, lightweight, rigid **Polystyrene** plastic widely available in various sizes and shapes. Styrofoam is very useful in property departments for making decorative props for dressing sets, foods for display (pies, fruits, eggs, meat, etc.), and ornamental pieces. Styrofoam is easily shaped with saws, knives or rasps and can be painted with any kind of paint except lacquer. A soldering gun may be used to sculpt; heat thus provided melts Styrofoam in a relatively clean cut. *Warning*: Styrofoam will burn but a soldering gun will not ignite it. Larger pieces should be painted with fire-retardant paint. Fumes HARMFUL. Fire: ease of ignition, READILY; non-self-extinguishing.

Foam, Urethane. A lightweight foam plastic similar to, but more close-celled than, Styrofoam. Urethane foam is a versatile plastic because it is available in liquid chemicals to be used in molds, as rigid sheets to be cut and shaped, and in flexible sheeting to be used as padding and upholstering. When ordering for stage, specify self-extinguishing urethane foam in order to meet the fire codes. Unlike Styrofoam, urethane is resistant to most chemicals and solvents such as lacquer thinners, alcohol, and acetone. A variety of adhesives can be used to fasten foam, but because the close-cell structure of urethane allows no evaporation from within, laminating foam to foam presents a problem. Hot, ground amber glue and contact cement seem to be among the most effective adhesives. When using contact cement, allow maximum time for drying before pressing the two pieces together. **Working with foam:** Urethane foam is the product of two chemicals that, when mixed and stirred vigorously, rapidly take on a new form. One gallon of the combined

chemicals will expand into approximately 5 cubic feet of cured urethane. Mixing should be done with a propeller-type blender in an electric drill at about 1000 rpm. Molds may be made of PLASTER OF PARIS, papier-mâché, or even urethane but they must be thoroughly covered with two or three coats of Johnson's paste wax to ensure release. Mixing time is 20 seconds, during which time the propeller should be moved up and down in the combined chemicals to ensure thorough mixing. Pouring into the mold should occur before foaming, when the mixture is a light brown color and about the consistency of molasses. The mold should be tilted from side to side during the pouring to make sure all surfaces are covered. With an open-faced mold, a piece of plywood should be cut slightly larger than the mold, waxed, and used to hold down the rising foam, forcing it into the outer extremes at the top of the mold. The resulting product should be removed from the mold in about 10 minutes or before heat generated from the chemical reaction dissipates and allows the wax releasing agent to solidify. The finished product should be cold before attempting to clean. Clean mixing blades with acetone immediately. Fumes: HARMFUL. Fire: ease of ignition, READILY; non-self-extinguishing.

Mylar. A thin **polyester** film used as a releasing agent for casting resins, color media, and a variety of reflective surfaces. Mylar is much more heat resistant than acetate and is therefore more suitable as a transparency for slides in certain PROJECTORS. Fumes: MODERATELY HARMFUL. Fire: ease of ignition, MODERATE; non-self-extinguishing.

Nylon. Sheet, rod, tube, filament, clear, colored. Very strong, used in ropes, fabrics, low speed-bearing surfaces, paintbrushes. Fumes: SOMEWHAT HARMFUL. Fire: ease of ignition, MODERATE; self-extinguishing.

Phenolics (Bakelite). Usually used as an insulating material in electrical work. Fire: ease of ignition, VERY DIFFICULT; self-extinguishing.

Polycarbonates (Lexan). Sheets, clear. A high impact glass substitute and good material for transparent stage floor. Fire: ease of ignition, DIFFICULT; self-extinguishing.

Polyesters, saturated (Mylar, Dacron).

Available in film and roll and fabric. Variety of uses on stage. Fumes: MODERATELY HARMFUL. Fire: ease of ignition, MODERATE; non-self-extinguishing.

Polyesters, unsaturated. Fiberglass uses a hardener; roll stock is impregnated with resin and hardener. Many uses for the stage. Also available in casting resin. Fumes: MODERATELY HARMFUL. Fire: ease of ignition, MODERATE; non-self-extinguishing.

Polyethylene (Atathou, Dow, Dylan, expanded polyethelene, Ethafoam). Films, sheets, rods, clear, colored adhesive by heat welding. Cuts easily, used in all areas backstage. A flexible, thin sheet plastic with many commercial and home uses. Fumes: SOMEWHAT HARMFUL. Fire: ease of ignition, READILY; non-self-extinguishing.

Polypropylene (Polypro sheets, filaments). Adhesive available, cuts easily, used in theatre primarily for ropes. Fire: ease of ignition, READILY; non-self-extinguishing.

Polystyrene (Dylene, Lustrex, Styrofoam). Sheets, cast, resin, clear, colored. Adhesive available. Cuts and melts readily, THERMOFORMS used for wide variety of things backstage. Fumes: HARMFUL. Fire: ease of ignition, READILY; non-self-extinguishing.

Polyurethanes (Polyfoam, Formthane). Rigid, flexible sheets, casting resin, cuts easily and self-adhesive. Often used with molds to make forms. Froth-pak handy method of texturing a stage or set. Fumes: HARMFUL. Fire: ease of ignition, READILY; non-self-extinguishing.

Polyvinyl chloride (vinyl, Krene). Clear, milky, colored. A self-extinguishing, flexible, thin sheet plastic suitable for many covering and draping purposes on stage. Although polyvinyl will burn, flames will be extinguished by the fumes as soon as the source flame is removed. Standard widths are 36", 48" and 54". Standard thicknesses are 4, 6, 8, 10 mils and up. Fumes: HARMFUL. Fire: ease of ignition, DIFFICULT; self-extinguishing.

Silicones (Silastic). Catalytic hardening material, colored, lubricants, mold material, thermal insulators.

Synthetic rubber (Polysar). Sheets, gray.

Self-adhesive, cuts well, even with scissors. THERMOFORMING. Used primarily in costumes and props.

PLASTIC SETS. Stage settings composed of three-dimensional platforms, ramps, stairs, and elevations. Plastic sets of formal or rectangular geometric designs can be made with standard PARALLELS or with platforms from stock equipment. Irregular ground such as mountainous exteriors, overhanging cliffs, boulders, etc., must be built for particular requirements. It is practical to use available platforms, wagons, and steps as a base on which to work. Sturdy boxes, crates, or blocks of wood can be added to fill out general contour. Old rugs, rug padding, jute, or old muslin from flats can be used to round out contour and fill in sharp, abrupt, or unnatural corners. Tarpaulin, canvas, or old muslin (painted side down) can be stretched and tacked over entire irregularity and painted to resemble rough terrain.

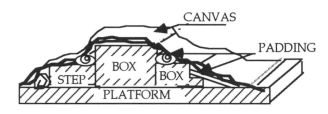

SECTION THROUGH PLASTIC SET

PLATE. A common wooden or metal decorative piece on furniture. See also CEILING PLATE.

Escutcheon plate. A decorative plate or shield used around doorknobs, locks, etc. Elaborate escutcheon plates can be made of cardboard or beaverboard.

Rosette. Name sometimes given to a circular plate between doorknob and door.

PLATFORM. An elevation. Most theatres find it advantageous to make collapsible platforms (PARALLELS) because they are easier to carry and store. See also RAMP; STOCK SCENERY.

PLEATING. Tying on drapes in such a way as to form fullness. Most common type is point-to-point tying, where the two ends are tied on then the center of the drape is located and tied to the center of the space between the two ends. Keep using this procedure till all the ties are tied.

PLIERS. Pincers used for gripping small objects and for bending or cutting wire. The most useful are electrician's pliers, carpenter's (slip-joint) pliers, and long-nose (needle-nose) pliers.

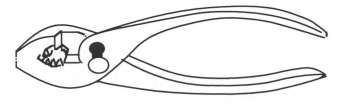

SLIP-JOINT PLIERS

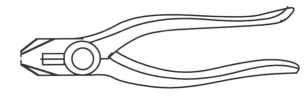

ELECTRICIAN'S PLIERS

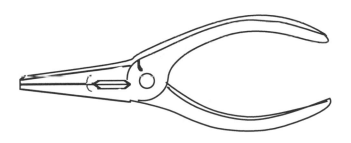

NEEDLE-NOSE PLIERS

PLOT. A floor plan or cue sheet or both, indicating location of lights, furniture, props, etc. Light plots, furniture plots, and prop plots should be made by the person responsible for each field, and notations of cues and changes should be clearly indicated. See also LIGHT PLOT; SOUND PLOT.

PLOUGH. To rip a DADO lengthwise in a board.

PLUG

    Flats. A small flat of less than standard dimensions, used to make special scenery. Standard flats with a plug battened between them top and bottom make an oversized window. Standard flats with a plug battened between them at the top make an oversized arch. Plugs are also used for GROUNDROWS and bushes with irregular cutouts applied.

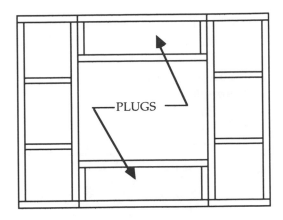

SCENERY PLUGS

    Lights. See under PLUGS, ELECTRICAL.

    Scenery. A piece of scenery fitting into a permanent skeleton set. See **Unit set** under SCENERY, SHIFTING.

PLUGGED OPENING (plugged arch). An opening or arch of a unit set that has been closed with another piece of scenery, e.g., windows, fireplace, curtains. See **Unit set** under SCENERY, SHIFTING.

PLUGGING BOX. A portable box for multiple electrical hookups. Plugging boxes are made to accommodate two or more plugs, usually **Stage plugs** (see under PLUGS, ELECTRICAL).

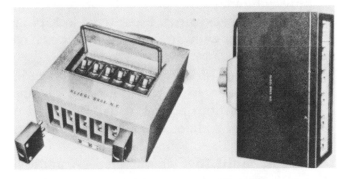

PLUGGING BOXES (KLIEGL)

PLUGGING PANEL. See **PATCH PANEL.**

PLUGS, ELECTRICAL. Electrical connectors of various types designed to make temporary connections in an electrical circuit. Most states require three-prong plugs for new installations, the third prong grounding the load. A female plug (body) contains one or more receptacles for prongs and fastens to the "line" (power supply). A male plug (cap) contains one or more prongs and fastens to the "load" (equipment to be used). Plugs in common use in the theatre include the following.

Edison plug. Standard type, not usually considered durable enough for stage use, but used for practical lamps, appliances, and shop equipment.

EDISON PLUGS

Multiple pin connector (spider). A female electrical connector to which more than one male connector can be attached.

Pin connector (slip connector). An electrical plug and receptacle particularly suitable to stage use because of its flat rectangular design (does not roll if stepped upon). Available in 20-, 30-, 60-, and 100-amp sizes. Most theatres try to standardize on one size, usually 20 amps for portable equipment.

Polarized plug. Electrical plug or receptacle designed to fit together in one way only and often used in switchboard hookups where interconnecting panels are used. Polarized plugs eliminate the possiblity of connecting equipment backwards. Most twist-lock plugs and all plugs with three or more prongs have polarity.

Stage plug (floor plug). A large plug designed for heavy loads of 20-, 30-, and 50-amps, fitting into a floor pocket, usually recessed in stage floor or wall, or into a portable plugging box.

Taps, multi (twofer, threefer). A multiple connector consisting of two or three female plugs attached to one male plug by a 2' or 3' length of cable or asbestos leads.

Twist-lock plugs. Round plugs that lock together when twisted, giving positive connections that cannot be pulled apart accidentally.

PLUGS, JACKS. A sound equipment term used to refer to male (plug) connector and female (jacks) connector. Two of the most commonly used in theatre are the XLR, used on most microphone cables, and RCA plugs, used on equipment and patch bays.

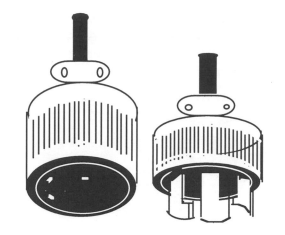

TWIST-LOCK PLUGS

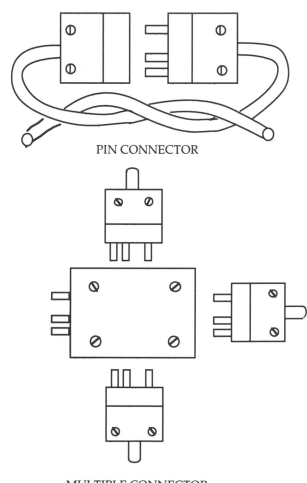

PIN CONNECTOR

MULTIPLE CONNECTOR

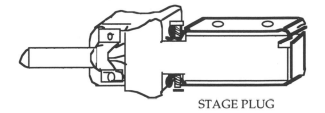

STAGE PLUG

PLUMB BOB. A small conical weight fastened to a cord and suspended to determine a perfect vertical line. Used to plumb or line up a set vertically.

PLUSH. See VELOUR.

PLYWOOD. Three or more thin laminates of wood glued together so that alternate grains run in opposite directions to make a stronger sheet of wood. Fir is generally the most reasonable and suitable for theatre use. Plywood is available in 4' widths and 6', 8', 10', or 12' lengths and 5' x 9' (Ping Pong tables). The most commonly stocked size is 4' x 8'. Longer lengths are expensive. Plywood is graded by letters from A to D with a separate letter for each side.

AA. Top grade both sides.

AB. Top grade on face with tight knots and circular plugs permitted on back.

AC. Top grade on face with small open defects permitted on back.

AD. Top grade on face with open defects up to 2 1/2" and pitch pockets permitted on back.

AC or AD grades are generally acceptable for theatre work. Plywood is sold by the sheet and priced by the 1,000 square feet. Prices vary with thickness. Common uses for plywood include the following.

1/8" door skin. This plywood consists of a thin sheet of expensive wood glued to less expensive sheets of plywood and used to face doors. In addition to standard 4' x 8' sizes, door skin is available in a 3' X 7' size, intended for standard doors. Used for thicknesses on arches or any facing requiring strength, light weight, and flexibilty.

1/8" plywood (three ply). Sometimes necessary for thicknesses of small-diameter arches and for facings on curved units and round columns.

3/16" or 1/4" plywood (three ply). Used for corner blocks, keystones, profiles, arch thicknesses.

5/8" or 3/4" plywood (five ply). Used for platform tops, steps, shelves, etc.

PNEUMATICS. Using compressed air or other gasses to power a variety of mechanical devices, usually tools and CYLINDERS.

POCKET. See FLOOR POCKET.

POCKET, CHAIN. See **Dye drop** under DROPS.

POINTILLISM. A system of painting by means of small dots of pure color applied with the point of a brush. **Spraying, Spattering, Stippling** (see under PAINTING TECHNIQUES) give effects similar to those of pointillism since separate dots of different colors respond to various colors of lights, giving three dimensional effect of solidity.

POLARIZED PLUG. See under PLUGS, ELECTRICAL.

POLE. One of the terminals (positive or negative) supplying electrical energy.

POLE, FOULING. See FOULING POLE.

POLYHINGE. See under HINGES.

POOL. An area covered by light from overhead spotlights in a near vertical position.

POPE COLOR WHEEL. A color wheel based on twelve colors.

PORTABLE BOARDS. Control boards lightweight enough to be moved from place to place and used to control lights, sound, hydraulics, curtains, etc.

PORTAL. A gate, door, or entrance, usually downstage on either side of stage. Portals can be either scenery constructed for the play or a permanent part of the proscenium. In many theatres of new design, portals are built as permanent side entrances to the apron.

PORTAL, LIGHT. Tall, narrow slot in side of proscenium or auditorium walls, where spotlights can be hung for proper lighting. Light portals should be included in theatre designs and should be a minimum of 18" wide, 6' above stage level, and 8' high. Portals should include masking pieces to conceal spotlights from audience and should provide access to the portal from behind to facilitate focusing.

POT. See POTENTIOMETER.

POTENTIAL. The tendency of an electric current to flow. Volts are measure of potential. Often referred to in terms of whether power is on or off. See also ELECTRICITY.

POTENTIOMETER (abbr. pot). A small variable resistance, similar to a radio volume control, used with electronic dimmers, sound equipment, etc., to vary the intensity of light or sound.

POT TIME. Time between introducing the catalyst (hardner) in fiberglass resin and and hardening of the plastic.

POUNCE BAG (chalk bag). See STENCIL.

POWER AMPLIFIER. See under SOUND EQUIPMENT: **Amplifier.**

POWER TOOLS. Electrically driven tools of various types. See also MOTOR, ELECTRICAL.

Bandsaw. A nonportable tool, having a continuous blade and used for cutting sweeps, curves, scrollwork, etc. The throat of a bandsaw (distance between the blade and the frame supporting the wheels) should be at least 18" in order to give adequate flexibility in use. Two-wheel and three-wheel saws are equally useful. Blades are sold by width and number of teeth: 1/4", six teeth, standard cabinet work; 3/8", six teeth, all-purpose cutting; 1/2", five teeth, heavy work and rough cutting. Skip-tooth blades are available in 1/4", 3/8", and 1/2" sizes; they are extremely durable. Skip-tooth blades can be used to cut aluminum and other soft metals.

Chop saw. A portable circular saw hinged on back side to a table. Comes down in a chopping motion on the material to be cut. Often used for metal and masonry.

Circular saw. See **Chop saw, Portable circular saw, Radial saw, Table saw.**

Cut-all. A portable cutter using a vibrating chisel as a blade. Very useful for fine scrollwork on beaverboard or 1/4" plywood.

Drills. Portable electric drills are designated according to maximum drill size accommodated by the chuck (1/4", 3/8", and 1/2"). 1/4" drill is usually adequate if a 1/2" drill press is also part of shop equipment. Attachments for buffing, polishing, grinding, sawing, and scrollwork are available and make drills doubly useful.

Drill press. A nonportable tool that attaches to bench or floor stand and is used for precision work. The drill press should accommodate drill shank of 1/2".

Electric screwdrivers. Usually cordless drills with the proper bit inserted. The 9.6- or 12-volt types seem to be most popular. Indispensable in driving **TEK screws** (see under SCREWS).

Grinder. Both portable and nonportable grinders are available. Useful for sharpening tools, polishing and cleaning metal, essential for welding.

Jigsaw. A nonportable tool, useful for fine scrollwork, but largely supplanted by the sabre saw and cut-all.

Jointer. A nonportable tool that has three rotating blades used to plane or smooth a board. Originally used to smooth for making joints.

Lathe. A nonportable luxury item for small theatre shops, but useful for turning ornamental pieces, furniture legs, etc.

Panel saw. A portable circular saw mounted on a moveable frame, leaning against a wall and used to cut or rip plywood or scenery panels.

Planer. A portable jointer; smooths and removes small amounts of wood.

Portable circular saw. Skilsaw (actually a trade name) is often used as a generic name. Useful for cutting large sheets of plywood or pieces too awkward to cut on a table saw. The portable circular saw is dangerous and should be used only by those who have demonstrated ability in the shop.

Radial saw (pull-over-saw). A nonportable circular saw cantilevered over the work and adjustable to any angle. Particularly useful for crosscutting at any angle but also designed for ripping and dadoing. Blades are interchangeable with **table saw** (see below) providing shaft sizes are the same. Preferred to a table saw for crosscutting long lengths of lumber, but a well-equipped shop will have both.

Reciprocating saw (Sawzall). A portable saw with the blade on the longitudinal axis of the motor and used primarily in remodeling work.

Router. A portable high speed wood shaper.

Saber saw (jitterbug, bayonet). A portable jigsaw that is most useful for cutting scrollwork or intricate designs from beaverboard or plywood.

Sander. The most useful of stationary sanders is a combination disk (or rotary) and belt. Portable disk sanders are best for medium to coarse work, and portable belt sanders are best for fine (furniture refinish) to medium work. Fine sanding is usually done by inline and orbital finishing sanders. Medium (no. 1) is all-purpose grit for most work, while coarse (no. 2 or no. 3) is used for heavy work, and fine (no. 2/0 or 0) is used for fine sanding, though on metal 6/0 is used.

Table saw. A nonportable, extremely useful power saw, used for ripping, crosscutting, ploughing, and dadoing. Blade diameters of 6", 8", 9", 10", and 12" are available. Combination blades (rip and crosscut) are generally best for all-purpose cutting. Tilting arbors are preferred to tilting tables.

Welder (arc, gas, TIG, MIG). The oxygen/acetylene welder is a gas welder. The others are all of the electric arc variety, with automatic self-feeding DC wire welders (TIG and MIG), using inert gases flowing over the molten metal, the easiest to use. A welder is essential in a medium-sized shop for joining metals.

PRACTICAL. Any prop or piece of scenery designed and constructed for actual use; e.g., windows and doors that open, fireplaces with lighting effects, switches on walls, etc.

PREAMPLIFIER (preamp). See under SOUND EQUIPMENT: **Amplifier.**

PREFOCUS BASE. See **Bases** under LAMPS.

PRESERVATIVES. See PAINT MIXING.

PRESET

Lights. A method of setting light intensity on a switchboard for one or more scenes in advance. When one scene is completed, a fader or master dimmer is used to fade lights down on one scene and up to preset intensities for the next scene. See **Computer terminology** under LIGHTING CONTROL.

Props. Setting properties onstage or offstage prior to their use in a production.

Scenery. Setting scenery in position ready for production. Scenery may have offstage presets for fast changes.

PRESET BOARD (console). A lighting control system by which one series of dimmers, controllers, or channels may be assigned a given cue while another series is assigned yet another cue. Preset boards often have from two to ten different presets depending upon the complexity of the system.

PRESET SHEETS. An additional cue sheet that gives only the presetting information on each cue. This type of specialization sheet is used usually on complicated shows. This type of fast-moving lighting is sometimes called a set-reset show.

PREVIEW

Lights (previewing cues). See **Computer terminology** under LIGHTING CONTROL.

Productions. A special performance of a production usually prior to OPENING and often one of the final DRESS REHEARSALS.

PRICKER (tracing wheel). A sharp-toothed wheel used for making perforations. Can be used to transfer wallpaper stencils to flats, or designs to fabrics for costumes, draperies, etc.

PRIMARY COIL. See TRANSFORMER.

PRIMARY COLORS

Lights. Red, blue, and green. See LIGHTING COLORS.

Paint. Red, yellow, and blue. See ADDITIVE METHOD OF COLOR MIXTURE; COLOR; SUBTRACTIVE METHOD OF COLOR MIXTURE.

PRIME (size). To cover with a first coat of paint to shrink and fill pores of muslin or canvas. See PAINTING SCENERY.

PRODUCTION MEETING. Planning meeting that usually includes director, stage manager, technical director, all designers, and any other people connected with preplanning a production.

PROFESSIONAL. Term used to refer to a theatre that usually employs union workers in some area within the production organization. See also UNIONS.

PROFILE (verb). To apply contours of profile board or beaverboard. See also GROUNDROW.

PROFILE BOARD. Three-ply 1/8", 3/16", or 1/4" thick, the name is derived from the common use of plywood on groundrows or set pieces where contours or silhouette outlines must be cut.

PROGRAMMABLE PATCH. See **Computer terminology** under LIGHTING CONTROL.

PROJECTED SCENERY. See also PROJECTORS. Scenery can be projected on a translucent screen with the projector located upstage, projecting from behind the screen, or onto an opaque screen with the projector located well above the floor in the downstage area. In either case, a certain amount of distortion (see KEYSTONING for illustration) can be expected because of the angle at which the beam of light hits the screen. Since most stages have limited space for projection, lensed projectors are usually located close to the screens and must be equipped with large, wideangle lenses.

Moving projections. Moving projections of abstract effects can be obtained by introducing a turntable or revolving disk at the focal point between the objective lens and the condensing lens of a projector, allowing metal cutouts or free-form abstractions placed on the disk to be rotated. *Warning:* The focal point is the hottest part of the light, and therefore, anything placed in this focus must be heat resistant. Moving projections may be achieved by using one of the following methods.

Cloud drum. Cutouts of clouds, hills, buildings, etc., fastened to a wire mesh drum 4' in diameter, rotating around a strong light source will cause shadows to move across cyc. The lamp must be clear (see PROJECTOR LAMPS) and have concentrated filament.

Sciopticon. An attachment for a spotlight consisting of a rectangular box housing a transparent disk, usually mica, on which clouds, rain, snow, waterfalls, flags, etc., are painted. A clock mechanism or electric motor rotates disk through beam of light, and an objective lens focuses image on sky drop. The sciopticon is available through most theatrical supply houses or stage lighting manufacturers.

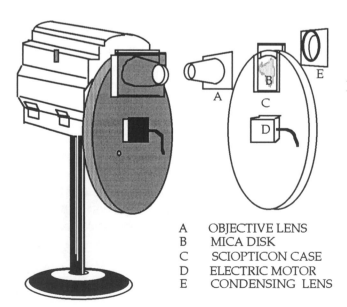

A   OBJECTIVE LENS
B   MICA DISK
C   SCIOPTICON CASE
D   ELECTRIC MOTOR
E   CONDENSING LENS

SCIOPTICON MOUNTED ON SPOTLIGHT

PROJECTION (art). See under DRAWINGS.

PROJECTION BOOTH. See BOOTH, PROJECTION.

PROJECTION SCREENS (sheets). A device used to show an image projected from the front or rear. Front projection screens have often been made of a highly reflectorized material such as glass bead screens. The more recent welded plastic screens have the advantage of taking the place of the traditional sky cyc and can be used from either the front or the back.

Front screen. A screen that must have the projector placed in front of it (audience side). Keystoning is a major problem with front projections since placing the projector in the optical axis of the screen is usually impossible. Front screens can be as simple as seamless muslin or scrim or a more elaborate reflectorized screen or a light-colored plastic.

Rear screen. A translucent screen that must have the projector placed behind it. The major problems associated with this type of screen are that it requires a large space behind it for projector throw and the hot spot of the light source is very often hard to disguise. Greatest advantage is the lack of keystoning because the projector can be placed at the optical axis of the screen.

Plastic screen. With the advent of welding on plastic material which is either opaque or translucent, the plastic screen became a reality. Depending upon the manufacturer, screens are available in several colors from white through cream to light gray, dark gray and black, and for front projection, rear projection, or dual projection.

PROJECTOR LAMP. Light sources for projectors have always been a leading problem in the development of projectors. Ideally the source should be a pinpoint of high-intensity light which is in the 3200 kelvin range and dimmable. Early incandescent lamps usually did not meet many of the requirements; the 2,100-watt 60-volt lamp was better, and the tungsten halogen lamp is better yet. With the advent of the encapsulated arc lamp (see HMI, XENON LAMP) the high-intensity, pin point of light requirement is certainly met; however, these lamps are still not the answer. Laser light sources may be used in the future or a yet undeveloped light source; only time will tell.

PROJECTORS. See also PROJECTED SCENERY. The simple projector consists of a high-intensity light source, a condensing lens for concentrating light, a slide holder, and an objective lens for focusing. A projector designed for one slide is called a uniplate, and a projector designed to accommodate several slides controlled remotely is called a multiplate. Focal length of objective lens will determine size of image on a screen. The following equation is used to determine necessary focal lengths for a given throw: $S/f = I/D$; in which S = slide size (height or width); f = focal length of lens; I = image size (height or width); D = distance from lens to image. Example: what focal length is needed for an image 30' wide at a distance of 20' with a slide 5" wide? $5/f = 30/20$, or $5/f = 3/2$, or $10/3f$, or f = 3.33 inches.

Linnebach projector (direct beam, lensless). A strong light source from a concentrated filament and a frame 3' to 5' away from the light source constitute this projector. Cutouts, paintings on transparencies, or combinations of both can be inserted in the frame for projection on cyc. This type of projector lacks the clarity obtainable with lens projectors. The best lamp for direct beam projection is one with a close filament. The light source must be of a high intensity and small, tight filament.

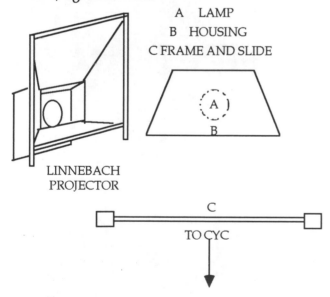

A   LAMP
B   HOUSING
C FRAME AND SLIDE

LINNEBACH
PROJECTOR

TO CYC

Overhead projector. Designed largely for classroom use, where the instructor writes on an acetate sheet with felt-tip pens and the writing is projected on a screen behind him; is also adaptable to rear screen projection. Since the slide used in this equipment is about 12" square, the designer is able to add a great deal more detail than is possible in smaller slides. 1,000-watt tungsten halogen lamps will provide sufficient intensity for pictures up to about 15' square, depending upon the opacity of the slide and the amount of AMBIENT LIGHT on stage. As with the slide projector, the fans of overheads must be left on full speed if the lamp is to be dimmed. Overhead projectors are great time savers in paint shops, where they may be used to project scenes, cartoons, wallpaper, etc., on drops and flats for quick transfer.

Rear-screen projector. Projector located behind a translucent screen. Such projectors generally have wide angle lenses so that distance between screen and projector can be minimized. It is necessary to keep the projector either below or above the direct line of vision of the audience. For screen see **Rear screen** under PROJECTION SCREENS; for a low budget screen see **Translucent drop** under DROPS.

Slide projector (carousel, tray type). For multiple screen or small-screen projections (up to about 10' square) the carousel or tray projector can be a very useful instrument. If the projector is to be dimmed, however, the fan must be rewired to a hot line. Most projectors of this type have many plastic parts, which will melt or distort beyond repair if the lamp is left on without the fan, or if the lamp and fan are turned off simultaneously after extended use. Tungsten halogen lamps and xenon light sources are preferred depending upon throw and size of image desired. The zoom lens has a distinct advantage in offering greater latitude in placing the projector while still filling the screen.

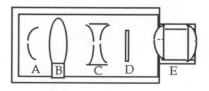

A = REFLECTOR B = LAMP C = CONDENSING LENS
D = SLIDE E = OBJECTIVE LENS

SIMPLE PROJECTOR

Stereopticon. Obsolete; a projection lantern that magnifies and projects pictures. Adaptations of stereopticons are used for projecting scenery of various kinds.

PROJECTOR SLIDES. Materials most commonly used for making slides are glass, Mylar, and acetate. On the rare occassion when the designer paints his own slides, he will have to check the heat within the projector and choose his material and dye paints accordingly. Glass withstands the most heat, with Mylar next and acetate following; acetate distorts at 130° F and melts by 250° F. ROSCODYE and alcohol-based felt-tip pens work well for most slides although it is advisable to test the medium used in the projector. Be aware that a small mistake, scratch, error, etc., made on a small slide becomes a big mistake when that slide is blown up to full size. Drawing in distortions to compensate for KEYSTONING, is very difficult. This problem is easily handled with the use of a bellows camera, which can, with some experimenting, photograph a picture or drawing with compensating reverse distortion.

PROJECTOR SPOT. See **Beam projector** under LIGHTING INSTRUMENTS, FIXED FOCUS.

PROMPT BOOK (book, script). Acting copy of a play used by the prompter or stage manager to help actors with lines, business, and cues.

PROMPTER (book holder). One who holds the script and follows the action during a play in case lines are forgotten on stage.

4,000-WATT PROJECTOR WITH MOTOR-OPERATED CARRIAGE FOR SIX SLIDES (STRAND)

5,000-WATT PROJECTOR (CENTURY)

CAROUSEL SLIDE PROJECTOR (KODAK)

MIGHTY MITE, 1,600-WATT XENON PROJECTOR
(STRONG ELECTRIC)

2,000-WATT SCENE MACHINE WITH SLIDE CARRIER
(THE GREAT AMERICAN MARKET)

PROMPT SIDE (PS). A professional stage direction in America, meaning the side of the stage on which the prompter was seated, generally stage right (see AREAS). See also OP; STAGE DIRECTIONS.

PROPERTIES. See PROPS.

PROPERTY MASTER. See under STAGE CREW.

PROPORTIONAL DIMMING. See **Electrical master** under DIMMERS, MASTER.

PROPS (properties). Stage furniture, set dressing, plus articles used in performance by actors. See under individual entries.

    Breakaway props. Props that are supposed to break as part of the action of the play.

    Dressing props (decorative props). Pictures, draperies, ornaments, centerpieces, flowers, bric-a-brac, etc.

    Hand props. Props handled by the actor but not carried on their person.

    Personal props. Any prop carried by actors. Pens, combs, money, paper, etc.

    Set props (floor props). Furniture, rugs, etc.

PROSCENIUM (proscenium arch). The frame separating stage from auditorium.

PANI PROJECTOR 4,000-WATT HMI (PANI)

False proscenium (inner proscenium). An inner frame set upstage of curtain to narrow proscenium or to set action further upstage to facilitate lighting.

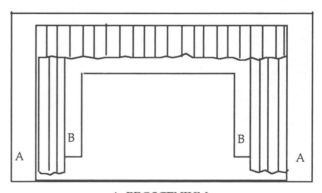

A PROSCENIUM
B FALSE PROSCENIUM

159

PROSCENIUM DOORS (vomitoria doors). Doors usually on the audience side of the proscenium leading off the apron.

PROSCENIUM LINE. A line drawn on the floor parallel with the upstage proscenium wall. Often used to measure scenic points on DRAWINGS. See also PLASTERLINE.

PROTOCOLS. See under DMX PROTOCOL.

PROSCENIUM STAGE. See under STAGES.

PRUSSIAN BLUE. A blue-black pigment used in scene painting for shadowing or for darkening other paints, including black. Prussian blue is both intense and expensive and therefore hardly ever used as a pure color. See also PAINT AND PAINT COLORS.

psi. A unit of pressure measurement, pounds per square inch.

PUBLIC ADDRESS SYSTEM (abbr. PA). An older sound system intended to amplify a speaker's voice in a large area and generally associated with poor directionality and fidelity. PA systems are comprised of microphone, amplifier, and speakers. See also SOUND EQUIPMENT; sometimes used as a generic term for a SOUND REINFORCEMENT SYSTEM.

PUDDLE PAINTING (wet blending). See under PAINTING TECHNIQUES.

PULLEY. See SHEAVE.

PURCHASE LINE. The operating line in a COUNTERWEIGHT SYSTEM. See also **Overhaul line** under LINE: **Rigging.**

PYROTECHNICS. Use of flash powders and other chemicals and explosives to make flashes, smoke, and special effects. The use of many new types of materials has tended to make this a highly specialized field, and, as such, expert advice is often required. A good starting point for that information is a supplier.

Q-FILE. Obsolete. Trade name of Century Lighting for a memory system of light control. See also LIGHTING CONTROL.

Q-MASTER. Obsolete; trade name for a single package dimming system by Century Lighting.

QUALITY OF COLOR. See COLOR.

QUARTZ IODINE LAMPS (quartz lamps, quartz halogen). A small, compact, long-life lamp used in various types of LIGHTING IN-STRUMENTS, largely replaced by **Tungsten halogen**; see under LAMPS.

QUICK-CONNECT PANEL. Obsolete. Brand name for a type of spring-loaded slider patch by Ariel Davis Dimmers. See also **Slider patch** under PATCH PANEL.

QUIET PLEASE (Command verb). Order for silence backstage; usually given just before curtain rises.Often understood to be unspoken part of the order PLACES.

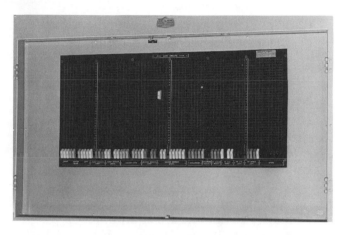

QUICK-CONNECT PANEL (ARIEL DAVIS)

R

RABBET. A groove or slot cut in the edge or face of one piece of wood to receive the edge of another. Commonly used to receive profile board. See also FURNITURE; GROUNDROW.

RACEWAY. See under WIREWAY.

RACK (noun)

   Scenery. Storage space or bins for scenery. Narrow racks of 30" to 36" are the most convenient.

   Sound. A metal container made to a standard 19" space between the steel uprights, used primarily to hold audio equipment.

RACK (verb). To put scenery into its storage space.

RACK AND PINION. A bar (the rack) with teeth that engage in the teeth of a gear (the pinion). Most older dimmers using mechanical interlocking banks made use of racks and pinions to transfer lever movement of the handle to rotary movement of the dimmer arm. See also **Mechanical master** under DIMMERS, MASTER.

RADIAL SAW. See under POWER TOOLS.

RADIO or STEREO, ONSTAGE. It is usually adequate to place a speaker from sound equipment behind the scenes in general vicinity of prop sound sources on stage. However, in arena staging and in certain other instances of more intimate staging, a small speaker may be mounted in the prop furniture and wired to offstage equipment.

RADIO FREQUENCY NOISE. Electrical disturbances from certain types of dimmers, picked up by intercom system or sound equipment. Equipment causing disturbance should be shielded in a metal box or separated. Radio frequency noise occuring in lamps is the audible vibration of lamp filaments caused by certain electronic dimmers. Most dimmers that might offend have built-in chokes to control filament vibration. If not, manufacturers should be consulted for correct choke.

RAIL, HAND. See BANISTER.

RAILING. See BALUSTRADE; BANISTER.

RAILS. Top and bottom crosspieces of a FLAT.

RAINBOW. Defective lenses, not corrected for chromatic aberration, can sometimes be masked so as to give a good rainbow effect on the cyc. **Linnebach projectors** (see under PROJECTORS) can be masked out to give a rainbow of the exact size and shape desired, and colored gelatine can be glued in strips over the cutout. Colors should follow the proper order of the spectrum: red, orange, yellow, green, blue, indigo, violet. In a primary rainbow, red is at the top and violet at the bottom; when a secondary rainbow appears above the primary, the spectrum is reversed, with violet at the top and red at the bottom.

RAIN EFFECT

   Sound. Effect achieved with a drum about 2' in diameter, covered with screen or tin and filled with dried peas or beans. Rain drums are suspended on a center axle and hung in supporting

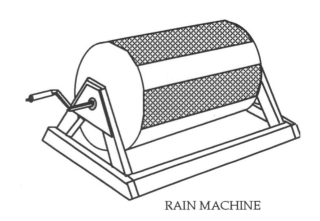

RAIN MACHINE

frames to revolve freely. Sound can be varied by wrapping the drum with padding or by substituting BBs, buckshot, or marbles for dried beans.

Visual. Rain is sometimes simulated by water dropping through perforated pipes above windows and doors, with catch pans to contain the water on the floor. Positive control of this method is difficult, and annoying dripping may continue long after the cue to stop. Fine-grain rice falling from a perforated cradle (see SNOW CRADLE) will, with proper lighting, give a realistic rain effect when rain is needed over large areas. Projected rain effects on a front scrim with some fog and appropiate sound effects also will work in some productions. See also FOG EFFECT.

RAKE

Scenery. To place a set or furniture at an acute angle to footlights. Sidewalls of a set are often raked to provide better sightlines. Proper rake is determined by the extreme seats in the first row. It is not always necessary to rake a set to the extent that the sidewalls are visible from extreme seats, but it is desirable to place set so that the actors will be in full view of the audience at all times.

Stage. To set stage or acting area on an incline with the downstage being low and the upstage being high. Most early stages were raked to improve sightlines from the flat level floor of the auditoriums. In recent years the raked stage has gained in popularity again and ramps are made by superimposing platforms or plywood legged to the desired pitch on the flat stage floor. Actors adjust readily to a 1" rise in 12" of floor space and may manage a 2" to 12" rake with a nonslippery surface; greater angles than this are not recommended. When a stage is raked the scenery and traveling wagons have to be modified to compensate for that rake, sometimes this is in the form of reverse rake. Furniture used on a raked stage is also sometimes adjusted to be perpendicular and level.

RAMP. An inclined or sloping platform. Ramps can be made with standard parallel tops placed on triangular frames of 1" x 3" stock lumber. The span between such supports should not exceed 30" and the maximum pitch should not exceed a 2" rise in 12" feet of floor space if the ramp is to be practical.

R AND R. Draftsman's symbol for reverse and repeat meaning to build another just like it only in reverse. See MIRROR IMAGE.

RAPIER. See SWORDS.

RASP. See FILES.

RATCHET, YANKEE. See YANKEE SCREWDRIVER.

RATTAIL

A form of ADAPTOR.

A kind of FILE.

RAW LUMBER. Unfinished or unplaned lumber.

RCA PLUG. See PLUGS, JACKS.

R CLIP (hitch clip). Used with hitch pin so the pin cannot vibrate out.

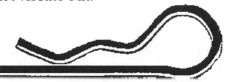

R CLIP

REACTANCE DIMMER. See under DIMMERS.

READER. Obsolete name for prompter or bookholder.

READING. The setting on a dimmer, sound equipment, or other device with a calibrated scale, usually a scale from 0 to 10. On computer boards, the setting may well be 0 to 100 using digital readouts.

REAMER. See under BIT.

REAR ELEVATION. See **Elevation, rear** under DRAWINGS.

REAR-FOLD TRAVELER. See TRAVELER.

REAR SCREEN. See under PROJECTION SCREENS.

REAR-SCREEN PROJECTOR. See under PROJECTORS.

RECEPTACLE. See PLUGS, ELECTRICAL.

RECESS. To set back or to set into a wall. A recess of 3" to 6" is sometimes used to eliminate unsightly cracks occurring when flats must be lashed together. See also ALCOVE; DESIGN.

RECORD. See **Computer terminology** under LIGHTING CONTROL. .

RECORDS (sound effects). Recordings available in vinyl disk, compact disk, and audio tape, covering every conceivable need are available on order from most larger recording companies. Specialized sound effects records, usually vinyl, are available from theatre supply houses. On occasion and in emergencies, some effects records may be borrowed from local radio stations. If tape equipment is available, location recordings may be made. See also SOUND EQUIPMENT.

RE-COVERING FLATS. See under COVERING FLATS.

REDWOOD. A very soft reddish wood of the pine family. Redwood is splintery and brittle, not satisfactory for flat construction.

REFLECTANCE. Reflected light divided by incident light and expressed in percentages.

REFLECTOR DROP. A plain or light-colored painted drop used to reflect light behind transparencies.

REFLECTOR LAMP (R lamp). See under LAMPS.

REFLECTORS. A reflector is usually a highly polished metal or mirror, concave in shape, used in spotlights. Floodlights and border lights generally have reflectors of a dull metal, either spun or stamped to shape. Efficiency of reflectors ranges from about 10% for light-colored surfaces to about 90% for mirrored glass or Alzak reflectors. Besides the white surfaces used on some types of general lighting equipment, there are four basic types of reflectors used in lighting equipment, each designed for a specific purpose in lighting. See also DICHROIC FILTERS.

Ellipsoidal. A reflector with two focal points. Ellipsoidal reflectors extend farther around lamp than parabolic reflectors, thus capturing more light rays, about 75%, and directing them to a second, or conjugate, focal point. Ellipsoidal reflectors are used in spotlights, and scoops. See also LIGHTING INSTRUMENTS, SPECIFIC.

Parabolic. Designed to reflect light from its focal point into parallel rays. Such reflectors are found in certain floodlights, beam projectors, scoops, and PAR lamps.

Spherical. Designed as a section of a sphere, with radial point the same as focal point. Light reflected from spherical reflectors returns and passes through the focal point, increasing efficiency by approximately 40%. Most plano convex and fresnel spotlights use spherical reflectors. Also used as front reflector in some beam projectors.

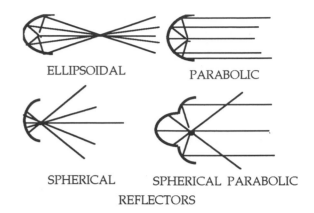

ELLIPSOIDAL

PARABOLIC

SPHERICAL

SPHERICAL PARABOLIC

REFLECTORS

Spherical-parabolic. This combination of spherical and parabolic reflectors is generally made of spun aluminum and is found in older types of borders and footlights.

REFRACTION. Bending of light rays when passing from one medium to another. A lens refracts light to concentrate on a given point called the focal point. Focal lengths are expressed in inches from the lens center to the point where rays of light converge.

REHEARSAL. A practice session of a production, during which time lines and blocking are learned, dances and music are integrated.

REHEARSAL PROPS. Simple, even crude, imitations of properties to be used in a show, basically to let the performer handle something. Often used until dress rehearsal.

RELAY. A remote switch, usually electromagnetically controlled.

RELEASING AGENT. A lubricant used to release material from its mold.

REMOTE CONTROL. Operation of lights, sound, hydraulics, pneumatics, or other device from a location remote from equipment. See also **Console** under LIGHTING CONTROL; CYLINDERS.

RESET BUTTON. See **Circuit breaker** under SWITCHES.

RESIN. Plastic resins are usually liquid until activated by a catalyst which hardens them. See PLASTICS.

RESISTANCE. Any conductor offers a certain amount of friction or resistance to the passage of electricity, depending upon the material, diameter, length, and temperature. This resistance is expressed in ohms. See ELECTRICITY; OHM'S LAW.

RESISTANCE DIMMER. See under DIMMERS.

RESPONSE TIME. The time it takes an operator of equipment to take a cue from the GO command of the cuer.

RETURN

A flat paralleling footlights and terminating the downstage wall of a set.

Two flats hinged at right angles to fold back to back.

REVEAL (thickness). Usually a 1" x 4" board fastened to the back of an opening of a flat to give an illusion of thickness to a wall. See also DOOR; WINDOWS.

REVERBERATION (reverb). The sound remaining in a space after the initial source has stopped. Sometimes called echo. Often part of creating the AMBIENT SOUND of a space and expressed in terms of time, usually parts of a second.

REVERSE VIDEO (highlighted). A shaded area used to show a particular piece of information on the display screen. See **Computer terminology** under LIGHTING CONTROL.

REVOLVER. See GUN.

REVOLVING STAGE. See under SCENERY, SHIFTING.

RF. See RADIO FREQUENCY NOISE.

RGB. Red, green, blue: a method of color blending using light primary colors. This method of blending is often used in AUTOMATED LIGHTS and DICHROIC FILTERS. See also COLOR; CYM.

RHEOSTAT. A variable resistor regulating current in a circuit by varying resistance in series with the load. See also **Resistance dimmer** under DIMMERS.

RIBBONS. A colloquialism for T-track lines (see RIGGING SYSTEMS) with mounting angle irons on the sidewall of the stage. Sometimes it is necessary to climb the ribbons to ride down an arbor.

RIDE THE LINES. To fly heavy scenery in a grid system without counterweights it is sometimes necessary for a stagehand to climb to the fly gallery and hang onto the lines, literally riding to the floor as others pull. This is obviously a dangerous practice and should not be encouraged. See also BULL LINE.

RIDING GAIN. The constant adjustment of a volume control necessitated by a variety of external factors. See SOUND REINFORCEMENT SYSTEM.

RIFLE. See GUN.

RIGGING. The use of ropes, wire ropes, pulleys, and other tackle. Any number of different kinds of rigging can be used onstage for as many given effects. Some of the constantly used devices are as follows.

Bag line. A line that lifts up a sandbag on a **sunday** (see under KNOTS) to gain a higher purchase on a set of lines. On lines that have very heavy weight, a bull line may be used to pull the set of lines down with a sunday.

Endless. A line that has a sheave top and bottom and the rope is spliced to run through the sheave. Sometimes used on certain sets of lines to slide a sunday up or down the lines; the endless must be free to move along with the sunday.

Spot line. A line that has a sheave only on top and attaches to something either offstage or onstage and then ties off on a belaying pin. Used to lift electric cables, sound cables, etc., to clear the floor.

RIGGING SYSTEMS

Hemp system. The basic system of three or more ropes (lines) (nine seems to be the limit, which is determined by the ability to get one's hands around the lines) running from one side of the stage through overhead pulleys (HEAD BLOCKS) to pulleys over the stage (LOFT BLOCKS) and terminating with a batten onstage. The addition of sandbags to the offstage lines counterbalances the weight of anything put on the onstage batten so a FLYMAN can lift a scene onstage up off the floor and out of sight (TAKE UP). The sandbag ends of the lines are then tied to the belaying pins on the pin rail located either on the stage floor or more often on the fly floor.

Counterweight systems

Chain drive system. System very similar to the T-track system but uses chain connected to motors to operate the arbor which is counterweighted.

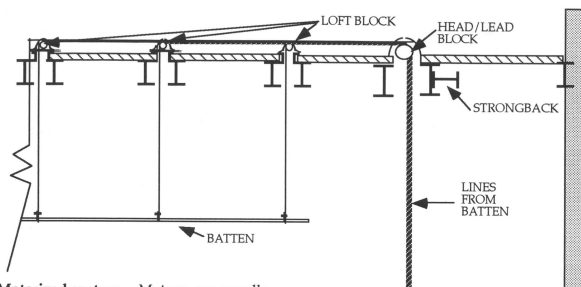

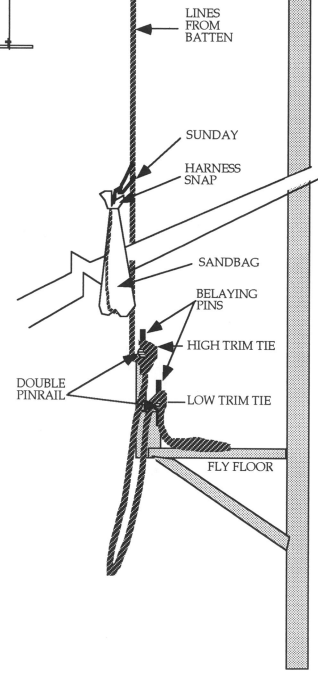

Motorized system. Motors are usually AC- or DC-powered electric or of the hydraulic type.

Self-climbing battens. A motorized winch that is mounted on a stage batten, self-contained, and operated by remote control.

Traction drive system. Similar to **Chain drive system** except the head block pulleys are motor driven (rather than arbor driven); also uses counterweights.

T-track system. A system of T-tracks or bars mounted on the sidewall of a stage which allows an arbor, holding counterweights, to slide up and down. The arbor is attached by wire rope through head (lead) blocks and loft blocks to a pipe batten onstage. The arbor is then operated by an overhaul line which attaches to the top and bottom of the arbor going over sheaves top and bottom and through a rope lock to complete the system (see illustration on p. 167).

Winch. Most of these systems do not use a counterweight arbor, but use a geared-down winch, a positive braking device with resettable trim switches. Some machines use variable-speed motors. All winch systems must be operated within the capacity of the unit.

Wire guide system. This system of counterweighting is the same as the T-track system except arbors travel within guy wires instead of on T-tracks. Although less expensive than the T-track system, the wire guide is less desirable from both operational and maintenance perspectives.

HEMP SYSTEM

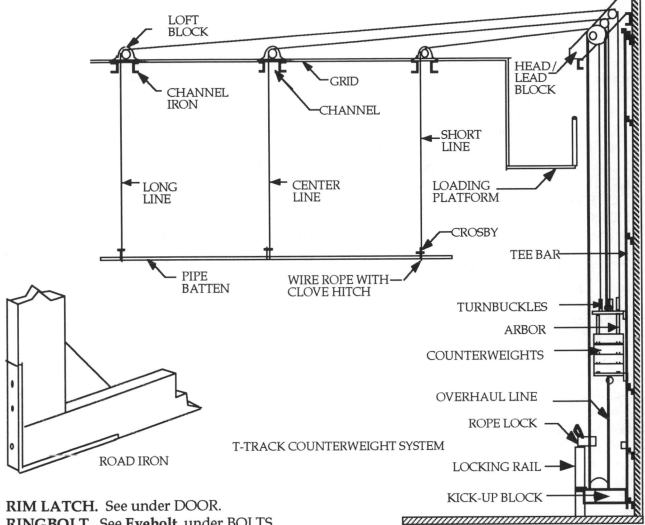

LOFT BLOCK
CHANNEL IRON
GRID
CHANNEL
SHORT LINE
HEAD / LEAD BLOCK
LONG LINE
CENTER LINE
LOADING PLATFORM
CROSBY
PIPE BATTEN
WIRE ROPE WITH CLOVE HITCH
TEE BAR
TURNBUCKLES
ARBOR
COUNTERWEIGHTS
OVERHAUL LINE
ROPE LOCK
LOCKING RAIL
KICK-UP BLOCK

ROAD IRON

T-TRACK COUNTERWEIGHT SYSTEM

RIM LATCH. See under DOOR.

RINGBOLT. See **Eyebolt** under BOLTS.

RIP IN FLAT. See **Flat patching** under COVERING FLATS.

RIPSAW. See under SAWS.

RISER. Technically, the height between treads on a step unit. Loosely used to refer to elevations or platforms on stage. See PARALLEL; STEPS.

RIVET. A metal pin with a head on one end, used to fasten things together by passing the rivet through holes in material to be joined and hammering the plain end down. Useful in fastening sheet metal, leather, fiberboard, etc. Three types most often used: split rivets, hollow rivets, and pop rivets. Split rivets have a split backside and the two sides are bent over against a washer holding the material together (leather harnesses often are fastened in this manner). Hollow rivets with washers are recommended in cases where both sides will be seen and on belts or clothing where underside would snag undergarments. Pop rivets are by far the most convenient to use and require a tool that can handle a number of sizes. The pop rivet contains a nail inside a hollow rivet that clinches the backside as it is pulled through the material by the tool.

R LAMPS (reflector lamps). See under LAMPS.

ROAD BOARD. A ROAD BOX specifically designed to enclose lighting dimmers and audio amplifiers and their related control equipment.

ROAD BOX. A box used for a touring show. See under BOXES.

ROAD CEILING. See **Roll ceiling** under CEILINGS.

ROADIE. Professional term for stagehand working a road (touring) show.

ROAD IRONS. Angle irons set into the corners of flats and used to protect the corners from splintering while on tour.

ROAD SHOW. Professional term for a touring show.

ROAD STIFFENER. A 1" x 4" batten, bolted or loose-pin hinged to two or more flats for the purpose of stiffening or strengthening the joints. See also **Battening** under FASTENING FLATS.

ROCKS. See PLASTIC SETS.

ROCOCO. An overelaborate style of decoration and design popular in the eighteenth century.

ROLL. See under PAINTING TECHNIQUES.

ROLL CEILING. See under CEILINGS.

ROLL CURTAIN. See under CURTAINS.

ROLL DROP

> **Drapery.** See **Roll curtain** under CURTAINS.
>
> **Scenery.** A telescoping or folding scenic unit that has to be raised and lowered into and out of view by a DRUM winch. When the unit is in the up position it is shrouded in black to "hide" it.

ROLLING SCENERY. See SCENERY, SHIFTING.

ROMANESQUE. Architectural style of the eighth to the twelfth centuries. Based on Roman principles and characterized by a round arch and solid appearance.

ROMEX (Loomex). A plastic- or fabric-covered wire containing two wires and a ground. Used in wiring homes and in-wall applications. All permanent wires onstage must be encased in EMT.

RONDEL. See ROUNDEL.

ROPE (line). Cords made of a variety of natural and artificial fibers, twisted or braided together. Braided Manila, sisal, and hemp should always be taped at each end to prevent unraveling. The best line for stage work is ship-grade long-lay Manila. Always tape before cutting; rose-pruning shears work well for cutting. New rope is rather oily and resilient; old appears dry and brittle. Always replace old rope before flying heavy scenic units. Cotton rope, though easy on the hands, stretches so much as to make it ineffectual. Some of the artificial fiber ropes also stretch (such as nylon) even though they are very strong. Sisal and hemp produce many slivers and are hard on hands. Soaking hands in vinegar helps toughen them up when working the rail. See also RIGGING.

ROPE LOCK. In a T-track or wire guide COUNTERWEIGHT SYSTEM, the rope lock se-cures the OVERHAUL LINE (operating line), thus locking the set of lines so it can not move. See illustration under RIGGING SYSTEMS.

ROSCODYE. Trade name for a dye with a binder from Rosco Laboratories, used for painting slides of glass, acetate, or polyester film; heat resistant.

ROSCOGEL, ROSCOLUX, ROSCOLENE. Trade names for COLOR MEDIA.

ROSETTE. See under PLATE.

ROSIN. Residue from distilled turpentine. Rosin aids in achieving certain sound effects (see BULL ROAR) and is used on the soles of shoes to prevent slipping on stage during scenes requiring fast footwork, dancing, dueling, etc. Available at paint and hardware stores.

ROSIN BOX. A low, flat, open box, large enough to stand in, containing powdered rosin. Usually located offstage close to an entrance or exit, where actors or dancers can rosin shoes or slippers quickly and easily.

ROTARY SWITCH. See under PLUGGING PANELS; SWITCHES.

ROTO DRAPER. Pivot device for drapery legs on a short pipe, which either clamps on a pipe or runs in a traveler track (with brake). Used in countless high schools. It is most important to check occasionally for loose parts.

ROTOLECTOR. Older trade name for a rotary switch used to interconnect dimmers and circuits. See **Rotary switch** under PATCH PANEL; SWITCHES.

ROTO-LOCK

> **Pipe** (rota-lok, rota-lock). A hardware item used to firmly attach pipes together in a 90° configuration for frames, platforms, and trusses. See also CHESEBOROUGH.
>
> **Scenery.** A rotating device used to attach butt ends (see **Butt joint** under JOINTS) together and often used on wagons. More properly called COFFIN LOCKS because they were originally used to latch down the tops of coffins.

ROTOR. In an electrical motor, that part of the motor which revolves within the stationary part (stator). See also **Inductor dimmer** under DIMMERS.

ROUGE CLOTH. A very fine abrasive cloth, using jewellers rouge, which works well for shining electrical contacts and armatures.

ROUGH LUMBER. See under LUMBER.

ROUNDEL (rondel). A round, heat-resistant, glass color filter available for certain types of border lights and footlights. Color selection in roundels is greatly limited in comparison with other types of color media, but colors will not fade or burn out. There is no lens value in roundels. See also COLOR MEDIA; LIGHTING INSTRUMENTS, GENERAL.

ROUND LUMBER. See DOWEL.

ROUTER. See under POWER TOOLS.

rpm. Abbreviation for revolutions per minute. Used for a variety of rotating devices backstage.

RUBBER-BASED PAINT. See **Acrylic latex** under PAINT AND PAINT COLORS.

RUBBING PAINT. Paint that rubs off because it does not have enough GLUE. See PAINT MIXING, DRY PIGMENT.

RULER

Folding ruler. An older measuring tool largely superseded by the tape measure.

Tape measure. A rewindable flexible steel tape available in a variety of sizes. The most useful backstage or in a scene shop are 1/2" or 3/4" wide x 12', 16', or 25' long.

Cloth or fiberglass tape. Ultraflexible tape in very long lengths of 50' or 100' or longer. Very necessary for backstage use.

Scale ruler. Architect's triangular scale ruler is used for making and reading scale drawings. Triangular scale rulers have ten scales ranging from 3/32" = 1' to 3" = 1', plus a standard 1" rule on one face. When rule is flat on table, two scales are exposed on top side, one reading from left to right and the other from right to left. Calibrations appearing before the zeros represent inches or, in larger scales, fractions of inches.

When measuring feet only, start from zero; when measuring fractions of a foot, start with number of inches desired before zero and proceed to additional feet desired.

RUMBLE CART. Obsolete. A sound effects machine for thunder, passing trucks, fire engines, etc. The rumble cart consisted of a 2' x 4' box equipped with 12" wheels on which lugs were nailed. The cart was filled with weight and rolled behind scenes.

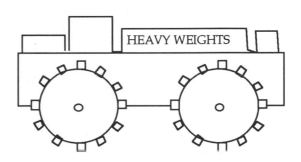

RUMBLE CART

RUN. Length of time a play is shown.

RUN A FLAT (running). To carry a flat. See under HANDLING FLATS.

RUN-THROUGH. An uninterrupted rehearsal of an entire play usually without technical support services or technical personnel.

RUNWAY (Jolson strip). Narrow extension or runway of stage into audience; common in Japanese theatre (hanimichi), used in some burlesque houses, and made very popular by Al Jolson in the United States in the first quarter of the twentieth century. The runway is commonly used in fashion shows.

S

S-4-S. Lumberman's symbol for "smooth on four sides," meaning LUMBER planed or dressed on all four sides.

SABER. See SWORDS.

SABER SAW. See under POWER TOOLS.

SADDLE

Door. Wooden threshold on a stage door. Used only for door casements and usually made of 1/2" plywood or 3/4" lumber with edges beveled to reduce tripping hazard. See also DOOR.

Rigging. A bronze or galvanized steel strap that holds a wire rope close to the top of a flat. This hardware is used when flying flats are rigged to trim from the bottom. Available from marine supply outlets. See illustration for use under TRIM (verb).

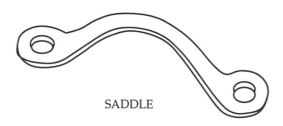

SADDLE

SADDLE IRON. See under STRAP IRON.

SAFE PATCH. A PATCH PANEL that cannot be patched hot. Obsolete. A brand name for a phone patch made by Kliegl.

SAFETIES. A chain, wire rope, or some kind of line used to secure COLOR FRAMES, INSTRUMENTS, TOOLS, and, in fact, anything overhead. See SAFETY LINE.

SAFETY. One of the major problems in theatre is the constant use of new materials with the accompanying lack of knowledge about the new product. Often it is found that health hazards exist with the material. It is imperative that theatre people protect themselves to the best of their ability when working with new items. Do not breath the fumes from a chemical or from its reaction with other materials or heat. Do not check on ignition of materials indoors. In short, protect yourself.

SAFETY FACTOR. Percentage exceeding rated load of ropes, wire, dimmers, etc. This factor is usually about 20 percent, but it is unwise to take advantage of a safety factor for any extended period.

SAFETY LINE

Electrical. Small-diameter wire rope or chain securing color frame to an instrument and the instrument to a pipe.

Personal. Using an ANSI-approved full-body harness on a wire rope with a stopping device that prevents unwanted downward movement. Must meet OSHA requirements.

Rigging. A line attached to rigging to prevent movement.

Tools. A small line used to tie tools to a person's belt when that person is working above people.

SAL AMMONIAC. Ammonium chloride used for FLAMEPROOFING.

SANDBAG. Canvas bags, varying in size, filled with sand and used to weight unused sets of lines, jacks supporting top-heavy scenery, etc. On stages with rope rigging, sandbags are tied to lines to counterbalance flown scenery in place of counterweights. Available at theatrical supply houses or can be sewn with double stitching in heavy 12 ounce canvas.

SANDER. See under POWER TOOLS.

SANDPAPER (emery paper, garnet paper, rouge paper). Used for smoothing wood. Sandpaper is available in many different grits: no. 2 or no. 3 for coarse work and no. 1/0 or no. 2/0 for fine work. Emery paper or cloth is a tougher abrasive and can be used on metals as well as wood. Garnet and rouge papers are fine grit and are used for polishing metals and cleaning electrical contacts on dimmers, etc.

SASH WINDOW. See under WINDOW.

SATURABLE CORE. See **Magnetic amplifier** under DIMMER.

SATURATED COLOR. Undiluted hue or pure color.

SAWHORSE. A support about 2' high, consisting of 2" x 4" lumber approximately 3' long with four 1" x 4" legs splayed at the bottom to give support. The sawhorse is valuable in shops as a rest for wood to be sawed or, in larger sizes, as a support for flats to be covered or washed.

SAWS. Thin metal blades with cutting teeth. See also POWER TOOLS.

Backsaw. Handsaw with a ridged reinforcing strip on the back edge; twelve to fourteen teeth per inch recommended. Used in miter box.

Coping saw (scroll saw). Small handsaw with a very thin, narrow blade used for fine scrollwork in thin wood. Occasionally useful.

Crosscut saw. A handsaw with teeth set at correct angle for cutting the cross grain of wood; twelve to fourteen teeth per inch recommended.

Dado blade. Thick blades for a circular saw, mounted together to cut a wide slot through a board. Useful for notching and dadoing.

Hacksaw. Small handsaw with fine teeth for cutting metal, sixteen and eighteen teeth per inch recommended.

Keyhole saw. Small handsaw, usually with a blade approximately 10" long with ten teeth per inch. Because the blade is narrow, keyhole saws will cut circles.

Ripsaw. Handsaw with teeth set at correct angle for ripping with the grain of wood, six to eight teeth per inch recommended.

SCAFFOLD CLAMP. A forged-steel rigid or swivel clamp used for overhead applications. See also CHESEBOROUGH; TRUSS.

SCALE DRAWING. See DESIGN; DRAWINGS.

SCALE RULER. See under RULER.

SCALE STICK. Synonym for architect's scale ruler; see RULER.

SCARF JOINT. See under JOINT.

SCENE

Acting. A subdivision of an act in a play.

Scenery. A vista or set in a play.

SCENE DESIGNER. A creative person who brings together the concepts of playwright, director, lighting designer, and costumer into a scene design. Ideally all this creativity results in wonderful visuals that are exciting and workable while staying within a budget.

SCENERY, SHIFTING. Moving scenery for scene changes. See also DESIGN; HANDLING FLATS. Methods of moving scenery include the following.

Elevator stage (hydraulic stage). Various types of elevator stages have gone through experimentation, but the initial expense of the elaborate mechanism has prevented widespread use. Radio City Music Hall in New York City has one of the few large elevator stages in this country. It consists of sections of stage which can be lowered or raised, permitting changes of scenery to be made under the stage. Most elevator stages are hydraulically operated. If an elevator stage is intended, stage should be trapped according to the dimensions best suiting size of scenery. Each TRAP is controlled by a hydraulic lift to raise or lower a specified distance. In this manner, the stage can be made varying heights by push-button control.

Flying scenery. If a COUNTERWEIGHT SYSTEM is part of stage equipment, or if grid is sturdy and counterweights and arbors are available for lines, scenery can be flown. Flown scen-

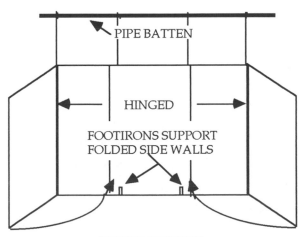

PIPE BATTEN

HINGED

FOOTIRONS SUPPORT
FOLDED SIDE WALLS

FLYING SCENERY

ery is generally limited to the backwall of a setting or to the backwall and as much of the sidewalls as can be hinged to the backwall. The balance of the set can be assembled manually. It is rarely possible or advisable to fly an entire set without folding to a more compact form. Before flying anything heavy, ropes and knots should be checked. Clove hitches tie to pipes, and bowlines tie to ceiling plates or hanger irons. For heavy scenery, lines should pass through ceiling

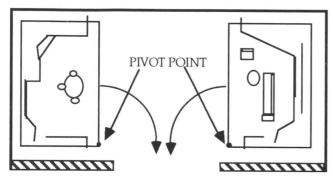

JACKKNIFE STAGE

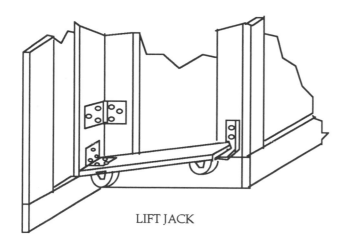

LIFT JACK

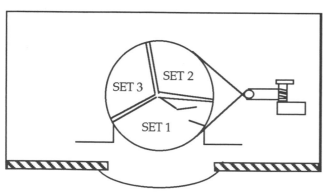

REVOLVING STAGE

plates at the top of the flats and tie to hanging irons on the bottom. If flown scenery is to be detached when it reaches the floor, a CARPET HOIST can be used, or a simple block and tackle can be rigged to keep counterweight suspended during the time scenery is removed from pipe batten.

Jackknife stage (pivot stage). Complete settings are mounted on two wagons. One wagon is placed on each side of the stage and pivoted on a pipe and flange on downstage, onstage corner. Pivot holds one corner on a spike mark while the other end can swing into or out of position. Extremely fast changes can be made with jackknife stages, since all props and even actors can roll in with the setting.

Lift jack. Casters are mounted on a 6" board, which is hinged to bottom of the flat so that closest caster can act as a fulcrum. When free end of the board is stepped on, the flat is lifted about an inch above floor level. A block or cleat is used to hold the board down while scenery is rolled offstage. Lift jacks are most useful for three-dimensional scenery such as window seats, alcoves, dormers, stairs, etc.

Manual shifting (gripping). Complete changes of sets made by crews, stagehands, or grips, without the aid of wagons, flies, revolving stages, etc. For manual changes, all scenery should be as lightweight as possible and at the same time strong and rigid. Keep separation points at a minimum, avoiding lashing except on corners. Design more corners in the form of setbacks or offsets if necessary for lashing. See also HANDLING FLATS.

Revolving stage (disk, revolver, turntable). A revolver is built into the stage floor as a permanent part of the theatre, whereas a disk sits on top of the stage floor. A turntable can be either a disk or a revolver. Box sets can be placed on the turntable so that they can be rotated into or out of position. Plastic sets, or settings using platforms, steps, and ramps, are particularly effective on turntable stages. Plays requiring treadmill movement on stage can make use of turntables to suggest movement from one location to another. Since a masking problem is always present downleft and downright, permanent pieces such as doors, portals, or flippers

172

are generally incorporated into sets. These pieces are usually painted a neutral color to blend with all sets on the turntable. The downstage flats in a wall are sometimes hinged to open off the disk for masking, and fold back onto the disk for the revolve. Always check relationship of curtain to revolver, and adjust design to avoid fouling scenery with act curtain during revolve. Two basic box sets can be placed back to back on revolver, and upstage set can be redressed while scene is in progress in downstage set.

Set within a set. One large set, parts of which can remain standing while a small set is brought in and assembled in front of it. Part of the wall of the large set on one or both sides of the stage must be movable, to allow manipulation of the smaller set. Heavy, bulky scenery and props in the large set should be confined to stationary part of setting.

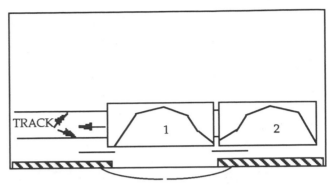

FULL WAGON STAGING
(SLIP STAGE)

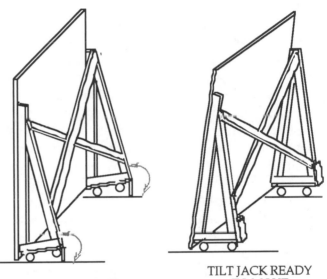

TILT JACK LOCKED

TILT JACK READY TO MOVE

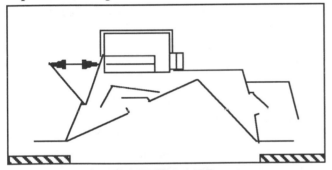

SET WITHIN A SET

Slip stage (sliding stage, slotted stage). A form of **Wagon stage** (see below) which travels in grooves set into a FALSE DECK. Common practice is to build a false stage 6" to 8" above stage level into which guide grooves are cut to receive a cleat or bracket attached to a wagon. Grooves are metal-lined with an angle iron countersunk in the false deck. Cables and winches are usually used to provide power to move slip stages, but PADDLE BOARDS can be used for limited travel.

Tilt jack (tip jack). A wall is fastened to the hypotenuses of at least two triangular jacks (tilt jacks) equipped with casters on the base. When in place, the wall is vertical and casters are off the floor. When wall is tilted so that casters touch the floor, it is ready to roll offstage. A similar tilt jack is made by hinging one end of a 6" board (on

which casters are mounted) to the bottom of a flat. A stage brace is then run from a brace cleat and fastened to the other end of the board. Tilt of the flat is adjusted by adjusting stage brace span. Two tilt jacks are required for any wall, and others can be added if necessary. Allow a minimum of 30" for jack base. Tilt jacks can be used for walls containing heavy fireplaces, bookcases, pictures, etc. Since door thicknesses will drag if tilted, tilt jacks cannot be used on doors.

Unit set. A permanent skeleton of three arches onstage and flats of various kinds used to plug the arches, thereby changing the setting. Stage right a window can be used for act I, a fireplace for act II, a door for act III. The center arch can be open for act I, double doors act II, curtained act III, etc. The unit set is the simplest way to change scenery for multiset shows staged in limited space.

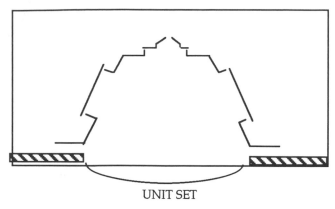

UNIT SET

Wagon stage. All or any part of a set can be mounted on 6" platforms equipped with casters, allowing scene changes to be made by merely rolling a set or part of a set on or off the stage. If space is available, elaborate use can be made of wagons large enough to accommodate entire sets. If space is limited, alcoves, staircases, fireplaces, etc., can be mounted on wagons to save time in shifting. If flats are hinged to fold against each other, a quite small wagon can accommodate the major part of a set. A wagon can also be set with scenery on two sides so that it can be turned to form the bulk of a second setting. Wagons are usually made in small units of 4' x 8' or in dimensions most adaptable to the stage and scenery. Small wagons are easily handled and stacked when not in use and can be bolted or clamped together in any desired numbers. Construction is usually with 1" x 6" lumber for the frame and 3/4" fiveply for the top. CASTERS are placed on 4' centers.

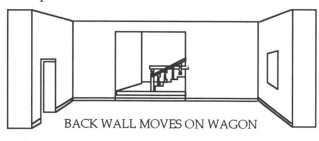

BACK WALL MOVES ON WAGON

PARTIAL WAGON STAGE

SCENERY PANELS

Beadboard. Two outside layers of heavy paper or cardboard with Styrofoam laminated in the middle.

Duraply. Heavy paper laminated on both sides of a plywood core.

Gatorboard. Same as beadboard.

Honeycomb. A honeycomb of aluminum laminated with outside layers of paper or veneer.

Thermoply. A paper board with foil laminated on both sides.

SCENERY SHOW. A show that has large scenery requirements.

SCENE SHIFTING. See SCENERY, SHIFTING.

SCENE SHOP. See WORKSHOP.

SCENIC ARTIST. The person responsible for painting the scenery. The artist works closely with the SCENE DESIGNER; often there are assistants who help with the painting. In some theatres the designer is also the scenic artist.

SCHEMATIC. A diagram of an electrical or electronic circuit using SYMBOLS showing all the components.

SCIOPTICON. See under PROJECTED SCENERY.

SCOOP. See under LIGHTING INSTRUMENTS, GENERAL.

SCR. See **Silicon controlled rectifier** under DIMMER.

SCREEN

Projection. A sheet of material on which an image is projected. See PROJECTORS.

Scenery. Gray fiberglass insect screening often used to simulate GLASS.

SCREW BASE. See **Bases** under LAMPS.

SCREWDRIVER. Tool for setting screws. Designated by head type, length in inches, and width by a number designation; has a metal shaft from tip to handle. Most useful for the shop are 6" x 0, 1, 2, or 3 for average work and 8" x 3 or 4 for heavy work. Electric screwdrivers and variable

SCREWDRIVER

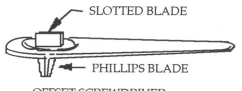

SLOTTED BLADE

PHILLIPS BLADE

OFFSET SCREWDRIVER

speed reversible cordless drills are both big timesavers. The electrical drivers usually work best with other than a slotted bit. Other screwdriver bits include Phillips, Reed and Prince, square drive (Robertson), and Torx. See also YANKEE SCREWDRIVER.

SCREWS. Used for temporary or permanent fastening.

Lag screw (lag bolt). Large wood screw with a square head. Used with a wrench. Lag screws are used in place of bolts where it is impossible or impractical to use a nut on the end of a bolt. Available in various diameters (1/16" intervals) and lengths (1/2" intervals).

Peg (patent peg, plug peg, stage screw). Large metal screw with a butterfly end, used to fasten stage braces, foot irons, and jacks to the floor. Screw and plug are used when the screw must be used in the same place several times. Sandbags or weights can be used where stage screws are not feasible.

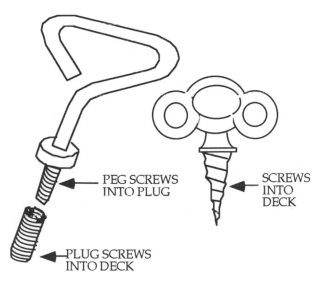

PEG SCREWS INTO PLUG

SCREWS INTO DECK

PLUG SCREWS INTO DECK

STAGE SCREWS

Plug (patent peg plug, screw plug). A short metal tube with wood screw threads on the outside (goes into floor) and metal screw threads on the inside (for **Peg**).

Screw eye. Wood screw bent into a loop at one end. Often used with a hook to fasten scenery temporarily.

Set screw. A screw with no head that fits flush to surroundings. Often tightened with an allen wrench.

TEK screw (tech screw). A hardened, low-root, heavy-thread screw with a square drive (Robertson) or Phillips flat head. TEK screws are often used to attach materials to metal-tubing frames.

Thumb screw. Screw or bolt with a flattened head that can be turned by thumb and forefinger.

Wood screw. Sold by the box (hundred count) and designated by flat or round head, blue or bright, diameter according to number, and length according to inches. The higher the number, the greater the diameter. Most useful in scene construction are the following:

3/4", no. 8, bright, flathead. For fastening threeply, hinges, lash hardware, etc.

1 1/2", no. 8, bright, flathead. For fastening wood to wood, battening flats, and for fastening hinges or hardware into the end or side grain of lumber.

1 1/2", no. 6; 2", no. 8 or 10; and 2 1/2", no. 10, are sometimes useful for furniture construction or special work.

SCRIM. A loosely woven material somewhat resembling cheesecloth and used on stage for window glass and special effects drops. If light is shone behind scrim, it becomes transparent. If light is kept in front of scrim, it is opaque. Scenes dye-painted on scrim as a drop can be used either as a solid wall or as a transparency, by changing light source. Scrim is available in widths up to 30' at theatrical supply houses. See also DROPS; FOG EFFECT.

SCRIMMING

Covering with muslin or canvas to make all components in a set accept paint in the same manner.

Covering an opening or window with SCRIM.

Covering plywood or lumber with any fabric.

SCRIPT. The acting edition of a play used in production.

SCROLL. Roll of PARCHMENT PAPER.

SCROLLER (scroll color changer). A device that attaches to the front of a lighting instrument and changes the color of light by rolling 10 to 12 different filters across the light. The individual filters use a special tape to attach them to one another. The unit is remote controlled and fairly fast, usually taking 2 seconds from one end to the other or stopping at any desired color.

SCROLLER CONTROL. A device that controls a color scroller. In computer-type units the numbers assigned to colored gels by their manufacturer are often programmed into memory. See also **Computer terminology** under LIGHTING CONTROL.

COLOR WIZ (GREAT AMERICAN MARKET)

SCULPT-O-FAB. See CELASTIC.

SCUMBLE. See under PAINTING TECHNIQUES.

SEALED BEAM LIGHTS. See **Parabolic reflector spot** under LAMPS.

SEATING, AUDITORIUM. National and local regulations are offered for the protection of audiences in auditoriums; although there are variations among locales, the following are minimum requirements most generally accepted for the different seating arrangements.

American-plan seating. A system allowing no more than 14 seats per row between the aisles.

Continental seating. Unlimited number of seats per row, 54" from seat back to seat back.

Intermediate continental. Maximum of 26 seats in each row or no more than 12 seats away from an aisle; 46" from seat back to seat back.

Normal seating. Maximum of 14 seats in each row or no more than 6 seats away from an aisle, 36" from seat back to seat back.

SECONDARY COIL. Output coil of a TRANSFORMER.

SECONDARY COLORS. See COLOR.

SECTION DRAWING. A drawing of a cutaway view through a three-dimensional object. See also DRAWINGS.

SEGUE (pronounced seg way). See under SOUND TERMINOLOGY.

SELECTOR SWITCH. See under SWITCHES.

SEMIPERMANENT SET. See under SET.

SEQUENCER. A processor or control that makes electrical functions work in a particular order. Often used to make lights flash on and off with **Chasers** (see under COMPUTERS).

SEQUINS. See GLITTER.

SERIES CIRCUIT. See under CIRCUIT, ELECTRICAL.

SET (setting). Scenery or background for a play. See specific item: DRAPERY, SET; DROPS; FIREPLACE; SET PIECE, etc.; see also DESIGN.

Permanent set. Stylized setting of a classic or nondescript nature that can be used for many scenes or plays. Setting for single-set play that can be assembled once and left until the play closes.

Semipermanent set (unit set). Usually neutrally painted frame of three arches or openings (downright, upcenter, downleft) in which a variety of decorative or practical pieces of scenery can be placed.

Skeleton set. A set containing only the essentials for a play. Usually staged in blacks with set pieces, such as freestanding fireplace, window, door, etc. The permanent portion of a **Semipermanent set** (see above).

SET-IN (in, hang, drag in). To move scenery into the theatre, put into place, set lights, and dress the stage.

SET LIGHTS. To focus the lighting equipment for a play. See LIGHTING STAGE, ARENA; LIGHTING STAGE, PROSCENIUM; LIGHTING STAGE, THRUST.

SET OF LINES. Refers to a fly system commonly using three or more lines in each set. See also COUNTERWEIGHT SYSTEM; GRID; RIGGING.

SET PIECE. Any free-standing scenery such as groundrows, detailed windows, doors, fireplaces, or other centers of interest. Set pieces are often backed with black drapes to suggest a setting. Many plays are most effectively staged in this simple manner.

SETTING
A SET for a play.
A reading on a dimmer or volume control.

SHACKLE. A U-shaped coupler with a pin closing the open end. Forged shackles are used in RIGGING.

SHACKLE

SHADE. A variation in color made by adding black. Distinguished from TINT.

SHADOW LINE. A contrast line representing a neutral shadow. Applied to scenery with 1/2" or 1" brush under moldings or in other places where shadows would fall from motivated light sources. Blue-black colors are preferred.

SHADOWS. Shadows or shades of light are essential to good lighting in order to achieve a three-dimensional effect. Lighting without shadows is ineffective and tends to wash out detail. Shadows of actors on the backwall are generally distracting and should be avoided, if possible, by placing spotlights at a greater angle to acting area. See also LIGHTING STAGE, ARENA; LIGHTING STAGE, PROSCENIUM; LIGHTING STAGE, THRUST.

SHAKESPEAREAN STAGE. Any stage resembling the Globe Theatre stage in shape. Generally considered to be a thrust stage extending into the auditorium with the audience on three sides and a backwall containing an inner below and an inner above. See illustration on next page. See also STAGE; INNER ABOVE; INNER BELOW.

SHALLOW STAGE. A stage lacking depth.

SHEARS. Large scissors for cutting cloth or metal.

SHEAVE (pulley) (pronounced shiv). The grooved wheel or pulley of a block, used for flying scenery. See also BLOCK; COUNTERWEIGHT SYSTEM.

SHEET BEND. See under KNOTS.

SHELLAC. A purified lac resin used in varnishes. See under PAINTS, MISCELLANEOUS.

SHIELD (props). Shields can be made of fiberboard, fiberglass, Celastic, plywood, or metal. If a metallic ring is needed, it can be made of 1/8" aluminum cut on a bandsaw with a skip-tooth blade. Shields can be made of 1/4" plywood with the grain running vertically so that the proper curve will result when the wood is fastened to a curved rib. Fiberboard, available in thicknesses from 1/32", will form reasonably well to a mold if soaked in hot water. FIBERGLASS can be made into any shape or form in a mold or on a cast. Authentic shield designs found in costume books or encyclopedias should be used.

SHIELD, LIGHT. See LIGHT SPILL CONTROL.

SHIM. A thin piece of any material used to raise a corner of a flat, platform, or any construction to level. Shingles make good shim stock for leveling platforms or plumbing walls.

SHIN BUSTERS (shin kickers, shin bangers). Lights mounted on low BOOMS in the wings. Used often for dance performances. Name refers to what happens if a dancer runs into the boom and instrument.

SHINGLES (exterior finish). Simulated on stage with beaverboard or cardboard or by painting, if for a distant scene. For extreme realism or close viewing, real shingles can be used, if properly flameproofed.

SHOE
Lights. See BRUSH, ELECTRICAL.
Scenery. A block of wood measuring about 1 1/2" x 16" and sometimes used in flat construction to make a stronger joint between toggle rails and stiles.

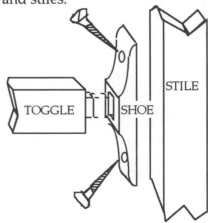

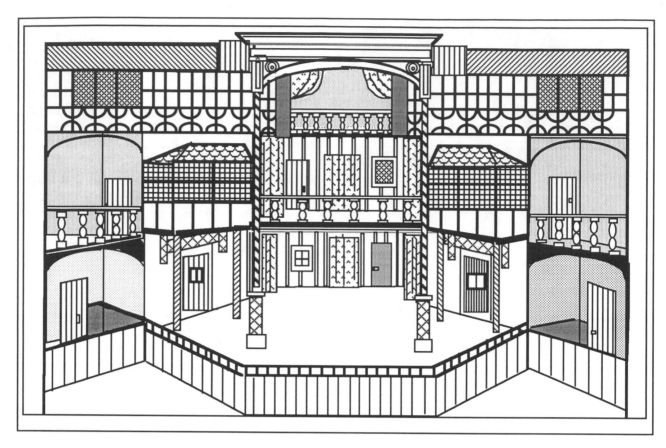

BASED ON A MODEL OF THE GLOBE THEATRE
AS RECONSTRUCTED BY JOHN CRANSTON ADAMS

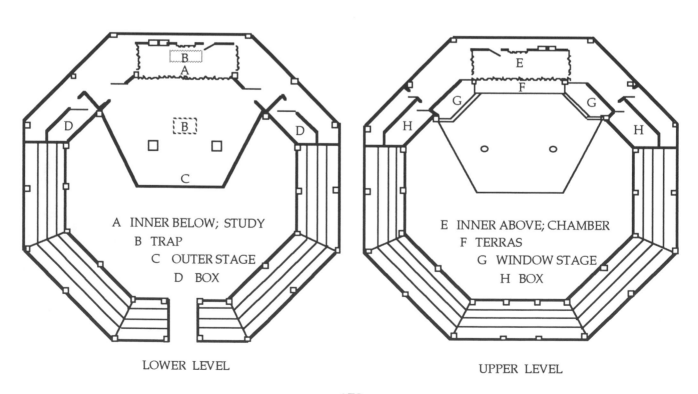

A INNER BELOW; STUDY
B TRAP
C OUTER STAGE
D BOX

E INNER ABOVE; CHAMBER
F TERRAS
G WINDOW STAGE
H BOX

LOWER LEVEL   UPPER LEVEL

SHOE FILE. A hand rasp with four different filing surfaces: flat (fine or coarse); convex (fine or coarse). See also FILES.

S-HOOK. See under HOOKS.

SHOP. See WORKSHOP.

SHORT CIRCUIT. To complete an open circuit by shunt of low resistance. Short circuiting results in blowing a FUSE. Before replacing fuses, try to determine the cause of the short and repair it. Replace fuses with correct sizes.

SHORT LINE. The shortest line in a set of lines strung from the grid. See COUNTERWEIGHT SYSTEM.

SHOT STICK. A 2' to 3' length of wood which when slapped against the floor sounds like a gun shot; used where guns are not permitted or their use is not feasible. One end of the batten is held about 18" above stage floor and the other end is placed under the operator's foot. Operator applies pressure with foot and releases the other end of the batten, which strikes the floor with a shotlike sound.

SHOW CURTAIN. An act curtain designed for a specific show. See also ACT CURTAIN.

SHRINK TUBING. A special plastic tube applied over wires; when heated with special hot air gun, tube shrinks over the wires making them into a compact bundle. Never use shrink tube gun for drying hair; it is far too hot.

SHUNT. A conductor, usually of low resistance, which is placed across two points of an electric circuit and through which part or all of a current can be diverted.

SHUTTER

    Lights. The framing device on an ellipsoidal spotlight. Occasionally refers to cutoff, blinder, or barndoor, but the latter words are preferred. See **Barndoor** under LIGHT SPILL CONTROL.

    Scenery. A wooden slat blind commonly used as a decorative piece.

    Sometimes refers to a door, as distinguished from door flat and door casement.

SIDE ARM. See **Lights** under ARM.

SIENNA. A reddish or yellowish pigment available in burnt or raw pigment and used for scene painting. See also PAINT AND PAINT COLORS.

SIGHTLINES. Lines of vision from seats in extreme positions in the auditorium. Sightlines are laid out on the floor plan to determine visibility of setting from the extreme seats and also to determine the number of masking flats necessary for all openings. If balconies are used, elevation sightlines should be plotted to determine masking for flies from first row and visibility of backwall from balcony.

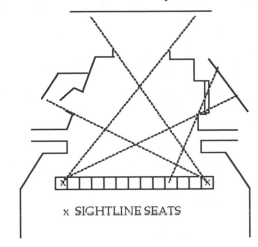

x SIGHTLINE SEATS

HORIZONTAL SIGHTLINES

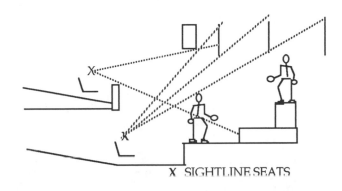

X SIGHTLINE SEATS

VERTICAL SIGHTLINES

SIGNAL LIGHT. A system of signaling cues from stage manager to electrician and sound technician or orchestra.

SILHOUETTE. See GROUNDROW.

SILICON CONTROLLED RECTIFIER. See under DIMMERS.

SILICONE LUB. A dry lubricant in powder or spray form used instead of GRAPHITE or oil. An advanced form has Teflon added to spray; extremely slick.

SILL. The lower thickness piece in a window frame or door casement. The sill of a door casement is called a saddle or threshold. See also DOOR.

SILL IRON. See under STRAP IRON.

SILVER PAINT. See **Aluminum paints** under PAINTS, MISCELLANEOUS.

SIMULTANEOUS STAGING. See under STAGING.

SINGLE POLE SWITCH. See **Toggle switch** under SWITCHES.

SINGLE THROW SWITCH. See **Toggle switch** under SWITCHES.

SIREN (sound effect). Use a hand or electric siren whenever possible. Recordings are good for distant or background sirens.

SIXTY-CYCLE HUM. Noise in sound systems caused by audio cables running parallel with 120-volt electrical lines.

SIZE (verb). See PAINTING SCENERY.

SIZE WATER. See under GLUE; see also PAINT MIXING, DRY PIGMENT.

SIZING (noun). See under GLUE.

SKELETON SET. See under SET.

SKILSAW. See **Portable circular saw** under POWER TOOLS.

SKY. See CYC, SKY; **Cyclorama colors** under LIGHTING COLORS.

SKY CYC. See CYC, SKY.

SLAM, DOOR. See DOOR SLAM.

SLAPSTICK. A kind of paddle used in comedy to hit a person, usually on the rump, making a loud slap noise. Made with two thin pieces of wood, 1/2" x 2" x 36" with a 1 1/2" spacer block/handle attached at one end.

SLAPSTICK

SLIDE PROJECTOR. See PROJECTORS.

SLIDING DOOR. See DOOR, SLIDING.

SLIP CONNECTOR. See **Pin connector** under PLUGS, ELECTRICAL.

SLIP STAGE. See under SCENERY, SHIFTING.

SLOTTED FLOOR. See **Slip stage** under SCENERY, SHIFTING

SMOKE EFFECTS. Can be produced in a variety of ways. The older method using ammonia and hydrochloric acid is considered hazardous because of the toxicity of the chemicals but was reasonably effective if great care was exercised.

Interesting classroom experiment: as shown in the diagram, two bottles, one containing ammonia and the other containing hydrochloric acid, are joined together by glass tubes through stoppers. A second tube is taken through the stopper of each bottle. Air blown or pumped through ammonia tube passes through the hydrochloric acid and comes out in the form of smoke (NH_3Cl). The odor is somewhat pungent, the risk of spilling is always present, and good ventilation is necessary.

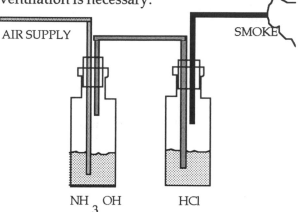

SMOKE EFFECT

Ammonium chloride. Will give smoke when sprinkled on a hot plate.

CO_2 fire extinguishers. Can be used for blasts of smoke if sound can be disguised.

Dry ice. Dry ice in hot water produces a

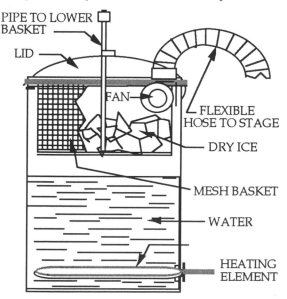

DRY ICE SMOKE MACHINE

heavy, white, foglike smoke, which will stay close to the ground unless agitated. Dry ice machine can be used, one on each side of the stage. Use a 55-gallon barrel on casters, with a clampdown top and 4" dryer hose coming out of the upper side with 120-volt squirrel cage fan; 220-volt hot water elements provide water heating; a wire mesh basket holds the dry ice, which can be lowered into the water via a rod. In operation, the water is heated, the basket is filled with up to 25 pounds of dry ice, just ahead of the cue the basket is lowered into the hot water, and on cue the fan is turned on; smoke flows out of the 4" tube end, which can be concealed wherever necessary; this smoke hugs the floor.

Flash box. A bright flash with a puff of white smoke can be made with a flash box and powdered potassium nitrate mixed with powdered magnesium. One half teaspoon of each is mixed and thoroughly ground in a mortar and pestle. The mixture is then placed in the flash box and ignited electrically. More potassium nitrate produces more smoke; more magnesium produces more flash. Chemicals will not ignite unless well powdered. Keep flash box away from costumes, draperies, etc.

Smoke machine (fog machine). A small, compact smoke machine is available through several theatrical manufacturers. "Fog juice" (basically a silicone-based liquid), available from the manufacturer, is vaporized into a non-toxic, white smoke by an electric element in the machine. Often blown over dry ice to increase smoke. Quantity is easily controlled. Both local and remote control available from scenery supply houses.

Steam. Dead steam (low pressure) can be used for effective smoke, if available.

SMOKE POCKETS. Metal grooves at each side of the proscenium in which asbestos or fire curtain slides. Smoke pockets are designed to prevent flame and smoke from escaping from stage into auditorium.

SMOKE VENTS. Louvres or traps in the stage roof that can be opened in case of fire by cutting a line to the stage manager's desk. When louvres are opened, a draft is created that tends to confine flames to stage house. Smoke vents should be provided with fuse links that melt at low temperatures, causing vents to open automatically.

SNAP BRACE (snap hook). A mechanical device that holds pipes or truss parts at a given distance.

SNAP BRACE

SNAP LINE. See CHALK LINE.

SNATCH BLOCK. A pulley or block with a removable side allowing the block to be inserted into existing rigging without restringing.

SNATCH CHAIN. See **Trim chain** under CHAIN.

SNATCHING. Hooking or unhooking flown scenery from a set of lines during a scene change.

SNATCH LINE. See under LINE.

SNEAK A LIGHT CUE (steal a cue). To slowly dim up or down at an imperceptible speed. It is sometimes necessary to set a mood with low intensity on stage at the beginning of a scene and to sneak lights up as the scene progresses.

FOG MAKER SMOKE MACHINE (MOLE-RICHARDSON)

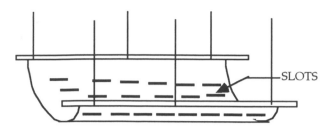

SNOW CRADLE

SNOW CRADLE. A long piece of canvas or muslin with battens on either side. The canvas is hung in the form of a sling or cradle on two sets of lines. Small slits are cut in the canvas at irregular intervals, and confetti, small bits of paper, or flaked Styrofoam are placed in the cradle. Pulling one set of lines releases the "snow," which falls through cloth slits onto the stage.

SNUB. To temporarily tie off a set of lines by wrapping the lines in a figure eight around a pin and holding the ends.

SOBO. A flexible white glue used with fabric. See also GLUE.

SOCKET. A receptacle for a LAMP.

SOFT LIGHT. A diffused light from a source with a frosted medium or a fresnel lens.

SOFT SET. A set composed of draperies, legs, borders, and drops, as opposed to a hard set, composed of flats, wings, and set pieces.

SOFTWOOD. A wood easily worked with shaping tools; accepts nails and screws with ease. Common softwoods include pine, spruce, and fir.

SOLDER. A metal or alloy melted to join wires. All electrical joints of a permanent nature should be soldered. Wires are held together and heated with a soldering iron; solder is dipped in flux (see FLUX, SOLDER) and touched to iron and wire. All joints should be thoroughly fused, with solder flowing freely. If solder stays in round drop without fusing, use more flux and heat. Solder is available as solid or with an acid or rosin core. Core solders require no additional flux. Because acid cores tend to corrode electrical joints, rosin cores are recommended.

SOLDERLESS CONNECTOR (wire nut). Used to join wires after they have been twisted together in a clockwise direction. The connector is screwed on in the same direction. Some of the larger ones use a bolt or set screw (see under SCREWS) to firmly hold the wires. See drawing under WIRE NUT.

SOLID STATE. In modern electronics, refers to dimmers such as the **Silicon controlled rectifier** and the **Magnetic amplifier** (see under DIMMERS), in which electrons are passed or blocked by other electrons of a like charge in a DC circuit. Many solid state devices are extremely efficient, take up very little space, and are as reliable as any previous device used for switching and dimming.

SOLVENTS. Liquids used for dissolving or thinning.

　　Acetone. Used for lacquers.

　　Alcohol. Used for shellac.

　　Lacquer thinner. Used for lacquers.

　　Mineral spirits. Used for oil paints and varnishes.

　　Paint thinner. Used for oil paints and varnishes.

　　Turpentine. Used for oil paints and varnishes.

　　Water. Used for latex, rubber base, and vinyl paints.

SONO TUBE. Cardboard tubes of varying sizes manufactured as forms for concrete and very useful on the stage as large columns. Available from large construction companies.

SOUND EFFECTS. Most sounds are available on record or tape. Some sets of sound effect records are of exceptional quality and great variety. DIGITAL AUDIO TAPE sound effects are very realistic. Certain sounds are more realistic if produced with a combination of recorded and live noise, e.g., crowd noises. Some sounds should be only live, e.g., glass crashing, close auto horns, close siren, etc. Certain sounds can be very well produced with older-type machines (which are fun to build and operate), e.g., rain, wind, thunder.

SOUND EFFECT SYSTEMS. Systems designed to play or create sound effects, preshow music, and intermission or production music. It is important that the amplifiers are of sufficient output wattage to give the desired volume. High-level recordings are necessary to produce high-volume playback. Effects system should have microphones available (see SOUND REIN-

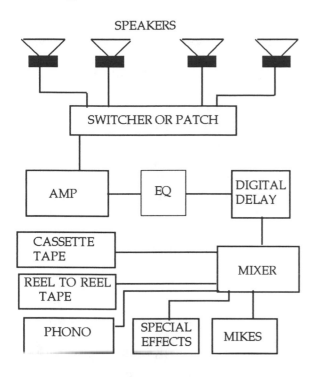

SPEAKERS

SWITCHER OR PATCH

AMP — EQ — DIGITAL DELAY

CASSETTE TAPE

REEL TO REEL TAPE

PHONO

SPECIAL EFFECTS

MIKES

MIXER

TYPICAL SOUND EFFECTS SYSTEM

FORCEMENT SYSTEM). A good system includes tape decks (reel to reel and cassette), phonographs, microphones, mixer, graphic equalizer, preamps, power amplifiers, speakers, and patch panel with wiring, connectors, and plugs necessary to connect all components. Other equipment to increase quality and flexibility: thunder screens, digital delays, cart tapes, compact disks, and digital audio tape.

SOUND EQUIPMENT. A number of electronic devices are available for both SOUND EFFECT SYSTEMS and SOUND REINFORCEMENT SYSTEMS.

Amplifier (amp). An electronic device that increases the volume of sound within it. Amplifiers often have a number of controls, one for each input (or a selector switch as in amps for home use), base and treble controls, and output gain. By raising or lowering the gain (volume control) sound levels are increased or decreased. Signal is measured in decibels on a dB meter or on a VU (volume unit) meter.

Power amp. An amplifier that usually has only a gain control for output power. Power is measured in watts.

Preamp. An amplifier that strengthens the signal from microphone, phono cartridge, tape, or disc player to a level useable by the power amp.

Cans. Headphones.

Cartridge. A device that converts mechanical movement of stylus into electrical pulses. A crystal or ceramic cartridge is used on a **Thunder screen** (see under THUNDER) and magnetic cartridges are used for most theatre phonographs.

Cassette player. An audio tape deck in cassette format. Not practical for splicing, use reel-to-reel tape deck. The cassette deck excels for music and **loops.**

Compact disc (CD). A small digital recording read by a laser beam and played back through a preamp mixer and amp. Extremely high quality recordings and playback.

Digital audio tape (DAT). A tape unit that uses the same digital technology as the compact disc with high-quality results.

Digital delay. An electronic device that provides adjustable time delay in playback. Similar to an echo effect but can be adjusted to change time of the second sound. Along with graphic equalizer, the delay helps in tuning a room or space to give a live presence.

Foldback monitor. Part of sound reinforcement system allowing performers to hear themselves, an onstage orchestra, etc. Often called monitors or onstage monitors, they face the performer.

Graphic equalizer (EQ). An electronic device that boosts or cuts specific frequencies to shape sound to a particular space or to the particular hearing of an individual.

Joystick (pot pan). A device that divides an input into several outputs via a small rotating handle, which activates the connected speakers. Often used in auditoriums to allow sound to travel around from one speaker to another.

Loop. An endless (circle) piece of audio tape used for repetitive sounds. Effective for such sounds as rain and those of a party or crowd.

Microphone (mike, mic). An electroacoustical device that converts sounds into electrical pulses. Since the pulse level of mikes is often very low, many need preamps to increase the signal to the amplifier. Omnidirectional mikes will pick up sounds coming from all directions while unidirectional mikes pick up sounds from only one direction. Types of mikes include the following.

Carbon mike. Cheapest, oldest, and one of the most widely used, somewhat noisy and not good for reinforcement systems.

Condenser mike. Must be placed close to preamp, has fewer moving parts than most, and quality is good to excellent. Requires a power source but is smooth and responsive.

Dynamic mike. Inexpensive for general use, good to excellent quality; top of the line are very expensive and are often the standard in the recording industry. Very rugged, popular with theatres because so dependable. A must if thunder is made with BBs in balloon; see THUNDER.

Ribbon mike. Used originally in movies and radio, not very popular with theatre.

Wireless m ike. These mikes broadcast their signals on FM frequency. Occasionally they have an interference problem from outside radio signals; quality is improving, though units of high quality are expensive. Require excellent receiver to ensure good quality interface to mixer.

Mixer. Used to mix incoming signals to an output. Many mixers have the capability of adding equalization, noise reduction, reverberation, foldback and other monitor circuits, etc. Mixers are necessary if using power amplifiers. Usually have preamps on each mike input and are referred to in terms of number of circuits "in" and number of circuits "out," e.g., 8 in 2 out, 12 in 4 out, etc.

Patch bay. A patch panel used either on input or output side or both. Used to gain maximum flexibility within any system.

Phonograph (phono, turntable). For sound effects and music, a three-speed phono is most flexible. Be sure to have replaceable cartridges and styli for both 78-speed and 33 1/3-speed records.

Speakers. Usually of dynamic or electrostatic design, speakers are an electromechanical device designed to change electrical pulses into audible sound. Speakers are basically as good as the enclosure surrounding them. Most enclosures are either infinite baffle, ported (vented), or of the horn design. A three-way system is common in a speaker enclosure: woofer (low frequencies), squawker (midrange), and tweeter (high frequencies), with crossovers to allocate the frequencies to each speaker. The folded horn design is the favorite of some audiophiles. A reasonably good speaker will have a frequency response in the 50- to 20,000-Hz. area; marvelous ones are 20- to 40,000-Hz. There should be speakers mounted in the house and on the stage; portability on the stage is desired. Either the speakers have some sort of switching system to move sound to the desired area, or, in top-of-the-line systems, each speaker is driven by its own amplifier and control is through the **Mixer.** Speaker enclosures are an emotional issue with many people; suffice it to say, get a multispeaker unit as good as budget will allow. It is wise to seek help in deciding upon type of system needed, whether to use switcher, 70-volt line outputs, etc.

Stylus. Diamonds are used with all records except 78s.

Tape decks. Reel-to-reel decks are the standard in theatres; they must be capable of at least 7-1/2" per second speed for highest quality and are considered the best for timing and splicing of audio tape. Cart tapes are the standard in radio for commercial spots. Because of their electronic cuing ability, they can be of use in theatre. Cassettes are usually good for preformatted tapes such as music, which is usually used for preshow, intermission, and postshow. Digital audio tape is the newest technology, which as yet has not been used in theatre.

SOUND PLOT. A formal presentation showing the usage of sound during a production. The plot often uses charts, drawings, possible cues, and rough settings to explain the concept of the designer.

SOUND REINFORCEMENT SYSTEM. Used to strengthen the voice for clear projection to a given space or location, indoors and outdoors. Systems include microphones, preamps, mixers, equalizers, amplifiers, monitors and speakers with necessary cables and hardware. To gain some insight into very complex systems, see a headliner rock group; they often have the best equipment available.

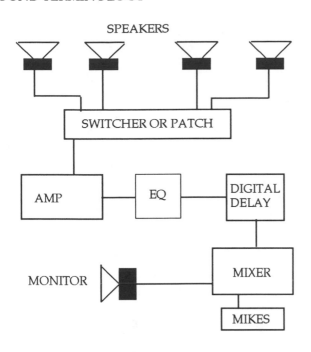

SPEAKERS

SWITCHER OR PATCH

AMP — EQ — DIGITAL DELAY

MONITOR

MIXER

MIKES

TYPICAL SOUND REINFORCEMENT SYSTEM

SOUND TERMINOLOGY

Audio tape. Acetate-backed tape is used for shows. Mylar tape stretches too much for repeated use.

Backup. A copy of a tape used in case the original show tape is ruined. After a master tape is made for production, it is important to make a dub as a backup. See **Dubbing** below.

Dolby, NR. A noise reduction system that takes tape noise out of nondigital tape.

Dubbing. Recording a tape from another recording, either tape or record.

Feedback. When a microphone is directly in line with speaker or gain is too high a loud howling is heard; reduce gain or change speaker location.

Leader and timing tape. Used to time each cue in sequence, spliced in between each cue on the show tape.

Monaural. Use of only one channel of sound. Theatre is best served by monaural sound since stereo cannot be heard by everyone in the audience.

Pot. The potentiometers used for a variety of things from gain to tone controls.

Segue (pronounced seg way). Sound term meaning to cross-fade two sounds by lowering one gain while raising the other gain.

Stereophonic. Use of two channels of sound. See **Monaural** above.

SPACE STAGING. See **Formal** under STAGING.

SPACKLE. A useful filler for cracks and imperfections in wood. Available in powder to be mixed with water or as paste in cans.

SPAGHETTI. Insulation tubing of varying diameters, which can be slipped on wires. Particularly useful for amplifier and radio circuits. See also SHRINK TUBING.

SPATTER. See under PAINTING TECHNIQUES.

SPEAKERS. See under SOUND EQUIPMENT.

SPECIAL. A spotlight set for a specific purpose for a specific play, as distinguished from standard area spotlights.

SPECIAL EFFECTS

Autopan, tilt, iris lights. Lights that pan left and right, tilt up and down and iris open and shut; all features remote controlled.

COLOR CHANGER ON TILT-PAN LIGHT
(DYNA-MIGHT)

Bubble machine. Blows bubbles and sends them into the air.

Chasers. Lights which seemingly move from one lamp to another as though they are chasing each other.

Color changers. Remotely controlled devices for changing color media. See SCROLLER.

Flicker lights. Little lamps that blink on and off rapidly.

Fog machines. See SMOKE EFFECTS.

Helicopter. A rotating head with 4 to 12 colored parabolic reflector spots.

Mirror balls. Motor-driven globes covered with squares of mirror into which spotlights shine and reflect the small squares all over the space.

Multiheaded lights. Many lights in circular pattern on floor. Often these lights spin or blink or chase.

Spinners. A light that spins its beams in a circle on the floor. This is usually accomplished with a rotating mirror.

Strobe. Intense light that shines on for a fraction of a second, goes off, and then repeats itself over and over. Controls can be set for speed of flashing; effect is much like that of a LOBSTERSCOPE.

Sweepers. Lights that pan or sweep back and forth across a given area. See also AUTOMATED LIGHTS; BATTERY OF LIGHTS; PAN AND TILT LIGHTS.

SPECIFIC LIGHT. An individual area or location of light, nongeneral. See LIGHTING INSTRUMENTS, SPECIFIC.

SPECTRUM. Divided wavelengths of light resulting in the colors of the RAINBOW.

SPEED-THROUGH. A rehearsal of a play in which the actors say their lines as fast as possible without emotion or pauses. Used to help performer memorize their lines.

SPHERICAL REFLECTOR. See under REFLECTORS.

SPIDER. See **Multiple pin connector** under PLUGS, ELECTRICAL.

SPIDERING (verb). To run electrical lines together with multiconnectors. Often used to connect orchestra lights. See **Multiple pin connector** under PLUGS, ELECTRICAL.

SPIGOT. See TRUSS CONNECTIONS.

SPIKE (verb). To mark a spot where a particular prop or set will be placed.

SPIKE MARKS. Marks put on floor to give the exact position of furniture or set. Spike marks can be painted with scene paint that will wash off or marked with various kinds of tape. Different colors used for different scenes will lessen confusion during fast scene changes. Spike marks should be small and accurate. See also **Spike** under TAPE.

SPILL. Stray light beams striking stage or auditorium in undesirable places. Spill is sometimes caused by imperfect lenses, which should be replaced, or by dusty lenses, which diffuse light. Keep lenses clean. See also ABERRATION; LIGHT SPILL CONTROL.

SPILL RING. See **Louvre** under LIGHT SPILL CONTROL.

SPINDLE. See BALUSTER; STEPS.

SPLICE (verb)

Rope. To fasten braided ropes or wire rope together or to make loops in the ends of braided ropes by interweaving rope ends.

Wire. To fasten electrical wires together by twisting and/or soldering and taping. Solderless connectors are often used for easy splicing.

SPLIT FADER. A fader that has two handles, each operating opposite the other so in effect when both are moved together a cross-fade from one scene to another is achieved. The advantage of the split fader is ability to perform time delays in a cross-fade, which cannot be done with a fader.

SPLIT STAGING. See under STAGING.

SPOKESHAVE. See DRAW KNIFE.

SPONGE. See under PAINTING TECHNIQUES.

SPOT (noun). Abbreviation for SPOTLIGHT. See also LIGHTING INSTRUMENTS, SPECIFIC.

SPOT (verb). To focus a spotlight or a followspot on an actor.

SPOTLIGHT (abbr. spot). Light equipped with a lens and, in most types, a sliding lamp socket and reflector for adjusting focus. A partial list of spotlights and spotlight data is given below. For a more detailed description of these and other spotlights, see LIGHTING INSTRUMENTS, SPECIFIC.

Type	Wattage	Position	Throw
Baby spot	250-400	On stage	Very short
Plano-convex	500-2,000	Any position	Short to medium
Ellipsoidal	400-3,000	Any position	Short to long
Fresnel	500-3,000	On stage	Short to medium
Arc light	2,500-10,000	Booth	Medium to very long

SPOT LINE. See under LINE.

SPRAY. See under PAINTING TECHNIQUES.

SPREAD OF SPOTLIGHT. Area covered by light from spotlight, determined by size, focal length of lens, and distance of throw. See BEAM ANGLE; FIELD ANGLE.

SPRUCE. A softwood; can be used for scenery if pine is not available. Sitka spruce is best. See also LUMBER.

SQUARE. A tool with a calibrated blade at right angles to a handle and used for marking lumber for a square cut. See also TOOLS, HAND.

Bevel gauge (sliding-tee bevel, bevel square). Adjustable tool used for setting and marking angles of any kind.

Combination square. Compact adjustable carpenter's square with settings for making angles of either 90° or 45°.

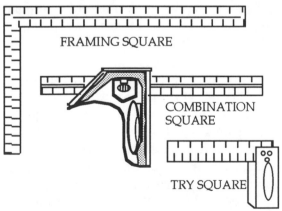

FRAMING SQUARE

COMBINATION SQUARE

TRY SQUARE

Framing square. Tool consisting of two blades set at right angles and calibrated for laying out various angles for rafters, stairs, etc. Used for squaring flats or other rectangular frames during construction.

Try square. Small carpenter's tool for laying out right angles.

T-square. A straightedge with a crossbar at one end. T-squares are used with triangles and drawing board to make working drawings.

SQUARE KNOT. See under KNOTS.

SQUEAKY DOORS (sound effect). Squeaking hinges are hard to find, but sometimes large hinges mounted at slight angles will work. A rosined string tied to the inside of the door near the hinge, run over a piece of 1/4" dowel, and tied to a weight will simulate a squeaky door. Some effects records have this sound.

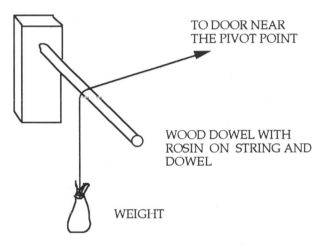

TO DOOR NEAR THE PIVOT POINT

WOOD DOWEL WITH ROSIN ON STRING AND DOWEL

WEIGHT

DOOR SQUEAK

SQUIB. A small explosive charge used to ignite a larger charge or used to break blood capsules, windows, etc. Squibs are electrically controlled, available through theatre supply houses.

STAB A LINE. To open the lay of a rope with a FID and pull a ribbon through to make a trim mark. See also FLAG.

STACK (pack). A pack of flats or scenery.

Live stack. Flats placed in the sequence in which they will be used.

Dead stack. Scenery which will not be used again during the performance. In multiple set plays it is common practice to take scenery from the live stack for set up and strike to dead stack when the scene is completed.

STAGE

Performance area or space.

The acting area behind the proscenium, enclosed by the stage house.

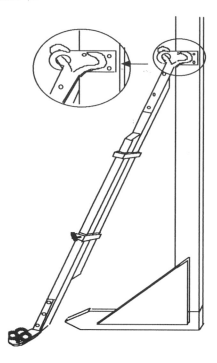

STAGE BRACE

STAGE BRACE. Adjustable hardwood brace with a hook on one end and a foot iron on the other, used to brace scenery. Always place the hook in a **Brace cleat.** See under FASTENING FLATS: **Lashing.**

STAGE CABLE. See WIRE, ELECTRICAL.

STAGE CARPENTER. See **Master carpenter** under STAGE CREW.

STAGECRAFT. Theatrical skill or techniques.

STAGE CREW. Personnel who work backstage during a production. The crew is made up of the following people, arranged in order of responsibility:

Stage manager. In complete charge of all performances after final dress rehearsals and responsible for calling special rehearsals for understudies or for disciplinary reasons. The stage manager also calls all light, sound, carpenter, fly, and crew CUES, checks entrances, often holds the prompt book, and keeps the show moving. In professional theatre and most other productions, the stage manager has attended all rehearsals and has recorded blocking, business, and changes in the master prompt script.

Master carpenter. Responsible for handling and repairing scenery onstage, in charge of set-in, scene changes, and strike. Responsible for overseeing the cleanliness of offstage areas.

Flyman. The person responsible for the rigging and its operation during a show. Reports to the master carpenter.

Flys. Part of the carpentry department and responsible to the flyman for rigging and its operation.

Second hand. The main assistant carpenter. If there is only one, the second hand is often in charge of the stage-left area during the run of the show. It is not unusual to have more than one assistant carpenter, who with a group of grips are assigned specific tasks. In the hierarchy of the carpentry department there can be a second hand (stage-left carpenter), a stage-right carpenter, and a winch operator, each person with a group of grips.

Grips. Work as carpenters and are responsible to the master carpenter and assistant carpenters. During scene changes they move all scenery except that allocated to the flymen.

Master electrician (juicer). In charge of electrical set-in, running lights during the show, and striking lights after the show.

Assistant electricians. Help the electrician with set-in and strike and run auxiliary boards.

Sound master. Responsible for all sound reinforcement and sound effects. Sometimes under the direction of the master electrician.

Sound crew. Sound technicians or assistant electricians will sometimes be included under the sound master.

Property master (prop master). In charge of all properties: hand, set, furniture, and dressing. Also responsible for overseeing the cleanliness of the onstage areas.

Property crew. Works with and under the supervision of prop master.

STAGE DIRECTIONS. Directions according to performers' right or left as they face the audience, and upstage or downstage in accordance with the sloped construction of early stages. Abbreviations are often used: DL, downleft; DCL, downcenter left; DR, downright, etc. See AREAS. Directions found in acting editions of old plays were based on entrances according to wings. These are used mostly in professional theatre and are sometimes confusing to the nonprofessional wishing to stage plays from original acting editions:

R.1 - Stage right, first entrance upstage of proscenium.

R.2 - Stage right, second entrance upstage of proscenium.

R.C. - Right center.

R.U. - Right upstage entrance.

O.P. - Opposite prompter (stage left).

P.S. - Prompt side (stage right, or side with curtain control).

(E) - Enter.

(X) - Crosses the stage.

STAGE DOOR. Backstage entrance to theatre.

STAGEHANDS. Those employed to work scene shifts, set a play, or strike a play, and those working props and sound. See STAGE CREW; UNIONS.

STAGE MANAGER. See under STAGE CREW.

STAGE PLUG. See **Stage plug** under PLUGS, ELECTRICAL.

STAGES. Acting areas designed in many configurations, some of which are identified below. There is some debate as to what constitutes a 3/4 arena versus a thrust stage. Here we assume the arena stage floor to be at the same level as or slightly lower than the first row of seats, with successive seats tiered, and the thrust stage to be a platform, with the first row of seats beginning slightly below the level of the stage.

Arena stages

Full arena. Acting area completely surrounded by audience. Successfully introduced in the mid-1930s by Professor Glenn Hughes, the father of the modern arena stage, who was inspired by the Paris one-ring circus. His first full arena stage was the Penthouse Theatre built at the University of Washington in 1940. Usually the floor level of the arena stage is either the same as or lower than the first row of seats. The lower acting area is preferred because it is easier to keep the lights out of the audience.

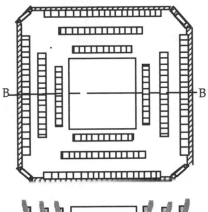

SECTION THROUGH B-B
ARENA STAGE
ELEVATED STAGE

Three-sided arena. Audience on three sides of the main acting area, which can be backed with a scenic wall. Sometimes this configuration is called the T- or U-shaped stage. It is similar to a thrust stage, except the first row of audience is usually on or slightly above the acting floor level.

Two-sided arena (sandwich arena, football field shape). A long, narrow acting area with audi-

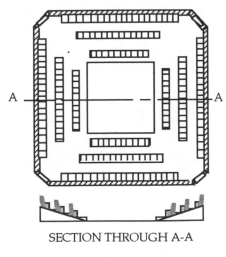

SECTION THROUGH A-A

ARENA STAGE
ELEVATED SEATS

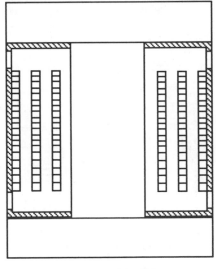

SANDWICH STAGE

ence on two sides. The audience seats are at stage level or slightly above, with successive rows tiered.

Apron stages

Extended-apron stage. Basically a proscenium stage with a large APRON supplementing the stage acting area. The apron often extends between 9' and 12' in front of the proscenium, with no provision made for seating on the sides. The extended apron is not as large as the thrust stage.

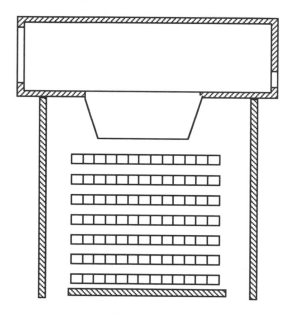

EXTENDED-APRON STAGE

Thrust stage. Follows the principles of the Shakespearean stage, with the acting area thrust into the auditorium and seating on three sides of the stage. The stage is elevated above the first row of the audience, and successive rows usually rise above stage level. The configuration can be confused with the three-sided arena.

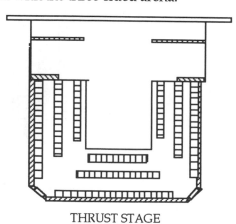

THRUST STAGE

Flexible stage (black box, open stage). Enclosed space equipped with seats on movable risers, permitting a variety of seating possibilities around an acting area. Larger flexible stages often have winch grids overhead. In some spaces the auditorium and stage are integrated into a single unit, with architectural TORMENTORS defining lateral extremities of the stage and serving as screens for entrances and exits.

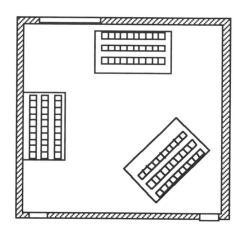

FLEXIBLE STAGE

Proscenium stage. Conventional stage separated from the auditorium by a PROSCENIUM, or "picture window." Usually the first row of the audience is seated below stage level, with successive rows tiered.

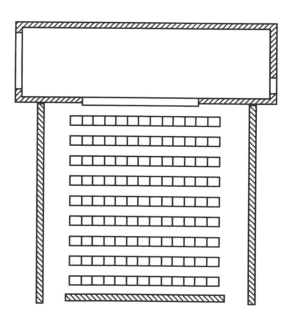

PROSCENIUM STAGE

Shakespearean stage. The SHAKESPEAREAN STAGE is a two-story thrust stage within an octagonal building. It has a curtained INNER BELOW and a curtained INNER ABOVE and boxes in conventional locations on the sides of the stage. The original apparently included an orchestra space on a third level. A reconstruction of this stage is the Globe Theatre in London, England.

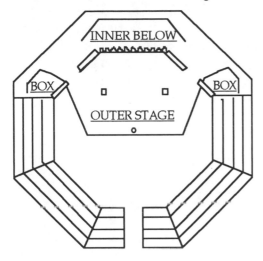

SHAKESPEAREAN STAGE

STAGE SCREW. See **Peg** under SCREWS.

STAGE SPACE. Refers to the actual physical space of the entire stage as opposed to ACTING AREA.

STAGING. Directing a play on stage, planning physical setting, lights, props, platforms, etc.

STAGING STYLES

Formal (space staging). Platforms, steps, ramps, etc., give varied and interesting levels for stage business and direction.

Naturalistic. Realistic box sets behind a proscenium.

Simultaneous. Action takes place on two or more separate parts of the stage, but not necessarily simultaneously. Simultaneous staging requires careful setting and focusing of lighting equipment to avoid spills or overlaps between any two areas.

Split. Simultaneous staging in which two unrelated scenes can be performed at the same time.

Symbolic. Backgrounds suggesting or enhancing plots or offering character interpretations.

STAIN. See PAINTING TECHNIQUES.

STAINED GLASS WINDOWS. See under WINDOWS.

STAINS. Scene paints will not cover all stains. Treat in the following ways:

Dye paint. If a small amount, coat with thin shellac before repainting. If large portion of flat has been painted with dye paint, recover flat.

Glue burn. If glue is still wet, sprinkle liberally with whiting and rub in. Allow to dry and brush off surplus whiting. If glue is dry, paint with thin shellac or rubber-based paint before applying scene paint.

Oil stain. Sometimes shellac will cover oil stains, but re-covering is recommended. Cut out small stains and patch hole. See **Patching** under COVERING FLATS.

Pitch stain. Before painting with scene paint, coat pitchy lumber with shellac to check discoloring or further bleeding.

Water stain. A thin coat of shellac over stains will prevent future bleeding, but re-covering of flat or painting entire flat with rubber-based paint is recommended.

Warning: Shellac tends to stiffen material and destroys the elasticity of canvas or muslin threads, causing material to wrinkle slightly and to fail to shrink at the same rate as the unshellacked portion of the flat.

STAIRS. See STEPS.

STAND (standard). A pipe in a metal base used to support a spotlight or floodlight. See also LIGHT MOUNTING DEVICES.

STAND BY (noun). A substitute or understudy.

STAND BY (verb). Warning for a cue.

STAPLE GUN (stapler, tacker). Tool for driving staples; an extremely useful tool in the shop. A 1/4" or 3/8" gun is sufficient for most work, but beaverboard or cardboard facings can be attached with the 1/2" or 9/16" staples used in larger guns. Compressed-air staplers capable of driving staples up to 1 1/2" long are available and can be used for fastening plywood, beaverboard, keystones, and corner blocks if a supply of compressed air is available.

STAPLES. Double-pointed tacks used for fastening. Staples can be used in place of tacks for flat covering, holding dutchman, upholstering, fastening opaquing cloth, etc. Available in a wide variety of types of finish, sizes, and crowns. Staples with fiber insulators at the top should be used for electrical wires.

STAR FROST. See under FROST.

STARS, PROJECTED. Laser-cut GOBOs make the best stars; insert in the pattern holder in an ellipsoidal reflector spotlight and focus. Or make pin scratches on a glass slide painted black and use in a projector or in any spotlight to which a second (objective) lens can be attached.

STATUE (prop). Buy plaster of paris figurines or make of PAPIER-MACHE or STYROFOAM. Cheesecloth dipped in SOBO or strong size water and draped over a suitable armature will retain its shape of robes or dresses when dry. See also MOLD, PLASTER OF PARIS.

STEAM. See SMOKE EFFECTS.

STENCIL. Template used to make wallpaper designs on flats. Lay designs on stencil paper or butcher paper and either cut with a razor blade or perforate with a pricker. If stencils are cut out, transfer design to flats directly with paint and brush, sponge, or spray gun. If stencils are perforated, pat a pounce bag containing dry scene paint or chalk dust against the stencil while it is held in place on the flat. Chalk dust transfers the perforations to the flat. The transfers are then painted freehand. Leaf patterns, fern patterns, geometric designs, and other interesting designs can be made by laying cutouts or real leaves on flats and spraying over them with a garden spray gun. After paint is dry, cutouts are removed and another color is sprayed to tone down effect. Wallpaper designs of all kinds should be **Sprayed** or **Spattered** (see under PAINTING TECHNIQUES) as a final coat to tone and blend the patterns.

STEP LADDER. See under LADDERS.

STEP LENS. See under LENSES.

STEPPING MOTOR. A type of motor that moves a step at a time, used for precision placement of a PARAMETER.

STEPS

    Onstage steps. Composed of the following parts: tread (step proper); riser (height between steps); stringer, carriage or step jack (side supports in which cuts are made to support treads and risers); legs (support for high end of steps). Stringers are made from 1" x 12" board or plywood by holding a large carpenter's square with 6" mark on one blade and 12" mark on the other blade to edge of board. Scribe along both outside

edges of square, making a 12" tread with a 6" riser at right angles. Repeat for as many steps as desired. Cut first riser short of 6" by thickness of lumber to be used for treads (usually 3/4"). Successive steps compensate themselves. Stringers are cut to marks, and risers applied. Treads rest on risers in front and risers drop behind treads in rear and nail to treads from under the step unit. Legs for small steps can be 1" x 3" lumber, bolted, hinged, or screwed to stringers. Long step units (those of four steps or over) are more easily stored if legs are bolted or hinged to fold. An X-bracing on legs is necessary for solidity. Stringers should be no more than 3' apart.

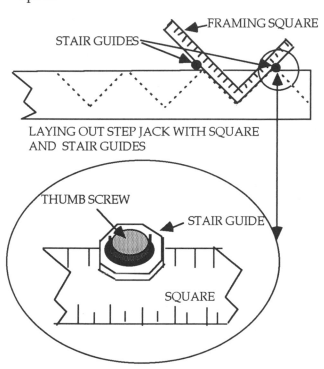

LAYING OUT STEP JACK WITH SQUARE AND STAIR GUIDES

    Offstage steps. Escapes, or carry-offs, are often made like ships' ladders, with widths of 2' to 3', 8" treads, and 9" to 12" risers. Stringers are made of 2" x 8" or 2" x 10" lumber rabbeted to receive the 2" x 8" treads. No riser board is used with this type of step. Batten handrails (1" x 3") are usually added as a safety precaution.

STEREOPTICON. A projection lantern which magnifies and projects pictures. Adaptations of stereopticons are used for projecting scenery of various kinds. See also PROJECTORS.

STICK. Vertical part of an A-ladder.

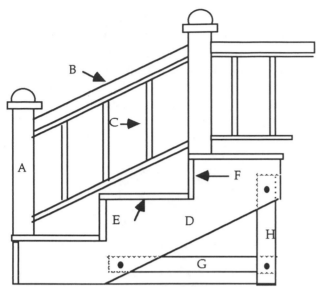

A NEWEL POST; B HANDRAIL(BANISTER);
C SPINDLE (BALUSTER); D STRINGER (JACK);
E TREAD; F RISER; G STRETCHER; H LEG.

STEP UNIT WITH BALUSTRADE   (A, B, C)

STIFFENER. Usually a 1" x 3" batten placed at right angles to a flat or piece of scenery, hinged on each side and used to increase rigidity of scenery.

STILE. The vertical side piece of a FLAT.

STILLSON WRENCH. See under WRENCH.

STIPPLE. See under PAINTING TECHNIQUES.

STOCK LUMBER. Generally 1" x 3", 1" x 6", or 1" x 12" white pine used for scene construction. See also LUMBER.

STOCK SCENERY. Building scenic units in pre-determined sizes. In nonprofessional theatre, it is considered economical and good practice to set standard widths and heights for scenery. Some university theatres avoid the concept.

Flats. In professional theatre, flat widths used to be standardized at widths of 5' 9" and heights of 12', 14', 16', and 18'. The 5' 9" width was originally limited by width of a boxcar door, but touring shows are trucked now and this restriction is no longer imposed; however air-freighting scenery has imposed all kinds of size restrictions, so check with airlines. Nonprofessionally, the same standard heights are used, but widths are more likely to be round figures of 1', 2', 3', 4', 5', and 6'. It is seldom wise to build flats wider than 6' because of difficulties in handling and storing. Some theatres standardize on one flat width of perhaps 5' and a jog width of 2 1/2' . The size, limitations, and storage space of any given theatre will help to determine correct widths. It should be noted that if only two sizes are used, a definite restriction is placed on the scene designer.

Platforms. Plywood sheets of 4' x 8' tend to set standards for platform width and length. Platform heights should be made in 6" modules, and multiples thereof will always fit to standard steps with 6" risers.

Steps. Standard steps for interiors should consist of a 12" tread and a 6" riser. Space staging or exterior designs may call for 4" risers, which permit more graceful movement on stage and still fit to 12" platforms..

STOP BLOCK. See under FASTENING FLATS: **Lashing.**

STOP CLEAT. See under FASTENING FLATS: **Lashing.**

STOP LINE. See under LINE.

STRAIGHTEDGE. Straight lumber or lattice, 4' to 6' long, with a slightly beveled edge to prevent smudging. Used as an aid for lining panels, baseboards, or wainscotings. See also PAINT-BRUSHES.

STRAINER. Lightweight sheet metal square, perforated with small holes and cut to fit in color frame in a spotlight. Strainers are designed to cut out light but maintain brilliance. See also MOONLIGHT EFFECT.

STRANDED WIRE. See under WIRE, ELECTRI-CAL.

STRAP HINGE. See under HINGES.

STRAP IRON. Strips of iron available in a variety of widths and thicknesses, with a corresponding variety of uses.

Angle iron. Usually 1/8" x 1/2" iron, bent at a right angle and used to reinforce the inside corners of frames and screens.

Corner iron. Small piece of iron cut at right angles and used as a plate to support corners of screens, frames, etc.

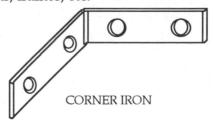

CORNER IRON

193

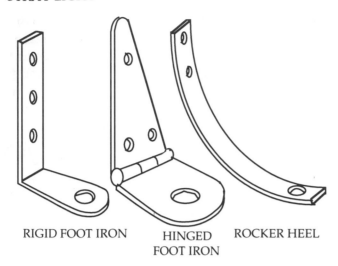

RIGID FOOT IRON   HINGED   ROCKER HEEL
FOOT IRON

FOOT IRONS

Foot iron (flat iron, floor iron). 1/4" x 3/4" iron, bent at an angle and drilled to accommodate a stage screw. Foot irons are used at the bases of flats, platforms, wagons, groundrows, stage braces, etc., to secure them to the floor. Hinged foot irons, which are less apt to snag or foul other scenery, are best for scenery that moves during changes.

Hanger iron. A 4" to 6" length of 1/4" x 3/4" iron with a 1" to 2" ring, drilled to accommodate screws. Used to tie off lines supporting scenery to be flown. Some hanger irons are bent at the free end and can slide under flats for maximum support.

Saddle iron. Strap iron fastened to the bottom of a door flat to maintain door opening width and flat rigidity. Saddle irons differ from **Sill irons** (see below) in that extra pieces are welded on the iron to fasten to inner stiles or verticals of door opening. Saddle irons are fastened in place with 2" (no. 8) flathead wood screws countersunk in the strap iron.

Sill iron. 1/4" x 3/4" strap iron fastened to the bottom of a door flat to maintain correct width of the flat and prevent rack. Fasten through countersunk holes with 1 1/2" or 1" (no. 8) flathead screws. Sill irons bent at each end and extending 8" to 12" up outside stiles of a flat provide greater strength.

STRAY LIGHT. Uncontrolled spills of light. See ABERRATIONS; LENSES; LIGHT SPILL CONTROL.

STRETCHER. Any brace going from one part of a structure to another; e.g., braces going from stair stringer to legs.

STRETCH HOSE OR WIRE (coil hose or wire). A hose or wire that is in a coil. The hose or wire is stretched out to work but coils back up when not in service.

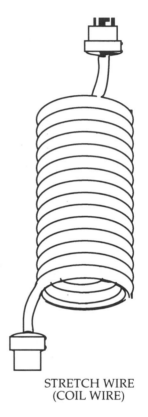

STRETCH WIRE
(COIL WIRE)

STRIKE A SET (strike). To remove all scenery and props from the stage.

STRINGER. See STEPS.

STRIP (verb). To glue a DUTCHMAN over a crack between two flats.

STRIP GLASS. Narrow widths of colored glass cut in strips to help withstand heat expansion. The strips are placed in a special color frame and used in close proximity to lamp. Occasionally two different colors are used in same frame to blend colors.

STRIP LIGHT. See under LIGHTING INSTRUMENTS, GENERAL.

STRIP OUT. To cover the stage with a wide beam of light from a followspot, as opposed to the general practice of following an actor with a narrow cone of light.

STROBE LIGHT. See **Strobe** under SPECIAL EFFECTS.

STUD. An upright timber in walls, usually measuring 2" x 4".

STYLES OF STAGING. See STAGING.

STYROFOAM. White, porous, lightweight, rigid plastic widely available in a variety of sizes, shapes, and thicknesses. Styrofoam is most useful in property departments for making decorative props for mantelpieces, foods for display (pie, fruits, eggs, meat, etc.), and ornamental pieces. Styrofoam is easily cut and shaped with a saw, rasp, or knife and can be painted with any available kind of paint except lacquer. A soldering gun can be used to cut or sculpt; heat thus provided melts Styrofoam in a reasonably clean cut as operator moves gun. *Warning:* Styrofoam is not flameproof; thus larger pieces should be painted with a fire-retardant paint. See **Foam, Styrofoam** under PLASTICS.

SUBTRACTIVE METHOD OF COLOR MIXTURE. Mixture of primaries of pigments (red, yellow, and blue) to obtain color. Called subtractive because pigments give color by subtracting, or absorbing, other colors of different wavelengths. See also ADDITIVE METHOD OF COLOR MIXTURE.

SUNDAY. See **Sunday knot** under KNOTS.

SUNLIGHT EFFECT. Best obtained from a single source, high-intensity light, such as a 1,000- or 1,500-watt ellipsoidal spotlight or narrow beam projector spot. Color should contrast with basic colors used for area; e.g., if amber is predominant on stage, sunlight through windows or doors should be clear; if blues or pinks are predominant, use light amber for sun. See also LIGHTING COLORS.

SUPPORTS, SCENERY. See DESIGN; JACK; STAGE BRACE.

SURF BOX (sound effect). A box 4' to 5' long by 12" to 18" wide made of 1" x 3" lumber with a 1/4" plywood bottom. BBs or buckshot are placed in the box and sound like rolling waves as they are rolled from one end to the other. Window screen tacked over the box will prevent spilling of BBs.

SWATCH. Sample of material or paint used for matching or demonstration.

SWEEP. Segment of a curved arch. See also ARCH; CURVED SCENERY.

SWITCHBOARD, LIGHTING CONTROL LOCATIONS. The ideal position is nonexistent; the advantages and disadvantages of various possible locations are listed below.

Downstage on control side of stage. Close contact with command control but apt to be in the way for multiple-set or large-cast plays. Poor visibility of stage.

Downstage above floor level on control side of stage. Close contact with command control, out of the way, better visibility of stage except for box sets with ceilings.

Downcenter stage in conductor's pit. Out of the way, good visibility of stage, but too close to perceive subtle changes.

AUXILIARY SWITCHBOARD WITH 8 STAGE PLUG OUTLETS, 4 1,000-W AND 2 500-W DIMMERS, 6 FUSED CIRCUIT SWITCHES, AND 1 MAIN SWITCH (CAPITOL)

MECHANICAL INTERLOCK WITH SLOW-MOTION MASTER WHEEL RESISTANCE DIMMER SWITCHBOARD

Control room in back of theatre. Out of the way, excellent visibility, best if stage manager is in same space, otherwise requires intercom system.

SWITCHBOARDS. Boards consisting of the switches, fuses, and dimmers necessary to control stage lights. Switchboards ideally have sufficient dimmers to control lights for each area of the stage, plus special effects lights, general toning lights, cyclorama lights, and house lights. For small theatres, between thirty and forty dimmers are needed to control light adequately. A system of mastering individual dimmers to one or two controls should be included by either mechanical interlocking or, preferably, electrical interlocking (see DIMMERS, MASTER). Dimmer controls should be compactly arranged for rapid manipulation and clearly marked to avoid errors. For dimmer protection, fuses or breakers should be placed in a readily accessible position between dimmers and circuits. Switchboards for small theatre should be capable of handling a minimum of 50,000 watts. Plugging panels should be provided close to switchboards, enabling the operator to plug any light or set of lights on any dimmer. See also DIMMERS; PATCH PANEL;

PIANO BOARD WITH TEN INTERLOCKING
RESISTANCE DIMMERS (KLIEGL)

LIGHTING CONTROL.

Piano switchboard. Obsolete. Portable switchboard mounted in a box shaped like an upright piano crate. Generally equipped with resistance dimmers and was used extensively on Broadway and for touring productions.

Preset switchboard. Obsolete. Switchboard with two or more controls to each dimmer; it was possible to adjust one set of controls for one

REMOTE CONTROLLED MOTOR OPERATED
RESISTANCE DIMMER (CAPITOL)

AUTOTRANSFORMER BOARD WITH MECHANICAL
INTERLOCKING CONTROL HANDLES (KLIEGL)

scene while another scene was in progress. During scene changes a fader was used to transfer power from one bank of dimmer controls to the other.

Remote control switchboard. Obsolete. Dimmers located in one part of a theatre and controlled from a more convenient location. Remote control, either electrical or mechanical, made it possible to place bulky parts of a switchboard in a less congested spot and concentrate

VITROHM, BANK OF INTERLOCKING RESISTANCE
DIMMERS (WARD LEONARD)

controls in a more compact unit, in view of acting areas.

SWITCHES. Make and break devices for electrical circuits.

Circuit breaker (breaker switch). Switchlike device used in place of a fuse that opens automatically if circuit is shorted or overloaded. Circuit can be closed again by pushing a reset button or by turning switch to "off" and then to "on" position. Breakers are commonly used because a blown breaker can be easily spotted and reset.

Knife switch. Obsolete. An open electrical switch composed of a copper blade hinged on one end and a spring copper receptacle. Contact was made by closing blade into receptacle. Simple knife switches were not enclosed and were therefore dangerous to use on anything but low-voltage, low-amperage circuits.

Master switch. Obsolete. Generally a knife switch enclosed in a metal box and equipped with a handle outside the box. Master switches were rated for maximum load of combined branch circuits and were fused accordingly. Many master switches provided for fusing within their boxes.

Mercury switch. A silent switch in which mercury makes contact in "on" position. Because they are noiseless, mercury switches are favored on switchboards close enough to the audience to be heard. Most mercury switches are designed to operate in vertical or near-vertical position and will not operate in a flat position.

Rotary switch. Switch with two or more contacts activated by rotating handle or knob.

Selector switch. A multiconnector rotary switch designed to connect lighting equipment and dimmers. See also PATCH PANEL.

Toggle switch. A major type switch used in PRESET BOARDS. Standard household switch.

Single pole–single throw. Designed for one side of the line, with one "on" position and one "off" position.

Single pole–double throw. Designed for one side of the line, with two "on" positions. Used in circuits where two switches in different locations control the same light.

Double pole–single throw. Designed for both sides of the line, with one "off" and one "on" position. Used in circuits where two switches in different locations control the same light.

Double pole–double throw. Designed for both sides of the line with two "on" positions.

SWORDS (props). Swords pictured in dictionaries and encyclopedias indicate the proper weapons for each period. Swords to be carried can be made of wood and painted with aluminum paint to look reasonably authentic. Swords to be used should be either dull foils or épées borrowed from gymnasiums or fencing instructors, or fairly broad swords made of 3/16" or 1/4" aluminum strips. Aluminum is available in many alloys, designated by number, and in several tempers, designated by the letter "T" followed by a number. Recommended alloys for swords bear the following designations: 60661-T6, 2024-T4, and 7075-T4. Thickness or gauge is designated by thousandths of an inch. Any thickness between 0.188" (approximately 3/16") and 0.250" (1/4") is recommended. If real swords are used, edges and points should be dulled to ensure reasonable safety. Prop departments should acquire a selection of swords, either homemade or made safe for stage use.

SYMBOLIC STAGING. See under STAGING.

SYMBOLS. Symbols used extensively in the theatre are shown on this and the next page. Shown are lighting instruments and electrical symbols that are sold as plastic templates. The floor plan symbols are usually drawn or stored in drafting libraries on computer drafting programs (CAD).

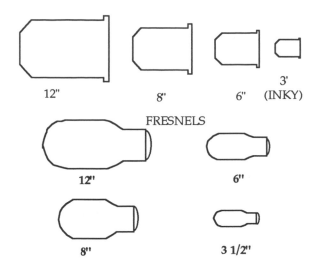

12"   8"   6"   3' (INKY)

FRESNELS

12"   6"

8"   3 1/2"

ELLIPSOIDAL REFLECTOR SPOTLIGHTS

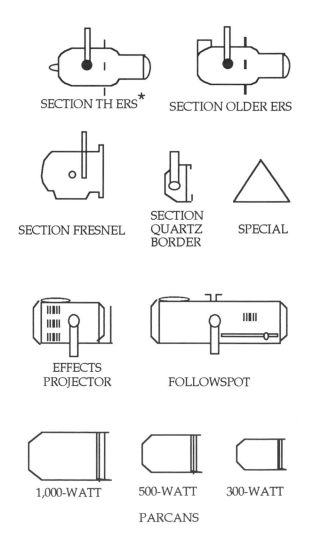

SECTION TH ERS*   SECTION OLDER ERS

SECTION FRESNEL   SECTION QUARTZ BORDER   SPECIAL

EFFECTS PROJECTOR   FOLLOWSPOT

1,000-WATT   500-WATT   300-WATT

PARCANS

LIGHTING INSTRUMENT SYMBOLS

*TH = Tungsten Halogen Lamp; ERS = Ellipsoidal Reflector Spot.

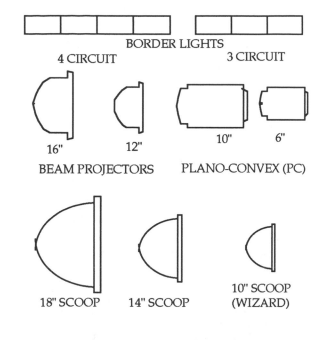

BORDER LIGHTS
4 CIRCUIT   3 CIRCUIT

16"   12"   10"   6"

BEAM PROJECTORS   PLANO-CONVEX (PC)

18" SCOOP   14" SCOOP   10" SCOOP (WIZARD)

LIGHTING INSTRUMENT SYMBOLS

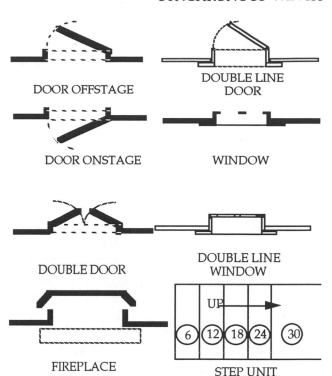

DOOR OFFSTAGE   DOUBLE LINE DOOR

DOOR ONSTAGE   WINDOW

DOUBLE DOOR   DOUBLE LINE WINDOW

FIREPLACE   STEP UNIT

UP
6   12   18   24   30

FLOOR PLAN SYMBOLS

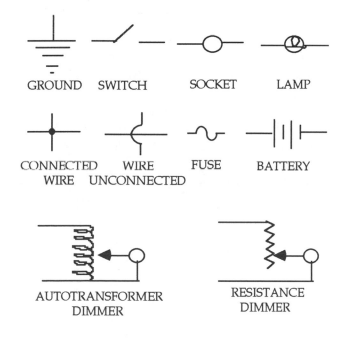

GROUND   SWITCH   SOCKET   LAMP

CONNECTED WIRE   WIRE UNCONNECTED   FUSE   BATTERY

AUTOTRANSFORMER DIMMER   RESISTANCE DIMMER

ELECTRICAL SYMBOLS

SYNCHRONOUS WINCH. A fly system, developed by George Izenour of Yale University, that uses motorized winches instead of counterweights. Individual motorized winches are mounted in loft above gridiron, and sheaves are designed to be moved in channels and locked in different locations on gridiron. A system of cross-patching permits any two or more winches to be ganged together on the same control so that any combination of winches can raise or lower a batten. Conventional counterweight systems operate battens parallel to footlights, while the synchronous winch system allows any placement of battens, from parallel to perpendicular. This versatility and the elimination of manual loading of counterweights to offset weight of flown scenery are obvious advantages of the synchronous winch system. See also COUNTERWEIGHT SYSTEM.

T

TAB CURTAIN. See under CURTAINS.

TABS. Wide drapery legs used as wings. Usually twice the width of a leg. Drops or draperies hung in the wings perpendicular to the footlights, masking the extreme sightlines in wide houses. Most often used in large theatres for large productions requiring crowd entrances and exits from the wing positions. Very often, tabs must be flown out for scene changes.

TACKER. See STAPLE GUN; STAPLES.

TACKS. Used for flat covering, groundcloths, and upholstering. No. 4 carpet tacks, bought by box or carton of boxes, are most useful. Gimp tacks are used for finished upholstering and, because they will show, have a small, round, sometimes ornate head. Colored, large-headed upholstery tacks may also be useful.

TAIL. The last several feet of a rope often hanging from a belaying pin on the rail. Often a tail is used as a temporary safety on the end of a set of lines or on the overhaul line of a counterweight set. See SAFETY.

TAKE A WRAP (Command verb)

> **Hemp house.** To take a turn around a belaying pin with a set of lines while checking trim, usually followed with the command "tie it off."

> **T-track house.** Push down and in on kickup block with foot, at same time grasp either front or back overhaul line depending on where weight is; quickly take the slack and wrap around other line three to five times. Flyman can hold a great deal of weight in this manner on a misweighted line.

TAKE OUT (take up). To fly out or raise scenery or a curtain.

TAKE-UP BLOCK. See under BLOCK.

TAP AND DIE SET. Tools for threading metal or pipes. Taps are used for inside threads (threading the hole) and dies are used for outside threads (pipes or bolts). Sets are designated by diameter of hole and number of threads per inch; thus, 1/4 x 20 equals 1/4" diameter with 20 threads per inch. Smaller taps and dies are coded by number in which diameter decreases as first number, and second number still designates threads per inch: 12 x 24, 8 x 32, 6 x 32, etc. (see chart). Dies for threading pipe are designated by inside diameter of pipe; thus a 1/2" pipe die threads a pipe with an inside diameter of 1/2" and an outside diameter of 3/4". Most useful pipe dies in the theatre are 1/2", 3/4", 1", 1 1/4" and 1 1/2". To tap holes for various sizes of bolts, use the chart to determine drill size. There are also snub-nosed taps called bottom taps, which are used where the hole is not drilled all the way through.

DRILL SIZES FOR TAPPING			
BOLT SIZE	OD (INCHES)	DRILL NO.	OD (INCHES)
2 x 56	.086	50	.070
6 x 32	.138	36	.106
8 x 32	.164	29	.136
10 x 24	.190	25	.149
12 x 24	.216	16	.177
1/4 x 20	.250	7	.201
5/16 x 18	.312	F	.257
3/8 x 16	.375	5/16	.312
7/16 x 14	.437	U	.368
1/2 x 13	.500	27/64	.422

TAPE DECKS. See under SOUND EQUIPMENT.

TAPES

Leader and timing tape (cueing tape). A special plastic tape used to splice on the front of audio tape recordings to give a warning of an upcoming cue. The 3M brand has distinctive markings every 7 1/2" to give 1-second warning at 7 1/2" per second speed.

Recording tapes. See MAGNETIC TAPE; VIDEO.

Tape measure. A flexible steel, fiberglass, or cloth tape calibrated to measure in feet and inches or in metric measure. Comes in 3' to 100' lengths. See under RULERS.

Tapes with adhesive:

Double-faced. A tape to attach carpets to floors, it has adhesive on two sides.

Electrical Scotch-type. Black plastic tape with high dielectric strength. Used as the standard for electrical wiring.

Florist. Strong green tape available in florist shops and useful for props.

Friction. Black electrical tape used sometimes for wiring, superseded by black plastic electrical tape.

Gaffers. Usually rug tape in black, gray or silver. Rug tape is backed with either plastic or cloth. Usually 2" wide though other sizes available. Used extensively backstage, it is the great mending material of every master carpenter.

Masking. Cream-colored tape used to hold paper to drawing boards and mask objects to be painted.

Rug. See **Gaffers.**

Scotch. Sticky clear tape used for paper and a number of uses.

Slide. Teflon-coated plastic tape is superslick and slides on smooth surfaces.

Spike. Plastic tape in wide variety of colors used to mark placement of furniture on floor of a set. Use a different color for each set or scene.

TEA. The basis for many BEVERAGES used in plays.

TEAMSTER'S HITCH. See under KNOTS.

TEARS IN SCENERY. See **Flat patching** under COVERING FLATS.

TEASER

Name of first border or drapery, hung in flies downstage, forming with tormentors an inner frame for the stage or simply masking the flies.

First border hanging downstage of act curtain, used to adjust proscenium height; also known as the grand valance.

TEASER BATTEN

First pipe or first border.

Pipe batten hung close to teaser and act curtain and used for lighting equipment.

TECHNICAL DIRECTOR (TD). In non Broadway theatres, the technical director is directly responsible for construction, execution of designs, lighting, and run of production, and for setting, shifting, striking, and disposing of scenery for each production. In many theatres, the technical director is also responsible for designing and painting.

TECHNICAL REHEARSAL (tech). A rehearsal scheduled for the crew in order to determine set-shifting routine, lighting cues and intensity levels, sound cues and volume levels, and everything involving the technical personnel. Occasionally performers will be involved so they may assist with cues involving blocking. It is critical that all sets and props be ready for the technical rehearsal.

TECHNICIAN (techie). Anyone working on a technical aspect of a production.

TECHNIQUES OF PAINTING. See PAINTING TECHNIQUES.

TED LEWIS. See **Top hat** under LIGHT SPILL CONTROL.

TEE. See under PIPE FITTINGS.

TEE-BAR (T-bar). A heavy T-shaped bar of steel attached to the stage wall behind the COUNTERWEIGHT SYSTEM, forming a track to guide the counterweight ARBORS.

TEE-NUT. Threaded sleeve with prongs for imbedding in wood. Used when it is necessary to bolt into wood, but difficult or impossible to place a nut on the inside. Available at hardware stores, most-used sizes on stage are 3/16", 1/4", 3/8", and 1/2".

TEE-PLATE. A steel plate shaped like a T used in place of a keystone.

TEE-SHAPED STAGE. See **Arena, tee** under STAGE.

TELEPHONE

It is popular to have telephone systems custom designed for large theatres. Pushbutton intercom systems are often placed on the phones so that by pressing a button a person has instant communication with anyone else on the system. A closed circuit–type phone communication between the stage manager and other key department heads was used prior to modern headphone systems. See INTERCOMMUNICATION SYSTEM.

Telephones for props. In most phones, the bell system is 45 volts AC; an autotransformer will supply that voltage; check with VOM. Since the divestiture of AT&T, period telephones are no longer being made and are, therefore, not available for borrowing by theatre groups. Any period phones already owned by a prop department should be kept under lock and key, and prop people should keep their eyes open for possible sources of additional phones to add to the collection.

TELESCOPTER (Genie, cable lift, lift). A telescoping frame that will lift people, lights, and other equipment into the air. See also GENIE LIFT.

TEMPER. To harden metal by cooling highly heated metal in various coolants to control the rate of temperature reduction.

TEMPERATURE. See KELVIN SCALE.

TEMPLATE

Drafting. A commercially manufactured pattern or guide used to lighten the work of the draftsperson by providing various patterns for tracing appropriate symbols. The theater technician will find the following templates of great value in drafting work:

Flat template. 1/2"=1' scale includes symbols for keystones, corner blocks, standard 3" stock lumber, toggle locations, hinges, lashing hardware, etc. See NAILING BLOCK.

Furniture template. Either or both 1/4" = 1' or 1/2" = 1' scales. Include standard sizes for beds, chairs, sofas, pianos, tables, etc.

Lighting template. Either or both 1/4" = 1' or 1/2" = 1' scales. These templates establish standard symbols for ellipsoidal and fresnel spotlights plus scoops, projectors, striplights, etc. Lighting templates are available in either floor plan symbols or elevation symbols; floor plans are probably more universally used.

Shop (template). A pattern made in the shop of thin material (cardboard, plywood, or the like) used as a guide for tracing or marking items to be cut.

TEMPLATE BENCH. See under BENCHES.

TENON. See **Mortise and tenon** under JOINT.

TENSION BLOCK. See **Take-up block** under BLOCK.

TERMINAL. One end of an electrical circuit usually providing a means of attaching a conductor.

TEST LAMP. A low-wattage lamp or neon lamp with short leads, used to test circuits. Two low-wattage lamps in series used for testing 220-V or 110-V circuits.

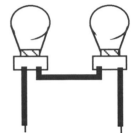

TEST LAMP

TEXTURE. One of the four aspects of visual manifestation, the others being line, color, and form. For methods of giving texture or a third dimension to a finished set, see PAINTING TECHNIQUES.

TH. See **Tungsten-halogen** under LAMPS

THERMOFORMING. Shaping plastic by the use of heat, pressure, and a mold.

THERMOPLASTIC. A plastic that will soften when heated and may be reshaped. The majority of plastics used in the theatre are of this type.

THERMOSETTING PLASTIC. These plastics set permanently when heated and may not be softened again. The urea resins and phenols fall into this classification and include the old switchboard panel favorite, Bakelite.

THICKNESS. See REVEAL.

THOMAS REGISTER. An extremely handy set of books that list all the companies in the U.S. and the products they manufacture.

THREADING PIPES. See TAP AND DIE SET.

THREE-DIMENSIONAL SCENERY. Scenery that will be seen from all sides, therefore finished on all sides.

THREE-FER. An electrical junction providing three outlets.

THREEFOLD. Three flats hinged with two folding face to face. To complete the folding a tumbler must be placed between flats 2 and 3 to allow 3 to fold over the other two. Dutchmans are applied over all cracks with a large one over the tumbler and adjacent stiles. The flat designed to fold in must be no wider than the center flat. In use, threefolds are held rigid by

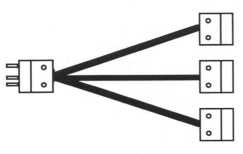

PIN CONNECTOR THREEFER

battening or by placing battens in S-hooks on the back. See **S-hooks** under HOOKS.

THREE PLY. See PLYWOOD.

THREE-WIRE SYSTEM OF WIRING. See **Three-wire single-phase circuit** under CIRCUIT, ELECTRICAL.

THRESHOLD. See **Door** under SADDLE.

THROW

Lights. Distance between lighting instrument and area to be illuminated. A light intensity of 35 footcandles is considered minimum for most stage lights; therefore, the practical throw of a given instrument is the distance between the instrument and an intensity reading of 35 footcandles on a photometer.

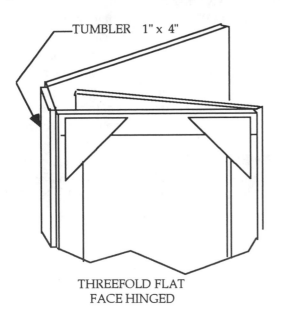

TUMBLER 1" x 4"

THREEFOLD FLAT
FACE HINGED

Rigging. To attach a rope or line in a particular manner to an object or other line.

THRUST. A stress tending to push a part of a structure out of position. In platform construction, the thrust is down; therefore, supporting legs should be placed under cross members or frames for maximum strength.

THRUST STAGE. See under STAGE.

THUMB SCREW. See under SCREWS.

THUNDER (sound effect). Recordings work well especially if augmented with any of the following:

Thunder sheet. Sheet metal 18 to 24 gauge, 3' x 6' or 8', suspended by a rope on one end and having a wooden handle on the other end. Best effects are achieved with long sheets.

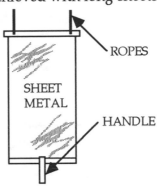

ROPES

SHEET METAL

HANDLE

THUNDER SHEET

Thunder drum. Bass drum, timpani, or a 4' x 4' wooden frame on which a drum head is stretched can be used as a thunder drum. If tension is lost through dampness, the heat from a lighted 500-watt floodlight hung near the drum for two or three hours will tighten head again.

Balloon with buckshot or BBs inside, hit and rotated against a dynamic microphone, will produce effective, controlled thunder.

Thunder screen. A crystal phonograph cartridge attached to a 30" square copper screen (insect type) via a soldered copper wire to the needle slot will amplify the sounds made with a sheepskin polishing mitt. Smack the screen with the back of the mitt on the hand for the crash of thunder and then run diagonally across the screen with the mitt for rumble. Use free hand to adjust the volume from loud to fadeout.

THYRATRON TUBE DIMMER. See under DIMMERS.

THYRISTER. European name for SCR. See **Silicon controlled rectifier** under DIMMER.

TIE-OFF (noun). See under KNOTS.

TIE-OFF (COMMAND verb). To secure a line or a set of lines to the belaying pin on the pin rail. To tie a line.

TILT JACK. See under SCENERY, SHIFTING.

TIMED FADE. A fade up or down according to predetermined speed as set by lighting designer and counted out or checked on the control board timer or clock. See also **Computer terminology** under LIGHTING CONTROL.

TIME LAG. Time lapse between activation and action; e.g., lag between time a switch is closed and filament of a large lamp reaches incandescence. Some SCR controllers have time lag, and require compensation by anticipation of cues. See **Silicon-controlled rectifier** under DIMMERS; HEAT UP.

TIME SHEET. Schedule kept by a stage manager to show the exact time of each act, scene, scene change, and intermission. Time sheets are an aid to the director and stage manager in maintaining the pace of a show over an extended run.

TINNING. Putting SOLDER and flux on wire to stiffen it or to facilitate soldering.

TIN SNIPS. Large, heavy shears used for cutting tin or lightweight metal. Duckbill snips are easier to use than straight-cut snips.

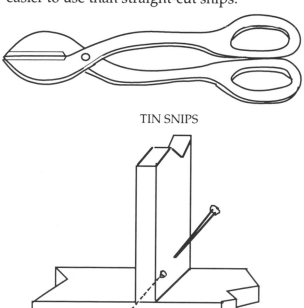

TIN SNIPS

TOENAILING

TINT. A variation in color made by adding white. Distinguished from SHADE.

TIP JACK. See **Tilt jack** under SCENERY, SHIFTING.

TOENAIL. To nail obliquely through an end or side of a board.

TOGGLE (toggle rail). Cross member of a FLAT.

TOGGLE SWITCH. See under SWITCHES.

TONING LIGHTS. Lights used for general color and mood. Used to set the tone of a play. See LIGHTING INSTRUMENTS, GENERAL.

TOOLS, AIR. See AIR TOOLS.

TOOLS, HAND. Scene shops should be provided with at least the following basic tools: hammers, screwdrivers, crosscut saw, ripsaw, keyhole saw, rasp, files, plane, chisels, mat knife, brace and bits, framing squares, combination square, bevel gauge, 12' or 16' tape measures, tin snips, pliers, long nose pliers, dikes, end cutter, crescent wrenches, socket set, wood vise, metal vise.

TOOLS, POWER. See POWER TOOLS.

TOP HAT. See under LIGHT SPILL CONTROL.

TORCH (prop). Made of sticks built up with papier-mâché to any desired shape and holding two flashlight batteries, a switch, and a flashlight lamp. Cover lamp with scraps of color media to resemble a flame. Colors should include frost, amber, straw, reds and blue. If gelatine is used, moisten it to make it self-adhering and it will hold most shapes. See wiring diagram under LANTERN.

TORMENTOR (torm). A masking piece used to terminate the downstage wall of a set on each side of the stage or to form an inner frame (inner proscenium) so that action can be set further upstage and in a better position for lighting. In the latter case, walls of the set are terminated by RETURNS. Tormentors are usually flats with a 6" or 12" thickness.

TORMENTOR LIGHT (torm light). Spotlights mounted upstage of tormentors on each side of the stage. Tormentor lights can be hung from BOOMS, LADDERS, or TREES (see LIGHT MOUNTING DEVICES).

TORN FLAT. See **Flat patching** under COVERING FLATS.

TOWER. See LIGHT MOUNTING DEVICES.

TRACING PAPER. Lightweight, semitransparent paper used for making drawings, especially drawings to be blueprinted. Available in sheets and tablets in various sizes at art and drafting stores.

TRACK. See **Slip stage** under SCENERY, SHIFTING; TRAVELER.

TRAMMEL POINTS. Adjustable clamps which slide on a bar to give variable radii and are used for scribing circles or arcs of large diameter.

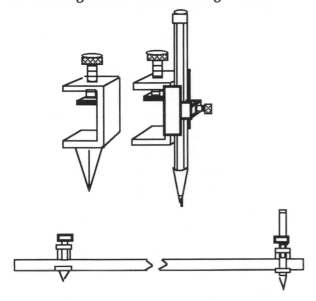

TRAMMEL POINTS

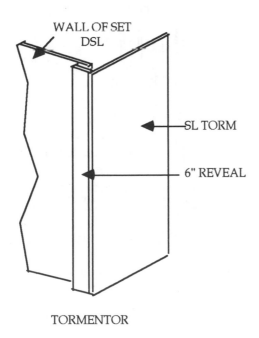

WALL OF SET
DSL

SL TORM

6" REVEAL

TORMENTOR

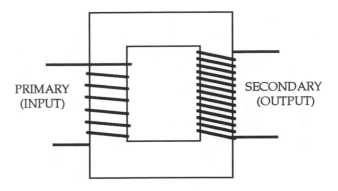

PRIMARY
(INPUT)

SECONDARY
(OUTPUT)

SIMPLE TRANSFORMER

TRANSFORMER. A core of laminated iron on which two coils of wire are wound. Primary coil, carrying an alternating current, induces an alternating current in secondary coil. Voltage in secondary coil is determined by ratio of windings on primary to windings on secondary. The more windings on secondary, the higher the voltage. Bell transformers, available in hardware stores, are of this type and are useful for door bells, buzzers, and chimes. See also **Autotransformers** under DIMMERS.

TRANSLUCENT DROP. See under DROPS.

TRANSPARENCIES. See SCRIM.

TRAP. Removable section of floor. Stage floors in many theatres are segmented so that sections can be removed for scenic effects, e.g., sunken stairs or scenery or disappearing actors. Traps for disappearing actors are usually rigged as elevators or as one end of an arm on a pivot (lever trap). In either case, the trap itself is made to ride in a track on each side and is given sufficient depth to prevent twisting or jamming in the track.

Elevator trap. Pulleys are mounted under the floor at each corner of the trap, and lines are run from corners of trap over pulleys to counterweights. Hydraulic pistons also work well for this type of trap.

Lever trap. Pivot point is established halfway between traveling distance of trap and several feet away from trap. A heavy timber (4" x 6" or 4" x 8") is fixed with a bolt to trap bottom, fastened to pivot point with metal strap, and counterweighted at end with sandbags or weights. An attendant must release a catch on the bottom of the trap. Large coil springs, spring cushions, or mattresses under the trap will help to break the fall and muffle the sound.

Macbeth trap. A special type of stage trap, originally used for the appearance of Banquo's ghost in *Macbeth*. A small section of floor is rigged to drop slightly below floor level and to slide to one side, allowing room for the actor to be lowered or pushed up through opening.

VAMPIRE TRAP

Vampire trap. A double-faced door type trap that pivots in the center and can be used for fast escapes or disappearing props fastened to the trap. The vampire trap may also be used for tables where props or place settings are fastened to the table top and pivoted under for very fast changes or disappearance scenes. *Warning:* These traps can spin so fast that they pose a hazard to crew members operating them; they must also have positive stops and locks.

TRAVELER. A track used for hanging **draw curtains** (see under CURTAINS). Metal travelers are more compact than wooden travelers, although they are apt to be noisier unless equipped with rubber or nylon carriers. Travelers should be long enough to provide for a minimum 2' overlap of curtain at center. Standard travelers gather folds as curtains are opened. Rear-fold or back-packing travelers are available which gather folds on the offstage part of the track when opening and closing, leaving onstage curtain taut. Particularly useful for scrim or show curtains.

TREAD. The actual step in a step unit. See STEPS.

TREE LEAVES. Muslin or canvas painted and cut to resemble leaf masses. A die in the shape of a leaf is useful in cutting green material for foliage effects. Die should cut all but stem of leaf so that leaf hangs from hole in material, making border three dimensional. Finger painting with green paste on muslin can also be effective. See also **Feather dust** under PAINTING TECHNIQUES; STENCILS.

TREES. Trees on stage are either two dimensional cutouts to be used as background or three dimensional trunks with two or three branches showing behind leaf borders.

Profile trees. Outline is laid out on three ply or beaverboard and sawed with a keyhole saw, saber saw, or bandsaw. The cut profile is then

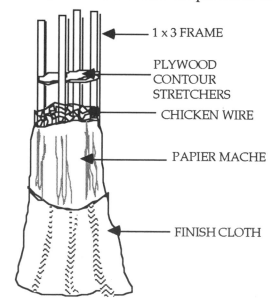

1 x 3 FRAME

PLYWOOD CONTOUR STRETCHERS

CHICKEN WIRE

PAPIER MACHE

FINISH CLOTH

THREE DIMENSIONAL TREE

framed with 1" x 3" battens on the back to provide rigidity. Less expensive profile trees can be made by using flats or plugs to which scraps of lumber are added for the outline or contour. Jacks or stage braces are used to support trees in position.

Three-dimensional trees. Frames are made of 3/4" plywood disks cut to conform to cross sectional contours at 3' to 4' intervals in trunk and branches. Disks are strung together with battens and covered with chicken wire, PAPIER-MACHE and then cloth.

Drapery trees. Can be most effective if used far enough away from actors to avoid contact. Contour sections are cut from five ply, and dye-painted muslin (see **Dye drop** under DROPS) is tacked or stapled in folds resembling bark to plywood sections. Trees are suspended from pipe batten behind foliage border. A sandbag or counterweight can be placed on lower plywood section to hold trunk to floor.

Practical trees. Should be built on a frame of 2" x 4" or 2" x 6" lumber strong enough to support weight of actors. The trunk shape should be formed around framework with chicken wire, papier-mâché, muslin or burlap. Coating the final covering with fiberglass resin will produce a hard surface and help make the unit rigid. As a safety precaution, practical trees should be supported with lines from a pipe batten.

TREES, LIGHT. See LIGHT MOUNTING DEVICES.

TRESTLE. A frame or horse used as a weight-bearing support for a platform.

TRICK LINE. A thin line used to trigger some trick device or special effect on stage during the show.

TRIM (noun)

Lights. A set of carbon electrodes in an ARC LIGHT.

Rigging. A high trim is the highest level that a drop is flown, usually out of sight, while the low trim is the lowest level a drop is set while in use. In certain applications there can be intermediate trims for scenery.

Scenery. See **Facing** under MOLDING.

TRIM (verb)

Lights. To replace carbon electrodes in an arc light. Arc lights will operate about one hour and twenty minutes on a trim.

Rigging. To level flown scenery so that it is parallel with floor.

Scenery. To cut canvas or muslin after gluing to a flat.

TRIM BLOCK. See **Trim clamp** under CLAMPS.

TRIM CHAIN (snatch chain). See under CHAIN.

TRIM CLAMP. See under CLAMPS.

TRIM HEIGHT. Predetermined height off the floor at which scenery will be hung or trimmed.

TRIM IT (Command verb). Mark rope when TRIM HEIGHT is reached.

TRIM MARK (ribbon, mark, flag). A piece of ribbon pulled through the lay of rope to mark or flag the location of the overhaul line to the top of the rope lock to give a particular point of reference. Usually the low trim (down mark) is made even with the top of the rope lock; the high trim (up mark) is either in the WELL or alligning mark on the backline with a horizontal angle iron holding the T-track at about eye level. See also FLAG.

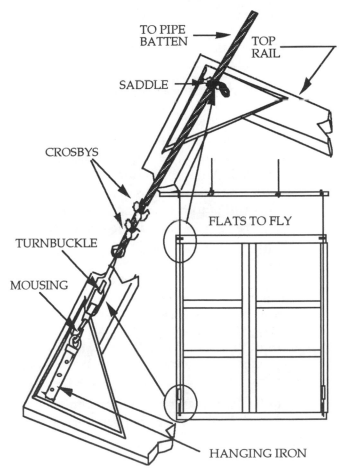

TO PIPE BATTEN
TOP RAIL
SADDLE
CROSBYS
TURNBUCKLE
MOUSING
FLATS TO FLY
HANGING IRON

TRIMMING A FLYING FLAT FROM THE FLOOR USING TURNBUCKLE AND SADDLE

TRIP

To pull flown scenery off vertical with another set of lines.

To fly drops or drapes on two sets of lines, one tied to top and the other tied to bottom of drop. Drops tripped in this manner require only one half the grid height required by a single set for flying.

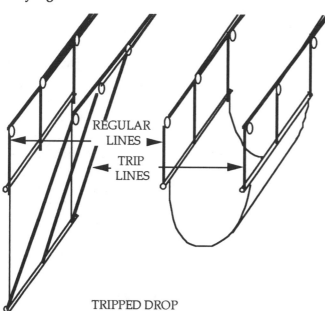

REGULAR LINES ►

◄ TRIP LINES

TRIPPED DROP

TRIP LINE. A special line or set of lines tied to a pipe batten and used to trip a batten upstage, downstage, left or right stage. See BREASTING.

TROMBONE. A hand-operated sliding device that holds the objective lens in a followspot. The action (similar to a trombone movement) of moving the lens via the handle makes the light beam go from small to large.

TROUGH

Obsolete. Sometimes used to refer to toning lights in metal trough reflectors.

Occasionally used in place of cradle in reference to snow trough, rain trough.

TROUPER. A trade name for a followspot by Strong Electric.

TRUCK.

A dolly for moving heavy equipment.

A two-wheeled barrow used for carrying trunks or heavy articles.

TRUSS

Scenery. Lumber or metal tubing or pipe used to brace, usually diagonally, a framework or structure.

Lights. A metal structure used to enclose or hold lighting instrument when a single pipe would bend. Often used sectionally and bolted together for touring shows.

TRUSS CONNECTIONS

Plate connection. Connection used to bolt together sections of trusses. Sometimes a CAMLOCK is used as a fastening device instead of a bolt.

Spigot connection. A type of connection used with some types of trusses. Usually uses a clevis pin or bolt to ensure a tight, secure fit.

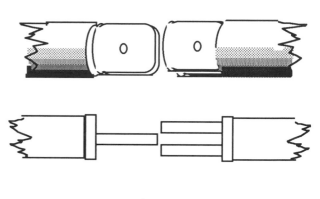

SPIGOT CONNECTION

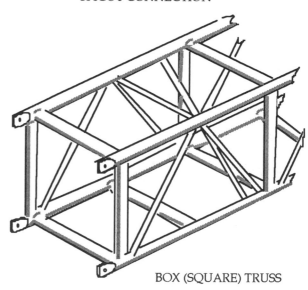

BOX (SQUARE) TRUSS

TRUSS, SHAPES

Triangle truss. Basically, a triangular unit.

Box truss. A square or rectangular unit.

TRY SQUARE. See under SQUARE.

T-SQUARE. See under SQUARE.

TUMBLER (wooden dutchman). Lumber 1" x 3" or 1" x 4" hinged between the second and third flats of a threefold, acting as a spacer and enabling the third flat to fold around the other two. Tumblers must be used in three, four, and five-folds if flats are to fold up compactly. See illustration under THREEFOLD.

TUNER CLEANER. A special cleaner made for TV tuners but which also cleans many other electronic parts, e.g., potentiometers.

TUNGSTEN HALOGEN LAMPS. See under LAMPS.

TURNBUCKLE. Two eyebolts, one right- and one left-hand thread, threaded into a sleeve, so that tension may be drawn by turning the sleeve. Some of the many uses for turnbuckles include tightening guy lines, tightening wires to be used as curtain travelers, straightening doors, and

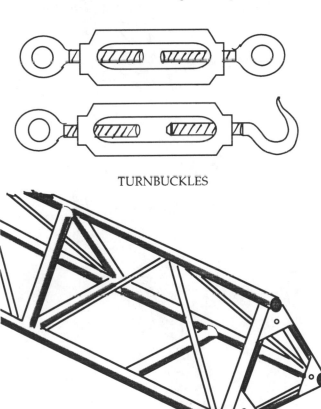

TURNBUCKLES

TRIANGLE TRUSS

taking sag from screen doors and various frames. See also MOUSING.

TURNTABLE

    Stage. Any revolving disk or platform capable of turning 360°. See **Revolving stage** under SCENERY, SHIFTING.

    Sound. The platen revolving on a phonograph, on which the record is placed. See SOUND EQUIPMENT.

TV (television, monitor). A method of seeing the action of a show using a TV set. A TV camera watching the stage is common to many productions, used by cast, crew, and front of house staff. Lighting computer consoles also use monitors for their readouts.

TWEETER. A small speaker which emits high frequencies used in a two- or three-way speaker.

TWINKY LIGHTS. A colloquial expression for a set of small lights which blink or Christmas tree lights which are used on stage and blink for special effects, often used for stars along with nonblinking, miniature lights.

TWISTLOCK. See under PLUGS, ELECTRICAL.

TWO BLOCKED. A term which denotes having the pipe on stage close to the grid and next to the loft block; thus the counterweight arbor is as close to the floor as possible. See also WELL.

TWO-DIMENSIONAL SCENERY. Flat scenery having no depth.

TWO-FER

    Box office. Two tickets for the price of one.

    Lights (Y). A short cable in the shape of a Y which has one male plug and two female receptacles. An electrical junction providing two outlets.

TWOFOLD. Two flats hinged to fold face to face. See also THREEFOLD.

TYP. Abbreviation for "typical" in drawing and drafting.

TYPE OF SHOW. See CLASSIFICATION OF SHOWS.

U

U-BOLT. See under BOLTS.

ULTRAMARINE BLUE. An intense blue pigment used in scene painting. See PAINT AND PAINT COLORS.

ULTRAVIOLET LIGHT (UV light, black light). Light rays, invisible to the human eye, which cause certain colors and materials to glow or fluoresce in the dark. If the source of light can be placed close to the object to be fluoresced, tubular UV lamps may be used. Available in 15- and 40-watt sizes, the tubular lamp has an advantage of having no warm-up period. Mercury arc lamps with UV filters require a 4- to10-minute warm-up period before they will operate. When turned off, about a 15-minute cooling-off period is necessary before they will turn on again. Despite the unfortunate lack of instant control, the mercury arc lamp remains the more efficient black light source for high-intensity concentration of light. Maximum throw distances recommended for effective use of mercury arc lamps are 15' to 20' for 100-watt flood lamp; 25' to 30' for 100-watt spot lamp; 30' to 35' for 150-watt flood lamp. Effective coverage or spread is about equal to the throw (e.g., 25' throw equals a 25' spread). Included among the many available fluorescent products are ribbons, fringes, paper, paints, dyes, crayons, various cloth materials, and artist's chalks and pencils in a wide variety of colors. Stage makeup is also available.

UMBER. Brownish color, low-intensity pigment, used for painting scenery. See PAINT AND PAINT COLORS.

UNBLEACHED MUSLIN. See **Muslin** under COVERING FLATS: **Materials.**

UNCLE BUDDY (rope clip, line lok, goat hook). A handheld locking device used for an overhaul line on a T-track system rather than taking a WRAP.

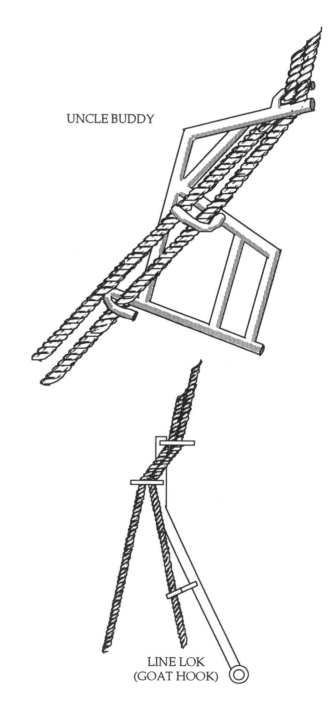

UNCLE BUDDY

LINE LOK
(GOAT HOOK)

UNDERCOAT. Paint applied to scenery before the final, finished coat. See PAINTING SCENERY.

UNDERLIGHTING. Low lighting intensity. If sustained periods of dark scenes are necessary, they should open with low-intensity, establishing proper mood, and then gradually build in intensity to a point beyond eyestrain.

UNDERWRITERS LABORATORY (U.L.). An independent laboratory that tests equipment to make certain it meets safety standards under proper usage. All electrical equipment used in the theatre should bear the U.L. label.

UNION, PIPE. See under PIPE FITTINGS.

UNIONS (associated with theatre)

AEA. Actors Equity Association.

AFM. American Federation of Musicians.

AFTRA. American Federation of Theatre and Radio Artists.

AGMA. American Guild of Musical Artists.

AGVA. American Guild of Variety Artists.

ATPAM. Association of Theatrical Press Agents and Managers.

IAIW. International Alliance of Iron Workers.

IATSE. International Alliance of Theatrical Stage Employees.

IBEW. International Brotherhood of Electrical Workers.

SAG. Screen Actors Guild.

SSDC. Society of Stage Directors and Choreographers.

TEAMSTERS. IBT. International Brotherhood of Teamsters.

USA. United Scenic Artists.

UNISTRUT. Trade name of slotted steel angle iron. Makes setup of structural units very easy by putting the required shape together and bolting the pieces.

UNIT (fixture, instrument, light, luminaire). See LIGHTING INSTRUMENTS.

UNIT SET. See under SCENERY, SHIFTING.

UNIVERSE. Reference to number of channels of control available. Presently 512 channels make up a universe. It is possible, however, to have more than one universe available within a system. See also DMX PROTOCOL.

UPSON BOARD. Trade name for BEAVERBOARD

UPSTAGE. That part of the stage closest to the backwall and farthest from the audience. Term is derived from earlier theatres in which stages were ramped for better visibility and upstage was literally higher than downstage. See STAGE DIRECTIONS; AREAS.

UPSTAGE DRAFT. When the air-handling systems volume in the house and stage does not match, it produces this draft, which makes curtains drift upstage. Causes fouling in the flies in a fast-moving show.

UPSTAGING

Acting. Moving upstage, forcing other actors to speak with their backs to the audience.

Scenery. So distracting it upstages actors by usurping audience attention.

URETHANE. See **Foams** under PLASTICS.

USITT. United States Institute of Theatre Technology. A national organization of designers and technicians. This group has subdivisions that investigate the need to set standards for various phases of backstage theatre operations.

V

VACUUM FORMING. Molding thermoplastic sheets by using a vacuum to draw heated plastic sheet into a mold. See also PLASTICS.

VALANCE

A short curtain or border hung across the top of a window.

A border or teaser used as an overhead masking piece.

The cloth border hung downstage of the main curtain and used to change the height of the proscenium opening.

VALUE. Refers to the amount of gray in a color. See also TINT.

VAMPIRE TRAP. See under TRAP.

VANDYKE BROWN. A low-intensity, dark brown pigment used for scene painting. See PAINT AND PAINT COLORS.

VANISHING POINT. The apparent point of intersection of parallel lines in perspective drawings.

VARATHANE. Trade name for a liquid plastic used as a protective coating for furniture and props. Relatively fast drying and very durable. Available in clear glossy, clear satin, and a variety of colors. Often substituted for VARNISH.

VARIAC. Trade name for an autotransformer. See under DIMMERS.

VARI-LITE. A brand name of a moving-yoke type of AUTOMATED LIGHT.

VARNISH. A liquid preparation consisting of a resinous matter dissolved in alcohol or oil base and used to provide a durable, glossy finish on furniture or floors. Available in many colors and shades. See VARATHANE.

VDU (CRT, monitor, display). Acronym for visual display unit.

VELCRO. A nylon material used for fastening and consisting of two dissimilar pieces of tape, one with tiny nylon hooks and the other with a bushy pile, that interlock when pressed together. Particularly useful for costumes or temporary fastenings of many kinds.

VELOUR (plush). Any of a variety of materials made of wool or synthetic fabrics with a pile or napped surface. Used for draperies and upholstery. See under COVERING FLATS: **Materials.** See also DRAPERIES.

VELVET. Closely woven fabric of silk, nylon, rayon, or acetate with a short, thick pile. Generally too expensive for scenic use; corduroy and velveteen are sometimes used as more reasonable substitutes.

VELVETEEN. Imitation velvet usually made of cotton twill. Generally very good for DRAPERIES and upholstery.

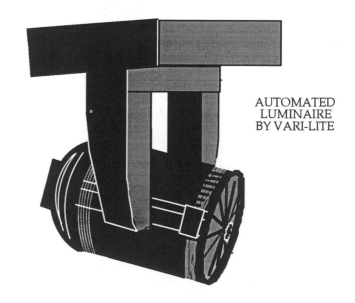

AUTOMATED LUMINAIRE BY VARI-LITE

VENEER. Technically, a thin layer of expensive wood used for inlay or glued to thicker, less-expensive wood. A term loosely interchangeable with PLYWOOD. See also DOOR SKIN.

VENETIAN RED. A brick-red pigment of low-intensity used in scene painting. See PAINT AND PAINT COLORS.

VERMILLION RED. A brilliant red pigment of high intensity used in scene painting. Vermillion red is too brilliant to be used on stage in great quantity, but intensity can be lowered by mixing with other pigments, or it can be used in pure form for highlighting or decorative effects.

VIDEO. Closed circuit videos are used in theatre to enable a hidden orchestra to view the production and enable the performers to view the conductor. TV monitors are often used backstage for one reason or another, and often in large theatres views of the stage are shown in the lobby for latecomers, who are not allowed to enter till a break or pause in the performance. VCRs are also used in the theatre to study rehearsals, dance technique, etc., and to keep a record of various areas of the building for security purposes.

VINYL. See **Polyvinyl chloride** under PLASTICS.

VINYL ACRYLIC PAINT. See **Acrylic vinyl** under PAINT AND PAINT COLORS.

VISE. A holding device consisting of two jaws that can be drawn together to hold objects securely. Shops should have at least one metal vise and one wood vise. Metal vises are designated according to number of inches jaws will open. Usually a 4" opening is adequate.

VOLT. A unit of electromotive force, or difference of electrical potential, that will cause a current of 1 amp to flow through a conductor against a resistance of 1 ohm. Most stage circuits in the United States carry a potential of 110 to 120 volts, and most equipment available for stage lighting is rated within this range. See also ALTERNATING CURRENT; ELECTRICITY.

VOM. A volt-ohm-millimeter indispensable portable device for testing electricity and electrical circuits, both AC and DC.

WAD. The plug that holds gunpowder in a blank cartridge. Since the wad is usually forced out of the muzzle of the gun when fired, guns should never be pointed directly at a person. See also GUNS.

WAGON. Rolling platform on which scenery can be placed for quick changes. See CARS; **Wagon stage** under SCENERY, SHIFTING.

WAINSCOTING. Paneling of the lower part of a wall. Wainscoting is usually 3' to 6' high and finished as wood paneling to form a contrast with upper wallpaper or plaster. A common practice is to fasten MOLDING to flats at desired height and paint flats below the molding as woodwork.

WALK IT UP. See **Lift a flat, walk up** under HANDLING FLATS.

WALK-ON. A small role in a production

WALL. One section of a BOX SET, e.g., stage right wall or stage left wall.

WALLBOARD. Fiberboard used to deaden sound and decrease echoes. Also used as bulletin boards. Wallboard is priced by the square foot and sold in 4' x 8' sheets.

WALL BRACKET. Various kinds of ornamental light fixtures designed to hang on walls and help establish period, decor, and location of the setting. Wall brackets provide the lighting designer with a MOTIVATED LIGHT source but they must be shielded to prevent glare and keep their intensity controlled. Low-wattage lamps are recommended.

WALLPAPER. Real wallpaper should not be used on scenery because it is heavy, expensive, and out of scale with stage settings. Appropriate designs should be enlarged to fit scale of the settings and stenciled on flats. See STENCILS.

WARM COLORS. See under COLOR.

WARNING CUE. Verbal notice or signal to get ready for a CUE. Warnings are given by the stage manager, through an intercom system, via a signal light, or visual contact 15 to 30 seconds before the cue is to happen. After the warning, the word "GO" is spoken to execute the cue if a CUE LIGHT system is not available.

Written notation on CUE SHEET anticipating a cue. See also AUTOFOLLOWER.

WARPED LUMBER. Warping is caused by crooked grain, improper curing, or uneven, careless stacking. Green, unseasoned lumber should be stacked straight with spacing boards between layers to allow for air circulation. Seasoned lumber should be stacked straight with ample support in the center to prevent sagging. Nothing can be done to salvage warped lumber; it can be used as battens to fasten scenery together or used in short pieces.

WASHING FLATS. See **Flat washing** under COVERING FLATS.

WASH LIGHT. Lighting instruments used in wide focus to provide general coverage FILL LIGHT as contrasted with sharply focused instruments used to highlight or illuminate a specific area. Wash lights are often used with strong color to provide mood. See also COLOR WASH; LIGHTING STAGE, ARENA; LIGHTING STAGE, PROSCENIUM; LIGHTING STAGE, THRUST.

WATER STAINS. See under STAINS.

WEBBING. Stout, closely woven tape. Drops, borders, cycs, etc., should be webbed with 2" to 3" awning webbing before GROMMETS are attached. Webbed drops and drapes resist tearing at tie lines. Best webbing sizes include 1" to

2" tape for lightweight drapes; 1 1/2" tape for medium weight drapes; 2" to 3" tape for heavy drapes. Gathering or pleating is seldom necessary for drops, but may be done if the effect is wanted for window draperies or theatrical curtains. Various kinds of curtain hooks designed to aid in pleating are available in dry goods stores. Furniture is webbed under the padding and springs with a jute webbing, tacked to the frame and woven tightly in a basket weave; 3" to 4" webbing is generally used. Available from tent and awning manufacturers and some mail order houses.

WEDGE. A tapered piece of wood sometimes needed as a shim to straighten a wall. Wedges are also used to prevent WAGONS from rolling off SPIKE MARKS while scene is in progress and often they are placed between stage braces and cleats to make bracing more rigid.

WEIGHT-BEARING STRUCTURE. See PARALLEL.

WEIGHTS (bricks). Counterweights that go onto the arbor are classified as full weights and half-weights. Cut steel weights usually are approximately 30 pounds and 15 pounds; and cast iron, 22 pounds and 11 pounds.

WELDER. MIG, TIG (inert gas arc welders), electric arc, and gas (oxygen, acetylene) welders are commonly used in scenery shops. See also under POWER TOOLS.

WELL. The area of a counterweight system below the locking rail and back to the ribbons. Placing the arbor in the lowest position ("in the well") places the pipe in its highest position ("two blocked").

WEST COASTING. Lowering flown draperies or legs directly from the pipe on which they are tied into a drapery bag.

WEST VIRGINIA FORMULA. W = VA. See under ELECTRICITY.

WET OR DRY PAPER. A sandpaper used on metal which is rinsed in water to clean the grit while sanding. Available at hardware stores in course (50) to superfine (200, 300, 400, 600) grits.

WHEAT PASTE. Inexpensive paste that can be used to glue covering on flats. Wheat paste can be used in its original form or mixed 1/3 paste to 1/3 hot gelatine glue to 1/3 water. Wheat paste

is less expensive than glue and almost as strong when mixed as above.

WHEELS. See CASTER; IDLER; SCENERY, SHIFTING; WAGON.

WHETSTONE. A stone used for sharpening cutting tools.

WHISKEY STICK. A shop-made marking tool, particularly useful for marking angles.

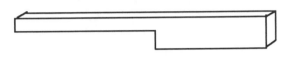

WHISKEY STICK

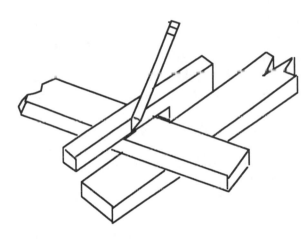

SCRIBING AN ANGLE WITH A WHISKEY STICK

WHITE PAINT. Avoid the use of pure white paint on stage if possible. Off-white will not reflect as much light and therefore will not be as distracting. See PAINT AND PAINT COLORS.

WHITE PINE. White pine is the best lumber for building scenery in spite of the fact it is expensive and sometimes hard to find. Flats constructed of white pine will outlast flats made of other woods because of the pine's strength and resiliency, thus effecting a savings in the long run. See also LUMBER.

WHITING. Powdered white pigment used in scene painting. See PAINT AND PAINT COLORS.

WIDTHS OF SCENERY. See STOCK SCENERY.

WIGGLE LIGHTS. A slang term for PAN AND TILT LIGHTS.

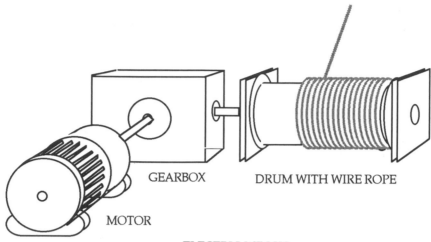

GEARBOX DRUM WITH WIRE ROPE

MOTOR

ELECTRIC WINCH

WINCH. A mechanical unit that can lift or pull using chains, rope, or wire rope via a capstan, drum, or chain hoist. This can be hand powered or motorized. Usually, a permanently mounted winch uses wire rope on a drum or capstan. The portable types are usually chain hoists. See also CHAIN HOIST; CHAIN HOIST CONTROL; DRUM; SYNCHRONOUS WINCH.

WIND MACHINE (sound effect). Recordings or tapes are most common solution for sound effects of all kinds at present. However, if such recordings or equipment are not available, yesterday's answers to the same problems are still valid. Probably the most durable of the old wind machines is the drum made by nailing 1" strips of lattice on wooden disks, suspended on a pipe axle in a cradle as illustrated. Heavy canvas, tacked to the frame at one end and hung over the drum and weighted at the other end, will make a windlike sound when the drum is turned. Another more advanced wind machine consists of four 1/4" dowel vanes, each about 2' long, attached to the pulley of a motor. A rather full range of "wind sounds" will result from varying motor speeds, and SCR dimmers will provide proper control. See **Silicone controlled rectifier** under DIMMERS. Vibrations and motor hums will be reduced if the motor is suspended on ropes in the flies. *Warning*: be sure to guy this machine from several angles to guard against torque recoil.

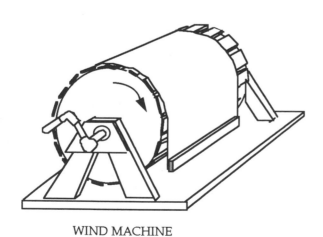

WIND MACHINE

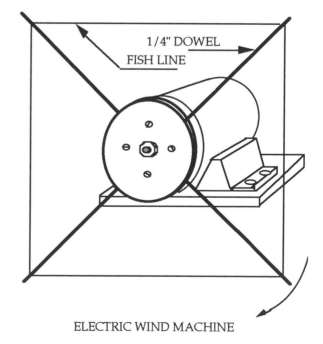

1/4" DOWEL
FISH LINE

ELECTRIC WIND MACHINE

WINDOW. See also **Window flat** under FLAT; GLASS. Types of windows include the following.

Casement window. Hinged to open out.

Sash window (double hung). Counterweighted with sash weights to raise or lower.

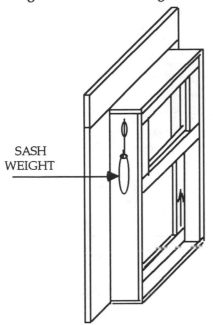

SASH
WEIGHT

SASH WINDOW

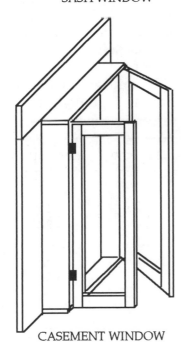

CASEMENT WINDOW

Stained-glass window. Small windows may be made of pieces of different-colored GELATINE cut to prescribed patterns and fastened together by wetting the edges and pressing together firmly. Black electrical tape over the joints simulates leading. Colored gelatine may also be used for larger windows by stretching cheesecloth on a frame, painting with clear, gloss latex, and applying precut gelatine to the wet latex. A second coat of latex over the finished product will ensure binding. Larger stained-glass windows are best made like DROPS, by dye painting unbleached muslin. The muslin must be stretched on a frame and flameproofed. After drying, the pattern is laid out with chalk or charcoal and dye is applied with a brush. Dye painting of this type may be done on other surfaces, including lightweight papers and sheer materials. Wax crayon lines between panels (leaded portions of window) will prevent dyes from creeping from one section to the other.

WINE. See BEVERAGES.

WING

Flats or drapes on either side of the stage, running parallel with footlights and used to mask offstage areas.

Offstage areas out of audience sightlines.

WING-AND-DROP SET. Consists of a series of false PROSCENIUMS made of wings or legs with borders masking overhead and painted scenic drops behind the openings. Scenery of the eighteenth, nineteenth, and early twentieth centuries was almost exclusively wing-and-drop type.

WING NUT. A nut with a flare on two sides permitting manual turning without a wrench. Wing nuts are most useful on bolts holding platforms together, fastening fireplaces, headers, etc., to flats, or for other semipermanent fastening jobs. Sizes correspond to bolt sizes. See also BOLTS; TAP AND DIE SETS.

WIRE. See also WIRE, ELECTRICAL.

Piano wire. Used to fly heavy scenery where top of scenery and supporting wire would be visible to the audience. Also used to fasten to harnesses for flying people, although wire rope (see below) is greatly preferred because it is much easier to handle. Piano wire is made of tempered steel, available in many sizes as designated by gauge and/or diameter expressed in thousandths of an inch.

Gauge	Diameter (inches)	Breaking strength (pounds)
13	0.031	279
20	0.045	518
26	0.063	1,038

Piano wire

Picture wire. Light, stranded wire available in several sizes and used for hanging pictures. Strength is usually indicated on package.

Pin wire. No. 14 gauge iron wire (0.080" diameter) used as pins for loose pin hinges. Cut in 6" lengths and bent at right angles, these pins are easily removed during quick scene changes.

Stovepipe wire. Malleable black wire used for guying tall GROUNDROWS or trees and for flying lightweight scenery where top is visible. Use no. 16 or 18 gauge, but be advised it is not tempered and therefore it stretches and is not very strong.

Wire rope, aircraft cable. This wire rope made as aircraft control cable is used extensively in theatre in place of piano wire for flying heavy objects. It is much more flexible than piano wire and therefore easier to work with, and when used in conjunction with NICO-PRESS sleeves, installation is much faster. Most commonly used sizes and strengths of aircraft cables from Bethlehem Wire Rope charts:

Diameter (inches)	Strands	Minimum breaking strength, approximate (pounds)
1/16	1 x 19	500
1/16	7 x 7	480
1/8	7 x 19	2,000
3/16	7 x 19	4,200
1/4	7 x 19	7,000

Designations refer to over all diameter plus strands of wire making up the cable: e.g., 1/8", 7

x19 equals 1/8" diameter, seven strands, each strand made up of nineteen small wires. The larger the number of small wires, the greater the flexibility.

Wire rope, galvanized. About half the price of stainless steel and just as suitable for stage work. *Warning:* When flying people, always consider LIVE WEIGHT as at least twice as heavy as dead weight, and choose accordingly.

Wire rope, counterweight cable. Cable used for counterweighting systems is known as extraflexible wire rope. This consists of eight strands, nineteen wires to the strand, and is especially designed to be used over small SHEAVES. The following table gives safe loads for most commonly used sizes in cast steel rope:

Diameter (inches)	Tensile strength (pounds)
1/4	700
5/16	1,100
3/8	1,600
7/16	2,100

WIRE, ELECTRICAL. The following table gives ampere capacities of various gauges of copper wire. Wire is usually referred to by the gauge and the number of conductors within a cable. Romex is 12/2 with ground. Border light cable may be 12/24 with ground, etc.

Gauge no.	Amp capacity
16	6
14	15
12	20
10	25
8	35
6	50
4	70
2	90

BX wire or cable. Obsolete; usually not legal to use. Metal sheathed wire formerly used for interior wiring, replaced by **Greenfield.**

Feeders. An entertainment-grade cable, usually 0000 gauge, that powers heavy electrical loads on a temporary hookup.

Greenfield. Flexible armored tubing.

Multicable. A flexible multiple wire (conductor) that is often used for wiring RACEWAYS and BORDER LIGHTS or as control wires for various types of equipment

Romex wire. Trade name for solid copper wire with a plastic covering, used for permanent interior wiring.

Shielded wire. Copper wire covered with insulation and braided metal shield, used for amplifiers and electronic equipment to reduce RF disturbances.

Solid wire. Single-strand wire used for permanent installations.

Stage wire or cable. Electrical cable used in theatres to connect lighting instruments must be stranded wire, 12/3 (12 gauge, 3 conductor), sheathed in a heavy insulation of rubber. For border or beam positions where a number of circuits are required, special border light cable containing multiple conductors in one flexible sheathing is used. Border light cable is not only less expensive per circuit than individual cables, it is considerably easier to handle and causes less clutter. Color coding circuits is obviously essential. All stage cable is sold by the foot, with a slight discount for 100' rolls. Available in most theatrical supply houses or wholesale electrical companies.

Stranded wire. Electrical conductors made more flexible by twisting together a number of small wires, necessary for any temporary installation made in the theatre.

WIRE CUTTERS. Electrician's pliers with a cutting edge for snipping wires, or any of a variety of plier-like cutters used for cutting wires, including end nippers, diagonals, dikes, needlenose cutters. See also PLIERS.

WIRE NUT. A plastic cap with interior screw threads that encloses twisted wires to hold them securely. See also SOLDERLESS CONNECTOR.

WIRE ROPE (cable). See under WIRE.

WIREWAY (gutter, raceway). Sheet metal trough designed to carry many wires or circuits in a safe raceway.

WIRING. See CIRCUITS, ELECTRICAL.

WIZARD. 10" scoop, often used as a BACKING LIGHT.

WOOD ALCOHOL. See under SOLVENTS.

WOOD DROP. Canvas or muslin drop painted to resemble woods scenes.

WOODEN DUTCHMAN. See TUMBLER.

WOOD SCREW. See under SCREWS.

WOOD WINGS. Flats with irregular edges painted to resemble trees and forests and used as WINGS. Profile edges are made of 1/4" three ply, cut to desired shape, nailed to stile with threepenny nails, and covered with muslin or canvas trimmed to profile edge. Wood wings are usually made as TWOFOLDS so they will be freestanding.

WORKING AREA. All space surrounding acting area.

WORKING DRAWING. See under DRAWINGS.

WORK LIGHT. Light or group of lights controlled independently of lighting control and used for working onstage or for rehearsals. Work lights should be provided with two-way switch so they may be controlled from light control, as well as stage proper.

Night-light (ghost light). A single naked lamp mounted on a standard and placed center stage after rehearsals and performances and used as a safety light.

WORKSHOP. Area devoted to building and painting scenery. Ideally, the workshop should have the following qualifications:

Location within the theatre with easy access to stage through doors not less than 8' wide by 16' high.

Sufficient height in shop (not less than 18') to permit trial setup of scenery for fitting and painting or for touch-up.

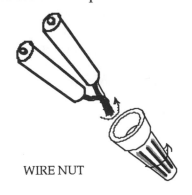

WIRE NUT

Storage space for tools in safe place, out of the way, but convenient.

Storage racks divided into 30" or 36" widths for vertical storage of flats.

Work benches about 3' high and large enough to accommodate the largest stock flats. Benches should be designed to collapse, roll out of the way, or be stacked on end to gain assembly space when needed.

Paint rack or free wall where scenery may be placed for painting. This space should be long enough to accommodate at least the entire wall of a large set. Ideally, paint racks should be motorized to move up and down so the designer-painter can step back from the work every now and then to get a perspective.

Storage space for paints, with enough room for stove, sink, brushes, spray gun, and other paint paraphernalia. Metal cabinets for flammable paints, lacquers, and solvents will be required by fire codes.

Sanitary facilities, showers, drinking water, and adequate space for changing clothes.

WRAP

Boxes. Lumber (often 1" x 3" white pine) used on road boxes (see BOXES) to protect the edges and corners. Wrap is usually screwed onto the plywood so it is easily replaced when damaged.

Electrical. Black aluminum foil used to prevent light leaks from INSTRUMENTS.

WRECKING BAR. See CROWBAR.

WRENCH. Tool used for loosening or tightening nuts, bolts, pipes, etc. Most useful wrenches in theatre are the following.

Crescent wrench. Adjustable wrench with jaws set at an angle to the handle. Most common sizes are 6", 8", 10".

End wrench. Stationary wrench with a different size on each end. Useful sizes include 3/8" to 3/4" at 1/16" intervals.

Locking plier wrench (vise grips). A wrench that adjusts like pliers, but locks in adjusted position. The 7 1/2" length is useful for mounting lights, bolting parts of sets, etc. The

10" length is also useful as a small pipe wrench.

Socket wrench. A set of sockets fitting progressively larger sizes of nuts and bolts and designed to fit one drive handle. Like other wrench sets many kinds and sizes are available but the standard SAE set of 3/8" to 13/16" sockets at 1/16" intervals with a 3/8" drive handle is probably adequate for the small theatre.

Stillson wrench. Adjustable wrench with jaws that grip and tighten as tension is applied. Used primarily for pipe, the most useful sizes are 14", 16", and 18".

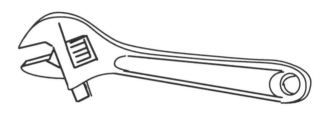

CRESCENT WRENCH

END WRENCH

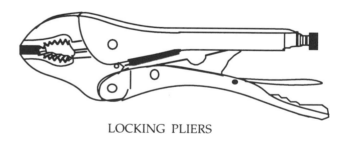

LOCKING PLIERS

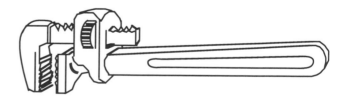

STILLSON WRENCH

X-ACTO KNIFE. Trade name for a small knife with precision-ground interchangeable blades. Very useful for wood carving, trimming muslin or canvas, stencil cutting, etc.

XENON LAMP. A very powerful, point source of light derived from the arc between two tungsten electrodes enclosed in a xenon gas–filled quartz envelope and used in projectors and large followspots. These lamps are designed for low-voltage, high-amperage direct current and must therefore be provided with their own power sources and igniters. Available in a wide range of wattages, lamp life in 1500-hour range. Since xenon is an arc, it cannot be electrically dimmed. Although the lamp produces ozone and ultra-violet radiation, it is used in projectors and followspots because of its small size and efficiency. See **Arc type** under LAMPS; PROJECTORS.

XLR PLUGS. A standard connector used with microphone cables and other sound equipment. See also PLUGS, JACKS.

X-RAY. A professional term used for any border light. Obsolete: an older ribbed glass reflector border; the concert border position (first border). See under LIGHTING INSTRUMENTS, GENERAL.

YANKEE DRILL. See under DRILL.

YANKEE SCREWDRIVER (ratchet driver). A spring return push-type spiral screwdriver. A variety of bits and sizes of bits is available. Tool comes in 12", 18", and 24" sizes, with the 24" size giving the best leverage.

YELLOW OCHRE. Pigment used for painting scenery. See PAINT AND PAINT COLORS.

YELLOW PINE. Classified as a softwood but considerably harder and grainier than white pine and therefore not as suitable for scenery construction. See also LUMBER.

YOKE. A U-shaped hanger for spotlights that bolts to the spotlight housing on each side. Yoke hangers are generally considered superior to other types because they give balanced support, making adjustments and focusing easier.

YOKE CLAMP. See under CLAMPS.

Z

ZINC WHITE. The whitest of white pigments used in painting scenery. See PAINT AND PAINT COLORS.

ZIP CORD (ripcord). Lightweight electrical wire of the type used for household lamps usually in black, brown, and white as both 18/2 (18 gauge with 2 conductors) and 16/2 (16 gauge with 2 conductors). Not acceptable for stage use except for practical lamps on stage and for low- voltage signal or speaker systems.

ZOOM FOLLOWSPOT. Trade name for a Century Strand followspot using a 1,000-watt tungsten halogen lamp. Designed for throws of up to 80 feet.

ZOOM LENS (variable focus). A system of lenses in which focal lengths can be changed either manually or electrically. Frequently used in moving pictures and television but also adaptable to the stage for projection equipment when an object is required to grow larger on the screen, e.g., an approaching ship.

Selected List of Manufacturers and Distributors

For a more complete listing of manufacturers and distributors of all theatrical equipment, the reader is referred to:

Theatre Crafts International, 32 W. 18th St., New York, NY 10011-4612 (http://www.elecnyc.net/tci/). *Theatre Crafts* has 10 issues a year and includes the Industry Resource and Buyers Guide. The Industry Resource, a directory of manufacturers and distributers, is on-line at http://www.etecnyc.net/ir. This is an extensive listing of products and services by company name. Also in the listings are the World Wide Web URLs (addresses) for the various companies that are on-line.

Lighting Dimensions, 32 W. 18th St., New York, NY 10011-4612 (http://www.elecnyc.net/ld/). This magazine is published 11 times a year and includes the Industry Resource and Buyers Guide.

The major designers and technicians organization in the U.S. and Canada is USITT. With over 10,000 members, the group is instrumental in setting standards for the industry. United States Institute for Theatre Technology, 6443 Ridings Rd., Syracuse, NY 13206 (http://www.ffa.ucalgary.ca/usitt/).

The Canadian Institute for Theatre Technology can also be found on the Web at http://www.ffa.ucalgary.ca/citt/.

The Professional Lighting and Sound Association, PLASA, 7 Highlight House, St. Leonard Rd., Eastbourne, East Sussex, BN21 3UH, U.K., is the major organization in England. Major information and links available at http://www.plasa.org.uk/.

Increasingly the Internet provides huge numbers of Web sites with information on the theatre industry. Many commercial sites not only discuss product lines but also have teaching resources available. The following organizations have a number of links to various source companies and even individuals that can be of great informational value to the theatre technician.

ESTA, Entertainment Services and Technology Association, 875 6th Ave., Suite 2302, New York, NY 10001. The members of this group have a large listing on-line at http://www.esta.org/memberslinks.html. The number of link sites for theatre technicians is becoming extremely large. The following listing of URL addresses is just a starting point.

http://www.yale.edu/dramat/sound/links.html

http://www.etecnyc.net/IR/index.html

http://waapa.cowan.edu.au/lx/index.html

http://www.stagelight.se/backstage/lighting_links.html

Explanation of designations used in the following entries:

Full service: Suppliers of theatrical equipment and materials, including counterweight and rigging systems, draperies, curtain tracks, electrical connectors, wire, stage lighting equipment, color media, followspots, lighting control, projections, gobos, fabrics, flameproofing, paints, dyes, tools, hardware, templates, shop supplies, makeup, wigs, and wig-making supplies.

Lighting control and instrument mfg.: Suppliers of control boards and lighting equipment only.

Lighting control mfg.: Suppliers of control boards only.

Lighting instrument mfg.: Suppliers of lighting equipment only.

Specialty: As listed.

Aero-go, Inc.
1170 Andover Park W
Seattle, WA 98188
Specialty: Air casters

Peter Albrecht Corporation
6250 Industrial Ct.
Greendale, WI 53129-2432
Specialty: Motorized stage machinery,
winches, rigging, shells

Alcone Co., Inc.
5-49 49th Ave.
Long Island City, NY 11101
Full service

Altman Stage Lighting Co., Inc.
57 Alexander St.
Yonkers, NY 10701
http://www.altmanltg.com/
Specialty: Lighting equipment

Barbizon
426 W. 55th St.
New York, NY 10019
http://www.barbizon.com
Full service

Bash Theatrical Lighting
3401 Dell Ave.
North Bergen, NJ 07047
http://www.esta.org/homepages/bash
Specialty: Lighting equipment

Broadway Press
3001 Springrest Dr.
Louisville, KY 40241
http://www.broadwaypress.com
Specialty: Theatre books

J. R. Clancy, Inc.
7041 Interstate Island Rd.
Syracuse, NY 13209
http://www.esta.org/homepages/jrclancy
Specialty: Stage rigging and
hardware mfg.

CM Lodestar
140 John James Audubon Pkwy.
Amherst, NY 14228-1197
Specialty: Chain hoists

Coemar Spa
2506 Freedom Broadway Trade Center
San Antonio, TX 78217
Specialty: Automated lights

Colortran, NSI Corp.
PO Box 635
Wilsonville, OR 97070
http://www.nsicorp.com
Lighting control and instrument mfg.

Compulite R & D
3 Haroshet St.
Ramat Hasharon
Israel, 47279
http://www.compulite.com/
Specialty: Lighting technology

Dyna-Might Sound & Lighting
3119-A S. Scenic
Springfield, MO 65807
Specialty: Special effects

Electronics Diversified, Inc.
1675 NW 216th Ave.
Hillsboro, OR 97124
http://www.edionline.com
Lighting control mfg.

Goddard Design Company
51 Nassau
Brooklyn, NY 11222
http://idt.net/~goddard
Specialty: Lighting technology

Gothic Ltd.
PO Box 189, 1 Continental Hill
Glen Cove, NY 11542
Specialty: Paints, dyes, binders, brushes

Great American Market
826 N Cole Ave.
Hollywood, CA 90038
Specialty: Gobos, filters, lighting
accessories

Grosh Scenic Studio
4114 Sunset Blvd.
Los Angeles, CA 90029
Specialty: Rental drops

Group One Ltd.
80 Sea Lane
Farmingdale, NY 11735
http://www.g1ltd.com
http://www.claypacky.it
Specialty: Clay Packy automated lights

High End Systems, Inc.
2217 W Braker Lane
Austin, TX 78758
http://www.highend.com
Specialty: Intellabeam automated lights

Hoffend & Sons, Inc.
34 E Main St.
Honeoye, NY 14471-9621
Specialty: Stage rigging, shells, lifts

Holzmueller Corp.
1000 25th St.
San Francisco, CA 94107
Full service

Lawrence Metal Products, Inc.
260 Spur Dr. S.
Bayshore, NY 11706-3917
http://www.tensabarrier.com
Specialty: Crowd control equipment

Le Maitre Special Effects
546 Sovereign Rd.
London, ON N5V 4K5 Canada
http://www.lemaitrefx.com
Specialty: Special effects, pyrotechnics

Lighting and Electronics, Inc.
Market Street Industrial Park
Wappingers Falls, NY 12590
http://www.le_us.com
Specialty: Lighting equipment

Lycian Stage Lighting
PO Box D, Kings Hwy.
Sugar Loaf, NY 10981-0214
http://www.lycian.com
Specialty: Followspots

McMaster-Carr Supply Co.
PO Box 54960
Los Angeles, CA 90054-0960
http://www.mcmasters.com
Specialty: Any building hardware

Mole-Richardson
937 N Sycamore Ave.
Hollywood, CA 90038-2384
http://www.mole.com
Lighting control and instrument mfg.

Musson Theatrical, Inc.
890 Walsh Ave.
Santa Clara, CA 95050
http://www.musson.com
Full service

Mutual Hardware Corp.
5-45 49th Ave.
Long Island City, NY 11101
Specialty: Stage rigging and hardware

Norcostco, Inc.
3203 N Highway 100
Minneapolis, MN 55422
http://www.norcostco.com
Full service

Oasis Stage Werks
249 S. Rio Grande St.
Salt Lake City, UT 84101
http://www.oasis.com
Full service

The Obie Company
19771 Magellan Dr.
Torrance, CA 90502
http://www.obieco.com
Specialty: Lighting equipment

Olesen
1523-35 Ivar Ave.
Hollywood, CA 90028
http://www.olesen.com
Full service

Packaged Lighting Systems, Inc.
PO Box 285, 29-41 Grant St.
Walden, NY 12586
Lighting control and instrument mfg.

Ludwig Pani
Kandlgasse 23
Vienna, A-1070, Austria
Specialty: High-performance projectors

Phoebus Manufacturing
2800 3d St.
San Francisco, CA 94107
http://www.phoebus.com
Specialty: Followspots

PNTA
333 Westlake Ave. N
Seattle, WA 98109-5282
http://www.pnta.com
Full service

Rosco Laboratories
52 Harbor View Ave.
Stamford, CT 06902
http://www.rosco.com
Specialty: Color filters, plastic projection screens

Rose Brand
517 W. 35th St.
New York, NY 10001
http://www.rosebrand.com
Specialty: Fabrics

SSR Stagelight AB
Box 406
S-90108
Umeå, Sweden
http://www.stagelight.se
Specialty: Gobos, lighting technology

Stagecraft Industries, Inc.
PO Box 4442, 1330 NW Kearney St.
Portland, OR 97208
http://www.stacrft.com
Specialty: Rigging, lighting, drapes

Strand Lighting, Inc.
18111 S Santa Fe Ave.
Compton, CA 90224-5516
http://www.strandlight.com
Lighting control and instrument mfg.

Strong International
4350 McKinley St.
Omaha, NE 68112
http://www.stronginter.com
Specialty: Motion picture projectors, followspots

Teatronics Lighting Controls, Inc.
1236-A Los Osos Valley Rd.
Los Osos, CA 93402
Lighting control mfg.

Theatre Effects, Inc.
642 Frederick St.
Hagerstown, MD 21740
http://www.theatrefx.com
Specialty: Fire, smoke, confetti

Theatrical Services and Supplies
1792 Union Ave.
Baltimore, MD 21211
http://www.esta.org/homepages/tss
Specialty: Rigging, drapes

Theatrix, Inc.
1630 W. Evan, Unit C
Denver, CO 80110
Full service

James Thomas Engineering, Inc.
10603 Lexington Dr.
Knoxville, TN 37932
http://www.jthomaseng.com
Specialty: Trusses, hoists, lighting

Tobins Lake Studio
7030 Old US 23
Brighton, MI 48116
Full service

Tomcat
2160 Commerce
Midland, TX 79703
http://www.tomcatusa.com
Specialty: Staging, lighting, trusses

Tools for Stagecraft
713 Quail View Ct.
Agoura, CA 91301
http://www.toolsforstagecraft.com
Specialty: Specialized tools for backstage

Valentino, Inc.
151 W 46th St.
Elmsford, NY 10523
Specialty: Recordings, tapes, sound
effects

Vari-Lite, Inc.
201 Regal Row
Dallas, TX 75247
http://www.vari-lite.com
Specialty: Vari-Lite automated lights

Wenger Corp.
555 Park Dr.
Owatona, MN 55060-4940
http://www.wengerusa.com
Specialty: Portable platforms, shells

Westsun, Vancouver
3700 Keith St.
Burnaby, BC V5J 5B5 Canada
http://www.westsun.com
Full service

Bibliography

SCENERY AND LIGHTING

Bellman, Willard F. *Lighting the Stage: Art and Practice.* 2d ed. New York: Crowell, 1974.

_____. *Scene Design, Stage Lighting, Sound, Costume & Makeup.* New York: Harper and Row, 1983.

Bennette, Adam. *Recommended Practice for DMX512.* London, England: PLASA, 1994.

Bowman, Ned A. *Handbook of Technical Practice for the Performing Arts.* Wilkinsburg, Pa.: Scenographic Medias, 1972.

Bowman, Wayne. *Modern Theatre Lighting.* New York: Harper and Bros., 1957.

Burris-Meyer, Harold, and Edward C. Cole. *Scenery for the Theatre.* Rev. ed. Boston, Mass.: Little, Brown and Co., 1972.

_____. *Theatres and Auditoriums.* New York: Reinhold Publishing Corp., 1949.

Fuchs, Theodore. *Stage Lighting.* 1929; reprint, New York: Benjamin Blom, 1963.

Gasner, John (ed.). *Producing the Play.* Rev. ed. New York: Holt, Rinehart, and Winston, 1953.

Gillette, A. S. *An Introduction to Scenic Design.* New York: Harper and Row, 1967.

Gillette, A. S., and J. Michael Gillette. *Stage Scenery.* 3d ed. New York: Harper and Row, 1981.

Gillette, J. Michael. *Designing with Light.* Palo Alto, Calif.: Mayfield Publishing Co., 1978.

_____. *Theatrical Design and Production.* Palo Alto, Calif.: Mayfield Publishing Co., 1987.

Glerum, Jay O. *Stage Rigging Handbook.* Carbondale and Edwardsville, Ill.: Southern Illinois University Press, 1987.

Gruver, Bert. *The Stage Manager's Handbook.* Rev. by Frank Hamilton. New York: Drama Book Specialists/Publishers, 1972.

Halstead, William P. *Stage Management for the Amateur Theatre.* New York: F. S. Crofts, 1937.

McCandless, Stanley R. *A Method of Lighting the Stage.* 4th ed., amended and revised. New York: Theatre Arts Books, 1958.

_____. *A Syllabus of Stage Lighting.* New York: Drama Book Specialists/Publishers, 1964.

McCann, Michael. *Artist Beware.* New York: Watson-Guptill Publications, 1979.

Oringel, Robert S. *Audio Control Handbook.* Rev. ed. New York: Hastings House Publishers, 1972.

Parker, W. Oren, and Harvey K. Smith. *Scene Design and Stage Lighting.* Rev. ed. New York: Holt, Rinehart, and Winston, 1968.

Pecktal, Lynn. *Designing and Painting for the Theatre.* New York: Holt, Reinhart, and Winston, 1975.

Philippi, Herbert. *Stagecraft and Scene Design.* Boston, Mass.: Houghton Mifflin Co., 1953.

Pilbrow, Richard. *Stage Lighting.* Rev. ed. New York: Drama Book Specialists, 1979.

Rubin, Joel E., and Leland H. Watson. *Theatrical Lighting Practice.* New York: Theatre Arts Books, 1954.

Selden, Samuel, and Hunton D. Sellman. *Stage Scenery and Lighting.* Rev. ed. New York: Appleton-Century-Crofts, 1959.

Sellman, Hunton D., and Lessley, Merrill. *Essentials of Stage Lighting.* 2d ed. Englewood Cliffs, N. J.: Prentice-Hall, 1982.

Smith, Howard M. *Principles of Holography.* Rochester, N.Y.: John Wiley and Sons, Inc., 1969.

Tremaine, Howard M. *Audio Cyclopedia.* 2d ed. Indianapolis, Ind.: Howard W. Sams and Co., 1969.

White, Glen D. *The Audio Dictionary.* Seattle: University of Washington Press, 1987.

Wilfred, Thomas. *Projected Scenery: A Technical Manual.* New York: Drama Bookshop, 1965.

BIBLIOGRAPHY

HISTORY OF SCENERY AND LIGHTING

Dunlap, William. *A History of the American Theatre.* New York: J. and J. Harper, 1932.

Fitzkee, Dariel. *Professional Scenery Construction.* Edited by Ellen M. Gall. San Francisco: Banner Play Bureau, 1930.

Hartmann, Louis. *Theatre Lighting.* New York: D. Appleton and Co., 1930.

Held, McDonald Watkins. "A History of Stage Lighting in the United States in the Nineteenth Century." Northwestern University, 1955. Doctoral Dissertation Series Publication no. 13,091.

Hewitt, Bernard. *Theatre U.S.A., 1668 to 1957.* New York: McGraw-Hill Book Co.,1959.

Hughes, Glenn. *A History of the American Theatre, 1700-1950.* New York: S. French, l951.

Krows, Arthur Edwin. *Play Production in America.* New York: Henry Holt and Co., 1959.

Lloyds, F. *Practical Guide to Scene Painting and Painting in Distemper.* New York: Excelsior Publishing House, [1883].

MacGowan, Kenneth, and William Melnitz. *The Living Stage: A History of the World Theatre.* New York: Prentice-Hall, 1955.

Rubin, Joel Edward. "The Technical Development of Stage Lighting Apparatus in the United States." Unpublished Ph.D. dissertation, Stanford University, 1959.

"Stage Lighting—a Survey since 1906." *Illuminating Engineering* (January1956):113-22.

Wolcot, John R. "Philadelphia's Chestnut Street Theatre: A Plan and Elevation." *Journal of the Society of Architectural Historians* 30, no. 3 (October 1971).

PERIODICALS

Lighting Dimensions. The magazine for the lighting professional. Published 11 times a year. Includes the Industry Resource and Buyers Guide. 32 W. 18th St., New York, NY 10011-4612.

Theatre Crafts International. A magazine for professionals in theatre, film, video, and the performing arts. Published 10 times a year. Includes the Industry Resource and Buyers Guide. 32 W. 18th St., New York, NY 10011-4612.

WORLD WIDE WEB

The following are most helpful (listed in order of usefulness for this book):

The Industry Resource
http://www.etecnyc.net/ir

ESTA
http://www.esta.org/memberslinks.html

Thomas Register
http://www.thomasregister.com

Theatre Crafts International
http://www.elecnyc.net/tci

Lighting Dimensions
http://www.elecnyc.net/ld

SSR Stagelight AB   http://www.stagelight.se

High End Systems, Inc.
http://www.highend.com

Vari-Lite, Inc.   http://www.vari-lite.com

Tomcat   http://www.tomcatusa.com

Clay Packy   http://www.claypacky.it

McMaster-Carr Supply Co.
http://www.mcmasters.com

USITT   http://www.ffa.ucalgary.ca/usitt

PLASA   http://www.plasa.org.uk

Also useful are:

Altman Stage Lighting Co., Inc.
http://www.altmanltg.com

Barbizon   http://www.barbizon.com

Bash Theatrical Lighting
http://www.esta.org/homepages/bash

Broadway Press
http://www.broadwaypress.com

J. R.Clancy, Inc.
http://www.esta.org/homepages/jrclancy

Compulite R & D   http://www.compulite.com

Electronics Diversified, Inc.
http://www.edionline.com

Goddard Design Co.   http://idt.net/~goddard

Group One Ltd.   http://www.g1ltd.com

Lawrence Metal Products, Inc.
http://www.tensabarrier.com

Le Maitre Special Effects
http://www.lemaitrefx.com

Lighting and Electronics
http://www.le_us.com

Lycian Stage Lighting   http://www.lycian.com

Mole-Richardson   http://www.mole.com

Musson Theatrical, Inc.
http://www.musson.com

Norcostco, Inc.   http://www.norcostco.com

NSI Corporation   http://www.nsicorp.com

Oasis Stage Werks   http://www.oasis.com

The Obie Company   http://www.obieco.com

Olesen   http://www.olesen.com

Phoebus Manufacturing
http://www.phoebus.com

PNTA   http://www.pnta.com

Rosco Laboratories   http://www.rosco.com

Rose Brand   http://www.rosebrand.com

Stagecraft Industries, Inc.
http://www.stacrft.com

Strand Lighting, Inc.
http://www.strandlight.com

Strong International
http://www.stronginter.com

Theatre Effects, Inc.   http://www.theatrefx.com

Theatrical Services and Supplies
http://www.esta.org/homepages/tss

Tools for Stagecraft
http://www.toolsforstagecraft.com

Wenger Corp.   http://www.wengerusa.com

Westsun, Vancouver http://www.westsun.com